Brexit

David Ramiro Troitiño • Tanel Kerikmäe •
Archil Chochia
Editors

Brexit

History, Reasoning and Perspectives

Springer

Editors
David Ramiro Troitiño
Tallinn Law School
Tallinn University of Technology
Tallinn, Estonia

Tanel Kerikmäe
Tallinn Law School
Tallinn University of Technology
Tallinn, Estonia

Archil Chochia
Tallinn Law School
Tallinn University of Technology
Tallinn, Estonia

ISBN 978-3-030-08784-5 ISBN 978-3-319-73414-9 (eBook)
https://doi.org/10.1007/978-3-319-73414-9

Printed on acid-free paper

This Springer imprint is published by Springer Nature
The registered company is Springer International Publishing AG
The registered company address is: Gewerbestrasse 11, 6330 Cham, Switzerland

Foreword

> Every time we have to decide between Europe and the open sea, it is always the open sea we shall choose

These words were spoken by Winston Churchill to Charles de Gaulle during a ferocious row in the lead up to the Allied invasion of France in 1944. Churchill wanted to make it clear that Britain would only act in conjunction with the USA. During the UK referendum, those words were hijacked by the Leave campaign, which stuck them together with sentences written by Churchill in 1930, and then claimed they were spoken in Parliament in 1953. The aim being to give the impression that Churchill was opposed to joining the European project, which was not true.

This act of subterfuge and the importance attached to it by the Leave campaign, is illustrative of the false thinking that runs through much of the British debate about Europe. Membership to the EU is not an either/or choice. Since joining in 1973, the UK has continued to be an influential voice in global affairs. It has retained its special relationship with the USA, which receives 17% of UK exports. The UK remains one of the most competitive economies in the world. It is true that by being in the Customs Union, the UK's trade is governed by the rules of the Union, but those rules have given the UK easier access to one third of the world's markets by value, and access to more markets than countries like Canada and Switzerland. EU mutual recognition agreements facilitate trade with China and the USA, among others. EU membership does not appear to hinder German's trade with China, which is three times bigger than the UK's. More important trade deals are in the pipeline. The reality is that far from being an either/or choice, EU membership is the best way for the UK to "have its cake and eat it."

Long ago, I concluded that the UK simply does not "get" the EU. It does not comprehend the EU's very nature. In particular, it has never really understood that the EU is not just an economic project, but also a political one.

When I first went into the European Parliament, I found myself among people who still had their concentration camp numbers tattooed on their arms. One of my neighbours in the Socialist group had been a leader of the Luxembourg resistance to the Germans. I once heard a Greek MEP apologise for his English, explaining that he had taught himself while he was in solitary confinement during the dictatorship of the Colonels. I became acutely aware of being surrounded by a driving determination that the awful history of Europe in the first half of the twentieth century must never be repeated. The UK mainland, for all its suffering during two World Wars, was never occupied, and has not had a dictatorship in modern times. Consequently, the UK approach to the European project is more detached, less emotional, and more pragmatic.

The failure to understand that the EU is a political project, as much as an economic one, explains some of the more delusional statements made by politicians in the UK. We are constantly being told that because Germany sells lots of cars to the UK, then Germany will be desperate to do a quick deal. It is true 7.5% of Germany's exports go to the UK, but that means 92.5% do not. British commentators cannot grasp just how seriously Germany takes its leadership role in Europe. It would be very reluctant to upset the other 26 Member States, even if that meant eventually agreeing to a deal that was not beneficial to Germany. Former Chancellor Helmut Kohl was often quoted as saying that the EU was in Germany's interest even when it was not in Germany's interest. That is a view most British would find incomprehensible.

Another aspect of the British psyche, which is important to understand, is that UK politics is confrontational. There is always a winner and a loser. Continental politics tends to be conciliatory, always trying to compromise and bring people together. This is a difficult lesson for British politicians to learn when they first enter the European Parliament, as I know very well. Some can never lose their confrontational attitude, and as result, make little practical impact on the Parliament. This is important because any negotiations about the future will be accompanied by the constant drumbeat of accusations of betrayal from the fundamentalist wing of the Leavers. Every compromise will be painted as a defeat.

The UK narrowly voted for Brexit for a myriad of reasons, some rational, some not. The British, as I have mentioned, lack an emotional attachment to the Project, and so have always been reluctant Europeans. We have a rabid anti-EU right press that helped blow up a firestorm over immigration, which drowned out all rational debate on the subject. The Leave campaign was based heavily on distorted information and downright lies. Their slogan "Take back control" had a resonance that the Remain campaign based on economics could not match.

Two aspects of the Brexit vote though stand out. Firstly, this was as much a vote about austerity as about the EU. Since the crash of 2008, real wages of the average British worker have fallen 10%, the longest sustained fall in average pay since the Great Depression. In addition, following the 2010 election, the Conservative Chancellor of the Exchequer, George Osborne implemented cuts in services and benefits, which have hit the poorest very hard, including those in work. People at the receiving end were angry and frustrated, particularly, as they believe governments were following policies that made their situation worse, notably not controlling immigration.

The second important aspect of the Brexit vote can be found in opinion polling done into voter's values and how they affected their vote. People in England were asked whether they felt mainly British or English. The more they said they felt English rather than British, the more likely they were to vote for Brexit. Similarly, people who strongly wanted the restoration of capital punishment or were anti-feminist or anti-gay rights or anti-environmental politics, voted for Brexit regardless of age, wealth, or education. In this sense, the vote represented a backlash against the modern world and modern politics. This was like the forces at work in the victory of Donald Trump in the USA.

Neither of these aspects are exclusively British. They form the backdrop of politics throughout the EU. Brexit should be a wakeup call to the European political establishment to act now before the populists sweep all before them.

The Brexit vote has left Britain divided and uneasy with itself. An increase in hate crimes being the worst manifestation of this. Sterling plummeted in value, which while it should help exports, is undoubtedly fuelling inflation so putting more pressure on the less well-off. The new Chancellor of the Exchequer, Philip Hammond, revealed in his Autumn Statement that there is a £59 billion "blackhole" in Britain's finances caused by economic growth weakening following the leave vote. Business is uncertain about the future that could affect investment plans. The Government got itself involved in an unnecessary constitutional battle with Parliament over who should trigger the Brexit process. Perhaps the worst consequence of the Leave vote is the way it dominates all political discourse in the UK at a time when attention should be focussed on some very big challenges facing the country.

The Brexit vote was clearly a vote against the status quo. What is less clear is what it was a vote for. Throughout the referendum campaign, the Leave camp were allowed to avoid setting out what the alternative to EU membership was. Consequently, the Government of Prime Minister Theresa May reached the end of 2016 without being able to articulate what it believes the future holds beyond repeating that "Brexit means Brexit." At times, it all seems straight forward. The Government has said it rejects free movement of labour, it rejects making any contributions to the EU budget and it rejects the jurisdiction of the European Court of Justice. All that points towards a straight forward clean break or "Hard Brexit". Yet, at the same time, the Government wants access to the Single Market. Those demands seem to be mutually incompatible.

Naturally the Government wants to ensure that the British economy will thrive after Brexit. It is the 6th largest in the world. That bold fact rather obscures some worrying weaknesses. The UK is heavily reliant on Foreign Direct Investment, which is equal to half its GDP. That is the largest proportion of any of the world's leading economies. The UK has a big trade deficit as it consumes a lot more than it produces. UK productivity is only 90% of the EU15 average, which is a consequence of poor skills and weak infrastructure. Most importantly the UK's economy is unbalanced. Manufacturing has declined dramatically, and services now make up 80% of the economy with financial services being the most important. Interestingly the strength of financial services in the UK is largely a consequence of the success of the Single Market. Economic theory states that in a single market, economic activities will become specialised in geographic areas where they enjoy most advantage. The City of London with its streamlined regulatory regime, flexible markets and, of course, English as a first language enjoys such economic advantages and so financial services have gravitated there.

A financial service company needs a passport to do business inside the EU. Around 5500 firms registered in the UK, with a combined turnover of £9 billion, rely on passporting. Clearly, if the UK were to leave the Single Market those passports would be lost, dealing a huge blow to the industry. There are alternative strategies companies can pursue, but they are all likely to result in a weaker and less dynamic industry.

There is another side to the issue of financial services. The Governor of the Bank of England, Mark Carney in November 2016 stated "The UK is effectively the investment banker for Europe. More than half the equity and debt raised (for European governments and business) is raised in the UK, quite often from investors based in the United Kingdom." Meaning, a weakening of the UK financial sector could weaken the EU as a whole.

Mark Carney's words remind us that Brexit is not just going to affect the UK. Economically, the withdrawal of the EU's second largest economy would be a shock to the system. The Euro would come under even greater pressure, at a time when most commentators feel the ECB has reached the limit of what it can do to protect the currency. The withdrawal of the UK's contributions would leave a €10 billion hole in the EU budget.

There would be compensations. There would be no British rebate, which will leave the largest financial contributors like France better off. All Member States would hope to benefit from any diversion of Foreign Direct Investment that could occur.

Politically, the damage done by Brexit to the EU could be considerable. As already mentioned, the forces that led to Brexit are present in most Member States. They could drive forward the populist revolt against the status quo destabilising European politics. Those forces could drive a wedge between Member States bringing forward ancient tensions, and dragging the European project backwards. At the time of writing, we are awaiting the outcomes of the Dutch, French, and German general elections, which will show us the likely future direction of the EU.

Perhaps the Member State with most to worry about is Ireland, which is closely tied to the UK. Ireland's 17% global trading relationship is with the UK. Anglo Irish trade is worth £1.2 billion a week. Most of Ireland's energy comes from the UK. The greatest concern though is with the border with Northern Ireland. If frontier and custom controls must be re-established, it could be immensely damaging economically and politically. There could also be a knock-on effect to the Peace Process. The Good Friday Agreement assumed that all parties would be EU members.

The loss of the UK will affect the EU in other ways. The UK has usually been a major player in the political processes of the Union. British pragmatism and focus on outcomes, rather than process, has helped drive forward the European agenda. In particular, the UK has prioritised the drive to complete the Single Market, and to reform the way the EU works. In the field of security, the UK has a key role, notwithstanding its complicated opt ins and opt outs. Britain is a major player in the sharing of intelligence and police cooperation. Further, the UK is a major military force.

The real danger for the EU is that it now must focus energies on the internal management of the Brexit process, at a time of so many external threats. Syria, Turkey, terrorism, future relations with the Trump Presidency, and the refugee crisis, all demand the undivided attention of Member States. Perhaps none more so than Russia where Putin has made no secret of his desire to break up the EU.

On the other hand, many will welcome the fact that the UK will no longer be able to obstruct future EU integration. Unfortunately, EU integration will possibly be the biggest casualty of this saga. Governments are likely to further embrace intergovernmentalism as a protection from domestic populist forces.

The EU is caught between two contradictory forces. On the one hand, the need to tame globalisation demands greater integration. For example, in stopping multinational companies playing Member States off against each other as a way of avoiding taxation. Yet, this very integration is anathema to the forces of nationalism growing throughout the continent. The danger for the EU is that it could be torn apart by these opposing forces.

It is obvious that it is in nobody's interest for Brexit to be an acrimonious divorce. The future prosperity of all concerned depends on finding a mutually acceptable way out of this crisis. It will not be easy. No big country has ever left the EU before. Nor for that matter does the World Trade Organisation have any experience of a major country leaving a customs union. We are all operating in the dark. We will stand or fall together.

The chapters of this book look at the evolution of the UK's relations with the EU, including Brexit in greater detail. When studying what inevitably will be dry facts, it will be worth remembering that politics is about people. The people whose vision built the EU, the people whose suffering was the motivation for those early visionaries, and the people whose livelihoods are at stake if we get this next phase wrong.

Gary Titley was a British MEP 1989–2009. Vice President of the Socialist Group responsible for Enlargement 2002–2004. Leader of the British Labour Group 2002–2009.

London, UK Gary Titley

Introduction

Brexit is currently a crucial issue in Europe and beyond and its impact to the current but also further European integration cannot be underestimated. While the discussions around Brexiters mainly focus on the referendum of 2016 or David Cameron's "great miscalculation" and its results, this book looks at Brexit as a process that started decades earlier. The current academic contribution analyses the EU-UK relations from a new global perspective, considering the historical background, political aspects, legal, and economic matters. The book provides a holistic understanding of Brexit, seeing the referendum and its outcomes as a culmination of a long process rather than a separated political occurrence designed within the corridors of Westminster or Downing Street 10. The book, therefore, contains main thematic issues, historical patterns of political and economic behaviour both within and beyond of kingdom, as well as possible future outcomes in the relations between the Union and one of its most important members.

The research is divided into different areas, as a historical approach of the UK in its relations with the EU to understand long-term political and economic patterns in their relations. Finally, the book discusses possible future scenarios of current events, analysing different fields of the relations between the EU and the UK, outlining key elements, important aspects and variety of possible options.

As the historical reasoning of the Brexit goes far beyond the *realpolitik* of British Islands, the co-authors of the book chapters come not only from UK, but also from other European Union Member States. Furthermore, they represent different disciplines such as history, law, political science, and economics—therefore providing expert views from different key fields of the whole process of Brexit and the EU-UK relations. Finally, the authors have a different background of being academic scholars and practitioners. Therefore, such composition of the contributors to the book and their fields of expertise allow covering variety of essential aspects of the EU-UK relations and combining multifold opinions on the process of Brexit.

The contribution is an attempt to explain why pro-Brexit "taking back the control" rhetorics met the fertile soil or, at least was taking the advantage of the narrative John Bull has believed in.

Tallinn, Estonia David Ramiro Troitiño
Tallinn, Estonia Tanel Kerikmäe
Tallinn, Estonia Archil Chochia

Contents

List of Contributors

Ondrej Blažo Institute of European Law, Faculty of Law, Comenius University in Bratislava, Bratislava, Slovakia

Archil Chochia Tallinn Law School, Tallinn University of Technology, Tallinn, Estonia

Andrea Circolo Faculty of Law, University of Naples Federico II, Napoli, Italy

Rasa Daugėlienė Institute of Europe, Faculty of Social Sciences, Arts and Humanities, Kaunas University of Technology, Kaunas, Lithuania

Ondrej Hamuľák Faculty of Law, Palacký University Olomouc, Olomouc, Czech Republic

Thomas Hoffmann Tallinn Law School, Tallinn University of Technology, Tallinn, Estonia

Andrea Hrebickova Faculty of Law, Palacký University Olomouc, Olomouc, Czech Republic

Liisi Keedus Department of Politics, University of York, York, UK

Tanel Kerikmäe Tallinn Law School, Tallinn University of Technology, Tallinn, Estonia

Nicole Lindstrom Department of Politics, University of York, York, UK

Davids Lipsens Sorainen Riga, Riga, Latvia

Holger Mölder Tallinn Law School, Tallinn University of Technology, Tallinn, Estonia

Paulius Puskunigis Institute of Europe, Faculty of Social Sciences, Arts and Humanities, Kaunas University of Technology, Kaunas, Lithuania

David Ramiro Troitiño Tallinn Law School, Tallinn University of Technology, Tallinn, Estonia

Rafał Riedel Institute for European Studies, Chemnitz University of Technology, Chemnitz, Germany

Lehte Roots Tallinn Law School, Tallinn University of Technology, Tallinn, Estonia

Christoph Schewe Faculty of Law, University of Latvia, Riga, Latvia

Olga Shumilo Yaroslav Mudryi National Law University, Kharkiv, Ukraine

Gary Titley Former Member of the European Parliament, London, UK

Andres Tupits Estonian Business School, Tallinn, Estonia

Part I
Historical Approach of UK to the European Integration

First European and Pan-European Integration Efforts and British Reluctance

David Ramiro Troitiño, Tanel Kerikmäe, Archil Chochia, and Andrea Hrebickova

Abstract The following chapter is about coherence between European countries during centuries and first proposals how to unify whole Europe in one big project as a cultural, political, and historical community. These tendencies were strong during First World War, when Europe had to face military conflict. This chapter therefore returns to Jean Monnet, the father of Europe, who was active in integration process together with Robert Schuman, who adopted the integration proposal, today known as the Schuman declaration. Second part of submitted chapter is dedicated to Coudenhove-Kalergi's pan-European movement, which organized first Pan European Congress with the aim to unify all European nations together to avoid war conflict. In this part, we can find also the attitude of UK towards the European organization and its reluctance to be one part of supranational organization.

1 The First European Integration Proposals

The process of building a European association or community is not something new, or just an idea of the twentieth century. There have been different ideas about Europe throughout history and from different cultures. The name Europe comes from different traditions, such as Greek or Jews. The Greek Europa was a Phoenician princess who was very beautiful, and the main god of the Greeks, Zeus, fell in love with her. But the father of Europa took care of her very carefully making the loving advances of Zeus impossible. The princess used to walk on the beach, Zeus transformed himself into a white bull, and Europa was tricked into riding the bull when suddenly Zeus started running over the sea until he reached Crete. There he

D. Ramiro Troitiño (✉) · T. Kerikmäe · A. Chochia
Tallinn Law School, Tallinn University of Technology, Tallinn, Estonia
e-mail: david.troitino@ttu.ee; tanel.kerikmae@ttu.ee; archil.chochia@ttu.ee

A. Hrebickova
Faculty of Law, Palacký University Olomouc, Olomouc, Czech Republic
e-mail: aabecedaa@gmail.com

D. Ramiro Troitiño et al. (eds.), *Brexit*,
https://doi.org/10.1007/978-3-319-73414-9_1

restored his shape and made her his mistress. Europa gave birth to Minos, Rhadamanthus, and Sarpedon.

The word Europe is also recorded in the Bible. After the great flood sent by Yahweh, when Noah and his children were to repopulate the world, Japheth, son of Noah, who was assigned the repopulating of Europe, was told by his father to populate the territories of Europe, and became the father of the Europeans.[1]

Other traditions link Europe with Semitic, Phoenician, or Arab words. The shape of Europe and its borders were defined according to how different people spoke about it, and meant that the borders of Europe were, and in fact are, more cultural than geographical. Europe became a Greek creation where Greek people lived. The Romans widened the concept, including more northern territories and more peoples in the concept of Europe.

Britain had established diplomatic and trade relations with the Romans over a century since the expeditions of Julius Caesar in 55 and 54 a. C. and economic and the cultural influence of Rome was a significant part of the late pre-Roman Iron Age Britain, especially in the south. Between 55 a. C. and 40, the policy of payment of taxes, exchange of hostages and vassalage of the British tribes, which began with the Roman invasion of Britain commanded by Julius Caesar during the Gallic War, remained without undergoing little change. Cesar Augusto prepared the invasion of the island three times (34 a., 27. C. and 25 a. C.). The first and third were aborted because of riots produced in other regions of the empire and the second because the British leaders seemed willing to reach an agreement to avoid war. According to Augustus Res Gestae, two British kings, Dumnovellauno and Tincomarus, traveled supplicants to Rome during his reign, and Strabo said that Britain paid more in taxes that could have course in total if the island had been conquered. After Claudio's invasion, Britain became a part of the Roman Empire, even if all the island was never occupied and revolts and social unrest were common, and part of the roman concept of Europe.[2]

The fall of the Roman Empire and the consequent chaos meant a period of social and political instability and a change for the concept of Europe, when finally, the rise of the Muslim religion and its occupation of the eastern and southern shores of the Mediterranean gave again a cultural identity to the concept of Europe, Christianity. This religion reached Roman Britain in the third century, the first martyrs registered in Britain are Saint Alban and Julius and Aaron Caerleon, during the reign of Diocletian (284–305). Gildas date the arrival of faith at the end of the reign of Tiberius (14–37), although the stories that connect with Joseph of Arimathea, Lucio, or Fagan are generally regarded as pious forgeries. Restituto, Bishop of London, is registered as attending the Council of Arles in 314, along with the Bishop of Lincoln and the Bishop of York. After the Romans left Britain, Christianization intensified and evolved into Celtic Christianity.

[1] van der Hulst (1999).

[2] Higham (1992).

The Christianization of Anglo-Saxon England took place mainly during the seventh century and was because of the combined action of the Gregorian mission of 597 and the missionary efforts of Irish and Scots who had started in the 30s. From the eighth century, British Anglo-Saxons missionaries would play a crucial role in the conversion of the inhabitants of the Frankish Empire. Ethelbert of Kent was the first king to accept baptism around 601. Shortly after would follow Raedwaldo (East Anglia) and Saeberto (Essex) in 604. However, Ethelbert and Saeberto were succeeded by pagan and hostile kings to Christianity who drove the missionaries and encouraged his people to return to their old ways. Christianity survived only with Raedwaldo, who worshiped pagan gods old with Jesus Christ.[3]

The turning point for the incorporation of Anglo-Saxon England to Christianity was the death of Penda of Mercia in 655 during the Battle of Winwaed. This made Mercia officially a Christian state, and allowed the return of Cenwalh of Wessex from exile, strengthening Christianity in Wessex. After 655, only Sussex and the Isle of Wight remained pagan, although occasionally Wessex and Essex would return to paganism. Arwald, the last pagan king, died in battle (686) and from then on, all the Anglo-Saxon kings were Christians, at least nominally. It incorporated Britain to the cultural idea of Europe.

As the two religions were reaffirming their influence over different areas, Europe became the main area for Christians, Africa and Asia for Muslims. The Europeans took over Al-Andalus in current Spain from their Muslim rulers after centuries of fighting led by different Christian kingdoms located in the north of the Iberian Peninsula with important help from fellow Christians from the rest of Europe, especially from France and England. Their main ideological justification for the war was liberating Europe from Muslim occupation. England participated actively expanding the Christian religion over Europe in different war scenarios, as the Iberian Peninsula or East Europe.

Europe was defined again as a cultural space more than a geographical area, and this helped to expand the concept of Europe eastwards, to areas populated by pagan tribes to convert them to Christianity. The idea that Europe was once Christian is obvious, and it has been an important fact in developing the European identity, but to link the origins of Europe with this religion is difficult because it does not consider the previous Greek legacy. Christianity has been very important in shaping the current concept of Europe, but has not been the only source, and the debate that has been opened with the rejected European Constitution and the possible inclusion in it of a reference to the Christian roots of Europe,[4] is completely wrong. The current Europe has had other influences, as from the French revolution and the separation of religion and politics, so the debate is completely sterile and demagogic, because Christianity is one of the roots of Europe, but not the only one.

---

[3]Lynch (1998).

[4]Kalyvas (1996).

The Speech to the College of Europe ("The Bruges Speech") of Margaret Thatcher emphasized the idea of Europe as a cultural, political, and historical community where United Kingdom has been a key actor during centuries:

> We British are as much heirs to the legacy of European culture as any other nation. Our links to the rest of Europe, the continent of Europe, have been the dominant factor in our history. For three hundred years, we were part of the Roman Empire and our maps still trace the straight lines of the roads the Romans built. Our ancestors—Celts, Saxons, Danes—came from the Continent. Our nation was—in that favourite Community word—"restructured" under the Norman and Angevin rule in the eleventh and twelfth centuries. This year, we celebrate the three hundredth anniversary of the glorious revolution in which the British crown passed to Prince William of Orange and Queen Mary. Visit the great churches and cathedrals of Britain, read our literature and listen to our language: all bear witness to the cultural riches which we have drawn from Europe and other Europeans from us. We in Britain are rightly proud of the way in which, since Magna Carta in the year 1215, we have pioneered and developed representative institutions to stand as bastions of freedom. And proud too of the way in which for centuries Britain was a home for people from the rest of Europe who sought sanctuary from tyranny. But we know that without the European legacy of political ideas we could not have achieved as much as we did. From classical and mediaeval thought we have borrowed that concept of the rule of law which marks out a civilized society from barbarism. And on that idea of Christendom, to which the Rector referred—Christendom for long synonymous with Europe—with its recognition of the unique and spiritual nature of the individual, on that idea, we still base our belief in personal liberty and other human rights. Too often, the history of Europe is described as a series of interminable wars and quarrels. Yet from our perspective today surely what strikes us most is our common experience. For instance, the story of how Europeans explored and colonized—and yes, without apology—civilized much of the world is an extraordinary tale of talent, skill and courage. But we British have in a very special way contributed to Europe. Over the centuries we have fought to prevent Europe from falling under the dominance of a single power. We have fought and we have died for her freedom. Only miles from here, in Belgium, lie the bodies of 120,000 British soldiers who died in the First World War. Had it not been for that willingness to fight and to die, Europe would have been united long before now—but not in liberty, not in justice. It was British support to resistance movements throughout the last War that helped to keep alive the flame of liberty in so many countries until the day of liberation. Tomorrow, King Baudouin will attend a service in Brussels to commemorate the many brave Belgians who gave their lives in service with the Royal Air Force—a sacrifice which we shall never forget. And it was from our island fortress that the liberation of Europe itself was mounted. And still, today, we stand together. Nearly 70,000 British servicemen are stationed on the mainland of Europe. All these things alone are proof of our commitment to Europe's future[5]

On the field on the field of integration one of the first proposals of a European organization was linked with the concept of Christianity. George of Poděbrady, 1420–1471, king of Bohemia, tried at joining Christian forces against the Turks. The king had a problematic relationship with Catholics and especially with the Pope, as he was member of the Hussites, a Christian movement based on the teaching of Jan Hus, and at the same time he was under threat from the Turks who had conquered Constantinople and most of the Balkan area in 1453. The Bohemian king through the Treaty on the Establishment of Peace throughout Christendom, proposed a European

[5]Thatcher (1988).

organization including the main Christian powers to settle disputes by peaceful means and act together against the Turkish threat. The European organization would work with common institutions, as a common parliament, a common secretariat, a supranational insignia, and a defense treaty. The main idea was an organization to protect Europe from external pressures, the Turkish, to protect Christian lands from Muslim conquer. Nevertheless, his proposal was not accepted by the other powers of Europe and never came into effect.

Another plan came from Charles-Irénée Castel, Abbot of Saint Pierre, 1658–1743. This French writer and politician can be included among the first men supporting the Enlightenment. His chief work, *Le Projet de paix perpétuelle* (1713; A Project for Setting an Everlasting Peace in Europe), exercised influence up to the twentieth century. Saint-Pierre proposed a European peace based on the Peace of Utrecht and assured by a European confederation that would name a permanent arbitration council. He thought about a European organization as a peace system by which to avoid conflicts between European states.[6] The organization would be based on different social improvements and common institutions, as a permanent secretariat where the main powers of Europe, as the King of France, the emperor of the German Empire, the King of Spain, the King of England, and the Pope would have a permanent seat, and other less powerful states would have a rotated seat in this council. He also proposed a Court of justice to solve the differences between the Member States peacefully. His idea based on a confederation rather than integration respected the national sovereignty but created diplomatic tools for solving European conflicts.

Immanuel Kant, 1724–1804, a German philosopher, also made his contribution to the development of a political organization in Europe as a peace system. He published his 1795 essay *Perpetual Peace: A Philosophical Sketch* pointing out that peace could be granted only if the following conditions were followed:

- No Treaty of Peace shall be held valid in which there is tacitly reserved matter for a Future War
- No independent states, large or small, shall come under the dominion of another state by inheritance, exchange, purchase, or donation
- Standing armies shall in time be totally abolished
- National debts shall not be contracted with a view to the external friction of States
- No State shall by force interfere with the Constitution or Government of another State
- No State shall, during War, permit such acts of hostility that would make mutual confidence in the subsequent peace impossible: such are the employment of assassins, poisoners, breach of capitulation, and incitement to treason in the opposing State

Kant believed that a perpetual peace could only be reached by a federation of Free states, a league of nations with a civil constitution, but not a state of nations, because

[6]Pentland (1973).

it could reproduce the conflicts between nations. The idea of the federation was based in common interest, peace, and development, with a big emphasis on freedom and cooperation without domination by any power inside the League.

The Influence of Kant's Philosophy on Europe has been outstanding, but not just in the cultural aspects, but also in politics. The foreign policy of Lord Palmerston to promote peace and commerce is highly influenced by the German philosopher, and several other British authors have developed the idea of peace and trade in the European, and world level.

United States of Europe was also the name of the concept presented by Wojciech Jastrzębowski in *About eternal peace between the nations*, (1831). The project consisted of 77 articles. The envisioned United States of Europe was to be an international organization rather than a federation.

Victor Hugo in 1847 used the term United States of Europe during a speech at the International Peace Congress (Paris in 1849). He favored the creation of "a supreme, sovereign senate, which will be to Europe what parliament is to England" and added "A day will come when all nations on our continent will form a European brotherhood . . . A day will come when we shall see . . . the United States of America and the United States of Europe face to face, reaching out for each other across the seas." His references to England and its exemplary parliamentary democracy shows the importance of the British democratic model for the rest of Europe and for the European integration process.[7]

The period including the end of the nineteenth century and the beginning of the WWI was very active in proposals integrating Europe where the focus was on cooperation rather than integration, even though the most used expression referred to the United States of Europe. John Stuart Mill, English philosopher, and one of the most influential thinkers in the history of liberalism, who contributed widely to social theory, political theory, and political economy, also joined Victor Hugo in his aspirations for a peaceful cooperation among the European states. The British philosopher participated actively in the Congress of the League of Peace and Freedom as member of the League's Organizing Committee.

An active period of ideas pursuing the European integration to united Europe against conflict, instability, and wars, was followed by the most terrifying war in human history, the First World War. More than 70 million military personnel, including 60 million Europeans, were mobilized in one of the largest wars in history. Over 9 million combatants and 7 million civilians died because of the war. It was one of the deadliest conflicts in history, and paved the way for major political changes, including revolutions in many of the nations involved.[8]

[7]Stirk (1996).

[8]Keegan (2014).

2 The WWI, Jean Monnet and the Allied Maritime Transport Council

Jean Monnet, 1888–1979, has a crucial influence in the creation of the first European Community and in the further development of the organization towards the current European Union. He is known as the father of Europe because of his commitment to the European integration and his active participation in the development of the process. Monnet was born in the region of Cognac, France, and soon started working in the family business related to the drink called after the region it was produced, Cognac. His relations with United Kingdom started at the age of sixteen, when he abandoned his university entrance examinations and moved to the United Kingdom, spending several years in London as an assistant in his father's company.

Because of his professional activity as merchant he travelled all over the world to sell its product, as the internalization of the Cognac was fundamental for its profitable activity. The concept of luxury united to Cognac was a great marketing operation that last until nowadays, and allowed Monnet to have contact with the higher part of the society, the customers of Cognac, wherever he travelled. This period of his life had a big influence in his further intellectual development, as he learnt from different cultures different understanding of the organization of the society.

It is remarkable how important was United Kingdom and the Anglo-Saxon world in his life and in his source of power. At the age of 16 he moved to London, during the First World War he was sent to London by the French Government. Right after the war he was appointed as Deputy Secretary General of the League of Nations with the support of Arthur James Balfour, 1st Earl of Balfour, a British Conservative politician who was the Prime Minister of the United Kingdom from July 1902 to December 1905, and later Foreign Secretary. Balfour had worked previously with Monnet when he was Foreign Secretary in David Lloyd George's wartime administration and Monnet was working in the Allied Maritime Transport Council.

Monnet travelled to Canada where he could examine the federal constitution of the country and its multinational internal composition. Monnet also lived several years in USA, where he developed a business career and political contacts in the highest level of the American administration. The United States was a model of integration for those who supported the creation of a European organization, and Monnet understood the American country best than most of his contemporary fellows. During the Second World War he was again sent to London by the French Government and was working all the war in close collaboration with the British and American authorities. He always supported the participation of United Kingdom in the European Communities and promoted the British enlargement as a key expansion for the success of the European dream.[9]

[9]Duchêne (1994).

Jean Monnet as a father of Europe, was involved in all the major event regarding the European integration after being involved in the League of Nations, as left the organization frustrated by its working system, mainly the decision making based in cooperation that made impossible almost any common decision. After the Second World War, Jean Monnet was designated by the French government as Commissar of equipment and modernization, coordinating the economic help of the USA via the Marshall Plan to aid in the recovery of the French economy. His strong relation with Robert Schuman, then Foreign Minister of France, helped to shape the first European Community. Then Jean Monnet presented his plan of an integrated community to Schuman, who adopted it; it was published in what we know today as the Schuman declaration.

Jean Monnet was appointed as the first president of the High Authority of the European Coal and Steel Community, embryo of the current European Union, and oversaw the development of the Community. Eventually, his confrontation with the president of France, Charles de Gaulle and the personal veto of the French president made him resign. Their confrontation was link with a different vision of the European project, basically integration versus cooperation.

Monnet followed his work in the European building process with other positions, less public but still influential as became the president of the Action Committee for a United States of Europe, a very persuasive private lobby. He was also active in pushing for the enlargement of the community to the UK, Ireland, and Denmark and was an important backstage figure in the creation of the European Communities established by the Treaty of Rome, especially with the EURATOM.[10] Monnet finally promoted the creation of the European Council, the meeting of the highest political representatives of the Member States of the Community. Jean Monnet was involved in all the major steps of the European building process, but mainly as a secondary actor, behind the scenes, using his influential relations to determine the mechanism of the integration. His intentions were clearly good, building a united community of states to avoid wars and increase the living standards of its citizens. He even wanted to expand the organization, when minimal requirements could be fulfilled by the candidates, to other parts of the world, in a process that could end with a World Federation, something like a World Union to substitute an inefficient United Nations.

Nevertheless, he has been criticized many times for is lack of democratic background because he never was appointed to any position in his life by democratic elections, being always designated by his influential friends. It means that somehow, he did not represent the people of Europe, that he was giving the Europeans what they needed but without consulting them. However, currently Jean Monnet is well respected symbol all over Europe, and his image evokes more an idealistic person than a totalitarian one.

[10]Helmreich (1991), pp. 387–410.

2.1 The Allied Maritime Transport Council

When Monnet, just 26 years old, met in 1914 with René Viviani, French Prime Minister in a private interview, he exposed his ideas regarding tight cooperation between the Allies, especially between the United Kingdom and the French Republic, as a basic requirement to win the WWI. The French government supported the vision of Monnet and the change in the French premiership from Viviani to Aristide Briand and further cabinet changes did not change the support he obtained from the French government.

His basic idea was the development of a multinational navy to manage the common external help in the war effort. He thought that as the Allies were facing a common enemy, they should have common answers to it. Cooperation was the basic theoretical concept behind the Allied Maritime Transport Council, an established functional organization respecting the sovereignty of the Member States with an executive body and common rules. As in later occasions, Monnet presented a plan in a moment of necessity to achieve his goals.

The Allied Maritime Transport Council was organized in February and March 1918. The members of the Council were ministerial representatives from the three main Allies and delegates from USA. Robert Cecil and Sir Joseph Maclay represented United Kingdom, Étienne Clémentel and Louis Loucheur France and Giovanni Villa and Silvio Crespi Italy. Raymond B. Stevens and George Rublee were the delegates of the United States of America.[11]

Rober Cecil was later involved very actively in the creation of the League of Nations. It was an intergovernmental organization base on cooperation acting as a forum where to solve the disputes between states without violence. It was founded on 10 January 1920 and was the result of the Paris Peace Conference that ended officially WWI. It was the first international organization whose main target was to keep world peace and respect the established international order. The disputes between Member States were to be solved inside the organization through negotiations and arbitration. It also included other aspects, as labour conditions, the relations towards native inhabitants in w world still dominated by Europe by vast colonial empires, and other issues related with criminality, security, and protection of minorities. The peak of Member States was between 1934 and 1935 with 58 affiliate states.

The idea of the League of Nations was appropriate for the British desires and necessities following the British tradition based on cooperation and unanimity in the international politics as the best way to protect the British Empire and the leading position of the United Kingdom in the world affairs. Obviously, there was no interest in UK sharing sovereignty in an organization based on integration with other states because the country was in the zenith of its power. Nevertheless, the League of Nations was inefficient, decision making based on unanimity was slow and ineffective, and the organization obviously could not attain its primary goal, world peace, as

[11]Guichard (1930).

the world faced another wide violent confrontation between 1939 and 1945. Hence, the organization was a complete failure.[12]

Robert Cecil soon afterwards was against the plan of Aristide Briand for a united Europe although the organization was also based on cooperation between its members, because it could influence negatively in the British colonies. Hereafter, the British Empire was the main priority in terms of international organizations, and a European organization could not interfere in the British common wealth even if UK was not going to be a Member State.

Sir Joseph Maclay was businessman and public servant. His business was related to shipping and therefor thanks to his expertise he was appointed Minister of Shipping from 1916 to 1921. His technical profile based on shipping made him appropriate for the Allied Maritime Transport Council but his later involvement in European integration affairs was zero.

The Allied Maritime Transport Council was divided in four main committees, but its leading entity was the Chartering Committee James Arthur Salter and Jean Monnet, the real directors of the organization. Salter was a public servant working previously in the worked in the transport department of the Admiralty. In 1919 he was appointed secretary of the Supreme Economic Council in Paris, an organization created to advise the conference on economic measures to be taken pending the negotiation of peace. The Supreme Economic Council was divided in several commission focus on particular issues, within the organization highlighted the commission responsible for the creation of the League of Nations. Next Salter was appointed as head of the economic and financial section of the League of Nations secretariat, and in the League secretariat at Geneva. His involvement in international politics went on as deputy director-general of the United Nations Relief and Rehabilitation Administration. Arthur Salter was a renowned economist highly respected in British politics holding numerous governmental positions in the British government and as external member of the Iraqi government's Development Board.[13]

Salter as one of the designer of the League of Nations, defended a model of cooperation in the field of economy without political integration. His ideas were against the creation of a European exclusive economic area because it would reduce the inter connection of the different European economies with the rest of the world. Despite his concerns of limited national markets in Europe unable to cope with a mass production modern industry he advised against the creation of a European common market proposed by the French government.[14] He defended an alternative inside the League of Nations promoting world trade, abolishment of national obstacles to trade and other measures to create a world market. The ineffectiveness of the organization unable to impose any rule over its members because of its decision-making system based on unanimity fostered the national barriers to trade in other to protect the local industry against foreign products, and hence reducing the

[12]Ramiro Troitiño (2008), pp. 139–152.

[13]Ramiro Troitiño (2017).

[14]Walters (1965).

market size and increasing the economic tensions between states. Nevertheless, besides his differences with Monnet regarding European Integration, their work relation was fluid and effective in what they themselves called international administration.

The Allied Maritime Transport Council held four formal meetings while the executive body carried on the daily business of correlating shipment requirements and allocating the resources. The high necessity of resources during the WWI increased the number of committees inside the organization to reassure that American resources were put to the best use in the war efforts. The AMTC had not a higher status of other committees during the Great War, but as it controlled the transportation, took a leading position over other entities.

The Council played a decisive role in the war efforts and was designed following the cooperation theory were unanimity or consensus was mostly needed to take decisions. It respected the national sovereignty of its members and theoretically all of them stood equally inside the Council. However, Great Britain was the only member that had tonnage beyond its own requirements because of its formidable navy merchant navy, obtaining a decisive voice in the decision making. The British Merchant Navy included the British merchant ships that transported cargo and people during time of peace and war. The facts that United Kingdom is an island, the world extension of the British Empire and the intensive economic relations with USA, made the British the merchant navy the largest merchant fleet in the world.[15]

The Allied Maritime Transport Council was operational until 1919 when was absorbed by the Supreme Economic Council and its executive committees were disbanded, but its prominence was reaffirmed with the appointment of Salter, functional leader with Monnet of the AMTC as head of the Supreme Council.

The importance of the Allied Maritime Transport Council was to reaffirm the effectiveness of international cooperation. Besides being a model for future developments in the field of international relations. The people involved in the highest positions of the Council later occupied high responsibilities concerning the process of European construction, as promoters or detractors. The British position towards any kind of European organization was also influenced by those who worked in the Allied Maritime Transport Council. Nevertheless, the active British role in the Council as a leading country because of the importance of UK in the WWI and its predominant merchant navy, proved the British capacity collaborating with other states in the international arena and its predominant vision for the following years based on cooperation rather than integration.

[15]Lewis (1959).

3 Coudenhove-Kalergi's Pan-European Movement

A Hungarian Count, Coudenhove Kalergi, 1894–1972, founded, in 1923, the Pan-European movement, and in 1926 organized the first Pan European Congress held in Vienna. He considered the Great War as a conflict between nations, provoked by the animosity between them. He proposed to avoid further conflicts and the collapse of Europe uniting all the European nations in a Union. In a supranational organization all its members could be acquainted with each other, understand each other, collaborate, and settle their disputes in a peaceful way. His political analysis situated France and Germany as the main obstacle and challenge to achieve this Union because of their rivalry. Any European organization should have included the most populated nations of Europe and major economies of the continent.

Europe is the birth land of political nationalism; its geography has allowed an important cultural diversity and the creation of a great variety of social cultural groups or nations. Nation is a concept coming from the American independence and the French revolution. A nation needs people, a group of population with an ethnic and cultural identity living in a geographical space essentially defined. These people are united by some cultural aspects creating a community with a common identity. Therefore, the nation unites the people and gives them the feeling of belonging to a group organization. From a politic and territorial approach, the nation is the space where men and women speak, generally, the same language; belong to the same ethnical group, share culture and history. In a world divided in nations, each one of them has an idea of itself and about the other nations because of their history and traditions. The nation must look for icons as a necessity in a psychological union of its members. It can be charismatic person belonging to the history of the nation, when the nation was pure, like El Cid in Spain, Robin Hood in England, Roland in France, Sigfrid for the German nation, Owain Glyndŵr in Wales or William Wallace in Scotland. Monarchy can also play the iconic role for a nation, as in the case of UK or Japan. Nations also are link with religion as they normally have their own national saint, as Saint George is the patron saint of England or Saint Andrew in Scotland, Saint David in Wales or Saint Patrick in Northern Ireland. Another important element for a nation is the home land, a local feeling that creates deep emotions among the members of the nation. It is normally represented by an iconic landscape, as meadowlands and pastures in England, the Highlands in Scotland, or hills in Wales.[16] The roots of the nation are collective egoism and pride. The nation represents the relation of 3 elements:

1. A part of the humanity: A Folk
2. A part of land: Geographical space
3. Spiritual conscience

The nation creates a strong emotional link between its members and a high level of loyalty.

---

[16]Elgenius (2010).

On a different scope, the state is a geographical space organized with a political system that cannot exist without land. The state is the political association of citizens (political subjects) to live in a community. The citizens share their freedom to create common rules allowing the live in a common society. The sovereignty is the will of the people to share their freedom to organize a common settle of rules that in some cases will restrict their personal freedom, but will allow a functional society life. To be a member of a State the only requirement is to become a citizen, a political subject without any cultural, religious, or ethnical implications. The relation between the citizen and the state is more aseptic as it is based on an agreement related to some specific interest, the common wealth.[17]

National state is a combination of nation (culture) and state (politics). Its function is giving political expression to the ideas of the nation and looking forward the good of the nation. Europe developed the idea of the identification of the nations with the political state, merging the cultural and political spheres, and exporting it to the rest of the world. Then the people are part of the society because they belong to a nation rather than being political subjects. The aggressive behavior of the national political states in Europe was understood as the main reason for the WWI by outstanding European intellectuals, as Einstein, Thomas Mann, Freud, Rilke, or Unamuno, and policy makers as Aristide Briand.

The best proposal to overcome the conflicts generated in Europe by the competition between national states was breaking the identification between nation and politics creating a supra national organization. However, a multinational state, as United Kingdom that entails different nationalities in a common political entity, has been traditionally the most reluctant state in the process of creating a European political entity based on the concept of citizenship rather than nationality. Hence, the British identity, above the national level, could be complemented with a European identity in a higher level, without competing with British, English, or Scottish identities.

Still, nationalism is still currently seen as the main source of social loyalty from the citizens towards the state because it is based on feelings and ideals, providing a strong cohesion to the society, and hence strong support to the political state. The lack of European national identity is one of the reasons of the low cohesion in social terms in Europe, and a handicap for the so much needed popular support of the European society to the European integration process, as it is based more on a rational approach rather than feelings and emotions.

The idea of Coudenhove-Kalergi was link with the aggressive behavior of nations and their constant confrontations. He proposed a European political organization with no a single nation backing it, but several nations working together in a common political environment to avoid conflicts, as a peaceful solution to the endemic wars of Europe.[18] His vision was supported by his personal situation, as on his father's side he was of mixed European descent (Flemish. Czech, Hungarian Greek), a

[17]Ramiro Troitino (2013).

[18]Coudenhove-Kalergi (2011).

Japanese mother, and relatives living in England, Italy, Belgium, Spain, and Norway. He became a Czechoslovak citizen in 1919 and then took French nationality from 1939 until his death.

He published his ideas in 1923 in *Pan-Europe*, where he explained his idea of a European organization in detail. The book soon became very influential in European politics in the post war context when policy makers were looking for alternatives to their political system to avoid a new confrontation in Europe after the horror of the Great War.

To spread his ideas, Coudenhove-Kalergui founded the Pan-European Union in 1923 as the first international non-governmental organization with members from all over Europe. The main goal of the organization was promoting the unification of Europe in a single political entity. The main investor of the organization was the banker Max Warburg, a wealthy German-Jewish banker who afterwards emigrated to the USA because of the Nazi rise. His financial support allowed Coudenhove-Kalergi to establish his first office in Vienna and increase the membership to Pan-European Union travelling around Europe and presenting his ideas to a broader European audience.

The proposal of Coudenhove-Kalergui was based a world of international relations based on five main world powers:

- The American continent with a prominent position of United States of America following the Monroe doctrine of America for the Americans, an expired proposal as the USA neither central and South American were interested,
- The Asian Union dominated by Japan and China including most of the Pacific. Again, a proposal with no chances of success as the rivalry between the two Asian countries was too strong, and the capacity of the Chinese state to exert an effective international influence was much reduced because of internal problems.
- The Eurasia entity, dominated by the USSR
- The United States of Europe, with Germany and France as its main powers, and including all the colonies of its members
- The British Empire all around the world, including all its possessions in the globe.

This division of the world areas of influence was erratic and out of reality, completely wrong and impossible to put in practice. The exclusion of United Kingdom from the European organization was a very popular during decades as the British Empire was vast and transferred a world entity to the British. It could even be linked with the position of Churchill when he spoke about three main circles for the British external actions, USA, the Commonwealth, and Europe.[19] But did not oversee the British opposition to a great Union in Europe that would exclude the British from the European market and threat the dominant position of UK in the world affairs. Hence, the proposed areas of integration were completely unrealistic and unworkable under any circumstances.[20]

---

[19]Ramiro Troitiño and Chochia (2015), pp. 55–81.

[20]Neumann (1996).

About the borders of Europe, or the possible members of the United States of Europe, Coundenhove-Kalergi situated Russia outside the organization because it was not a democratic country. Regarding United Kingdom, he included the country and Ireland in the geographical space of Europe, and an important part of the European civilization, but the British Empire could not be considered as a European State. The only possibility would have been the dissolution of the British Empire, incorporating its main parts to other Unions, as Canada to Pan America, Australia to the Asian Union, etc. But even in this case, the incorporation of UK to the European Federation will not be positive as the British, Europeans in Geography and history, are strongly link with USA trough language, ethnics, and culture. These ties, according to Kalergui, were more important than any European link with UK.

The British Empire was bigger in terms of extension and population than Europe and was united, not by geography, but language, the culture of the English nation as dominant partner in the Empire, and the wisdom of the imperial authorities. Because of these reasons, the British area could not take part in the European integration. Nevertheless Coudenhove-Kalergui warned against the possibility of building a European Union against the British, because a friendly relation between both entities would have benefited both areas and the British could have benefited from its intermediate position between America and Europe.

Hence the collaboration between the British Empire and the European organization was a main pillar in the process constructing Europe. A hypothetical confrontation between both entities would have been negative for the British, as they still had to digest the expansion of the Empire and they had much more to lose than to win, and for Europe, as its possible expansion was limited by geography and culture with clear borders with Russia and Turkey. Then Europe would not really win anything with a confrontation with the UK. As both areas would have been more interested in peace, the cohabitation, respect, and collaboration would have been the natural relation between both powers. The Count counselled against any European integration proposal threatening the UK, because the British would have opposed it using all its power, as they had done historically during centuries in the continental Europe affairs, fighting against any hegemonic attempt to build a European Empire. A peaceful European Federation would have counted with the British support if democratic, because working as a peaceful system, no more wars would have dragged UK to a European confrontation where the British would not have had the possibility to remain neutral to keep their Empire intact. An additional reason for UK to support the creation of Pan-Europe given by Coudenhove-Kalergui was the danger of a Russo-German Union threatening all Europe and the British dominions if the European organization was not constituted.[21]

The agreement between the hypothetical Pan-Europe and United Kingdom was described by the Count based on seven points:

1. The creation of a binding Treaty between both entities.

---

[21]Marcussen et al. (1999), pp. 614–633.

2. Disarmament of the European submarine fleet
3. Agreement about future development of air forces including USA to grantee the safety of UK
4. Exchange of colonies in Africa to create more homogeneous areas of influence of both entities.
5. The British forces will protect the European colonies in Asia against any aggression. Pan-Europe will collaborate in the defense of United Kingdom against any possible aggression from Russia.
6. Equal treatment for British and European citizens in the dominions.
7. United Kingdom will become the referee in any internal conflict of the members of the European organization.

The importance of United Kingdom in the proposal for a Pan-European organization was outstanding but neglected the British interest of collaboration inside the League of Nations rather than supporting the constitution of a possible rival for world supremacy. The predictions of Coudenhove-Kalergui regarding the British involvement patronizing some sort of European States of Europe were to be proved wrong in the following years.

On the Pan-Europe itself, the issue of national sovereignty was not clearly address, as the proposal names the organization in several occasions the United States of Europe. A federation is based on common sovereignty on such sensitive issues as common army, common Foreign Policy, common citizenship, or common market. But other times, the book refers to some sort of European Confederation where all the Member States can keep their national sovereignty intact as the decision-making was to be unanimity.[22] These kinds of contradictions repeat on several issues and many occasions.

His idea of a European pseudo-federation/confederation was based on the necessity of Europe to keep its international influence in the world affairs that certainly would decline unless the continent was united, with an equilibrium between freedom and organization of the European capabilities including as much autonomy inside the Union as possible and as much federal as possible in Foreign Policy. The European organization was the only manner to avoid a German-Russian Union or a Russian invasion of Europe, pointing Russia as the main external threat for the European civilization. His vision included democracy as the basic requirement for a functioning Union where the political rights of the citizens would have been above the nationalities.

Many intellectual Europeans before him had addressed the problem of nationalism, but he introduced a novelty promoting a European national identity to be created by the Federal authorities following the example of the European states. There are two main schools concerning national states in Europe, the French school that defends that the state creates the nation, and the German school that supports the idea that the nation exists beforehand and provides itself with political power to

[22]Braghiroli (2007), pp. 358–380.

obtain freedom. Koudenhove-Kalergui, following the French school proposed the creation of European symbols to unite the people of Europe in a common identification with the same items all over the continent, as a permanent capital, located in Paris, the creation of a European day resembling the national days of the European states or a common European anthem. It was him who suggested Beethoven's hymn as the EU's national anthem, and was very active about the design of the EU flag. He also proposed a common language, English to be included as co-official in all the members of the organization.

The designs of Richard von Coudenhove-Kalergi were not very well grounded from a theoretical perspective, somehow were completely out of reality mixing ethnicity, religion, colonial exploitation, racism towards black people, elite approach, hate towards Russians[23] and proposing an impossible Union based on unrealistic conditions. Nevertheless, his importance lays on the debate he generated in Europe and his capacity to attract distinguished intellectuals, politicians, and businessmen to his project.

References

Braghiroli S (2007) The challenges to democracy in the interwar period: lessons from the past relevant today. Poland, Lithuania, and Czechoslovakia in an extended Rokkanian perspective. CEU Polit Sci J 4:358–380

Coudenhove-Kalergi RN (2011) Pan-Europa, vol 4. Encuentro

Duchêne F (1994) Jean Monnet: the first statesman of interdependence. Norton, New York

Elgenius G (2010) Symbols of nations and nationalism: celebrating nationhood

Guichard L (1930) The naval blockade, 1914–1918. D. Appleton & Company, New York

Helmreich JE (1991) The United States and the formation of EURATOM. Dipl Hist 15(3):387–410

Higham NJ (1992) Rome, Britain, and the Anglo-Saxons. Trafalgar Square

Kalyvas SN (1996) The rise of Christian democracy in Europe. Cornell University Press, Ithaca

Keegan J (2014) The first world war. Random House, New York

Kohn H (1960) Pan-Slavism: its history and ideology, vol 710. Vintage Books

Lewis MA (1959) The history of the British Navy. Essential Books

Lynch JH (1998) Christianizing kinship: ritual sponsorship in Anglo-Saxon England. Cornell University Press, Ithaca

Marcussen M, Risse T, Engelmann-Martin D, Knopf HJ, Roscher K (1999) Constructing Europe? The evolution of French, British and German nation state identities. J Eur Publ Policy 6(4):614–633

Neumann IB (1996) Russia and the idea of Europe. A study in identity and international relations. London

Pentland C (1973) International theory and European integration. Macmillan Pub Co.

Ramiro Troitiño D (2008) De Gaulle and the European Communities. Proc Inst Eur Stud (4):139–152

Ramiro Troitino D (2013) European integration: building Europe (European political, economic, and security issues). Nova Science Publishers Incorporated

[23]Kohn (1960).

Ramiro Troitiño D (2017) Jean Monnet before the first European Community: a historical perspective and critic. Trames no. 3
Ramiro Troitiño D, Chochia A (2015) Winston Churchill and the European Union. Balt J Law Polit 8(1):55–81
Stirk PMR (1996) A history of European integration since 1914. Pinter Pub Limited
Thatcher M (1988) Speech to the College of Europe ("The Bruges Speech"), download at http://www.margaretthatcher.org/document/107332
van der Hulst H (1999) Word prosodic systems in the languages of Europe, vol 20, no 4. Walter de Gruyter
Walters FP (1965) A history of the league of nations. Oxford University Press, Oxford

The First Attempts to Unify Europe for Specific Purposes and British Flexibility

Tanel Kerikmäe, Archil Chochia, David Ramiro Troitiño, and Andrea Hrebickova

Abstract This chapter describes the initial effort of Briand, who presented his proposal for the creation of the United States of Europe through memorandum. This organization had to be based on peace like the League of Nation and had to create European market, which meant criticism from the UK as a protagonist of liberalization of trade and the main reason this attempt failed. Second part of the chapter is about Anglo-French Union, which had as a goal the protection of France against defeating by Germany and it was the only possibility how to keep France in the war. This proposal of Anglo-French Union had many similarities with the previous proposal of Briand.

1 Aristide Briand and Memorandum on European Unity

The twentieth century started in Europe with the Great War, 1914–1918, a war pitting almost all the continent one against the other, and inflicting a high number of casualties, around 37 million between dead and wounded. It was a shock for the whole society, and the nationalistic conflicts between France and Germany were thought to be one of the main reasons for this war.

Aristide Briand, 1862–1932, was a French politician who served several terms as Prime Minister of France from 1910 till 1929, and collaborated closely with Gustav Stresemann, 1878–1929, a German politician who was Chancellor and Foreign Affairs minister during the Weimar republic.

Briand studied law and became journalist in the publication La Lanterne. He was one of the founders of the French Socialist Party, but he was expelled from the party in 1906 as he accepted the ministry of Education and Culture, as part Sarrien cabinet

T. Kerikmäe (✉) · A. Chochia · D. Ramiro Troitiño
Tallinn Law School, Tallinn University of Technology, Tallinn, Estonia
e-mail: tanel.kerikmae@ttu.ee; archil.chochia@ttu.ee; david.troitino@ttu.ee

A. Hrebickova
Faculty of Law, Palacký University Olomouc, Olomouc, Czech Republic
e-mail: aabecedaa@gmail.com

D. Ramiro Troitiño et al. (eds.), *Brexit*,
https://doi.org/10.1007/978-3-319-73414-9_2

minister, starting then his relations with the radical-socialist group. He participated as a member of cabinets on five occasions during the first quarter of the twentieth century.

Since 1925 and continuously until 1932, he was minister of Foreign Affairs of the French Republic, supported on several occasions by Poincaré and Painlevé. His main achievements as Foreign Affairs Minister of France were the Locarno Pact in 1925, which was an important milestone improving relations with the German Empire, and the Kellogg Briand Pact of 1928, renouncing war as a tool for establishing national policy. His political view was based on peaceful means directing the foreign policy of France and conciliation with Germany after the WWI, against the popular tendency based on militarism as an expression of the State might and revenge towards Germany. This outstanding attitude was rewarded with the Nobel Peace Prize in 1926, shared with Gustav Stresemann, German Foreign affairs minister of the Weimar Republic.

Briand and Stresemann launched a proposal to avoid conflicts in the future between Germany and France, a plan for a European organization. The idea was presented by Briand in the League of Nations in 1929.[1] The concept was developed afterwards in a memorandum for the French government about the European Federal Union. The main target of Briand was the end of the conflicts between France and Germany via a common organization where sharing economic and political aspects would have made any war between the members impossible.[2] His economic proposals were based on a common market, as well as free movement of persons, merchandise, service, and capital, very similar to the current Single Market started by the Single European Act in 1986.

On the other hand, his political approach to the organization was link with intergovernmental cooperation between the Member States, rather than integration. According to his proposal the sovereignty of the states was kept intact and the decision making was based on consensus and unanimity. Good faith between the members of the organization was crucial for its functional capacity. Nevertheless, the creation of a common market somehow needs some level of integration, at least to abolish national obstacles to trade created by the national governments to protect their local economic sectors. The Briand proposal might have developed in a supranational organization forced by the obvious necessities of the market, as a logical evolution of the economic integration. Nevertheless, the economic proposal without political integration was, and still is, a popular idea among the British. The British Premier David Cameron have asked in several occasions to increase the development of the European market and decrease the political integration, position defended also by Margaret Thatcher and other influential British politicians since the debate of Europe was opened. Neither of them have explained how the economic integration can be achieved without political integration to harmonize the common rules of the common market without national distortions affecting trade. The idea of

[1]Braghiroli (2007).

[2]Oudin (1987).

the market ruling itself, as the major expression of British liberalism could have been a theoretical option until the crisis of the beginning of twenty-first century, where the intention of the states was needed to save the economic situation.

However, the most important project of Briand since the late twenties was the proposal for the creation of the United States of Europe. In a speech delivered on 5 September 1929 at the Tenth Assembly of the League of Nations, launched to the international community the proposal to create a United Europe. The proposal was intentionally ambiguous in the real objectives and conditions to create the European Federal State, fostering the debate about how the new political form should be defined. The own Briand defined in greater detail his plan for the United States of Europe in another historical speech at the Hôtel des Berges, during a meeting attended by representatives of several European countries as the British Arthur Henderson, Stresemann, Hymans (Belgium), Motta (Switzerland), the Italian Scialoja, Benes from Czechoslovakia or Quiñones de León representing Spain.

Arthur Henderson, the British representative was a politician belong to the Labour Party, he was the first Labour cabinet minister and was active in British politics over decades. During his early life he was working in the Iron industry and became a trade union leader. Joining afterwards the Labour party where he held numerous positions. He was a supporter of the League of Nations, and other forms of cooperation in the international arena to reduce the tensions among the main powers. He worked with the World League of Peace and chaired the Geneva Disarmament Conference, and in 1934 he was awarded the Nobel Peace Prize.

The positive impact that caused the speech of Briand and the possibilities of the proposal to achieve a peaceful cohabitation among the European powers led to French Politician commissioned by European governments to the developing a Memorandum on European unity. The memorandum included a detailed plan for the creation of the United States of Europe as a peace organization with the main task of avoiding further confrontations in Europe, especially between France and Germany, as the rivalry between these two countries was considered the main source of conflict in Europe.[3] Regardless the federal essence of the name United States of Europe, the Briand proposal was fundamentally intergovernmentalist. The involvement of United Kingdom in the new proposed organization faced a contradiction in the own spirit of the memorandum as cooperation following the model of the League of Nations fitted perfectly the British political positions towards a European organization, but the economic integration was against the British international position influenced by the British Empire and their support for liberalization of trade. United Kingdom, the greatest world empire at the time, must have chosen between the markets of its possessions, or the European market, as both would have not been accepted by the other European partners. The full membership in the European market of the whole British Empire would have change the essence of the European market towards a world market, and could have led to a British dominance over the common market because of the Empire extension and economic capacity.

[3]Briand (1927).

Obviously, the British Empire was more important than a hypothetical European market for the British authorities, and the British involvement in the Briand proposal was not a real possibility.

On 1 May 1930 the elaboration of this Memorandum was completed. The report was sent to each European government involved in the idea of a European organization. Nevertheless, the responses were not enthusiastic as the popularity of a European understanding was losing ground because of the beginning of an important economic crisis and the national unilateral actions to mitigate the negative impact on the national economies of an international economic crisis. The failure was alleviated at the Eleventh Assembly of the League of Nations where Briand proposal was presented. The ancestor of United Nations a Commission for the Study of the European Union, outlining the cooperation essence of the project, as the League of Nations itself was working more as a forum where the states could solve their differences peacefully through dialogue and negotiations.

The institutions of the organization proposed by Briand were mainly three, copying the working system of the League of Nations:

1. European Conference: A General assembly with a consultancy power.
2. European Committee: Similar to the Council of the League of Nations and decision center of the organization where unanimity and consensus were to be the voting system.
3. Secretariat: The working body of the organization.

Thomas James Tyrrell, a British politician from Australia, member of the Labour party, supported the Briand proposal, and lobbied for a positive response from the British government.[4] His main argument laid on the positive consequence of an active British involvement in European affairs. Nevertheless, the British Board of Trade prioritized the principle of most-favored-nation in trade relations, against the idea of a European Market close to its members with some sort of common trade policy and a custom union. The Board of Trade did not consider the possible preferential trade relations of the European custom union in way potentially similar to the imperial preference system of the British Empire, focusing on hypothetically customs preferences between the members of the European market. The main fear of the British authorities was the discrimination to no Member States or trade areas, against the principle of free trade dominating British politics at the time.

Briand wanted to discuss his plan with Henderson in May 1930 in Paris, but the Foreign Office advised against it until the intentions of Briand were clearer and the discussion was then postponed. Henderson, previously interested in the project of a European organization because of the international situation, was keener to reinforce the special relation with USA rather than getting closer to the French Republic. Later, Briand exposed to Henderson the master lines of his proposal, emphasizing the respect to the national sovereignty of its members. A clear sign of an organization based on the principles of the League of Nations, on cooperation, far from the federal

[4]Duroselle (1979).

idea entailed in the name of United States of Europe. The issue of national sovereignty was crucial for the British and Henderson promised to study the plan, but just if it will not interfere in the special relations between UK and USA, or in the case the European organization could be used against America.

Henderson concerns are a constant in the later relations between the EU and the UK, respect to national sovereignty and not using the European organization by any mean against the USA.

The final proposal of Briand incorporated the British desires,[5] downgrading the economic integration for more concerns related to security. His light proposal was not accepted by European countries interested in economic cooperation and neither by the British authorities. The efforts to include UK in the new European organization ended up in a general rejection of the premises included in the project by all the potential members.

Britain was supported by Baltic and Scandinavian states, Belgium and Austria because they saw United Kingdom as a counterbalance to the Franco-German power in the hypothetical European organization. Alan Leeper, first secretary in the League of Nations and Western department of the Foreign office drafted the response of the British government to the Brian memorandum. He was concern with the American economic expansion as a threat to the European dominance on the world, but also saw it as an example for the European economies. He saw many problems for UK in the proposal, as full membership meant a break with the Dominions, a formidable obstacle impossible to take over. However, he did not want to undermine the position of Briand, a peace seeker, in French politics, so he drafted a response without British fully involvement but expressing sympathy to the idea.

Noel Baker, professor of international relations, advised Henderson about the creation of a European organization without UK as a dangerous potential rival for British interest. Robert Cecil, 1st Viscount Cecil of Chelwood, one of the architects of the League of Nations, awarded with the Nobel Peace Prize in 1937, a Tory politician with expertise in international relations advised against the European organization because it could promote the idea of similar organizations in other parts of the world, as America or Asia. According to this idea, it was a great danger for the British Empire, as Canada could become part of an American organization or India part of an Asian Union, a main threat to the British Empire. Sir Arthur Salter warned about the inefficiency of the European small market units influenced by mass production industry comparing with other world economies as USA,[6] but the creation of bigger markets entities could have been done inside the framework of the League of Nations without political integration or without creating new trade blocs. According to this idea, the proposal of Briand was a threat for the League of Nations, and Salter proposed to support it but exclusively inside the International organization, as a part of the League of Nations in a worldwide context.

[5]Briand (1998).

[6]Ramiro Troitino (2013).

The position of Henderson and the British government was associated with the ideas of Sir Arthur Salter, respecting the concerns of Cecil and Baker, without confronting aggressively France, by supporting a European tariff truce and concerted economic action under the institutional umbrella of the League of Nations.[7]

The British involvement in the negotiations of Briand's proposal was important, but not decisive, for the failure of the first serious attempt creating a European organization with a common market and some political cooperation between its members.

2 WWII and a Franco-British Union

Despite of the signals, efforts and projects, Europe confronted again in a deadly conflict in 1939–1945. The contenders were like those of the WWI, a bad peace agreement, irresponsible behavior of the Allies, nationalism, economic crisis, and Nazi rise led to the European resurgence of violent conflict in its maximum expression.

The Allies, again under the umbrella of France and United Kingdom were facing an almost mighty Germany under the rule of the ruthless German National Socialist Party. Reediting the previous agreements and situations, the French government sent Jean Monnet to London to increase the effectiveness of the cooperation between both countries. Monnet kept still influential contacts in British politics and his previous work in the Allied Maritime Transport Council, were fundamental to nominate him as head of the Anglo-French Coordinating Committee in December 1939, just 5 months before the German occupation of France.

The function of the Anglo-French Coordination Committee was harmonizing the war economies of both states. It was divided in several executive thematic committees. The British contribution was calculated in 60% of the total economic effort, France backed the remaining 40%. The value of currencies of both countries were to be fix to provide as much stability as possible to the agreement. It was a clear common economic solidarity going beyond the traditional alliances. Jean Monnet worked again hand to hand with Salter, who was his colleague during similar task in the WWI. After his experience in the League of Nations, both men were convinced of the futility of intergovernmental institutions that kept intact the national sovereignty of the Member States of the organization and were supporters of integration rather than cooperation.

Also working with them was René Pleven, a supporter of the European integration who as French Prime Minister in 1950 proposed a European Defense Community. His plan was based on the success of the first European Community proposal just a few months before, the European Coal and Steel Community. The European states were willing to cooperate among themselves because of the benefits of

[7]Boyce (2009).

integration and because an important external reason, the USA idea of Europe as one more scenario of confrontation in the world war against communism, an important area that needed to be strong to resist Soviet expansion, as the Soviet Union wanted to spread its political system to Western Europe at a time there were important communist parties in such important countries as France and Italy.[8]

France, was also concerned about an independent and strong German. The French government led by Pleven thought of integrating the military field as the best way to avoid an independent German army. The proposed European Defense Community entailed France, West Germany, Italy, and the Benelux countries, already members of the ECSC, but not United Kingdom, the most powerful Western European Army due to the British concerns about integration and their support to other alternatives, as the intergovernmental military alliance based on the North Atlantic Treaty, which was signed on 4 April 1949, NATO. The European Defense Community was based in similar terms of integration than the ECSC but with tighter control from the national governments.

It was proposed to have a common budget, common institutions, and a common army; but in reality, the military forces were going to be under strict control from their respective national parliaments, except West Germany that was going to be under the surveillance of the common institutions.

The plan was not popular in the French Parliament, because the communists, an important force, saw it as an instrument of the USA to fight against communist ideas, while the supporters of de Gaulle thought of it as an attack on French sovereignty, a way to mutilate the military independence of France. Other members of the Parliament were concerned about the absence of the UK.

Nevertheless, the main obstacle was that an army is one of the main pillars of a state, and there was going to be a common army without a common state, and hence no common institution was to oversee the army. The Italian government then sponsored a plan, based in deeper political cooperation, to save the EDC; it was called the European Political Community and was drafted by the Common Assembly of the ECSC in 1952, but was too ambitious for the political moment of Europe at that time.

Finally, the French Parliament rejected the EDC in 1954 by a vote of 264–319, and the EPC was forgotten. Currently the development of a Common European Defense system has become again a priority, and probably in the coming years there will be outstanding developments in this field.[9]

Other British personality involved in the Anglo-French Coordination Committee was Lord Stamp, economist expert on taxation and statistics kill by a German bomb in a raid against London in 1941. He was assisted by Henry Clay, a close associate, and by H.D. Henderson, an economist and adviser to His Majesty's Treasury from 1939 to 1944.

[8] Young (1984).

[9] Thomson (1966).

The Franco-British collaboration was enhanced with other initiatives, as a Supreme War Council, the Anglo-French Industrial Council, and collaboration between their colonial forces.

The leadership of Monnet was uncontestable because of his contacts in British and French politics, his expertise in the field and especially because of his connections with USA. The idea of Monnet was to establish the closest possible economic integration between France and United Kingdom. The short-term results would have been more economic efficiency in the war, and in the long term, after the war, the tight economic collaboration between French and British should have led to the political union of Europe.

Jean Monnet with the essential collaboration of Salter, his vice-chairman on the Coordination Committee, presented drat on the Anglo-French unity, used next as the main source for the Vansittart draft on June 1940.[10] The proposal was influenced by previous statements from Alfred Duff Cooper, first Viscount Norwich and prominent conservative politician, who had argued about sharing resources with France already in 1938 as the only way to keep the independence of both states and Europe. Arnold Toynbee, a leading specialist on international affairs, professor of international history at the London School of Economics and director of studies at the Royal Institute of International Affairs in London, who even had a private meeting in 1936, wrote on September 1936 about a hypothetical Anglo-French union as the center of the great European Union. Sir Orme Sargent, one of the most important men in the Foreign Office during the 1930s, proposed in February 1940 a permanent system of collaboration between UK and France in politics, economy, and defense to counterbalance the German power in the post-war period. He was aware that his idea of a European federation with France and UK at its nucleus would generate tensions among the British citizens, but he thought as a solution to increase the educational work on the British citizens about the positive effects of such a union, peace. The ideas of Sir Orme Sargent reached the highest level of British politics. The period was also very active among French intellectuals, politicians and business men supporting the idea of an Anglo-British union.

Edward Frederick Lindley Wood, first Earl of Halifax, Foreign Secretary between 1938 and 1940 and from 1941 to 1946, British Ambassador in Washington, took seriously the idea presented by Sir Orme Sargent. The British Foreign Secretary asked the minister of information to increase the popularity of the Anglo-French union among the British citizens, and created an expert committee to discuss about how the idea could be applied in the reality. It would have taken years to apply the idea of first educating the British about the benefits of an Anglo-French union and develop the effective tools for it. Hence, it was seen as a notion to be developed in the long term, especially in the post war period.[11]

The German invasion of France began in May 1940, just 4 weeks after the French army was overwhelmed by the circumstances and close to the absolute collapse. The

[10]Ramiro Troitiño (2017).

[11]Beloff (1970).

French authorities were seriously thinking about an armistice, rejecting the idea of any desperate defense because it would destroy the country without serious chances of success rather than delay the defeat. But the British authorities, especially Winston Churchill, were trying to influence the French government to resist at any cost and continue the war, even if the mainland was occupied, from North Africa.[12]

On 14 June the German troops entered Paris and the French government moved from Tours to Bordeaux, increasing the pressure over the French government to reach an armistice with Germany unilaterally leaving UK alone against the German threat. Leo Amery, a British Conservative Party politician and journalist, secretary of State for India, drafted a paper the same day Paris surrendered, where he reaffirmed the Anglo-French Union as the only practical solution to keep France in the war. The main concerns of the British government were link with the French navy and its vast colonial empire that under the German power would have been deathly for the British aspirations in the war.

According to Churchill:

> In these days the British War Cabinet were in a state of unusual emotion. The fall and the fate of France dominated their minds. Grief for our ally in her agony, and desire to do anything in human power to aid her, was the prevailing mood. There was also the overpowering importance of making sure of the French Fleet. It was in this spirit that a proposal for an 'indissoluble union' between France and Britain was conceived.[13]

Also, on 14 June, Sir Robert Vansittart, the Principal Private Secretary to the British Prime Minister from 1928 to 1930 and Permanent Under-Secretary at the Foreign Office from 1930 to 1938 and later Chief Diplomatic Adviser to the British Government, had a meeting with Monnet, Pleven, and Morton to discuss the Anglo-French Union under the supervision of Lord Halifax. Sir Robert Vansittart was known for his fierce contempt for Germany, as he saw the Germans as an aggressive nation since the times of the Roman Empire, being the Nazis no more than the expression of the German spirit. According to this idea he proposed that Germany after the WWI must be stripped of all military capacity, including its heavy industries, and re-educating the German people intensively for at least a generation to change their aggressive behavior. Sir Robert Vansittart was himself a strong British nationalist and truly believed that the hegemonic role of United Kingdom in the European affairs should be defended at any cost. Morton, a British civil servant, was Churchill's personal assistant when he became prime minister in 1940, after the war he served on the UN's in the Middle East in 1949.

The four men with so different backgrounds produced a draft about the Anglo-French union to be used as the foundation for the final proposal by the British government. At first Churchill did not welcome the proposal because according to his own words:

> My first reaction was unfavorable. I asked a number of questions of a critical character, and was by no means convinced. However, at the end of our long Cabinet that afternoon the

[12]Ramiro Troitiño and Chochia (2015).

[13]Churchill and James (1974).

> subject was raised. I was somewhat surprised to see the staid, stolid, experienced politicians of all parties engage themselves passionately in an immense design whose implications and consequences were not in any way thought out. I did not resist, but yielded easily to these generous surges which carried our resolves to a very high level of unselfish and undaunted action.[14]

General de Gaulle, recently appointed Under-Secretary of State for National Defense arrived to London on 16 June to arrange the transportation of French troops to North Africa,[15] met with Monnet and the French Ambassador. Both men presented the Anglo-French Union as the only possibility to avid French defeat and urged the French general to express his support to the plan to the British Prime Minister[16] who finally supported the idea.

De Gaulle informed his government and prepared a final version of the declaration of Union with Jean Monnet, Pleven, and Vansittart. The French General later will be the main obstacle to British participation in the European Communities, but accepted an Anglo-French union as the only hope for France to keep on fighting. He presented the draft to Churchill and convinced him that it was the only possibility to keep France in the war. Finally, the British government accepted the idea, and after making some modifications to the draft, the Prime Minister of United Kingdom on 16 June 1940 made an official solemn proposal for an Anglo-French Union:

> At this most fateful moment in the history of the modern world The Governments of the United Kingdom and the French Republic make this declaration of indissoluble union and unyielding resolution in their common defense of justice and freedom against subjection to a system which reduces mankind to a life of robots and slaves.
>
> The two governments declare that France and Great Britain shall no longer be two nations, but one Franco-British Union.
>
> The constitution of the Union will provide for joint organs of defense, foreign, financial, and economic policies.
>
> Every citizen of France will enjoy immediately citizenship of Great Britain; every British subject will become a citizen of France.
>
> Both countries will share responsibility for the repair of the devastation of war, wherever it occurs in their territories, and the resources of both shall be equally, and as one, applied to the purpose.
>
> During the war there shall be a single War Cabinet, and all the forces of Britain and France, whether on land, see, or in the air, will be placed under its direction. It will govern from wherever it best can. The two Parliaments will be formally associated. The nations of the British Empire are already forming new armies. France will keep her available forces in the field, on the sea, and in the air. The Union appeals to the United States to fortify the economic resources of the Allies, and to bring her powerful material aid to the common cause.
>
> The Union will concentrate its whole energy against the power of the enemy, no matter where the battle may be.
>
> And thus we shall conquer.[17]

---

[14]See 16.

[15]Ramiro Troitiño (2008).

[16]Dinan (2004)

[17]See 16.

The proposal was enthusiastically received[18] by the head of the French government, Reynaud, but not by its War Cabinet, where an important part of its members thought better to reach an agreement with Germany than become a part of the British dominions. Reynaud lost the support of its cabinet and Mariscal Petain assumed the power, reaching an armistice with Germany, meaning the demise of the project.

The Anglo-French union proposal was vague because of the short time the British government had at his disposal to influence the French government. Nevertheless, the master lines of the Union were included in the declaration. Joint citizenship for British and French that in practical terms meant the unification of their political systems, as the citizen, as a subject, is the main pillar of a democratic state, hence the British parliament and the French national Assembly would have been united in a single chamber or at least be formally associated. The difference between these two conceptions lay on the essence of the union, federal for a united parliament or confederal in the case of a formal association. It also established a single currency for the new political entity, as economy was a crucial art of the Union, including foreign trade and a custom union. It also included defense aspects with a common war cabinet and common military command.

The Anglo-French Union had many similarities with the previous proposal of Briand after WWI, but was clearly define and can be considered more as a declaration of intentions than a specific plan for uniting United Kingdom and France in a single state. The historical context of the declaring and the vital necessities of the British under the German threat highly influenced the proposal. The Anglo-French Union probably would not have worked as most of France was under German occupation, and perhaps would have dissolved after the resolution of the war as for some British government members was a temporal solution for a temporal necessity and was not meant to be indissoluble.

Nevertheless, the plan was a long-term solution for a short-term necessity. It failed in his primary target, to prevent the surrender of France. Its long-term implications as an embryo of a future European Union or just a war time resolution that would expire after the conflict belong to the realm of speculation. The main certainty about the Anglo-French Union is that UK could become a leading force in terms of integration, reducing its autonomy, national sovereignty and even its currency if the external stimulus were strong enough. The British showed enough flexibility to adapt and change their statements, for example the British rejection to Briand's proposal, to obtain a higher reward.[19]

References

Beloff M (1970) The Anglo-French union project of June 1940. Intellect Polit: 172–199

[18]Gates (1981).

[19]Shlaim (1974).

Boyce RWD (2009) British capitalism at the crossroads, 1919–1932. Cambridge Books, Cambridge
Braghiroli S (2007) The challenges to democracy in the interwar period: lessons from the past relevant today. Poland, Lithuania, and Czechoslovakia in an extended Rokkanian perspective. CEU Polit Sci J 4:358–380
Briand A (1927) Paroles de paix. E. Figuière
Briand A (1998) Mémorandum sur l'organisation d'un régime d'Union fédérale européenne. In: Le Plan Briand d'Union fédérale européenne. Perspectives nationales et transnationales, avec documents. Actes du colloque international tenu à Genève du, vol 19. pp 569–582
Churchill W, James RR (1974) Winston S. Churchill: his complete speeches, 1897–1963: his complete speeches, 1897–1963. Chelsea House Publications, New York
Dinan D (2004) Europe recast: a history of European Union, vol 373. Palgrave Macmillan, Basingstoke
Duroselle JB (1979) La décadence, 1932–1939: 1932–1939. Impr. nationale, Paris
Gates EM (1981) End of the affair: the collapse of the Anglo-French alliance, 1939–40. University of California Press, Berkeley
Oudin B (1987) Aristide Briand: la paix, une idée neuve en Europe;[biographie]. Laffont, Paris
Ramiro Troitiño D (2008) De Gaulle and the European communities. In: Proceedings of the Institute for European Studies, no 4, pp 139–152
Ramiro Troitino D (2013) European integration: building Europe (European political, economic, and security issues). Nova Science Publishers Incorporated, Hauppauge
Ramiro Troitiño D (2017) Jean Monnet before the first European Community: a historical perspective and critic. Trames no. 3
Ramiro Troitiño D, Chochia A (2015) Winston Churchill and the European Union. Balt J Law Polit 8(1):55–81
Shlaim A (1974) Prelude to downfall: the British offer of union to France, June 1940. J Contemp Hist 9(3):27–63
Thomson D (1966) The proposal for Anglo-French union in 1940. Clarendon Press, Oxford
Young JW (1984) Britain, France, and the unity of Europe, 1945–1951. Leicester University, Leicester

Cooperation or Integration? Churchill's Attitude Towards Organization of Europe

David Ramiro Troitiño, Tanel Kerikmäe, Archil Chochia, and Andrea Hrebickova

Abstract This chapter analyzes Churchill's regard on European integration mainly through his political speeches, especially one in The Hague Congress and one in the University of Zurich. First part provides historical context, political ideas of Churchill, his attitude to European integration and the process of integration itself. The chapter also shows us the original plans for creating of European Union, Churchill's support of League of Nations, and his scepticism about integration. Through his participation in the process of European integration, we can see obvious British influence and we can understand the traditional British approach to the EU.

1 Winston Churchill: Eurosceptic or European Integration Supporter?

The main problem for researching the contributions of Winston Churchill to the current EU is the lack of specialised literature focused on the topic. Nevertheless, much has been written about Churchill, from different perspectives, including an outstanding number of general biographies, sectorial works focus on his different activities, his own writings, his own autobiography, and the record of his numerous speeches. Nevertheless, there is not relevant literature focus on his involvement on the European integration affairs rather than ethereal references to his famous speech in Zurich (1946) calling for the United States of Europe, that mostly is limited evoking the title of the speech rather than its content.

Churchill's work as historian includes several important books, as his history of the English-speaking peoples (Churchill 1958), The Second World War (Churchill 1953) or The World Crisis (Churchill 1931). His narrative history earned him the

D. Ramiro Troitiño (✉) · T. Kerikmäe · A. Chochia
Tallinn Law School, Tallinn University of Technology, Tallinn, Estonia
e-mail: david.troitino@ttu.ee; tanel.kerikmae@ttu.ee; archil.chochia@ttu.ee

A. Hrebickova
Faculty of Law, Palacký University Olomouc, Olomouc, Czech Republic
e-mail: aabecedaa@gmail.com

D. Ramiro Troitiño et al. (eds.), *Brexit*,
https://doi.org/10.1007/978-3-319-73414-9_3

Nobel Prize in Literature but is strongly link with the British affairs, hence the interest of Churchill obviously was not, at least from the historical approach, focused on the European affairs as a whole, rather than with the British involvement in the world affairs as a world power and active player in the international relations. The work as historian of Churchill has been carefully analyzed by Maurice Ashley,[1] literary assistant to Winston Churchill and historian himself.

The writing career of Churchill contains dozens of books on different topics, mostly link with his living experiences, novels, and even fictional works. His literature career has been analyzed by several authors, as Carter,[2] Alldritt[3] or Rasor.[4] On his more artistic sphere, his painting activity is less relevant for this research, but still important to understand Churchill, as clearly, he himself pointed out in his work *Painting as a Pastime* (1948). Coombs[5] has made a detailed research about Churchill's painting and its influence in his life. His military activity has attracted more attention, mainly in his early days as a young officer serving in the British Empire and his military activity in the Western front during the WWI. Authors as D'Este,[6] Russell[7] or Thompson[8] have deeply research the topic, highlighting his personal bravery, his tactical developments, and his command skills. His life as adventurer has attract lots of devotion, thanks to his own writings about the different campaigns he took part of, and the myth of a young hero built around the figure of Churchill, as brilliantly pointed out Cannadine.

The extended political career of Churchill has been widely discussed from different perspectives, as emphasizing his political beliefs Gilbert,[9] Addison[10] and Charmley.[11] These three authors, among others, explain properly the main political ideas of Churchill, but their outstanding works do not include enough information about the political beliefs of Churchill referring to the European Integration rather than mere indirect references. The biographies of Churchill are also countless, including several brilliant works, especially the works published by Gilbert[12] and Roy Jenkins.[13] Nevertheless, these well documented books analyzed deeply the life,

[1]Ashley (1968).

[2]Carter (1965).

[3]Alldritt (1992).

[4]Rasor (2000).

[5]Coombs et al. (2004).

[6]D'Este (2010).

[7]Russell (2005).

[8]Thompson (1973).

[9]Gilbert (1983).

[10]Addison (1980).

[11]Charmley (2014).

[12]Gilbert (1992).

[13]Jenkins (2012).

actions, and ideas of Churchill, but their references to the role of Churchill as a father of Europe are not properly addressed.[14]

Hence the best approach to understand the real thoughts and contributions of Winston Churchill to the European integration are his own speeches, his wide correspondence with the main political leaders of the twentieth century, his prolific correspondence with his wife, and his participation in different historical events shaping the current European Union. Thanks to the literature skills of Churchill, he mastered the elaboration of speeches, and used their publication to spread his ideas. The great edition of Robert Rhodes[15] includes the most relevant speeches of Churchill's long political career; like his famous *we shall never surrender* included in his speech *We Shall Fight on the Beaches* (4 June 1940) addressed to the House of Commons, or the reference to the Iron Curtain included in his speech *The Sinews of Peace* (5 March 1946)[16] in Missouri, USA. The main speeches related to the European integration, and basic pillars of this research are *the United States of Europe* (19 September 1946) in the University of Zurich, his speech to the Council of Europe (17 August 1949, Strasbourg) and his participation in the debate about the Schuman plan in the House of Commons (27 June 1950). As a complementary source, his wide correspondence with political leaders and close associates include some valuable information about the ideas of Churchill related to the European integration. Finally, his participation in The Hague Congress (1948) provides us with important information about the real involvement of Winston Churchill in the European movement and his position about the possible shape of the future organization.

The combination of the primary sources with a critic analysis to the extensive literature provides this research with information to clarify Churchill's ideas about the political and economic integration of Europe and establish his real role in the process uniting Europe.

1.1 Churchill. Personal and Historical Context

Winston Spencer Churchill was born in an English aristocratic family with a socialite American mother in 1874. He chose the military career and served in different locations of the British Empire, as India, South Africa, and Sudan as an officer. He showed courage in his war actions and combined his military activity with a work as war correspondent. His literature work was outstanding, being awarded with the Nobel Prize for Literature in 1953, thanks to different biographic and historical books, his series of articles and his speeches. Being the last highly influential in the world politics, as his speech encouraging the British to resist the German threat and

[14]Churchill (1968).
[15]Churchill and James (1974).
[16]Churchill (1946).

his famous we shall never surrender (We Shall Fight on the Beaches, 4 June 1940), when the German troops seemed unstoppable.

Before the WWI he was already and active politician, using his growing popularity as a war hero and as a writer to join the House of Commons of United Kingdom. He served as President of the Board of Trade, Home Secretary, and First Lord of the Admiralty as part of Asquith's Liberal government. The disaster of Gallipoli led to his resignation and he resumed his military activity in the Western front as commander of the sixth Battalion of the Royal Scots Fusiliers, where once again he showed his personal bravery in several war actions. He returned to government as Minister of Munitions, Secretary of State for War, and Secretary of State for Air. In 1921–1922 Churchill served as Secretary of State for the Colonies, then Chancellor of the Exchequer in Baldwin's Conservative government of 1924–1929.[17] During this period in governmental positions he took controversial decisions as supporting the gold standard, or rejecting the home rule of India and opposing the abdication of Edward VIII.

During the 1930s, Churchill became a strong critic to the Western inactivity towards Nazi Germany and campaigned for rearmament. He was again appointed First Lord of the Admiralty and following the resignation of Neville Chamberlain on 1940, became Prime Minister, leading the British Empire and the allies in the war effort against the Nazis.

The elections of 1945 send him to the opposition, being an active period in European affairs, with several conferences and his active participation in The Hague Congress in 1948. The post war period was crucial for the creation of the current European Union and other European initiatives as the Council of Europe. The participation of Churchill was very important because of his immense personal prestige and his support to the integration process in Europe under special conditions, not necessarily matching with the current trends of integration. Nevertheless, his return to Downing Street as Prime minister from 1951 till 1955, reduced his participation in the process and increased the British-American axis, separating UK from the first European Communities.

Winston Churchill died in 1965, being his last remarkable speech link with his nomination as honorary citizen of the United States by President John F. Kennedy. The last years of Churchill were negatively influenced by sickness and physical problems, reducing his personal participation in the European affairs, as for example in the case of the personal veto of the French president, de Gaulle, to the British petition of membership to the European Communities, where Churchill did not intervene regardless his solid personal connections with the French general.

[17]Churchill (1930).

1.2 Political Ideas and Main Contributions

The long political career of Churchill was defined by three different factors; pragmatism, tenacity, and innovation. His political life was divided between two of the main parties of UK, the conservatives, and the liberals, but his ideas remained substantially similar in his double way journey across the benches of the House of Commons. The analysis of Churchill's political work helps us to understand his vision about UK, as an active British statesman, and the international affairs, as a world leader. Nevertheless, this analysis should be cautious, as it is an indirect source open to interpretations and because Churchill was a politician, open to change his positions according to the social necessities. All the actions of Churchill must be understood under the prism of the historical situation, as the zenith of the British Empire, the WWI, the Interwar period, the WWII and the Cold War.

Winston Churchill was a fervent supporter of free trade, when at the time the British politics were dominated by the debate of the economic model of the state; open to the world economy fostering trade, or more restrictive access to the British market protecting the British industry from more competitive foreign companies. The result of the internal debate was favourable to Churchill's option, influencing the British economic development during the twentieth century and its relations with the European Communities.

The creation of the ECSC, the embryo of the current European Union, was an interesting project to the British authorities as the mining sector was important for the British economy. It was seen as a free trade area in the markets of coal and steel, but the inclusion of integrational elements meant the British withdraw from the negotiations. Afterwards the British government created an alternative model of cooperation based exclusively on industrial free trade, the European Free Trade Association, signed in Stockholm in 1960 by Austria, Denmark, Norway, Portugal, Sweden, Switzerland, and the United Kingdom, including later other European states. The association sponsored by the British government lost its importance with the enlargement of the European Communities to UK, Ireland, and Denmark. Nevertheless, the British once inside of the EEC have been constantly pushing in the direction of a free trade economy in Europe rather than political integration. The contributions of Margaret Thatcher to the Single European Act (1986) were crucial to create the Single European Market, and even in the current times, the British government lead by Cameron is constantly proposing increasing the freedom of the market to foster trade, but reducing the political integration, a constant in most of his predecessors. The influence of Churchill in the traditional British approach to the European Integration, as a free trade area rather than a political project, is obvious as he was crucial in the internal debate of UK leading to the implementation of a free trade policy. Nevertheless, the idea of Churchill was link with the conception of the British Empire as a world free trade area, but if we extrapolate this idea to the European stage, the current British position is a result of the ideas developed and supported fervently by him.

Churchill regardless his aristocracy origins included in his political actions numerous actions favouring the less fortunate British citizens, as an example of pragmatism accepting the new necessities of the British society against the privileges of his own social class, the imperial aristocracy. He introduced the Trade Boards Bill setting up the first minimum wages in Britain, he helped drafting the first unemployment pension legislation of the country, the National Insurance Act of 1911, and he also assisted and supported the people's Budget, creating new taxes on the wealthy to finance social welfare programs. His ideas were somehow included in the essence of the European Union as the solidarity between Member States is one of the main pillars in the organization, and did not differ from the ideas of the Christian democrats designing the European integration process. It also shows the great social adaptability of Churchill to new ideologies and the idea of a constant social evolution. It suggests adaptation to the European society demands and hence a flexible approach to the European building process according to the necessities of the society, in constant evolution.[18]

His capacity to compromise and accept creative and innovative political solutions was shown in the aftermath of the Second Boer War, also known as the Second Anglo-Boer War and the South African War (11 October 1899–31 May 1902), were he participated officially as a war correspondent combining it with active involvement in the fighting. After the military British victory, Churchill supported the Transvaal Constitution delegating a greater proportion of power to the Boers themselves. Regardless the British success in the war, he pointed out that any government imposed by London without including the Boers would lead to a repetition of the conflict. Integration between victors and losers was the best solution for a peaceful and prosperous coexistence in South Africa in the framework of the British Empire. It was the same essential idea that years later would lead to the creation of the European Communities, including Germany in the European integration as an equal partner.[19] Churchill showed a similar approach in the European scenario; at the Second Quebec Conference in 1944 he drafted and, together with Roosevelt, signed a less-harsh version of the original Morgenthau Plan, in which was pledged to convert Germany after its unconditional surrender into a country primarily agricultural and pastoral in its character. He remarkable changed his original position towards Germany promoting a strong and free Western Germany in the context of the Cold War.

The tenacity of Churchill could be defined as providential. His ardent opposition to the Communist regime in Russia, after the WWI, and his call for a military intervention to prevent future threats were dismissed by a British government and a British society exhausted by the war efforts. His resistance against the Nazis, against any logic as UK was standing alone against Germany after the Germans pact with the USSR, the French surrender, and the USA neutrality, prevented the Hitler's triumph and paved the way to victory. During the war he again showed pragmatism,

[18]Ramiro Troitiño and Chochia (2015).

[19]Braghiroli (2007).

as he collaborated actively with an unexpected ally, the USSR, regardless his opposition to the communist ideas. Right after the war he became a public advocate of freedom and democracy against the totalitarian system imposed by the communist regimes all over central and east Europe supported by the Red Army, and his speech *The Sinews of Peace* (5 March 1946)[20] encouraged the Europeans to stand firmly in the context of the Cold War against the aggressive behaviour of the Soviet Union and its world revolution. Churchill's opposition to the Communist expansion also helped the European Integration, as a united Western Europe was crucial to stand against the Soviet threat. The desirable collaboration between West Germany and France cannot be understood without the external influence of the Cold War.[21]

The capacity of Winston Churchill to adapt and implement innovations in different fields was one of his outstanding skills. He launched a program to replace coal power with oil power, among other innovations in the British navy as First Lord of the Admiralty, a controversial initiative as UK was an important producer of cool, and back then its oil reserves mere minimal. Nevertheless, his risky reform paid out during the WWII as the Royal Navy stood firmly in different war scenarios against the German Kriegsmarine. He also was a keen supporter of other military innovations, as the development of a tank force and the investment in aircrafts. His measures provided the RAF with enough strength during the Battle of Britain (1940) to contain the Luftwaffe and prevent any amphibious invasion. This fact proved that Churchill was not afraid of innovations; on the other hand, he supported them in any field, as military or politics. Hence the innovative approach of the European Communities, an integration process between enemies, would have not hesitated him.

An important feature of Churchill's life, in the political and personal sphere, was his relation with the United States of America. His mother, Jennie Jerome, was born in New York in 1854, in a rich family with a financier and speculator father, and a rich heiress mother, influencing Churchill's approach to USA. In political terms, his relation with Roosevelt and the collaboration between UK and USA during the WWII was crucial to defeat the Germans. The important influence in Churchill's life of USA has been analyzed by his own homonymous grandson, Winston S. Churchill, *The Great Republic: A History of America* (2001) and the outstanding book of Martin Gilbert *Churchill and America* (2005). Also, Churchill's own writings refer to the matter, as his book *A history of the English-speaking peoples* (2013) includes constant references to the special relations between United Kingdom and USA, as part of the same political and cultural space with common traditions and goals.

Winston Churchill visited for the first time USA in November 1895, on his way to his first military adventure, in Cuba. In 1900 Churchill returned for a comprehensive lecture tour across the eastern United States and Canada. During 1929 he repeated successfully a lecture tour all over USA, even visiting the West Cost, and again in

[20]Churchill (1946).

[21]Russett (1994).

December 1931 was in New York. As British Prime minister he visited USA five times during the WWII. On 1946, already out of office, he took a vacation in USA, and by 1953, again as British Prime Minister he visited again the USA with the Cold War as a main objective of discussion. In May 1959, at the age of 84, Churchill returned to the United States as a personal guest of the President Eisenhower, and 1961 he made his last visit to the States.

Already during the First World War the Americans honoured him with the Distinguished Service Medal in 1919 and after the WWII he was awarded with honorary American citizenship, a rare privilege. The special relation of Churchill, a major politician in the British Empire, the world power then, with three USA presidents, during the emergence of the United States as a major power was essential for the international affairs. The transition from the British leadership to the current USA position of world power cannot be understood without the friendly attitude of Churchill towards America. Even though Jean Monnet, another so called father of Europe and main architect of the European Coal and Steel Community, also had strong relations with USA, his approach was different, as he saw the Americans as the needed sponsors for building the European States of Europe. Churchill saw the Americans as an equal partner to the British Empire, and an ally to keep the British status as a world power, including a combined sponsorship on the European Integration. The special relation between USA and UK fostered and promoted by Churchill, did not really fit with the European integration process, as the relations with USA, according to Churchill, were the priority of the British government in foreign affairs. The transatlantic cooperation was more important than the European domestic issues, as the vision of Churchill was influenced by a global perspective provided by the conception of the British Empire as a world leader. The fluid relation with the USA was shadowed by different disagreements, as the problems with USA about the Treaty of Versailles after WWI or the Churchill's critics about US Sec of State John Foster Dulles' domino theory or some disagreements with Eisenhower about the European integration. Nevertheless, he had a strong relationship with U.S. President Franklin D. Roosevelt—between 1939 and 1945 they exchanged an estimated 1700 letters and telegrams and met 11 times; Churchill estimated that they had 120 days of close personal contact.

The special relation between UK and USA was, among other reasons, used by the French president de Gaulle to reject twice the British application to full membership to the European Communities.[22] The intentions of de Gaulle of building a third way in the Cold War independent from USA and USSR, and promoting the French role as a world leader, colluded with the Anglo-American relations. The French statesman even thought of UK as a Trojan Horse of USA in the European Communities. Other British prime ministers as Margaret Thatcher or Tony Blair also adopted Churchill's position towards USA. It has been a constant since then in British politics and it has highly influenced the British actions inside the EU.[23]

[22]Ramiro Troitiño and Chochia (2015).

[23]Ramiro Troitiño (2008).

1.3 Churchill's Main Ideas and Contributions to the European Integration

There are different direct sources to analyze Churchill's position towards the European integration process. His political activity provides important information for the research on Churchill's approach to the European integration, as the Declaration of Union between France and UK, adopted by the British government and announced by Churchill in June 1940,[24] his support to the European Defence Community,[25] Churchill's membership in the European Movement, and his relations with the European Communities in his second term as Prime Minister from 1951 to 1955.[26]

His public speeches are traditionally the main source used to explain the relation of Churchill with the European Integration; basically just one speech has been quoted constantly to explain Churchill's position, the famous 1946 Zurich speech.[27] It, obviously has created a distortion around the real position of Churchill towards the European Integration as most of the authors mostly refer exclusively to this speech to explain Churchill's ideas related to Europe, as the former president of the European Commission, Barroso did in 2013. Nevertheless, there are many other direct sources to investigate Churchill's position about European affairs, as important speeches in the Congress of Europe, the opening meeting of the Council of Europe in Strasbourg, his interventions as Chairman of the European Movement, international conferences, especially in USA, the mail correspondence with his close collaborators, and his interventions in the House of Commons, especially regarding the debate about the Schuman Plan.[28]

1.4 Winston Churchill and the European Building Process

Churchill has been used as an icon against the European Integration in British politics, UKIP leader Nigel Farage has stressed Churchill's opposition to the European Communities and his commitment to the independence of UK against any supranational intervention and even important scholars have written about the rejection of Churchill to join the European integration process. On the other hand, Churchill is included by the European Union as one of its founding fathers and an example of British support to the European Union when the relations between UK and the EU are conflictive, as previous president of the European Commission,

[24]Shlaim (1974).

[25]Duchin (1992).

[26]Young (1985).

[27]Barroso (2013).

[28]Churchill (1947b).

Mr. Barroso, pointed out in a Special Churchill Lecture in the university of Zürich (8 November 2013).

The apparent contradiction can be clarified through the own words of Churchill and his own European political positions. Churchill wrote to his foreign secretary, Anthony Eden, on 21 October 1942: 'Hard as it is to say now… I look forward to a United States of Europe, in which the barriers between the nations will be greatly minimized and unrestricted travel will be possible.' Clearly, he liked the idea of some kind European Integration as a novelty to prevent conflicts, because these words must be understood in the context of the WWII. Churchill made public his support to the European integration in his Zurich speech of 1946 as he said: 'We must build a kind of United States of Europe'. His words are clear as he used WE instead of THEY, showing his support and possible participation in the new process uniting Europe. At London's Albert Hall, in May 1947, just a few months after his Zurich speech, Churchill spoke as Chairman and Founder of the United Europe Movement to 'present the idea of a United Europe in which our country will play a decisive part.' His support to the novelty of uniting Europe was clear, including UK in the process. Nevertheless, the role of UK in the integration was not explained in detail in this occasion beside the reference about sponsoring it. He argued in the same speech that Britain and France should be the, 'founder-partners in this movement' and concluded, 'Britain will have to play her full part as a member of the European family'. In May 1948, Churchill said in the opening speech to the Congress of Europe in The Hague 'We cannot aim at anything less than the Union of Europe as a whole, and we look forward with confidence to the day when that Union will be achieved.' Again, making clear his support and involvement in the European integration in front of an audience debating about the model of the future integration. Nevertheless, Churchill did not present clearly his position about the level of British involvement and the way the integration should follow. At a speech, again given for the European Movement at Kingsway Hall, November 1949, Churchill argued: 'The British Government have rightly stated that they cannot commit this country to entering any European Union without the agreement of the other members of the British Commonwealth. We all agree with that statement. But no time must be lost in discussing the question with the Dominions and seeking to convince them that their interests as well as ours lie in a United Europe.' It expresses again the support of Churchill to the European integration, and adds a new element, the inclusion of the former British Empire countries included in the Commonwealth in the process. These declarations, during a long and stable period, reject any Eurosceptic sentiment in Churchill and understandably are not referred by those using the iconic force of Churchill against the European Union.

It is evident that Winston S. Churchill supported the process of the European integration as he expressed several times during his political life. Hence, the real debate should then be about what kind of Europe he supported, as there were, and still are, different visions about the process uniting Europe and not just a unitary position.

2 Churchill's Idea of Cooperation Versus Integration

Winston Churchill supported the creation of the League of Nations, even though he complaint bitterly about the incapacity of the organization to prevent the WWII because of its incapacity to treat fairly the defeated Germany. After the WWII he promoted the United Nations, a new world organization heir of the League of Nations.[29] Obviously the international cooperation was a priority for Churchill to keep peace and stability, basic for the international economic development. Both organizations were based on cooperation, rather than integration; it provides an example of Churchill's ideas about international integration. Nevertheless, the UN differed from the League of Nations in several crucial points, as more executive powers to the Security Council and the creation of armed forces provided by the Member States to serve as peace-keepers or to repel an aggressor. The Security Council had five permanent members, United States, the Soviet Union, China, France and Britain, plus other countries serving 2 years terms on it. The veto power of the permanent members over the decisions made by the Security Council express the idea of cooperation rather than integration, as a single member can blockade any decision against its national interest; a facto way to keep intact the national sovereignty. It resembles the actions of de Gaulle inside the European Communities and the agreement of Fontainebleau after the empty chair crisis where it was accepted a voting system based on qualified majority accepting the veto of any Member State if its national interest was at stake.[30] As Churchill was one of the main architects of UN and promoted it on USA and even with Stalin, we can assure that his commitment with international cooperation, and even with some sort of integration, was clear, but establishing some safeguards to the national sovereignty avoiding full integration.

Churchill made several statements linking the European integration and the new world organization, in his view complementing each other. Churchill's speech in La Hague 1948 outlined: 'we must endeavour by patience and faithful service to prepare for the day when there will be an effective world government resting on the main groupings of mankind.'[31] The reference of main groupings of mankind refers to Europe, Asia or America as an integral part of the organization. If UN would be organized by regional unions rather than countries, obviously these regions should be organized in a similar way than the United Nations. Hence, it is likely that Churchill thought of the future European Union as an organization organized as a forum where to solve the problems between the Member States by peaceful meanings with a regional security council including the most powerful Member States with veto rights. This idea is reinforced by Churchill's speech at the University of Harvard on September 1943: 'Let us have a world council and under it regional or

[29]Hughes (1974).

[30]Ramiro Troitiño (2008).

[31]Churchill (1949).

continental councils'[32] According to these ideas, Europe should work as a regional council integrated in a world council, as a part of the United Nations. Hence the European organization should not lay on political integration rather than an organization based on collaboration between its members. Churchill argued about the needed leadership of UK and France in the new organization, the only two European members of the Security Council of the UN with veto right. At London's Albert Hall, in May 1947, speaking in a meeting of the United Europe Movement to 'present the idea of a United Europe in which our country will play a decisive part....' Churchill supported that Britain and France should be the, 'founder-partners in this movement'. It could suggest that the Security Council of the UN, formed by USA, UK, France, USSR, and China was representing the major civilizations of the world and the leaders of their respective regional areas.

In October 1948 during a Conservative Mass Meeting at Llandudno, Churchill made clear that Britain held a unique position at the heart of 'three majestic circles': the 'Empire and Commonwealth', 'the English-speaking world' and a 'United Europe'. It would have made UK member of different regional organizations part of the United Nations. Obviously in a model following the pattern of integration, it would have been impossible to be part of different regional areas at the same time. For example, the European Coal and Steel Community created a common market with common external borders, these would have prevented the simultaneous membership of different regional organizations simultaneously. Hence, the idea of Churchill about the European integration differed strongly from the path chosen by Europe leading to the current European Union. In the same speech he continued with: 'we are the only country which has a great part in every one of them. We stand, in fact, at the very point of junction, and here in this Island at the centre of the seaways and perhaps of the airways also, we have the opportunity of joining them all together.'[33] Besides a British centred point of view in international relations, normal in a politician born in the British Empire, Churchill made clear his position towards the model of integration, as just with an organization as United Nations, could UK be part of different regional levels.

Reinforcing the idea of the European integration as a regional part of the world organization, Churchill made a speech in Fulton in 1946 declaring himself against Europe becoming a Third Force between America and USSR and creating a neutral geographical bloc in the context of the international relations.[34] As USA and UK were defending universal rights, principals common to all humankind being aside them during the Cold War, was standing for freedom and humanity, somehow representing the world. The idea of the European Communities as a third independent way in the Cold War was applied by de Gaulle in his attempt of recovering French international prestige and influence in the world affairs. Nevertheless, his

[32]Churchill (1944).
[33]Churchill (1947a).
[34]Churchill and James (1974).

position did not survive his office term, as Pompidou already changed the French Foreign Policy.[35]

According to the public positions of Churchill we can only guess what kind of organization he wanted in the European level. He was very ambiguous about it, but we should not forget that at that time a new process of integration started, something never done before in human history, without a clear map road to support or reject. Nevertheless, there are some red lines in Churchill's ideas about the European integration that should be respected to the full membership of UK in the organization, and the British were seen by him as a crucial part of the European future as he wrote in a private letter in 1963, just 2 years before his death:' The future of Europe if Britain were to be excluded is black indeed.'

The best source to obtain Churchill's views about the European organization are his interventions in the debate of the House of Commons to discuss a united Europe in June 1950, because it was a debate about Europe, a discussion related with the model of Europe suitable for UK. Churchill said that he could not 'at present' foresee Britain being 'a member of a Federal Union of Europe'. However, Churchill went on to explain that this was primarily because of Britain's position, 'at the centre of the British Empire and Commonwealth', and, 'our fraternal association with the United States of America.' Hence Churchill's ideas about the European integration were not link with federalism, but he was a supporter of UK participating in the project for the good of Europe and UK. The idea of Great Britain participating in different regional organizations, as Europe, transatlantic relations, or the Commonwealth, would have been possible in a scenario based on cooperation where the relations with the members of the organization will not be exclusively, as a common market with common external tariffs rather than a free trade area without integration.

Nevertheless, Churchill's pragmatism was present in this debate, complaining about the obstructive attitude of the British Socialist Government to the European Integration and the Schuman plan, converting UK an enemy of Europe. According to Churchill, if the British government persisted in its position, the influence of UK in Europe would decline. So, even if he did not want UK as a part of a federal Europe, he was open to negotiations to try to find the best solution for the British and European interest. The strategy of the British labor government was to delay as much as possible the European integration in a way to divert the path from integration to cooperation, earning for UK the European suspicious about the real involvement of the country in the European building process, that last until nowadays.[36]

Churchill was not against sharing sovereignty as a principle, as he reassured himself in the House of Common, when he argued:

> To win the war we agreed to put our armies under S.H.A.E.F., a great Anglo-American organisation that was for the tactical and limited purposes prescribed. No one would ever have suggested that General Eisenhower should have had the power to say what units of the British Army should be suppressed or disbanded, or how they should be raised or

[35]Ramiro Troitiño (2008).

[36]Ramiro Troitiño (2013).

> remodelled, or anything like it. All these remained questions within the control of the autonomous sovereign States which were willing to agree to a larger unity for certain well defined functional—I use the "functional" because it is coming into use—functional purposes. Surely, this is one of the points we could have urged, and even have made conditional upon our agreement to any final scheme.[37]

It is again a clear approach to the cooperation theory as the best option to coordinate the common efforts, where autonomous partners are under a common authority taking the decisions by consensus. Churchill's references to functions are link with the back then popular theory of integration developed by David Mitrany, functionalism, a liberal tradition based on a positive approach that accepts as a fact that humans are rational and wish peaceful progress, that conflict and disharmony are not endemic to the human condition. Essentially it claims that the main target of any kind of integration is ending the conflicts of the world through international organizations. The shape of the organization, its name, or other symbols, are not important; what matters is the achievement of the goals. Functionalism stresses the functions of the organization over any other consideration. The priority of the organization should be the human needs or the public welfare of its members, the people, forgetting any kind of ideology because of its tight framework, the results and not the method. It is a technocratic vision: people who know best about any job are the ones who should do it to succeed. Technicians must rule over the areas where their expertise provides them with the wisdom to offer the best solutions to the problems of the people or the members. On the other hand, functionalism does not trust politicians because their goal is keeping their power rather than the common good. Mitrany argued that transnational organizations were more effective than national entities, as they were more efficient and hence could solve the problems of the people. This efficiency would transfer the loyalty of the people from the national level to the international one, ending wars and conflicts. The concept of flexibility is very important in this theory, because human needs, and not the creation of a supranational state, are the priority. Thus, functionalism can adopt different forms, different names, and different means to achieve its target. Mitrany thought that the European Communities were just reproducing the functions of the states in a supranational level, keeping intact the decision making of the states, leading to the domination of the main states over the other members of the organization.

Functionalism is too technocratic; it is mainly based in professionals doing the job, with a minimum involvement of other important actors, such as politicians, diplomats, and mainly citizens. The idea of building a community without counting on the people is very close to a dictatorship of the social elite. But even if its intentions are good, it is impracticable in the present time where democracy has become the main method of organizing European societies. It also has too much faith on humans and in their capacity to act rationally in all the situations. Churchill's position towards functionalism was friendly but without full support. This approach to the integration reflected somehow his pragmatic vision of politics in the

[37] Churchill and James (1974).

international level, and the several occasions when Churchill referred to the United States of Europe fit with the functionalist idea that the denomination of the organization does not matter rather than the functions. Obviously, Churchill was not a supporter of the idea of a European Federation, link with the reproduction of the USA in the European level, hence his call to the United States of Europe as early as 1930 in an article in the Saturday Evening Post[38] must be understood under the prim of functionalism. But at the same time the combination of rejection of politicians involved in the project and the lack of democracy of the future institutions, made it unacceptable for Churchill's world vision.

During the debate about the British involvement in the Schuman plan, Churchill openly supported the idea of cooperation in Europe, as in his intervention proves:

> I would add, to make my answer quite clear to the right hon. and learned Gentleman, that if he asked me, "Would you agree to a supranational authority which has the power to tell Great Britain not to cut any more coal or make any more steel, but to grow tomatoes instead?" I should say, without hesitation, the answer is "No." But why not be there to give the answer?

It clearly shows the opposition of Churchill to full integration in the European level, but not full rejection to the process, as he himself points out, UK should be in the negotiations to defend its position towards the model of future Europe. This reference against a strong influence of the Communal authorities over the domestic policies of its members can also be link with the idea of subsidiarity, where the most efficient level of decision making will manage the issues in a common association. Hence, the highest level will just deal with aspects influencing the whole community, leaving to the members the management of domestic issues or the application of the common rules according to the national traditions, as currently the European Union directives do. The idea of subsidiarity is included in the European Union as a main pillar of the integration, respecting the national, regional, and local authorities. Perhaps, the main difference between Churchill's ideas about subsidiarity and sharing sovereignty and the European Union, is the voting system in the highest level of decision making, unanimity versus majority, or at least some veto capacity for the Member States when outvoted and their national interest is at stake. As he clearly made public in the same speech about the Schuman plan in the House of Commons:

> Nothing is said about the method of voting. We know nothing about the method by which voting power will be allotted to the different members of any supra-national authority which may be set up. But it is quite certain we should not agree to become members of it—and that we should have every right to disagree—if our great preponderance in coal and steel production did not receive full recognition. Then there is the question of the right to terminate such an agreement. That is surely a matter we could have looked at after discussion.

Obviously, Winston Churchill was asking for greater power to the UK in the European organization, as it has in other international organizations, as United

[38]Bruyning (1990).

Nations. His position of Member States having the possibility to withdraw the European organization if it was their national interest is another pillar to the cooperative essence of the new community, following Churchill's ideas.

His opposition to the federal proposal for building Europe was expressed in the House of Commons in his intervention in the debate about the Schuman plan:

> Such a tremendous step as the federal union of Europe as something like a United States of Europe is not a matter which rests with us to decide. It is primarily one for the peoples of Europe. In our European Movement we have worked with federalists, and we have always made it clear that, though they are moving along the same road, we are not committed to their conclusions. Personally, I have always deprecated in public our becoming involved at this stage in all the tangles and intricacies of rigid constitution-making, which appeals so strongly to a certain type of mind. I was sorry that the hon. Member for Coventry, East, should have marred an able speech, as he so often does, by a gross misstatement when he says that European Union 'is run and financed by federalists.

Most of European citizens, was, and still is, against the idea of a European Federation. Even Altiero Spinelli, a prominent federalist, had a big bang approach to the issue to break the popular resistance to the creation of a European Federation; basically, the federation should have been done at once, from the top, without the consent of the European people, who afterwards would have recognized the benign effects of it and support it. Churchill's delegation of the decision about a European Federation to the European people matched his idea about Europe, without any political cost or political erosion. His opening speech at the Congress of Europe in May 1948, includes this idea presenting the European building process: 'should be a movement of the people, not parties'.[39]

The European Movement included the supporters of the European federalism even if Churchill's opinion was against the inclusion of some kind of constitution or legal document binding the members, main pillar of a Federal State. Nevertheless, if continental Europe was going to move in the federal integration model direction, Churchill did not want UK to be a member, but neither an obstacle, collaborating with the hypothetical European Federation following his idea of the three magic circles, Europe, the Commonwealth, and USA, where UK could be associated with all of them:

> I cannot conceive that Britain would be an ordinary member of a Federal Union limited to Europe in any period which can at present be foreseen. We should in my opinion favour and help forward all developments on the Continent which arise naturally from a removal of barriers, from the process of reconciliation, and blessed oblivion of the terrible past, and also from our common dangers in the future and present. Although a hard-and-fast concrete federal constitution for Europe is not within the scope of practical affairs, we should help, sponsor and aid in every possible way the movement towards European unity. We should seek steadfastly for means to become intimately associated with it.

Sponsoring the process would have given the British government the possibility of influencing the development of the integration according to its interest and keep good diplomatic relations with the states involved in the process, a basic movement

[39]Churchill (1949).

in a gradually more global world where the independent European states were losing its predominance in the international relations.

Hence, the most likely theoretical approach to Churchill's vision about Europe is Intergovernamentalism. This theory is based on agreements between States supporting coordination as the way to solve conflicts between the members of the organization because the states are accepted as the last recipients of sovereignty. Churchill was not against the transfer of loyalty as a principle, as he himself proclaimed in his last speech about Europe at London's Central Hall, Westminster in July 1957; some 4 months after six founding nations established the European Economic Community by signing the Treaty of Rome:

> The Conservative and Liberal Parties declare that national sovereignty is not inviolable, and that it may be resolutely diminished for the sake of all the men in all the lands finding their way home together.

But he wanted to include veto powers for the Member States, following the model of United Nations, if the decisions of the European organization were going to harm the UK. This power in reality means a strong brake for the autonomous decision making of the organization.

Moravcsik, supporter of Intergovernamentalism, highlights that cooperation between states is possible only when they share some common interest or common values. The basis of the European integration should be agreements between states and good faith in their relations. The common institutions should be just common forums at which to negotiate and solve different problems. It fits perfectly the idea of Churchill of building Europe based on common principles, as freedom or human rights in opposition to the Communist area dominated by USSR.

Nevertheless, Churchill did not radically reject the British involvement in the European integration process based on integration, as he declare at the European Assembly in July 1949, where he addressed the intergovernmental-federal debate by suggesting that all possibilities be explored. On the other hand, in a 29 November 1951 Cabinet memorandum, Churchill affirmed that Britain should not become an "integral part of European integration" as it would "forfeit our insular or commonwealth-wide character." Obviously, he was open to the debate and some kind of compromise to reach a satisfactory solution for all the parts involved in the process, as he expressed in the House of Commons:

> The French Foreign Minister, M. Schuman, declared in the French Parliament this week that, "Without Britain there can be no Europe." This is entirely true. But our friends on the Continent need have no misgivings. Britain is an integral part of Europe, and we mean to play our part in the revival of her prosperity and greatness.[40]

In Churchill's head, there was no doubt of the European necessity of UK to succeed and the British necessity of involvement in a process of peace and prosperity. Hence, negotiation was the solution. When the British government rejected the invitation to participate in the ECSC Churchill bitterly attacked the British

[40]Churchill and James (1974).

government for isolating the country and not even present their ideas about Europe. The British absence from the Messina conference held from 1 to 3 June 1955 leading to the creation of the EEC, current European Union, occurred under the premiership of Anthony Eden, Churchill's successor in Downing Street since 6 April 1955 because the health conditions of Churchill were deteriorating incapacitating him for a daily intense political activity.

The last years of a Churchill affected by sickness entailed some references to the European integration, in August 1961, Churchill wrote to his constituency Chairman: 'I think that the Government are right to apply to join the European Economic Community…' and in 1963, he wrote in a private letter: 'The future of Europe if Britain were to be excluded is black indeed.' Because he warned: 'If, on the other hand, the European trade community were to be permanently restricted to the six nations, the results might be worse than if nothing were done at all—worse for them as well as for us. It would tend not to unite Europe but to divide it—and not only in the economic field.'[41]

It reassures Churchill's support to the European integration and the British involvement in the process, just leaving open the questions about what kind of Europe was desired by him and the British capacity to effectively negotiate with its European partners and the flexibility of the European Communities to accept the British singularity.

3 Churchill's Model of Europe

Two European organizations reflect the vision of Churchill about a united Europe because of his direct involvement in its creation, as the Council of Europe, and because it follows his statements in British politics and it was implemented by his closer collaborator Harold Macmillan, the European Free Trade Organization. The combination of both organizations provides us with a global vision of Churchill's proposals for uniting Europe as an integral part of a world organization. NATO is the third pillar of his idea about Europe, including defense.

The Council of Europe is the result of the Congress of Europe, where Churchill made the opening speech in The Hague in 1948. He proposed a European 'Charter' and 'Court' of Human Rights, assuring in his opening speech: 'We aim at the eventual participation of all the peoples throughout the continent whose society and way of life are in accord with the Charter of Human Rights.'[42] The meeting was a milestone in the European integration, where people all over Europe met to discuss the possibilities of a European organization. The meeting was presided over by Winston Churchill and brought representatives from different countries and different ideas about how to build a joint Europe. The participants were politicians,

[41]Ibid.

[42]Ibid.

intellectuals, and major representatives of the European culture who took three main positions towards European integration: the unionist, the federalist, and the supporters of Pan-Europe.

The unionists were under the moral leadership of Winston Churchill and entailed mainly Anglo-Saxon and Nordic people who were keener supporters of European cooperation among states. According to their ideas, any European organization could just work based just on agreements between governments. The decision making could still be in the hands of the Member States, adding economic cooperation based on free trade agreements, not on a common market. The federalists supported a European federation like the United States of America. They wanted to build a European State integrating economy and politics. Their main leader in the Congress was Altiero Spinelli, an important figure in the further European Communities where he was Commissioner of the European Commission and afterwards an important leader of the European Parliament. The third group, the supporters of pan-Europe, had a middle approach, between federalist and unionist, suggesting a Confederation of European states, deeper than the cooperation of the unionists, but far from the federal idea of one European state.

The Council of Europe is an organization outside of the European Union and based on common general principles, as defense of human rights, democracy and cultural understanding. It was created in 1949 by the Treaty of London, reassuring the prominent role of UK in its foundation, including ten members, Belgium, Denmark, France, Ireland, Italy, Luxembourg, the Netherlands, Norway, Sweden, and the United Kingdom; five out of the six original members of the European Communities took part in this European initiative. Currently it has 47 Member States. The institutional framework of the Council of Europe was organized based on three main institutions, a Committee of Ministers, a Parliamentary Assembly, and a Secretary General, very similar to the institutions of the European Coal and Steel Community. But the main difference resides on the power of the common decisions, not binding in the case of the Council of Europe in opposition to the supremacy of the communitarian law over the national legal systems in the European Union; a model based on cooperation versus a system based on integration.

The EFTA was somehow a British answer to the creation of the European Common Market by the treaty of Rome in 1957, establishing the European Economic Community in 1958 by the Member States of the European Coal and Steel Community. The main force leading to the Treaty of Stockholm in 1960 was UK and its Prime Minister, Harold Macmillan, who was a political protégé of Churchill. He served as Foreign Secretary and Chancellor of the Exchequer under Churchill's successor and close political ally, Sir Anthony Eden. When Eden resigned because of the Suez Crisis in 1957, Macmillan succeeded him as Prime Minister and led the conversations for the new European organization, the EFTA, following the pattern already established by his mentor.

Winston Churchill had become a defender of free trade in his early political career when the British economic model was under discussion and supported it as a valid model for Europe to foster trade and economic development to achieve social stability and peace. The EFTA followed the ideas of Churchill with a free trade area without common external customs, as the EEC, allowing the Imperial Preference system of the Commonwealth to continue. The EFTA worked well economically fostering trade between the members from 3.22 to 7.5 billion euro between 1959 and 1967, like the growth rate in the EEC. The EFTA mostly included just industrial production and excluded agricultural products and maritime trade, and again, it was based on cooperation against the EEC model of integration, which eventually followed a model closer to cooperation through the-decision making based on unanimity, but was open to future integrationist reforms, as the Single European Act in 1986, that really created the European market. The EFTA excluded similar future actions and lost its importance with the British, Danish, and Irish membership to the EEC in 1972; eventually the remaining members were absorbed by the European Union with the creation of the European Economic Area.

The third organization representing Churchill's approach to Europe is NATO. His involvement in European military association dates back to 1950, when Churchill called for the creation of a European Army'...under a unified command, and in which we should all bear a worthy and honourable part.'[43] just 1 year after the creation of NATO. He presented a motion to the European Assembly creating a European Army, which was adopted by the Committee of Ministers of the European Council. The proposal expressed the defensive essence of the new military association, the creation of a common leadership through a European minister of defense under the supervision of the Member States, democracy and freedom as principal common values, active collaboration with USA and Canada (NATO) and integration as a regional force in the United Nations.

Nevertheless, the French proposed another path for the military collaboration between Western European States based on integration rather than the collaborationist proposal of Churchill. The European Defence Community included the original members of the ECSC, and hence excluded the UK. A treaty was signed on 1952 but it never came into force as the French National Assembly rejected the idea because of fears about national sovereignty and the strong opposition of de Gaul and the French Communist. Churchill's proposal included national divisions, as the EDC, under the command of a civilian in the European level following the SHAEF model, rather than common institutions as in the alternative proposal, and the Member States governments controlling all the process against the French proposal including several supranational elements. After the French National Assembly rejection, NATO, an organization supported by Churchill and following his ideas about regional cooperation based on major principles, became the centre of the European defence system, including currently all the Member States of the European Union except for Austria, Ireland, Finland, and Sweden. Hence, Churchill's ideas succeeded this time in the European level over other proposals.

A combination of the Council of Europe, based on political and cultural values, as major principles as democracy or human rights, the EFTA, based economic relations, and NATO, based on military relations, was Churchill's idea about the

[43]Ibid.

European Integration. The British government took a leading position in the three organizations, but France, Germany, the Benelux, and Italy follow a different approach with the ECSC and the EEC. Nevertheless, Churchill argued against the development of the European integration without the involvement of UK, consequence of British lack of interest for integration models and the lack of flexibility of the European Communities to negotiate the British proposals and reach a compromise. Churchill in his speech to the House of Commons during the debate about the Schuman plan affirmed: 'the absence of Britain deranges the balance of Europe. I am all for a reconciliation between France and Germany, and for receiving Germany back into the European family, but this implies, as I have always insisted, that Britain and France should in the main act together so as to be able to deal on even terms with Germany, which is so much stronger than France alone. Without Britain, the coal and steel pool in Western Europe must naturally tend to be dominated by Germany, who will be the most powerful member.'[44] This idea was already mentioned in 1946 when Churchill visited Holland: 'the cornerstone of the new organization would be Anglo-French friendship'. So, the participation of UK in the European integration was needed to keep the organization balanced. This debate is currently important again, as Germany is taking the undisputable leadership of the European Union with a depress France and a reluctant Cameron after an initial political French domination led by de Gaulle in the European Communities, followed by an equal tandem between Mitterrand and Kohl. Obviously, Churchill's vision is link with his state centre organization approach, because another way to decrease German's influence in the EU would be increasing the level of integration and hence decreasing the power of the Member States of the organization. In a Cabinet memorandum 29 November 1951, already back as British Prime Minister, Churchill said that UK should not become 'an integral part of European integration'[45] leaving open the participation of UK in the process from another perspective different than full membership.

In the debate about Schuman plan, Churchill asked rhetorically about: 'what association should Britain have with the Federal Union of Europe if such a thing should come to pass in the course of time?' The word association provides us with an important hint of Churchill's ideas about the relation of UK with the European integration. Once the British proposals towards a united Europe were not adopted by the main continental powers, France and Germany, Churchill wanted to associate UK to the integration process without full membership: 'there is the question of whether there could be two grades of members of such a body—full members and associate'. An idea expressed in the early stages of the debate about the future European organization: 'If at first all the States of Europe are not willing or able to join the Union, we must nevertheless proceed to assemble and combine those who will and those who can.'[46] Opening the possibility of a multi-speed Europe, which as

[44]Ibid.

[45]Young (1985).

[46]Churchill and James (1974).

the matter of fact is currently working in the European Union, with UK keeping his national currency outside if the Eurozone, control over its borders outside the Schengen area, and not adopting the Social Policy of the European Union.[47] The incapacity of both areas to compromise influenced Churchill's diplomatic inactivity regarding European integration affairs, after his return to Downing Street in 1951.

Winston Spencer Churchill was an outstating man who owned an enormous personal prestige because of his political leadership of the United Kingdom and somehow the free world against totalitarianism. His iconic aura was supplemented with writing skills, a past as young adventurer, a warrior, a gentleman, and a painter. This combination has given Churchill a prestige compared to those figures ruling the human history. Hence, the importance of his real ideas about the European integration come from his own stature as a statesman. The Eurosceptic need Churchill to gain the popular support against the European integration; the European Union needs his support to bring closer to Europe the always recalcitrant and suspicious British. The lack of any other British personality link with the creation of the European Union and the immense power of Churchill over the British and world popular imaginary led to his nomination as a founder father of Europe.

Churchill was a Europeanist without any rational doubt, as has been shown in this research, but his model of Europe differed from the current European Union. Currently there are mainly two possibilities in the European debate, to be for or against the EU, but there were other options in the early stages of the integration, and Churchill was the main advocate of a third way. Nevertheless, Churchill's attitudes towards a united Europe cannot be understood without the historical context of his time and his well-known pragmatism and flexibility adapting his views to the social necessities.

Hence, the use of Churchill by the Eurosceptic is due to partial use of history, usually citing literally quotes from Churchill without contextualizing them and using them as absolute truths. Even those supporting a special British association with the European integration use Churchill for their political purposes when Churchill repeated in numerous occasion his will to commit the UK fully in the process. Just the political circumstances, as the Cold War, the intention to keep influence over the former members of the British Empire and the federal approach, made Churchill support a special relation of UK with the European Communities. Hence, it was a pragmatic approach rather than a dogmatic position.

On the other side, the inclusion of Churchill in the list of founding fathers of the European Union lacks respect to the own Churchill's proposals. It is a clear attempt to include UK through his most iconic figure in the European building process based on integration. He was a supporter of Europe, but his ideas did not fully match with the current European Union.

Churchill's position should enrich the debate about the future of the European Union rather than being used in partisan fights. As the historical context of Europe has dramatically changed since Churchill's times, we cannot know what would be

[47]Ramiro Troitiño (2009).

his position today towards the integration, but we still can learn from his visionary actions, his open mind to new creative solutions, his pragmatism and his dialogue capacity, to build a better world.

References

Addison P (1980) The political beliefs of Winston Churchill. Trans R Hist Soc., 5th ser. 30:23–47

Alldritt K (1992) Churchill the writer: his life as a man of letters. Hutchinson, London

Ashley M (1968) Churchill as historian. Charles Scribner's Sons, New York

Barroso JMD (2013) 'From 1946 till today – a European success story. Why leadership matters' download at http://europa.eu/rapid/press-release_SPEECH-13-900_en.htm

Braghiroli S (2007) The challenges to democracy in the interwar period: lessons from the past relevant today. Poland, Lithuania, and Czechoslovakia in an extended Rokkanian perspective. CEU Polit Sci J 4:358–380

Bruyning LF (1990) Italy-Europe. Rodopi, Amsterdam

Carter VB (1965) Winston Churchill: an intimate portrait. Hartcourt, Brace & World, New York

Charmley J (2014) Churchill: the end of glory: a political biography. Faber & Faber, London

Churchill W (1930) A roving commission: my early life. C. Scribner's Sons, New York

Churchill W (1944) Speech at Harvard University, 6 September 1943, Onwards to Victory

Churchill W (1946) Sinews of peace (iron curtain speech). Westminster College, Fulton

Churchill W (1947a) Speech at a conservative mass meeting, Llandudno, 9 October 1948. In: Randolph SC (ed) Europe Unite–speeches

Churchill W (1947b) Speech to the house of commons, the official report, house of commons (5th Series) 444

Churchill W (1949) Europe unites: the story of the campaign for European Unity, including a full report of the congress of Europe held at The Hague, may, 1948. Hollis & Carter, London

Churchill W (1968) Marlborough, his life and times, vol 1. Scribner, New York

Churchill W, James RR (1974) Winston S. Churchill: his complete speeches, 1897–1963. Chelsea House Publications, New York

Coombs D et al (2004) Sir Winston Churchill: his life and his paintings. Running Press, Philadelphia

D'Este C (2010) Warlord: the fighting life of Winston Churchill, from soldier to statesman. RUSI J 155(5):95

Duchin BR (1992) The "agonizing reappraisal": Eisenhower, Dulles, and the European defense community. Dipl Hist 16(2):201–221

Gilbert M (1983) Finest hour: Winston S. Churchill 1939–41. William Heinemann, Portsmouth

Gilbert M (1992) Churchill: a life. Henry Holt and Company, New York

Hughes EJ (1974) Winston Churchill and the formation of the United Nations organization. J Contemp Hist 9(4):177–194

Jenkins R (2012) Churchill: a biography. Pan Macmillan, London

Ramiro Troitiño D (2008) De Gaulle and the European Communities. In: Proceedings of the Institute for European Studies, Tallinn University of Technology, no 4, pp 139–152

Ramiro Troitiño D (2009) Margaret Thatcher and the EU. European Union: current political and economic issues

Ramiro Troitiño D (2013) European integration: building Europe. Nova Science Publishers, New York

Ramiro Troitiño D, Chochia A (2015) Winston Churchill and the European Union. Balt J Law Polit 8(1):55–81

Rasor EL (2000) Winston S. Churchill, 1874–1965: a comprehensive historiography and annotated bibliography. Greenwood, Bengaluru

Russell D (2005) Winston Churchill – soldier: the military life of a gentleman at war. Conway Maritime Press

Russett B (1994) Grasping the democratic peace: principles for a post-Cold War world. Princeton University Press, Princeton

Shlaim A (1974) Prelude to downfall: the British offer of union to France, June 1940. J Contemp Hist 9(3):27–63

Thompson RW (1973) Generalissimo Churchill. Blue Cloud Books, Phoenix

Young JW (1985) Churchill's 'no' to Europe: the 'rejection' of European Union by Churchill's post-war government, 1951–1952. Hist J 28(04):923–937

Part II
British Strategy to the European Communities Before Accession

The First European Community and the British Position

Archil Chochia, David Ramiro Troitiño, Tanel Kerikmäe, Olga Shumilo, and Nicole Lindstrom

Abstract This chapter traces the role of the United Kingdom (UK) in the European integration process, from the founding of the European Communities to its eventual membership in 1973. It considers several key factors leading to the UK's exclusion from the European Communities in the 1950s and 1960s, including economic factors related to its coal and steel industries, its relationship with the Commonwealth, as well as diplomatic concerns within the realm of 'high politics.' The chapter also considers the UK's role in creating alternative integration arrangements, namely the European Free Trade Association (EFTA) and the European Economic Area (EEA). The chapter provides a historical foundation to understanding the UK's relationship to the European Community as an 'awkward partner,' shedding light on its eventual exit from the EU four decades after joining.

1 Introduction

The proposal for creating the European Coal and Steel Community (ECSC) included the French plan of Aristide Briand as an example of the commitment of France to the peaceful building of Europe. It underlined the crucial relation between France as Germany as the centre of the process, but at the same time, remaining open to other European states. This Community was just the first step in building the European federation, following the neo-functionalist logic of incremental integration of different economic sectors. Since the first moment of European integration, it was clear

A. Chochia (✉) · D. Ramiro Troitiño · T. Kerikmäe
Tallinn Law School, Tallinn University of Technology, Tallinn, Estonia
e-mail: archil.chochia@ttu.ee; david.troitino@ttu.ee; tanel.kerikmae@ttu.ee

O. Shumilo
Yaroslav Mudryi National Law University, Kharkiv, Ukraine
e-mail: shumiloolja@gmail.com

N. Lindstrom
Department of Politics, University of York, York, UK
e-mail: nicole.lindstrom@york.ac.uk

D. Ramiro Troitiño et al. (eds.), *Brexit*,
https://doi.org/10.1007/978-3-319-73414-9_4

that the goal of many of its primary architects was the eventual creation of a European federation. Yet, this would be achieved at the level of 'low politics,' gradually integrating the economies of the Member States of the organization, with the aim of confining interstate conflicts amongst them to the past.

Jean Monnet was appointed as the first president of the High Authority where he oversaw the development of the Community. Eventually, his confrontation with de Gaulle and the personal veto of the French president led him to resign.[1] Monnet followed his work in the European building process with other, less public positions. Yet, he was still influential as president of the Action Committee for a United States of Europe, a very influential private lobby. He was also active supporting the enlargement of the community to the UK, Ireland, and Denmark. Monnet was playing an imperative role in the establishment of the European Communities established by the Treaty of Rome, especially the EURATOM.[2] Finally, he promoted the creation of the European Council.

After the Schuman declaration of 9 May 1950, an agreement was signed in 1951 in Paris creating the ECSC with France, West Germany, Italy, Belgium, Luxembourg, and the Netherlands. This document, considered the founding charter of the European integration process, was the result of cooperation between Jean Monnet and Robert Schuman. The inclusion of France and Germany as the centre of the community was a way to end the confrontation between both countries. Both states were also the most influential European states in Europe in both economic and population terms, along with the UK. They were the heart of the new community, their power and importance overshadowing other members.

The ECSC was a big novelty compared with other international institutions, introducing a new concept of 'supranationality'.[3] That is, Member States shared their sovereignty under the umbrella of common institutions that focused on the common good rather than the interest of each individual Member State. It is important to differentiate this concept from losing sovereignty, or freedom, in an international community. The Member States of the ECSC were looking for a common goal and the shared the power given by their citizens in a wider entity. To deal with common sovereignty, the Member States of the ECSC created different institutions with clear roles. The High Authority was the highest executive power of the new community, being independent from the Member States, which, according to some later scholar reviews, was the most supranational element of the generally not-so-intrusive ECSC.[4] It had a similar role to the current European Commission but with wider and stronger powers. It was the institution in charge of the Community and the frontrunner of the integration in the coal and steel sectors.

The council of the ECSC was the legislative power, and the Member States were represented there. It could be identified with the current Council of the European

---

[1]Ramiro Troitiño (2008).

[2]Ugland (2013).

[3]Mason (1955).

[4]Groenendijk and Hospers (2002).

Union but with the latter having more power and greater influence in the working system of the Union. There was also an Assembly in the ECSC where representatives from the parliaments of the Member States were to gather. It was the origin of the current European Parliament. This institution changed mostly because of the first European democratic elections in 1979 and the introduction of the co-decision system. But the Assembly of the ECSC yet had not very much power and was merely a body of political representation. Its creation was mainly based on democratic principles of the integration process and for the further development of the institution. Moreover, the European Court of Justice played a key role in the development of the European Communities. As the Community had common rules to be applied and respected in equal terms to all the economic and political agents included, it needed an independent body to ensure fulfilment of these rules without national interference. The ECJ was the highest legal institution in the fields included in the ECSC, higher than the national tribunals, their governments, or any other institution of the Member States. The main role of the Court of Justice was supervising the good working of the community. The ECSC also included the ECSC Committee, a consultative body with no power in the decision-making or working system of the community. The members of this Committee were the social agents involved in the field of coal and steel, as trade unions, companies, or independent professionals. According to a neo-functionalism, it is necessary to include in the integration process actors other than political institutions, as economic or social agents, to lobby their respective governments to achieve deeper integration. The creation of the ECSC Committee follows this pattern and is the example for different committees in the European Union, as the European Economic and Social Committee or the Committee of the Regions.

The ECSC did not include the United Kingdom as its founding members. The British economy had strong links with coal and steel and its government was interested in a Community based on this economic field, but its interest was based on cooperation and not on integration. The UK was interested in participating in the new community to fund the deficit of the sector and gain access for British producers to the German and French markets but not at any cost. The issue of securing imperial preferences and special political and economic ties to the United States was more important for United Kingdom than any hypothetical economic benefit for a sector in decline in Britain.[5] Although coal and steel sectors were in crisis, they had much power in British politics through the influence of the British trade unions. There was another important reason of the British government to avoid the participation of the country in the first European community: most of British companies related to coal and steel had been nationalised in February 1951 by the Atlee Labour Government.[6] Most of the key industries of the post-war economy tumbled into the public sector, where they were subject to elaborate planning controls. For the most part the takeovers were highly popular; none more so than the nationalisation of the

[5]Efron and Nanes (1957).

[6]Ellis (2012).

coalmines. Pit owners employed a high number of workers, many of them in dire and dangerous conditions. The new national coal board was seen as much as a humanitarian institution as an economic one. The National Coal Board became the largest industrial employer in Western Europe with 500,000 employees that formed the backbone of the labor movement. It was the beginning of the British welfare state.[7]

The public control over these industries was not compatible with the essence of the European Coal and Steel Community because a common market without national obstacles to trade would have cut the state subsidies to these industries. Theoretically all the companies operating in the market, public and private, should have competed in equal conditions without interferences by the Member States. Any distortion to the market to support inefficient companies were forbidden, especially those based on national grounds to support the local industries against the companies of the other members of the Community. It was unacceptable for a government that had nationalized these industries although the possible gains from a scale economy of a larger market could have been very positive. Hence, the British government was just interested in a free trade area where it could manage its own industries according to its necessities. The UK sent some delegates to discuss the preliminary negotiations for the creation of the ECSC, but they withdraw when the principle of national sovereignty was not respected, pointing out their interest in a trade area and cooperation in political terms, but not by any means integration.

2 The Treaty of Rome

The leaders of the Member States of the ECSC plus the UK met in 1955 in Messina in a conference where they agreed upon the creation of a preparatory committee for the construction of a common market and a community based on atomic energy. It was a year after the rejection of the European Defence Community, and all the parties involved were very cautious to avoid another failure that could have doomed the whole European project. Two new communities, the EURATOM and the European Community, were created by the Treaty of Rome in 1957, deepening integration in Europe. These two communities were independent from each other, and from the previous ECSC. The first was based on atomic energy and was a consequence of the lobby made by Jean Monnet and his supporters. He thought that atomic energy could be the new source of energy of the future because it could be locally produced in Europe, avoiding the dependency from oil coming from other parts of the world and because it was relatively cheap source of energy. The changes in the European economic model, the exhausting reserves of coal on the continent, and the independence of former European colonies rich in oil, led to an energy crisis with higher prices. It was a danger affecting the recovery of the European economy after the devastation of the WWII. Atomic energy seemed the solution, and Monnet

[7]Ramiro Troitiño (2014).

wanted to use this new energy source from a common perspective, building a community where the development of this energy would be the result of common work. It would avoid the military use of this energy among the Member States of the organization, as the technology would be shared, and could also increase the integration between the Member States.

Monnet thought of the potential spill over effect of this energy as an important tool for the creation of a European political entity. Nuclear energy was essential as well in the new making of war, as the nuclear powers felt safer from aggressions from external threats. It was an international mean based more on prevention than aggression. As steel had been basic for making weapons before, nuclear energy was thought to be the future in the military field. Sharing the technology and facilities under a common institution might avoid the possibility of using it against each other, reassuring peace and increasing the integration among the Member States. Also, Europe needed to work together in this field to gain independence from the unstable international situation. As the president of Egypt decided to nationalize the Suez channel, France, the UK, and Israel attacked Egypt. This was a fundamental transportation hub for the European economic interest because most of the oil was coming to Europe via Egypt, a much cheaper and faster way than circumnavigating Africa. The crisis was solved with the involvement of the USA supporting its Egyptian ally, crucial in the context of the Cold War, for the American interest in the Arab world.[8] The European powers had to withdraw from the area, making clear their minor role in world affairs dominated by the USA and the Soviet Union. A European community in the atomic field could help European powers increase their political influence in the world, or at least their independence in the context of the Cold War.

These were the theses supporting the creation of EURATOM, but the real situation was different. The other Member States did not trust the real intentions of France, because they thought that the French government wanted to use this community to have free access to German technology and to a common budget to develop French nuclear weapons.[9] The mistrust among the members, the stabilization of the price of oil, and the temporary end of the energy crisis were the reasons to lead to an empty community with no real power.[10] EURATOM had its own independent institutions, but finally in 1967 these institutions were merged with the European Community institutions, thus losing their independence. The current situation is again opening the debate about nuclear energy because of similar reasons as in the 1950s plus environmental and security concerns. But the position of the European Union is based on national independence in this field, promoting or not of nuclear energy depends on the governments of the Member States. Some of them, as France or Finland, are keen to build new nuclear facilities, another, Spain, is closing nuclear plants. It means that it is a policy out of the European influence, involving

[8]Marston (1988).

[9]Eunjeong (2013).

[10]Mathijsen (1961).

just national actors, even when its consequences are global, and not regional. It is because the political consequences of a common energy policy are very important, and the European building process still has not reached enough level of integration to deal with such a problematic issue.

The relation of UK with the nuclear energy was a matter of prestige and power, beside energetic supply. Already in 1947, the British government decided to develop their own nuclear program, mainly as a security measure and to keep the superpower status for the country. Ernest Bevin,[11] a British statesman, trade union leader, and Labour politician, was Secretary of State for Foreign Affairs (1945–1951), oversaw the nuclear development program of the country, and defined it as a matter of both prestige and national security. Nevertheless, the cost of the British nuclear program was very high and difficult to bear the cost of the operation. Finally, the superpower attempt weighed more than the potential economic gains of a common budget, common technology, and common development in EURATOM. United Kingdom was the only world nuclear power alongside USA and the USSR, so it did not have real motivation to join the EURATOM formed by countries trying to obtain the status UK already was holding.

The same treaty of Rome gave birth to the European Economic Community, which was meant to be mainly a common market with free movement of people, services, goods, and capital.[12] The idea was to create a large market for the economies of the Member States to increase trade and wealth.[13] It also had other less pragmatic reasons, as accelerating European integration. Having a common market with common rules, the European economies would integrate step by step, finally creating a single market. The economy was chosen to be the first field to integrated, leaving politics for a future stage. Each Member State also had its own interest in this common market. Germany was an economy based on exports, as it still is, and was keen for a market where no technical, legal, or economic barriers would decrease its activity. Fewer borders between the Member States economies made it easier for West Germany to export.[14] It meant an important increase in German economic activity. On the other hand, Germans were afraid of other policies included in the Treaty, as the Common Agricultural Policy, very expensive and likely to spend most of its budget in France. Nevertheless, the competitiveness of the German economy made this country the main beneficiary of this common market, but also made Germany the main contributor to the common budget. The German government currently still obtains important economic benefits from the European market because the economic activity is higher than without a common market; around two thirds of German exports are within the European market. The German companies benefiting from the European market pay taxes in Germany, with the consequent benefit for the German state. Germany pays more than other countries

---

[11]Deighton (2006).

[12]McKelvey (1989).

[13]Lindberg (1963).

[14]Dinan (1999).

because its economy is bigger than the other Member States economies and hence gets a bigger benefit from the common market.

France was less enthusiastic about the common market, because its economy was less competitive than the German, but free competition was thought of as a shock therapy where the French companies had to adapt to the new rules to survive, in the process winning global competitiveness. On the other hand, other policies, as the CAP, were going to mean a huge influx of capital in its important agricultural sector. The relations of the new community with Africa could also finance the external influence of France in the African continent,[15] something it could not afford alone in the context of the Cold War because France did not have enough muscle to compete with the USA or the USSR. Italy also supported the common market because of the heavily industrialized northern area of the country and the poorer southern part of Italy. The north was interested in a free market to export to the rest of the Member States competing on equal terms with German or French companies. The south was more interested in the free movement of people, to export workers to other parts of Europe without restrictions or discriminations. Also, the inclusion of the Common Agricultural Policy meant an important benefit for the agricultural sector of this part of Italy, focused on Mediterranean production, mainly market access and domination of the European Market on Mediterranean products through temporal restrictions to other Mediterranean producers.[16] Finally, the BENELUX countries had no other option than joining a market where Germany and France were present. It is because of obvious economic reasons, because the economies of the three states highly depend on the German and French market, and they could have had tough times without access to them.

There were economic reasons to create the common market, but also there were political reasons in terms of integration, and thirdly, each Member State had its own interest. These reasons made possible the creation of the EEC and the Common Market. At the beginning the Common Market encountered many problems, becoming basically just an industrial market based on free trade and an agricultural market based on market protection. To solve the problems of the Common Market, deeper integration was needed. The main target was increasing the economic competitiveness and wealth of Europe, and a new reform creating the Single Market was launched and signed in 1986. Again, the problems of the Communities were solved with deeper integration.[17] The way the European Economic Community was developed following the example of the ECSC, a supranational community with common rules, the same rights and duties, plus common institutions. The main supranational institution was the European Commission, the executive body, holding exclusively the right to initiate new legislation. It was designed as an independent body from the influence of the Member States, acting just for the common good of the community,

---

[15]Brown (2017).

[16]Trevor (1968).

[17]Moravcsik (1991).

leaving aside the national interest of each Member State. It worked in a collegial way and had its own staff.

The Council was the most powerful institution, and it represented the national interests of the Member States. It decided most of the matters related to new legislation, approving, rejecting, or reforming it. The main decision-making process was based on unanimity; that meant that if just one state rejected any measure, it could not be passed. This way was decided upon to break the resistance of those who thought that the new community was a threat to national sovereignty. The evolution of the Council shows that each treaty or reform of the Union locate more policies under another form of decision making, qualified majority, where not all the countries have to agree, and most of them, can pass legislation even if other Member States are against it. Mainly new policies are under unanimity, and when they are already properly working and there is no longer fear about the national interest of the Member States, they are transfer to a qualified majority system.

The Assembly was a copy of the ECSC, with no real power, but necessary for giving a democratic face to the integration process. Step by step the Assembly got more power, and finally was elected in a democratic way in 1979. From that point on, the European Parliament got more power, being currently a powerful institution that can stand almost on equal terms with the Council. It was clear from the beginning of integration that a European state was wanted, and this state should be democratic, with a common parliament elected by the Europeans.[18] At the end of the process the parliament will probably become the main institution of the European Union, so it is very likely that it will win power in each new treaty until the European state is created. Another important institution was the High Court, the sentinel of the common rules with power to force the Member States to follow the Communitarian law. It was something like the ECSC and different from the rest of the international organizations of the world that usually lack this kind of institution. Finally, there was an Economic and a Social committee, to involve in the process other actors such as workers, trade unions, companies, or liberal professions. Its powers were minimal; it was just a consultation body.

The EEC was the real start of integration in Europe because its spill over effect led to deeper and deeper integration, in a process that could probably lead Europe to the United States of Europe.[19] The common market in reality was just an industrial market, but was working well. Afterwards, new integration was needed to increase the effectiveness of the economic system and solve the problems created by the common market, so a single market was created, where there were fewer borders to trade. It led afterwards to the adoption of the common currency to avoid barriers to the market, and it is supposed to lead to an economic government in the European Union to fix the problems generated by the common currency. This would be the last stage in the creation of the European state. Nevertheless, the Treaty of Rome meant the disappearance of the word federation from the treaties of the EEC and the EU. It

[18]Pivoda (2007).

[19]Laurent (2011).

was like accepting the process, accepting the consequences of the new legislation, policies, and treaties, leading the Member States to the United States of Europe but hiding it from the citizens and, of course, avoiding any kind of publicity about it. In this sense the treaty of Rome was a step back in terms of European integration because the model chosen for the integration did not count on the European people.

The development of two key polices was also included in the treaty of Rome: the Common Agricultural Policy[20] and a united trade policy. Both were handled in a Communitarian way and had a huge influence on the image of the European communities at home and abroad. The French influence is clear in the Treaty of Rome, and its political predominance over other partners was important in the development of the Union for many decades. It was the Member State that obtained more economic benefits and political hegemony in Western Europe. It is important to remember that WWII, having occurred not much more than 10 years earlier, was still fresh in the minds of Europeans. Germany was still willing to pay for normalizing its relations with the rest of the international community and accepted this French leadership. Hence an important benefit for West Germany at that moment was political. The other members of the community could not challenge French dominance either, and their dependency on the economies of Germany and France gave them no real option to stay aside from the new community. As the Economist magazine pointed out "The French have a good claim to have invented the EU and have traditionally felt a sense of ownership over it",[21] and it can explain different attitudes in European Union history, as Chirac, president of France, calling the Member States of the Union that supported the war in Iraq anti-Europeans, even when there were more countries in Europe supporting the war than against it. He meant anti-French instead of anti-European and made a clear identification of France and Germany as Europe.

The British position in Messina was influenced by the British believe that what was proposed would have certainly led to a federal union in Europe. Following the theoretical approach based on Neo-functionalism, The European Economic Community would provide benefits to its members, but also new problems that could be solved just with deeper integration.[22] Perhaps the British officials were more aware of the future consequences of the EEC than most of the Member States of the organization. Obviously, the Federal Europe was not an option for United Kingdom back then, and it is not an option for the country currently. The British economy was one of the most important economies of Europe, but still not the most important, so its participation in the EEC was seen as a possible economic dominance over the British economy from other Member States.[23] It is also important to recall that the British economy at the time of Messina, still had more interconnections with the

[20]Common Agricultural Policy (CAP) (2004).

[21]A severe crise d'identité (cover story) (2005).

[22]Morris (1991).

[23]Thompson and Marsh (1962).

British Empire and the USA than with the continental Europe.[24] Hence, to integrate its economy with Europe breaking the well-established connections with other parts of the world, was a mistake according to the British government. Obviously, they could not oversee the future decline of the dominions in the external trade of the UK.

On the international sphere, United Kingdom had also other priorities than Europe, basically the special relation with USA, because a powerful Europe integrated could have become an alternative to the influence of the Americans in the Western World. The British power could disband in an integrated Europe that would become the central partner of the USA in the Western World. So, to keep the Anglo-American relations at its peak, UK could not ever join the European Communities. Because of the Ottawa Conference of 1932, the UK abandoned free trade and created a system promoting economic exchanges of the British dominions called the Imperial Preference. It created an exclusive economic area protected from the international competition by high custom fees. The relation with the Commonwealth was essential for UK and unquestionably was going to be negatively affected by the membership in the EEC because of the Common Agricultural Policy was entailed in the Treaty of Rome. The agricultural trade between the members of the Commonwealth was very important, and the CAP was to be protectionist towards international agricultural producers, affecting negatively the imports from the Commonwealth. Also, the Common Market included common customs, influencing the international trade agreements of its members that subsequently would have become trade agreement between the whole EEC and the international partners, or most probably, according the interest of the whole community, just dissolved.

The United Kingdom during the preliminary negotiations proposed instead of a common market a common trade area for industrial goods excluding agricultural production, and national autonomy to negotiate trade agreements with other partners to protect the British interest in the world and participate in a European market. The initial position of UK was considered in Messina in 1955 for further discussions, and just 1 year later in 1956 the French Prime Minister Guy Mollet approached the British Government suggesting the idea of an economic and political union between France and Great Britain, following the pattern of the Anglo-French union of 1940. The request was rejected by the Prime Minister of UK Anthony Eden closing also any association of France with the Commonwealth. Finally, the French rejected the British premise of a free trade area with the support of the other five members, and the EEC was created without the British participation.

3 The EFTA As an Alternative Plan

The European Free Trade Association was signed in 1959 in the Treaty of Stockholm by Austria, Denmark, Norway, Portugal, Sweden, Switzerland, and the United Kingdom. Finland joined in 1961, Iceland in 1970 and Liechtenstein in 1991. The

[24]Ellis (2012).

leader member of the association was UK that promoted an alternative European market for its products.[25] The European Free Trade Association (EFTA) was an intergovernmental organisation set up for the promotion of free trade and economic integration to the benefit of its Member States. The immediate aim of the Association was to provide a framework for the liberalisation of trade in goods amongst its Member States. At the same time, EFTA was established as an economic counter-balance to the more politically driven European Economic Community (EEC).[26] The British fear of being isolated from Europe was overcome with the association with those Western countries outside of the EEC. Nevertheless, the relations with the EEC were at the core of EFTA activities from the beginning. In the 1970s, the EFTA States concluded free trade agreements with the EC. It provided with more negotiation power to the British to deal with their relations with the EEC, the main market of Europe. The British design of the organization was based on two main points: (1) Tariff reductions between the member; and (2) No compromise to the national sovereignty of its members.[27]

Denmark and Norway had important economic links with the UK, and hence needed to be in the same economic organization than the UK to have access to the British market. Austria, Switzerland, and Sweden had the status of neutrality in the Cold War, and could not join the European Communities because they were seen by the Soviet Union as a capitalist organization against the workers of the world supported by the USA and hence against the communist intentions to protect the workers of the world. Joining the organization meant lining up with USA against Soviet Union in the context of the Cold War. On the other hand, Portugal was not a democratic country as it was under the power of the dictatorship built by Salazar, and democracy was a requirement for joining the European Communities.[28] The more politically orientated European Communities needed a homogeneous political system among its members, the EFTA based on trade agreements without political implication did not require political aspects. The EFTA gave international backing to the Portuguese regime plus the important economic ties the country had with the UK.

The new organization proposed a different model uniting Europe, one mainly based on trade and common agreements, without integration or any loss of national independence, following the ideas expressed by the UK previously. The working system was based on the good faith of the partners and their will to collaborate among each other, reaching common positions basically based on consensus. In practical matters it was an organization focusing on industrial production trade, excluding agricultural products and maritime trade, an area of free trade based on the British traditional posture without any political meaning. The EFTA would permit the UK to keep intact its economic relations with the Commonwealth increasing its market scope in Europe.

---

[25] Gardener (1991).

[26] Kaiser (2001).

[27] Aitken (1973).

[28] Andresen (2007).

The organization worked at the beginning as it increased the trade between its members despite this modest initiative. The financial results were good, as it stimulated an increase of foreign trade volume among its members from 3.5 to 8.2 billion US dollars between 1959 and 1967.[29] It made the EFTA more attractive to other Western European states to apply for membership. Europe was then divided in two main markets, in two main economic areas, in two different approaches to the European integration. The EFTA was organized with its own institutions reflecting the essence of the organization. The EFTA Council was the highest governing body meeting at the ambassadorial level (heads of permanent delegations to EFTA) and less often at Ministerial level.[30] In the Council meetings, the delegations consulted among them, negotiated, and decided on policy issues regarding the organization necessities. Each Member State was represented and had one vote, though decisions were usually reached through consensus. The idea of one state, one vote, did not consider the economic size of the state, or its population, or its political power. It was a clear example of cooperation based on the principle of an association of independent states collaborating without sharing their national sovereignty.

The Council discussed the main issues related to the good working system of the organization, especially relating to the development of EFTA relations with third countries and the management of free trade agreements. It had a broad mandate to consider possible policies to promote the overall objectives of the Association and to facilitate the development of links with other states, unions of states or international organisations. The Council also managed relations between the EFTA States and had a rotating presidency. Under the Council, a substructure of committees had evolved to deal with more specific necessities. The Committee on Third Country Relations, the Committee on Customs and Origin Matters, the Committee on Technical Barriers to Trade, the Budget Committee, and the EFTA Board of Auditors were the main working groups of the organization. Its organization based on public servants from the Member States expert on the issues discussed was clearly intergovernmental. The Consultative Committee provided a forum for representatives of companies and trade unions of the Member States to discuss the developments of the EFFTA and provided valuable inputs to the Council. The Parliamentary Committee provided a forum in which members of the national parliaments of the Member States could discuss about the impact of the EFTA and their concerns with the working system of the organization acting as a forum without real political implications or independent political body to control the development of the organization from their position of holders of the national sovereignty. Additionally, several committees in specialised fields were set up under the EFTA Convention.

The Secretariat oversaw the daily working of the organization and was headed by the Secretary-General. The division of the Secretariat reflected the internal organization of EFTA's activities.[31] The Secretariat employed a reduced number of

[29] Aitken (1973).

[30] Szokoloczy-Syllaba (1971).

[31] Corbet and Robertson (2016).

workers as the main activity of the EFTA was led by the Member States. By any circumstance could be comparable the EFTA Secretariat with the European Commission of the European Communities although while working at the Secretariat, staff members are servants of the Association and therefore not responsible to their national governments. The EFTA convention establishing the organization included the main targets of the organization: (1) To promote a continued and balanced strengthening of trade and economic relations between the Member States with fair conditions of competition, and the respect of equivalent rules, within the area of the Association; (2) The free trade in goods; (3) To progressively liberalise the free movement of persons; (4) the progressive liberalisation of trade in services and of investment (5) To provide fair conditions of competition affecting trade between the Member States; (6) To open the public procurement markets of the Member States; (7) to provide appropriate protection of intellectual property rights, in accordance with the highest international standards.[32]

These targets emphasized the economic orientation of the organization and the lack of political implications beside the agreements between the governments of the Member States. The EFTA included in its evolution an important concept in terms of integration, solidarity between its members, when the Portugal Fund was created. The concept of solidarity is strongly link with the current European Union as a pillar of the integration process in which the Member States contribute to the European budget that dedicates several funds to the development of the less advanced areas of Europe. The Cohesion Fund was based on solidarity between states, redistributed wealth from the better-off members of the Union to those above the European Union average GDP. Currently the idea of solidarity is not any longer focus on states but less developed European regions. The Portugal Fund was established in 1975 when Portugal was still a member of EFTA.[33] It followed the idea of internal solidarity in the organization took the form of a low-interest loan from the EFTA Member States to Portugal, to the value of 100 million US dollars. It showed the state control of the funds and limited solidarity bounded by the national sovereignty of Member States.

The historical development of the economies of the Member States of the European Communities was higher than in the EFTA. As the UK was being left behind France and Germany, and its economy was in crisis, their government had no other choice than asking for membership in the European Communities, even when this decision was against the British political beliefs based on cooperation and free trade. In parallel with the EC accession of Denmark and the United Kingdom, a series of bilateral free trade agreements were negotiated between the other EFTA States and the European Communities in the early 1970s, most of which came into force in 1973. These ensured that by mid-1977, duties on virtually all trade in industrial products between EFTA and the EC were eliminated. The wider European market had to respect the Communitarian legislation related to the European Market, to be applied to all the members of the trade area on the areas

[32]Aitken (1973).

[33]Eaton (1991).

included in the agreements. It means an important reduction of the autonomy of the EFTA because as no members of the European Union, cannot participate in the decision making of new legislation link with the European market, but as members of the EFTA must apply these legislation in their national territory if it affects the agreements between both entities.

In response to concerns relating to European competitiveness in the early 1980s, a first meeting at Ministerial level between the EFTA States and the EC was held in Luxembourg in 1984 to explore possibilities for further enhancing economic cooperation in Western Europe. The resulting Luxembourg Declaration laid down a program for the development of future European economic cooperation that would become one of the largest free trade system in the world.[34] The European Single Act treaty creating the European Single Market as an improving of the existing Common Market increased the scope of the European market and its level of integration. It led to a revision of the agreements between the European Communities and the EFTA Member States in 1989. The new partnership was based on of free movement of goods, services, capital, and persons. It practically meant the full integration of the economies of the EFTA states in the European economic market under the umbrella of the European institutional framework.

The negotiations began in 1990 and an agreement was signed in 1992 entering into force in 1994, forming the European Economic Area (EEA). It included recently born European Union and the back then Member States of the EFTA, Austria, Finland, Iceland, Norway, and Sweden. Switzerland, however, following a rejection of EEA membership in a referendum in 1992, proceeded to conclude two sets of bilateral agreements with the EU in 1999 and 2004. Liechtenstein became a member of the EEA on 1 May 1995. Since the accession of Austria, Finland, and Sweden to the EU in 1995, three EFTA States have thus been participating in the EEA: Iceland, Liechtenstein, and Norway. The EEA Agreement has now been in operation for more than a decade. It extends the Internal Market of the European Union to Iceland, Liechtenstein, and Norway. Because of EEA, economic operators in the EEA EFTA States can conduct their business under the same legal framework and are subject to the same rights and obligations in areas covered by the Agreement as operators in the EU States.

To achieve the goal of a homogeneous single market, the Agreement provides for the incorporation of new EU Internal Market acquis—the EU's rules and regulations—into the EEA through amendments to its numerous annexes and protocols. Since its entry into force, more than 5000 new legal acts have been incorporated into the EEA, in addition to the original 1500 acts.[35] The unbalance power in economic terms between the European Union and the European Economic Area Member States reduced the negotiation capacity of the EEA to a mere acceptance of what has been decided inside the EU. The EEA Agreement also provides for cooperation on horizontal issues affecting the members of both organizations, as Environment.

[34] Hurni (1986).

[35] Fredriksen and Franklin (2015).

And for the participation by the EEA EFTA States in various EU programs. On the other hand, respecting the national sovereignty of the EEA Member State and their will to be politically independent from the Union, the agreement does not include these policies of the Union not related to the Internal Market, as trade with other partners of the world, although the agreement includes several clauses to avoid a distortion of the market eliminating the possibility of accessing the Internal Market from the EEA states to international trade agents.

Agriculture and fisheries are not included either in the agreement, but its protective spirit inside the Union does not generate problems in economic integration between the EEA and the EU. Nevertheless, the current liberalization of the European agricultural sector is increasing the separation with the EEA states that include in their national priorities the protection of their farmers and fishermen. Monetary Union is an important issue in terms of economic integration but is not included in the agreement with the EEA states, but as even members of the European Union are not members of the Eurozone, it does not generated problems between both areas. As the EEA is basically a common market, it would be logical to have a common currency in the market to increase the trade connections between its members eliminating the uncertainty link with the changing value of the currencies. But the political implications of the Monetary Union for the further political integration of the EU, or at least of the members of the Eurozone, preclude the extension of the agreement to the EEA states.

An elaborate institutional framework known as the two-pillar system was established to manage the Agreement. This includes a set of common institutions – the ministerial-level EEA Council, the EEA Joint Committee of senior officials, and subcommittees and working groups of officials and the EFTA Court, which plays a role to that of the European Court of Justice in the EU's Internal Market including the supranational sphere in the agreement as the court decisions are above the national sovereignty and must be respected by all the members of the organization.[36] The EEA Agreement contains provisions for input from the EFTA side before new legislation is adopted. Input can take the form of participation of EFTA experts in EC committees or the submission of EFTA comments and the adoption of resolutions responding to Commission initiatives. Basically, it means that the EEA Member States can participate in the elaboration of new legislation related to the European market but cannot intervene in the proper decision making about these legislations. They provide information, expertise and their necessities to the legislative process but they cannot assure that they will be considered when the final decision is reached. The expansion of the European Union through its consecutive enlargements has meant the expansion of the EEA as any candidate to European membership shall apply to become a party to the EEA. The EFTA States thus closely followed the negotiations on EU enlargements.

To manage the contributions, an autonomous Financial Mechanism Office (FMO) administratively linked to EFTA was established to handle the bulk of the

[36]Baudenbacher (2004).

approximately €1.3 billion contribution from the EEA EFTA States for the 2004–2009 period to the European Union budget.[37] The Agreement on a new financial mechanism for the 2009–2014 period was reached at the end of 2009, providing for an annual contribution from the EEA EFTA States of €357.7 million. The European Union Member States financial contributions to the European budget are in some cases partly recover by those Member States nett contributors via the EU policies. The problem of the EEA states is that as nett contributors to the EU budget because of their participation of the European market, cannot reduce their contribution via the EU policies because as officially no-members of the EU, the policies of the organization (with some exceptions) do not apply in their territory. There other states of the EU that receive more funds from the Union that their contribution to the budget thanks to the solidarity principle included in the EU. The European Union Budget allocate more funds on those policies link with the development of the less fortunate areas of the territory of the organization. Obviously, the members of the EEA will receive more funds from the EU budget if they would members of the organization, reducing their global contribution to the EU budget in practical terms. But it will not make them nett receivers of funds, as their economic level is higher than the average of the European Union. It could also affect negatively some national policies, as their support to national farmers that is significantly higher than the support provided by the EU to the European farmers. The EEA countries, if members of the EU, should assimilate the EU level of protection decreasing the real protection of farmers and fishermen.

EFTA's trade strategy goes beyond the European Union to comprise today one of the world's largest networks of free trade relations. The first free trade agreement negotiated by the EFTA States as a group was with Spain in concordance to the preferential trade agreement signed between the Spanish and the European Communities. The EFTA-Spain trade agreement entered into force with the political normalization of Spain as a functional democracy after the death of the dictator Francisco Franco and the collapse of its authoritarian regime.[38] The EFTA trade agreements inside Europe were seen as a part of the pre-accession strategy to the European Union. The EFTA has trade agreements with the southern shores Mediterranean states, agreements with Canada, several countries in Latin America, Asia, and Africa. Nevertheless, the internationalization of the EFTA agreements has not declined the dependence of the organization on European trade, still the main market for their products.

[37]van Randwyck (2011).

[38]Hurni (1986).

4 The First and Second Petitions of Membership

The British encountered many problems in joining European Communities with two rejections. France had many concerns about the true intentions of the British and their commitment to the political integration process.[39] Also, the dominant position of France inside the Communities could be undermined with the membership of a great power as United Kingdom. Germany fully backed the French reluctance to the British accession because of the division of the country because of the Cold War between West Germany and East Germany. The USA, fully supported by the UK, accepted the division of Germany into two parts, alienating the British from West Germany authorities. It meant the support of Germany in favour of the French negative position towards the UK in this matter. On the other hand, other Member States were interested in the UK's being inside the Community, because they had important economic links with the British, especially the Netherlands, but their influence could not stand up to the French rejection. Other supporters of British membership were important personalities linked to European integration, as Jean Monnet, the so-called father of Europe, but they could do nothing against the combination of the French and German positions.

France had many reasons for rejecting the British application, first, the leading position of France inside the Communities as its main political actor. The Second World War was still recent and Germany was willing to cooperate with international partners to show their good faith. The inclusion of West Germany in the European Communities was a big step in rehabilitating this state in the international arena. The other Member States, as the Benelux countries and Italy, did not have the power to challenge the French position. So, France was the leading political force of the Communities, a position that could be in danger with another heavyweight, as the UK, inside the Community.[40] The problem of the British relation with the Commonwealth also had a negative influence on the relation of the Communities with its former colonies via the Lomé agreements; of all the members of the European Communities, but only France had ex-colonies of importance.

Finally, the Common Agricultural Policy was still under discussion, without its final shape, and the French government was concerned of the UK's changing the rules of this policy because the British agricultural sector was very different from the French and had other needs. Any candidate state when joining the European Union must accept the whole of it, without any possibility to become a partial member of the organization. Once a full member of the Union, any Member States can influence the development of European policies on the common ground of the European institutions with two main possibilities: (1) Rejecting new policies as unanimity is required for including new areas under the umbrella of the Union. In practical matters, the new policies included via European treaties must be supported by all the Member States as unanimity is required; (2) Signing a special protocol to leave a

[39]Dinan (2004).

[40]Miller and Spencer (1977).

Member States outside a new policy. Any enlargement of the European Communities and of the current European Union requires the unanimity of its members, providing the veto right to all the Member States of the organization. The rejection to the British membership also included Denmark, Ireland, and Norway that had applied commonly with the UK. The British application of 1961 was personally conducted by Harold Macmillan, a British Conservative politician who served as the Prime Minister of the United Kingdom from 1957 to 1963. He was known for his pragmatism and his capacity to adapt to the new necessities of his country, recovering the relations with USA, damage by the Suez channel conflict and redesigning the relations with continental Europe. Macmillan overcame the division of its government regarding the membership of the European Communities with a major Cabinet reorganisation in 1960.[41]

The fundamental reason for UK applying for membership in the European Communities, just 2 years after creating the EFTA, was basically link with fears rather than support to the European building process. The British government was concern about the development of the European Communities would affect the British role in world politics. The Member States of the European Communities were growing economically more than the British economy because of different factors, but essentially the new possibilities of a wider economic area promoting economic relations among the economic agents of the Member States. During the 1960s French gross national product grew at an average of 5.8% a year, meanwhile the British growth continued to struggle, at about only half the rate of that of Germany or France at the same time.[42] Nevertheless, it was a period of prosperity and rising living standards in UK, but also of decline in the relative competitiveness leading to a UK trade deficit with the European Communities very large, and was also influenced by the decision to retain a strong pound. The economic situation of United Kingdom was strong, with a stable growth, the industry had remained strong economic pillar in the post war period, and extensive house building and construction of new commercial developments and public buildings also helped unemployment stay low throughout this time. The main issue was that the Member States of the European Communities were growing more, decreasing the British weight in the overall European economy and, hence, decreasing the influence of UK in the international arena.

The British application was paved with the disappearance of a traditional obstacle in the relation between the UK and the European integration process, the Commonwealth. The already mentioned Ottawa conference established a facto common trade area with the different units forming the British Empire. The Commonwealth was officially created in 1949 by the London declaration in the post-war period to keep the British international influence in the context of the Cold War. It was designed as an intergovernmental organization working with consensus with a reduced common Secretariat. Currently it counts with 53 Member States that work on the principals of

[41]Ludlow (1997).

[42]Headley (2012).

equality and freedom as they do not have any legal obligation to one another. Imperial Preference was system on tariffs or free trade agreements between the dominions and colonies of the British Empire. It was considered a method of promoting unity within the British Empire and sustaining Britain's position as a global power as a response to increased competition from the protectionist Germany and United States in the beginning of the twentieth century.

During the 1920s, Imperial Preference became popular again as Prime Minister Baldwin became a full supporter of the establishing the Empire Marketing Board to encourage Britons to 'buy Empire' in 1926. But Winston Churchill, always a free trader, was an opponent to the idea, promoting free trade to increase the British competitiveness in a more global world.[43] Nevertheless, the conservative position did not obtain popular support in UK as it was seen as a threat to local jobs from industries located in other part of the world with lower standards. In 1932, representatives of Britain, the Dominions, and the Colonies held the Commonwealth Conference on Economic Consultation and Co-operation in Ottawa, initiating the agreement on Imperial Preference.[44]

The main partners of the organization from an economic perspective were UK, Canada, Australia, New Zealand, and South Africa, with active economic relations that for the British, was four times larger than trade with continental Europe at the time of the ECSC. Although the Commonwealth did not consist on multilateral trade agreements the trade between its members has been important during its existence. Britain's entry into the European Economic Community (EEC) in 1973, as a full member of the Common Market based on Common Customs and Common Trade Policy, meant the practical dissolution of the Imperial Preference System, as the European Communities acts as a representative of all its members in any international trade agreement.[45] The idea of a Free Trade area among the members of the Commonwealth has been discussed in several occasions, becoming a dream of the Eurosceptic in the UK as an alternative to the European Union market, but the integration of some members in other organizations based on free trade or common market, as the European Union, the Caribbean Community, or North American Free Trade Agreement, makes it unrealizable. Moreover, the EU has free trade agreements with South Africa and is negotiating new agreements with India.

The initial success of the Imperial Preference system boosting trade between its members suffered from the relation of the economic interest of its main partners. Canada has chased deeper economic collaboration with USA, including free trade agreements, because the importance of the American market in the economic system of the country is bigger than the relations with any member of the Commonwealth, including UK. Currently 75% of Canadian trade takes place with countries no-members of the Commonwealth. Australia, previously an important trade partner of UK, was focusing its priorities to the Asian and American markets, Singapore

[43]Ramiro Troitiño and Chochia (2015).

[44]Miners (2002).

[45]Parr (2006).

economic relations are also strongly link with USA and China. New Zealand has a free trade area with Australia and its economic priorities are similar, but the weight of their exports to the European market is still notorious.

The long-term decline on trade between the Commonwealth members and UK removed an important obstacle to the British application to membership in the European Communities. Between 1954 and 1960 Commonwealth trade with UK was increasing just at a reduced rate of 1% as the trade of the most prominent Member States of the organization was growing much faster because of the relocation of their trade priorities. The importance of UK in the Commonwealth was declining, threatening the British with international isolation.[46] As the international status was a priority for Macmillan, the petition to become a member of the European Communities became the only logical movement to preserve the power and prestige of United Kingdom in the world. The special relation with USA was also damaged because of the American world leadership removing the British influence for its own in many places in the world. It removed another obstacle for the British to apply for membership to the European Communities. The lower intensity between UK and USA were focused on the problem of decolonization and the influence of UK on its previous dominions that often did not match the American priorities in the context of the Cold War. The most notorious episode of this growing distance between both countries was the issue related to the Suez Channel, when the British had to withdraw and abandon a key maritime transportation hub because the president of Egypt, Nasser, was supported by the Americans. The relation was also affected by the full support of USA to the European Communities in particular and the European integration in general, as the perspective of a unite Europe working closely with USA in the world affairs was more appealing than a weak and divided Europe. Churchill's proposal of three main circles dominating the British international position was falling apart.

The stability of the European Communities also influenced the British petition for membership, as different reports from the Foreign Office outlined the difficulties of the project and the high possibility of collapsing in a short period of time because the tensions between the members. The political essence of the Communities had not been revealed during the first steps of the integration, focusing on economic matters. But the increasing economic integration would at some point evolve to the development of an institutional framework. These institutions would need to become democratic because otherwise the Community would have been dominated by a board of experts without any link with the people. At that point, the British expected the nationalism of the Member States of the Communities would have collapsed the organization. This error of prediction as the European Communities were stable and working in deeper integration, revealed the British necessity to become a member of the organization to keep its own status and influence the development of the process from inside. Finally, the support of some Member States of the European Communities, as Holland, to include somehow UK in the project, led to the Bonn declaration

[46]Henderson (1979).

of 1961 that emphasized the commitment of the European Communities members to develop further the integration but at the same time, to open to new members.

On July 1961 the British Prime Minister Harold Macmillan communicated the House of Commons the intentions of the British government to apply for membership in the European Communities, publishing in November a white paper that included the British claims and intentions.[47] Macmillan officially accepted the whole Community rules and policies, but expected to obtain exceptions for UK in the form of special protocols, especially in relation with the relations with the Commonwealth, still more important for UK in economic terms than the European new-born market. The Communitarian rejection to include exceptions for the British and negotiate just based on the Treaty of Rome meant the blockade of the negotiations and the final French veto. The same situation was repeated in 1967, when UK was not accepted in the European Communities because of the personal veto of de Gaulle and a very dramatic TV speech.[48] The British negotiators, Edward Heath, and Sir Eric Roll, were outmanoeuvre by the French unexpected movement, closing temporally the door to the British aspirations by dismissing the lobby of some members of the Community to accept the British membership.

Edward Heath was conservative politician who hold numerous positions in the British politics, and a supporter of the integration of the membership of UK in the European market. He tried to negotiate on the already mentioned basis of special protocols for the UK inside of the Communities and finally, as British Prime minister, oversaw the successful application a decade later. Eric Roll was an economist, banker, and public servant in charge of more technical aspects of the British application. The veto of de Gaulle was presented by most of the British politicians because of the pride, Anglophobia, and French chauvinism without a real analyzation of the real reasons behind the rejection. Nevertheless, a British re-application was always expected and after two unsuccessful applications the UK became a member of the European Communities in 1973.

References

A severe crise d'identité. (cover story) (2005) Economist 375(8428):27–29

Aitken ND (1973) The effect of the EEC and EFTA on European trade: a temporal cross-section analysis. Am Econ Rev 63(5):881–892

Andresen N (2007) The Salazar regime and European integration, 1947–1972. Eur Rev Hist: Revue européenne d'histoire 14(2):195–214

Baudenbacher C (2004) The EFTA Court: an actor in the European judicial dialogue. Fordham Int Law J 28:353

Brown M (2017) Drawing Algeria into Europe: shifting French policy and the Treaty of Rome (1951–1964). Mod Contemp Fr 25(2):191–208

[47]Bulmer and Burch (1998).

[48]Ellison (2006).

Bulmer S, Burch M (1998) Organizing for Europe: Whitehall, the British State and European Union. Public Adm 76(4):601–628
Common Agricultural Policy (CAP) (2004) Europe: a concise encyclopedia. pp 31–34
Corbet H, Robertson D (eds) (2016) Europe's free trade area experiment: EFTA and economic integration. Elsevier, Amsterdam
Deighton A (2006) Entente Neo-Coloniale?: Ernest Bevin and the proposals for an Anglo–French third world power, 1945–1949. Diplomacy Statecraft 17(4):835–852
Dinan D (1999) Ever closer union: an introduction to European integration. Hampshire, Basingstoke
Dinan D (2004) Europe recast: a history of European Union, vol 373. Palgrave Macmillan, Basingstoke
Eaton M (1991) Industrial assistance in Portugal: the role of the EFTA fund. Tijdschr Econ Soc Geogr 82(3):163–176
Efron R, Nanes AS (1957) The common market and Euratom treaties: supranationality and the integration of Europe. Int Comp Law Q 4:670
Ellis C (2012) Letting it slip: the labour party and the 'Mystical Halo' of nationalization, 1951–1964. Contemp Br Hist 26(1):47–71
Ellison J (2006) Separated by the Atlantic: the British and de Gaulle, 1958–1967. Diplomacy Statecraft 17(4):853–870
Eunjeong C (2013) EURATOM: bridging 'Rapprochement' and 'Radiance' of France in the post-war. J Int Area Stud 20(2):51–65
Fredriksen HH, Franklin CK (2015) Of pragmatism and principles: the EEA agreement 20 years on [article]. Common Mark Law Rev 3:629
Gardener EPM (1991) The European free trade association and the European Community. Int Lawyer 1:187
Groenendijk N, Hospers G (2002) A requiem for the European coal and steel community (1952—2002). De Economist (0013-063X) 150(5):601–612
Headley K (2012) Back when Britain was banging on Europe's door. The Guardian. Access mode: https://www.theguardian.com/commentisfree/2012/oct/13/britain-europe-david-cameron-eu
Henderson N (1979) Britain's decline; its causes and consequences. De Economist 2:29–41
Hurni B (1986) EFTA-EC relations: aftermath of the Luxembourg declaration. J World Trade Law 20:497
Kaiser W (2001) Culturally embedded and path-dependent: peripheral alternatives to ECSC/EEC "core Europe" since 1945. J Eur Integr Hist 7(2):11–36
Laurent W (2011) De Gaulle as a father of Europe: the unpredictability of the FTA's failure and the EEC's success (1956–58). Contemp Eur Hist 4:419
Lindberg LN (1963) The political dynamics of European economic integration
Ludlow NP (1997) Dealing with Britain: the six and the first UK application to the EEC, vol 56. Cambridge University Press, Cambridge
Marston G (1988) Armed intervention in the 1956 Suez Canal crisis: the legal advice tendered to the British government. Int Comp Law Q 37(04):773–817
Mason HL (1955) The European coal and steel community: experiment in supranationalism. Martinus Nijhoff, The Hague
Mathijsen P (1961) Problems connected with the creation of Euratom. Law Contemp Probl 26 (3):438–453. https://doi.org/10.2307/1190660
McKelvey MD (1989) European economic community: research policy, political ideology, and the decision-making process. Research Policy Institute, Univ. of Lund, Lund
Miller MH, Spencer JE (1977) The static economic effects of the UK joining the EEC: a general equilibrium approach. Rev Econ Stud 44(1):71–93
Miners N (2002) Industrial development in the colonial empire and the imperial economic conference at Ottawa 1932
Moravcsik A (1991) Negotiating the single European act: national interests and conventional statecraft in the European Community. Int Organ 45(1):19–56

Morris TGN (1991) Reassessing neo-functionalism: structure and process in the contemporary community. Archive of European Integration, EBSCOhost. Accessed 30 July 2017

Parr H (2006) Britain, America, East of Suez and the EEC: finding a role in British foreign policy, 1964–67. Contemp Br Hist 20(3):403–421

Pivoda RM (2007) The Rome treaty—50 years building Europe: short history. Annals: Economic Science Series: Timisoara, 13374-380

Ramiro Troitiño D (2008) De Gaulle and the European Communities. In: Proceedings of the Institute for European Studies, no 4, pp 139–152

Ramiro Troitiño D (2014) The British position towards European integration: a different economic and political approach. Balt J Eur Stud 4:119–136

Ramiro Troitiño D, Chochia A (2015) Winston Churchill and the European Union. Balt J Law Polit 8(1):55–81

Szokoloczy-Syllaba A (1971) EFTA: the settlement of disputes. Int Comp Law Q 20:519–534

Thompson D, Marsh NS (1962) United Kingdom and the Treaty of Rome: some preliminary observations, the [article]. Int Comp Law Q 1:73

Trevor P (1968) The EEC's common agricultural policy: the longest marathon. World Today 1:36

Ugland T (2013) Placing the supranational politics of Jean Monnet in time. Int J Can Stud 47:171–186

van Randwyck H (2011) EFTA or the EU. The Bruges Group, London

De Gaulle and the British Membership in the European Communities

David Ramiro Troitino, Tanel Kerikmäe, and Archil Chochia

Abstract While de Gaulle has been comprehensively studied on the EU level, this is—to a large degree—not the case for his influence on the British involvement in the European integration process. As this influence will cease to apply once the UK is no longer a member of the Union, the Brexit will cause essential challenges for the British, especially for the rural areas and for the EU-British future relations.

This research points out the main contributions of de Gaulle to the European integration process and their impact on the European-British relations from an historical perspective that can help both areas to improve their future relations as probably international partners.

1 Introduction

There have been several personalities with great importance in the European building process and the inclusion of United Kingdom in the European Communities. Most of them were supporters of European integration, such as Jean Monnet, Spaak, Spinelli, etc. Generally, they can be capsulated into two main streams and two different ideas of Europe.

One of these two streams was that of the followers of integration i.e. the creation of a supranational power and the creation of a new political superstructure, a European Federal State. One of the most important figures in this group was Jean Monnet, a French citizen who believed in a united Europe, where real and effective power would be in common institutions. Monnet lived in London several occasions during his life and was working very close with the British and French governments during the WWI and WWII. He was a fervent supporter of UK inside of the European Communities regardless the British negative attitude towards integration.[1]

[1]Werth (1966).

D. Ramiro Troitino (✉) · T. Kerikmäe · A. Chochia
Tallinn Law School, Tallinn University of Technology, Tallinn, Estonia
e-mail: david.troitino@ttu.ee; tanel.kerikmae@ttu.ee; archil.chochia@ttu.ee

D. Ramiro Troitiño et al. (eds.), *Brexit*,
https://doi.org/10.1007/978-3-319-73414-9_5

The second group, less heterogeneous and more differing in ideas, supported European cooperation, emphasizing the role of national states in some sort of confederation, with all power concentrated in national governments and not held by any outside institution. Charles de Gaulle was a member of this latter group, maybe the most important of them in European history, because his long term as president of France gave him the opportunity of leaving a deep imprint in the European building process. At first sight de Gaulle shared the vision about the Europe of the nations with United Kingdom, but the French president rejected twice the British membership application and the Anglo-Saxons were not accepted in the European Communities until Pompidou became French President and de Gaulle was retired. The Fouchet proposals were clearly very much of the British taste of Europe but it excluded the British participation.

Hence the most logical ally of de Gaulle in the European Communities from a conceptual approach were not accepted as such by de Gaulle because of several reasons as the own life experiences of de Gaulle, the Great Design the French president had for Europe with a structure with no room for several dominant powers, specific issues with the British as agriculture, relation with USA, balance of power in the context of the Cold War, and others discussed in this paper from a global European Franco-British perspective.

2 Facts About de Gaulle

Charles de Gaulle was born in 1890 in Lille, a French city near the border to Belgium. He was given a conservative, catholic education and soon decided to follow a military career, studying in various military schools until he graduated. He fought in WWI, was injured a few times showing bravery. In the beginning of the battle of Verdun he was injured again and was taken prisoner. He made several attempts to escape, but failed. De Gaulle was a good officer by then, but not yet a well-known figure in the French army. Until the beginning of WWII when he became a public figure, a leader, thanks to his theoretical knowledge and various writings, which had a great impact on France.[2]

At the beginning of WWII and after the decisive defeat of the French Army in a very short period, he showed strong determination to go on fighting and resisting the German occupation. He flew from England to France, urging the French government to go into exile and continue the war from the French possessions in Africa. This was his first contact with the concept of integration. Jean Monnet was in Britain and elaborated a plan to keep France fighting against the Germans.[3] His idea was that both countries, France and UK, would unite to defeat their common enemy, sharing the same rights and duties. The best way to effectively unite both countries according

[2]Jouve (1967).

[3]Ramiro Troitiño (2017).

to Jean Monnet was by integrating them, creating a new political structure, combining both countries to the extent of a common citizenship. De Gaulle, a French nationalist, convinced of the greatness of the French nation and its privilege to become one of the main world powers,[4] accepted this plan as the only way to keep his country fighting, as the only way to save French honor, even though he disliked Monnet and any supranational organization, even if it was temporal.[5]

This was not the last time that he sacrificed his political views for the sake of France; it was also evident in his foreign policy and his relationship with the European Community. De Gaulle made many political mistakes in his long career; many times, his actions were old fashioned and unrealistic but he showed a strong pragmatic sense, being able to adapt to new situations and transform his ideas. The plan itself did not work as the French government rejected it and surrendered to the Germans. De Gaulle stayed in London and tried to gain the leadership of "Free France." Once he was recognized as the person in charge (thanks to the help of Jean Monnet), he struggled to maintain the illusion that France was still at war and that France was one more of the allies. As leader of a country with no power, supported by the allies as a secondary actor to maintain the illusion of a national French opposition against the Germans, he tried to act as the head of government of one of the most important countries in the world, equal to the US, Britain, or the Soviet Union—the natural position of France according de Gaulle. But in fact, he was just a general commanding a small group of soldiers fighting for a flag that had no more territory than its colonies. This was the source of some of de Gaulle's problems with the USA and Britain. The American president F. D. Roosevelt did not like de Gaulle, his pretentious manners and his thoughts of greatness that did not fit with his stature. The French contribution to the war compared to the US was minored so Roosevelt treated de Gaulle as what he was, a minor figure in the World affairs.[6]

De Gaulle never forgot this personal affront, but was obviously he was more pained for his country and in the following decades he tried to avoid situations where France could be mistreated by the Americans. The British premier Winston Churchill had a good personal relationship with de Gaulle, but he was beholden to the USA. Britain could not face the power of the Germans without the support of the Americans and the former world power now found itself in American hands. Once France was liberated by the allies, comprising American and British forces and some token French unit, de Gaulle was appointed by the Allies as head of the provisional French government. His main aim was to normalize the French political life and restore the prestige of France by behaving like one of the powers that had won the war. That illusion was tolerated as such by the rest of the allies but, in reality, France never had an effective say or even an influence in the main post war decisions.

In May 1953 de Gaulle withdrew from active politics, but was ready to come back when the circumstances would permit it. Already in 1958, the Fourth Republic was

[4]Marcussen et al. (1999).

[5]De Ménil (1977).

[6]Ramiro Troitiño and Chochia (2015).

threatened by certain factors, mainly economic, but also those concerning the colonies, especially Algeria. That was when de Gaulle appeared again to save France from its enemies, as he liked to point out. Once elected as president of the Fifth Republic, he took measures to reform the French economy succeeding. In the political sphere, he drafted a new Constitution and decided to solve France's main problem, the colonies, by withdrawing from Algeria thus ending the colonial system. It did not mean that he was convinced of the rightness of such an important measure but France was simply not strong enough to keep its colonies in the context of the Cold War. De Gaulle showed that he could sacrifice his ideas for the sake of France; his dream of France as a world power, an active participant in the world affairs was unattainable. France lacked the power to maintain its influence in the colonies. After the French withdrawal from Algeria, the political and economic situation stabilized (Still, supporters of French Algeria tried many times to assassinate de Gaulle). Then, de Gaulle turned his eye towards Europe.

3 De Gaulle and Europe

After WWII the world was divided in two main blocks: the USA with its allies and the USSR with its supporters. While the two superpowers were fighting in the Cold War for world supremacy, the dreams of de Gaulle of restoring France greatness were impossible to achieve by conventional means. He needed a new approach a new way to increase the French power to keep the independence of the country and spread its influence. At the beginning, he tried to maintain a policy of independence from foreign powers, mainly from the United States. The American influence would have meant in his eyes the end of French independence. He was aware though that Europe was defended against the Soviets only by the American army and was aware that Western Europe rested free only thanks to the collaboration with the USA. So, he started working in two ways, reassuring French independence and developing nuclear facilities in France. The latter, according to de Gaulle, would again take France to the top league of global politics and keep away the threats. Harold McMillan, Prime Minister of the United Kingdom from 1957 to 1963, Nicknamed "Supermac", was known for his pragmatism, wit, and unflappability, in fact tried to convince de Gaulle to support the enlargement of the European Community to the United Kingdom, offering nuclear technology in exchange, but the French president rejected this offer. British nuclear technology was reliant on the USA, on the Polaris missiles, and de Gaulle wanted full autonomy. Getting the American missiles would have meant dependence on American supplies.

As a political gesture he moved the headquarters of NATO from Paris to Brussels and withdrew France from the military structure of NATO. It was clear that his country alone could not stand independent in the world, so he had to look for partners that would accept the preeminence of France, or at least an equal partnership. The British were close allies of the USA and hence could not join an alliance with France. His partners should help him creating a third way in the bipolar affairs of the Cold War and should not be tied to either side. With the intention of getting France recognized as a third force in world politics, he went to Moscow and other Soviet countries, but came back with minimal results: the only effective consequence of these trips was propaganda. France alone was too weak to play an active role in the world as it lacked economic and military resources to do so. Here, the French president made another change in his political views. The only possibility of an effective alliance would be West Germany and not the United Kingdom, traditionally an ally of France against the German aspirations in Europe.[7]

As a prisoner in WWI, de Gaulle had declared that cooperation between the Germans and French would be impossible in the future because the lack of harmony between their societies and their principals.[8] After WWII, he had supported the idea of allied domination over West Germany as the only possible mean to prevent another rise of German power again. But in the 50s, cooperation with the eternal enemy of the French nation would be the only possibility to rebuild the greatness of France. In other words, his political vision was old fashioned and unable to understand the new circumstances of the world. It could be said that luckily for him and for the Germans, the USA did not accept the ideas of de Gaulle. The United States gave full independence to West Germany because they were interested in a strong West Germany as the first battlefield in a hypothetical European war against the Soviet Union. De Gaulle always preferred bilateral contacts between the two countries but most of the Franco-German relations were done under the umbrella of the European Communities as the German wanted. The French president promoted meetings with Adenauer, the Chancellor of West Germany, to discuss community issues, trying to reach an agreement with the Germans and then to present a common position with them in the Community meeting. A common position of the two most important Member States was unlikely to be rejected. The influence of this bilateral conception and the influence of de Gaulle can still be noted in our days and obviously left no room for the incorporation of UK to the European Communities. The issue of West Germany shows a change in de Gaulle's political views, because according to his ideas, the nation was the last political structure, there was nothing beyond that, but if he wanted to cooperate with the Germans he had to do it through the European Communities, the diplomatic channel open between both countries. And the essence of the Community was supranational institutions where the national states shared sovereignty to an upper sphere, the common institutions. So, de Gaulle accepted the cooperation with Germany through the EC because it was the only possibility to increase the influence of France, and because he was wise enough to realize that many economic problems of his country could be solved in the framework of the EC thanks to the economic power of West Germany. This shows that he had the illusion that he could change the essence of the Community from within, from supranational to intergovernmental without further enlargements, but he failed in this.

[7]Hoffmann (1964).

[8]Braghiroli (2007).

West Germany from its perspective was eager to embrace the collaboration with France as it was the country defeated in the war, many millions had been killed and the Germans were still blamed for it. They needed to get over their past, so they needed to normalize their diplomatic relations with the rest of the world and they needed to demonstrate German generosity and solidarity through such an idealistic project as the EC. Also, they could minimize the French influence over West Germany in a wider Community with four more members and even more as the Germans were keen to accept the British as full members of the Communities. Hence, for West Germany to be accepted by France as a partner in the Community, with the political preeminence of France and an economic cost for Germany as the main contributor to the common Budget of the EC, was seen as a fair price to pay for the normalization of West German external relations.

De Gaulle also provided the Germans with some kind of diplomatic maintenance by supporting a united Germany against the division of the country in two parts. This issue was of great importance for Adenauer, after the de facto recognition by the USA and the UK of East Germany, which ended in the partition of the country.[9] It helped to cool the German eagerness towards the British enlargement or any other agreement between the Communities and the British.

Hence de Gaulle found a perfect partner to improve France's economic and political position and his acceptance of the EC can be understood as a mean towards his ambition to restore French greatness. But he did not accept the development of the EC into a supranational entity and he fought against it from within and even tried to change the whole Community through his Fouchet Plan, supporting the power of the national states. In a Community of six of France, West Germany, The Netherlands, Belgium, Luxembourg, and Italy, the preeminence of France meant that in a Community lead by states France could play the main role without the risk of national ideas melting in supranational institutions or in a 'European' influence. The idea of de Gaulle using the EC for the benefit of France was clear during all his years as president and this influence can be seen in the main issues of de Gaulle's relations with the EC and the British candidate, i.e. the Common Agricultural Policy (CAP), the empty chair crisis, the enlargement negotiations and the Fouchet proposals. The heritage of de Gaulle is still alive in many circles of French society and France's actions as an EU member are still influenced by his legacy.[10]

4 The Enlargement to the United Kingdom

The European Community began as the European Coal and Steel Community (ECSC) in the 1950s. Since the beginning of the negotiations the UK was interested in the new project, but as a supporter of national sovereignty opposed to

[9]Costigliola (1984).

[10]Dinan (2004).

supranational power, it supported a Community of intergovernmental cooperation instead of the integration of the ECSC. Hence the UK retired from the negotiations and later created another model of a European Community. This was based on a free trade area without common power institutions able to impose resolutions on the Member States, working through negotiations and agreements between the Member States. The creation of the European Free Trade Association with the Treaty of Stockholm in 1959 expressed the wishes of the British. When the idea of a Common Market was launched in the Treaty of Rome, the UK was again interested, but retired from the preliminary discussions in Messina for the same reason, opposition to supranational power.

Afterwards, because of different reasons such as the economic crisis in the UK or the success of the EEC, the British tried to join the Community. Logically the ideas of the British government about Europe should have coincided with those of Charles de Gaulle. It was even considered that since France had a new president in 1958, the character of the new Europe might be moving away from dogmatic emphasis on supranational technocracy. Both countries agreed with the idea of primacy of national sovereignty over any common institution and political cooperation as opposed to political integration. But, in reality, de Gaulle became a bitter enemy of the British application, blocking the enlargement twice, in 1961 and 1967. The reasons for de Gaulle's vetoing of the UK's admission laid mainly in the links between the UK and the USA that were viewed negatively, the British threat to the hegemony of France in the EC and as a result a threat to developing the CAP.

In de Gaulle's time the Community was clearly dominated by France and the French had and still do have some sense of ownership of the EC. De Gaulle viewed the EC as an instrument to empower France, this being the only reason for him to be inside it. Other European countries entering the association would not have been a problem, since their size in terms of population and economy were relatively small, but Great Britain was a big country, powerful enough to maintain its independence and hence, to dismiss the influence of France. This new member would rival the influence of France and could ruin de Gaulle's desire of placing France at the center of the European stage. It was also a threat to the perception of a close relationship with West Germany. The French president thought that a powerful and independent big country in the EC could overshadow the influence of France and could also affect the development of a Franco-German alliance, which had acquired symbolic force with the signing in 1963 of a friendship treaty between West Germany and France. This alliance was the core of French influence. It was clear for de Gaulle that there was not enough room for two main powers in the Community and hence the enlargement to Great Britain had to be blocked. Nevertheless, the hypothetical British influence inside of the Communities was to be proven false after the incorporation of the country. The special situation of the country and its reluctance to be fully involved in the European affairs dismissed any possibility of leadership in Europe.[11] It can be said that the lack of interest of the British in the Communitarian

[11]Beloff (1963).

affairs beyond the European market based on liberal principals proved wrong de Gaulle in his estimation on the British influence over other Member States, especially Denmark and Ireland, countries who applied at the same time than UK for membership.[12]

The special relationship between the UK and the USA also played an important role in the refusal of the French president to the enlargement. De Gaulle was suspicious of the UK's close links with the USA, and thought that UK would pave the way for American penetration into and domination of Europe and consequently, of France. According to the ideas of de Gaulle, France had to stand independently between the great powers, the USA and the USSR. De Gaulle was scared that with the UK the Americans would join the Community from the back door. He was afraid that the UK would promote a free trade agreement with the USA and Canada inside the Community and this of course was unacceptable, because the economic power of the USA would lead to economic domination of the EC. France would lose the European market, which at that moment was an indispensable market for such sensible French products as the agricultural ones. In his speech announcing his personal veto to Britain's entry, de Gaulle claimed that Britain was not yet sufficiently "European" in her outlook, and still too closely tied to the USA.[13] Nevertheless, after the enlargement no free trade agreement was signed with USA and just recently in 2017 the European Union has signed a free trade agreement with Canada, again proving wrong the theories of de Gaulle.[14]

The third reason, and probably main reason, for de Gaulle's personal veto against the UK was the Common Agricultural Policy. This European policy was settled in the Treaty of Rome, but did not start working until some years later, even after de Gaulle's term as president of France. It was still under discussion at the time of the petition of Britain to join the EC and de Gaulle did not want the British to interfere in the negotiations or the result of the communitarian agreement, because he thought that it might be against the interest of France. The CAP was a good deal for France and represented many benefits for French farmers. Agriculture was still very important for France and it needed huge subsidies to face the cheaper production of other parts of the world, like Argentina, Canada, or Australia. The French state was having considerable financial problems because of support to agriculture, so the Community was going to pay for this European policy for the benefit of French farmers and their government. On the other hand, the high artificial prices of agricultural products because of the subsidies lead to a boom in production—farmers produced as much as possible because the guaranteed prices supported by the government made production profitable. As they produced more than the French market was able to absorb, they created a tremendous surplus. France had to sell this surplus in the international market, because these were perishable products and could not compete with cheaper international prices. It meant that they had to sell below cost, losing money and

[12]Lieshout et al. (2004).

[13]Costigliola (1992).

[14]Newhouse (1970).

creating a supply distortion in the international agricultural products market, which in turn meant a decrease in international prices. The idea of the CAP was to get finances from the European Community and at the same time dealing with the surplus on the European market.[15]

The CAP was going to become the most important policy at the European level in terms of finance, absorbing most of the European budget—around €23.2 billion, making France one of the most important beneficiaries. The UK had developed another type of agricultural system than most of continental countries in Europe based on imports and the liberalization of the market. It meant a reduction in the importance of the English national agricultural sector but low prices and advantages for the colonies and British industry, which could access the labor liberated from the countryside. De Gaulle was concern that with the UK as a full member of the Community, the CAP that was against British interests would disappear or lose designed entity. The negotiations were not finished during the British application to membership to the Communities, so it was crucial for France to keep Britain out of the EC over this period—according to Community law, any country that joined the organization had to fulfill different requirements, one of them was to accept all the rules, laws, and policies of the EC. Once the CAP was approved by all the Member States, the UK had no choice but to accept it if it wanted to join the Community, so it was very important to keep the UK out of the EC until an agreement was reached on the CAP.[16]

Once the CAP was approved one of the main obstacles to the enlargement to UK was lifted, influencing the own internal agricultural sector in England, Scotland, and Wales. Obviously, the previous British system based on imperial preferences was cancel; priority was given to European agricultural production and farmers from Great Britain were encouraged by Community payments to increase their activity. It was a long-term process lasting for several decades but consequently an important local agrarian sector was created. BREXIT has created uncertainty about the future of the British farmers as the European payments will stop and the position of the British government is still not clear if they will return to the previous system of liberalization and massive imports of agricultural products from other parts of the world or a system based on national protection of the farmers reproducing the European model.

5 The Empty Chair Crisis

De Gaulle was against any supranational integration that could reduce the independence of France, but he had to accept the Community for the good of France. During his mandate he had numerous clashes with the European Commission president, the

[15]Ramiro Troitiño (2008).

[16]Serfaty (1968).

German Wallenstein, a supporter of European integration. The main crisis is known as the "Empty Chair Crisis" and came from the opposition of de Gaulle to the advance of integration in the Community; this consisted mainly of proposals to allow the Community its own income and to award greater powers to the Common Assembly. De Gaulle was also against what he saw as the increasing political importance of the Commission and against the imminent prospect of the Community moving into a stage of development in which there would be more majority voting in the Council, all proposals leading to the implementation of a supranational Europe. Accepting that decisions would be made by the majority could have meant in de Gaulle's eyes that France would be forced to accept the orders of the EC if the other five members supported any proposal against the interests of the French. It was a big change, because the Community was mainly working with a voting system based on unanimity, based on agreementbetween all the Member States. The French option was clearly in the same position than the British proposals and political options. The demands of de Gaulle in the empty chair crisis resemble enormously the British position in Westminster during the debates about the European integration after the WWII.[17]

De Gaulle could not accept the reform in the voting system of the Communities because his political beliefs were based on national sovereignty and because of his nationalistic views on France and the Community. European Integration was supposed to be a tool to increase the power of France, not decrease it. When Community income was discussed, De Gaulle yielded, even though he believed that the EC should get its income from the national contributions, never from its own sources, again a position that could have been easily defended by the British government. The economic independence of the European Institutions could make them dangerous and out of the control of the national governments and too independent and hence a threat to national autonomy.[18] In that respect, there is an obvious parallelism with the British complains of the size of the EU institutions and the necessity to reduce its numbers and powers. But on the other hand of the negotiation table there was the issue of financing the CAP, which was going to give huge benefits to France. To get the money required for the CAP, de Gaulle accepted the EC sourcing its own income. The CAP itself was another important factor in the crisis and a constant issue in de Gaulle's relationship with the EC. The negotiations to implement this policy were blocked because other members of the EC did not want to finance the farming sector of France. De Gaulle threatened his European partners with leaving the Community if the CAP was not approved. De Gaulle withdrew the French ministers from the meetings of the Council, stopping the activity of this important institution. The crisis continued for 6 months and ended only after the French government, under strong pressure, accepted a deal at a special Council meeting in 1966, known as "The Luxembourg Compromise". The accord meant that in the case of decisions, which could be made by a majority vote, any Member State could veto

[17] Bozo (1993).

[18] Bozo and Emanuel (2002).

it if its national interests were at stake. In other words, national governments were to keep their sovereignty in sensitive issues. The compromise had no constitutional status, but it had a huge influence in the decision making of the Council. Therefore, most decisions were to be made by letting deliberations and negotiations run until an agreement finally emerged. The national veto was invoked less than a dozen times between 1966 and 1985, but its effect on the negotiations made the Community slow and ineffective. The influence of de Gaulle through the "Luxembourg Compromise" lasted until 1986, when the Single European Act expanded the circumstances in which a simple majority vote was allowed, leading to the final demise of the Compromise.[19] The Compromise was perfect according to the British interest and helped in the integration of the country inside the Communities, not as a regular practice but as a last tool to protect the British national sovereignty. Nevertheless, the Single European Act, ending this practice, was signed by Margaret Thatcher, the British premier known for her concerns about Europe and her fierce defense of the British sovereignty, a contradiction difficult to explain.

6 Common Agricultural Policy

The CAP was a constant issue in the relationship between de Gaulle and the European Communities as we have already seen and it was also one of de Gaulle's biggest successes at the European level, influencing the British membership and the current negotiations of the BREXIT. In 1961 agriculture in France still accounted for 25% of all employment and state subsidies and gave a huge boost in output and caused downward pressures on prices. The living standards of millions of small farmers were threatened and the consequent movement of people from the countryside to the cities where jobs were scarce and no housing was available made agriculture the main issue in French domestic politics. Farmers kept the land through state subsidies and the expenditure was heavy and difficult for the French Republic to afford. When de Gaulle took power in 1958, France's farm surpluses had already reached crisis point. At a crisis Cabinet meeting in August 1962, de Gaulle declared that agriculture was "the most important problem" France had to face. Even de Gaulle affirmed that if the problem was not solved "we will have another Algeria on our own on soil". The problem of the state subsidies was that production increased because of it, because it altered the market balance between supply and demand, artificially raising the prices and hence production. De Gaulle had to find new markets for the surplus of French farmers and he also had to find another way of financing this policy because it cost a lot and the revenues of the state were exhausted. The situation was dangerous and again de Gaulle had to choose between his political convictions against supranational institutions and the French national interest. He, as before, showed pragmatism and chose the latter. The CAP was

[19]Ledwidge (1982).

already included in the Treaty of Rome, but just as vague declarations. In 1958 the conference of Stresa developed this policy, but it was almost 11 years before full agreement was reached thanks to de Gaulle's work, even though the final negotiations finished under the mandate of Pompidou, successor to de Gaulle. France secured the economic support of the rest of the Member States of the EC, especially that of West Germany when the policy was made European, changing the national subsidies into European subsidies. It also secured the European market for French production, as a high level of protectionism in agricultural goods at the borders of the European area was agreed to. Imports from Argentina, Canada or Australia had to face high custom duties when crossing into the borders of the Member States of the EEC.

It is clear that France obtained the CAP as a reward for its membership in the EC and Europe, especially West Germany, paid for the CAP to have France as a partner in the European building process. It was a great success for de Gaulle, because it was his personal veto of enlargement to the UK and his threats to the EC of France withdrawing from the organization and the "empty chair crisis" launched to blackmail the other Member States that led to an agreement on the CAP. In other words, de Gaulle's lack of commitment to European integration, his full dedication to France and his intransigence made great benefits for France possible and created the most important European level policy up to now.[20] The influence of de Gaulle can still be felt nowadays, with the biggest share of the European budget going to the CAP (around 40% of the European Budget) and several problems with the British agricultural sector. The British developed their own domestic sector after the membership in the European Communities influencing their traditional policy based on free trade and liberalization of the sector. The British farmers received in the year 2015 from the European Union payments for €3.1 billion in direct payments and have access to the €5.2 billion pot of funding that has been allocated to the UK for rural development projects over the period 2014–2020, including €2.3 billion that has been transferred from the BPS to the UK rural development programs. It is estimated that around 55% of the farmers' incomes in UK come from the EU and the redesign force by the BREXIT will influence enormously the countryside of UK.[21]

Nevertheless, it is a contradiction that British farmers, mostly conservative as in the rest of the world, and rural areas in UK where the support for the BREXIT was higher than in the cities, will suffer more during the BREXIT process as the British government will not replace the European support with a national plan because of lack of funds, exclusion from the European market and economic necessities based on free trade with other parts of the world that will force the British government to sacrifice the agricultural sector to benefit services and financial sectors in the global economy. Hence, those who supported firmly the BREXIT will suffer the most.

[20]De Gaulle (1994).

[21]Moravcsik (2000).

7 The Fouchet Proposals

If the CAP was a great success of de Gaulle's policies, the Fouchet proposals were the biggest failure. De Gaulle tried to change the Community from the inside to a model closer to his beliefs. It is clear that he did not like the supranational character of the EC but was forced to collaborate with the Community because of the various reasons discussed above. He thought that once inside and securing benefits for France, he could transform the essence of the EC "into an intergovernmental framework which has already become a Community" according to Jean Monnet. To achieve this transformation, de Gaulle proposed through the Fouchet Committee, which was dominated by him, a new Community composed of a voluntary union of independent states.[22] He also proposed moving the location of the institutions from Belgium, Luxembourg, and Strasbourg to one location, Paris, where the new secretariat would work instead of the European Commission, an institution that represented the European level. The French president wanted to have the institutions in Paris for his country to benefit from the presence of a center of power. Moreover, he thought that if the European institutions where located in Paris, the French government could control them better and the influence of France could grow, creating an association of Western European countries with France, which was different from the original idea of a Community where all the members had the same rights and duties. His ambitions to substitute the Commission with a secretariat were an obvious attack on European integration, substituting the independence of the Commission for national control, mainly French control. And its commitment to the European good made this institution the representative of all de Gaulle hated. He attacked the Commission constantly, accusing Wallenstein of behaving like a head of state without legitimacy, complaining about it mot being representative of the European societies it was meant to serve, in other words a dictatorship created by civil servants without any democratic support. A very similar statement to the views expressed in several occasions by Margaret Thatcher, British Premier.

An Additional proposal was, of course, an extensive national veto over common policies, which in reality meant cooperation instead of integration and a safeguard of the national sovereignty of the Member States. All these proposals could have meant the end of the European building process and the end of the Community as we currently understand it, but would have avoid the BREXIT as the proposals followed the main British claims concerning the issue of sovereignty.[23]

Nevertheless, in a Union of States, de Gaulle pretended to maintain the influence of France over the other members without any commitment from France itself, expressing the real point of view of de Gaulle about the Communities—they were to be a toy in the hands of France, for the benefit of France. It obviously leads to the conclusion that if the Fouchet proposals were approved, UK would have never become a member of the European Communities.[24]

[22] Camps (1965).

[23] Ramiro Troitino (2013).

[24] Young (1990).

On this occasion, de Gaulle miscalculated the muscle of the European dream of a union between equals, the power of the people who were working for a European supranational state and of course, he overestimated the power of France. This time West Germany stepped aside and did not support the reforms proposed by de Gaulle, defeating his aims, and making the Fouchet proposals the biggest failure in de Gaulle's policy. Denying the reality of the European Community, not accepting the fact that the world was changing, trying to go back one century to restore great France, de Gaulle showed his limited political understanding of the world. His position would have meant a reduction of the European Community to a minimal expression, articulating an idea removed from reality from a politician too old to understand the new realities. It could have meant the final fall of Europe from world affairs and hence of France, the end of the independence of Europe and of France, because in a globalized world the influence of separate European states would be minimal, far less than the central role he wanted.

8 Conclusions

De Gaulle had a huge influence in developing the European building process, in slowing the speed of integration, but he could not change its essence. He made the mistake of thinking it was possible to have a nationalist approach more typical for a politician of the nineteenth century, still worried about the greatness of France, not realizing that the only option for France was to stay inside a strong Community and to never again be a sole power. His biggest value was a capacity to adapt and change his views as many times as needed for the sake of his country, treating the integration into the EC as a minor ill.

His influence on the British involvement in European affairs is obvious in different spheres, as the double rejection of membership, the inclusion and design of the CAP and the defense of the national sovereignty as the last barrier to the European development. The rejections served to force the British government to accept all the European requirements during the final negotiations for the membership. It meant a bad agreement that had to be reformed in a few years and generated a negative feeling towards Europe inside of the UK. The CAP changed the internal social composition of the British rural areas as it boasted the British agricultural production, the prize of land, the incomes of Farmers and the rural development. It remains as a big challenge for the British government to deal with the new situation of the countryside after the BREXIT and the end of the European support to farmers and rural development. Finally, the Fouchet Proposals and the renationalization of policies could have succeeded if de Gaulle would have count with the British support, natural ally in these matters related to sovereignty, but the strong French nationalism and the idea of using the Communities for the benefit of France were more important for de Gaulle. Hence, for the following decades the British were the only European power advocating for more cooperation rather than integration.

References

Beloff N (1963) The General says no: Britain's exclusion from Europe. Penguin Books
Bozo F (1993) Deux stratégies pour l'Europe: De Gaulle, les Etats Unis et l'Alliance atlantique: 1958–1969. Doctoral dissertation, Paris 10
Bozo F, Emanuel S (2002) Two strategies for Europe: De Gaulle, the United States, and the Atlantic Alliance. Rowman & Littlefield Publishers
Braghiroli S (2007) The challenges to democracy in the interwar period: lessons from the past relevant today. Poland, Lithuania, and Czechoslovakia in an extended Rokkanian perspective. CEU Polit Sci J 4:358–380
Camps M (1965) What kind of Europe? The community since De Gaulle's veto, vol 8. Oxford University Press
Costigliola F (1984) The failed design: Kennedy, de Gaulle, and the struggle for Europe. Dipl Hist 8 (3):227–251
Costigliola F (1992) France and the United States: the cold alliance since World War II, vol 9. Twayne Pub
De Gaulle C (1994) A concert of European States. In The European Union. Macmillan Education UK, pp 25–41
De Ménil LP (1977) Who speaks for Europe? The vision of Charles de Gaulle. Weidenfeld & Nicolson
Dinan D (2004) Europe recast: a history of European Union, vol 373. Palgrave Macmillan, Basingstoke
Hoffmann S (1964) De Gaulle, Europe, and the Atlantic Alliance. Int Organ 18(1):1–28
Jouve E (1967) Le Général de Gaulle et la construction de l'Europe (1940–1966), vol 25. Librairie générale de droit et de jurisprudence
Ledwidge B (1982) De Gaulle. Weidenfeld and Nicolson, London
Lieshout RH, Segers ML, van der Vleuten AM (2004) de Gaulle, Moravcsik, and the choice for Europe: soft sources, weak evidence. J Cold War Stud 6(4):89–139
Marcussen M, Risse T, Engelmann-Martin D, Knopf HJ, Roscher K (1999) Constructing Europe? The evolution of French, British and German nation state identities. J Eur Publ Policy 6(4):614–633
Moravcsik A (2000) De Gaulle between grain and grandeur: the political economy of French EC policy, 1958–1970 (part 2). J Cold War Stud 2(3):4–68
Newhouse J (1970) de Gaulle and the Anglo-Saxons. Viking Adult
Ramiro Troitiño D (2008) De Gaulle and the European Communities. Proc Inst Eur Stud 4:139–152
Ramiro Troitino D (2013) European integration: building Europe (European political, economic, and security issues). Nova Science Publishers Incorporated
Ramiro Troitiño D (2017) Jean Monnet before the first European Community: a historical perspective and critic. Trames no. 3
Ramiro Troitiño D, Chochia A (2015) Winston Churchill and the European Union. Balt J Law Polit 8(1):55–81
Serfaty S (1968) France, De Gaulle, and Europe: the policy of the fourth and fifth republics toward the continent. Johns Hopkins Univ Pr
Werth A (1966) De Gaulle; a political biography, vol 793. Simon and Schuster
Young JW (1990) France, the Cold War and the Western Alliance, 1944–49: French foreign policy and post-war Europe. Burns & Oates

Great Britain and Differentiated Integration in Europe

Rafał Riedel

Abstract The United Kingdom has always been a special case in the European integration project. The British *exceptionalism* manifested in various forms and ways over the history. June 23rd 2016 delivered another culmination point in the story of the *stubborn European's* relations with its continental partners. The so-called *Brexit* referendum, which brought about victory for the supporters of the UK leaving the European Union, marks an important milestone in these relations. It has never been an easy marriage and many times threatened by the divorce. Instead of becoming *ever closer*, the European Union becomes *ever loser* and the UK is *ever closer to leaving*. Brexit is not only vital for the British, it is potentially destructive for the EU from the core. The UK changes its status inside from an integration-tolerant country (not a very ambitious one anyway), to integration unfriendly country, which endangers the very fundaments of the integration process. It produces externalities to be consumed by other Member States and non-members as well.

Accordingly, the main purpose of this chapter is to shed light on the positive discrimination of the UK inside the EU and its entertaining the status of a preferential membership. The referendum is seen as a game in which London tried to win even more beneficial conditions inside the EU and now, after the referendum, will try to build a status of a preferential non-membership. From this perspective, this process can be seen as an exercise in searching the limits of differentiated integration. The problem has always been there, the Brexit referendum made it crystal clear. It may serve as a wakeup call for the necessary reforms of the EU.

Based on the analysis of the existing literature about the differentiated integration, this contribution sees the June 2016 Brexit referendum as a structural problem for the EU. Following the logic of the integration evolution from one crisis to another one, it is possible to interpret the Brexit decision as an opportunity for the EU's reforms. The reformist impulse of Brexit may enhance the European integration in two various possible ways. First, it may help to reform the EU into a more differentiated

R. Riedel (✉)
Institute of Political Science, Opole University, Opole, Poland
e-mail: riedelr@wp.pl

D. Ramiro Troitiño et al. (eds.), *Brexit*,
https://doi.org/10.1007/978-3-319-73414-9_6

system that will allow accommodate countries willing to integrate at various speeds and extends. Secondly, once "getting rid" of the major troublemaker and marauder, that is Britain as a country opposing the further integration, the EU may accelerate now towards the "ever closer union".

1 Introduction

The existing literature on Great Britain and its place in the European integration process focuses predominantly on the existing descriptive models of various forms of differentiated integration. The concepts used range from the *Europe a'la Carte* metaphor, through Europe of different speeds, concentric circles, differentiated geometries, up to the diversified hemispheres of integration.[1] However, the June 23rd 2016 Brexit referendum brought some new stimulus to the reflection on the various forms of differentiation in Europe. Never has the existing Member State decided to leave the EU. At the same time, never has a Member State been so internally divided about its attitudes towards Brussels. To such an extent that directly after the Brexit referendum, many parts of the British society (including the Londoners, the Scotts and the Northern Irish), sympathizing with the European integration project, called for a new referendum or for a secession from the United Kingdom. Especially in the Northern part of the island, the Brexit referendum results stimulated the appetite to reconsider the independence and revisit the question of leaving not the EU, but the UK.

With its imperial past and a long-lasting tradition of the "splendid isolation" logic in its international relations, London has never been an easy partner for the other continental Europeans (this statement is even more true for the Irish). It is true that the United Kingdom, historically speaking, had a specific attitude to the European integration project (which is elaborated in other chapters of this book), however, the Brexit referendum brought about some new quality in the debate on the differentiated integration in Europe. It is one of the most important old Member States (though not the founding member), with one of the most powerful economy and high recognition in international relations. The above mentioned created a relative bargaining power for the United Kingdom and as a result an exemptive type of differentiation in the European Union.[2] London's divorcing Brussels may provide a strong disintegrative impulse for the whole project. And as such, it has a deconstructive potential for the post-WWII economic and political order in Europe. The *tsunami effect* of Britain going out of the European Union may be felt not only by the entrepreneurs operating across the Channel, but on the whole single market, including the barriers in migration traffic, capital flows, deficits in the EU funds and policies. Brexit is a structural problem for the EU.

[1]Further see: Andersen and Sitter (2006).

[2]For details see Schimmelfennig (2014).

The observed increase in differentiation came to the limits in which it carries the potential for disintegration. Exemptions from the Eurozone and Schengen area have already been quite prominent examples of differentiation. But undermining one of the four freedoms (free movement of people) attacks one of the fundamentals and questions the very idea of the European integration project. Openly opposing the very core of the Single Market turns the direction of the integration trajectory. The economic theories of international integration inform us that it is not only the free movement of products and services, which constitutes a common market. But for its creation and functioning, it is conditional to liberalize also the free movement the factors of production: the capital and the labor. Therefore, the four freedoms were treated as far as the inseparable four elements of one concept.

Both in academic deliberations and in the real-life politics, the differentiated integration concepts offered, so far, a way out from the dichotomous thinking between full membership and full non-membership. The British way of thinking about the UK's participation in the EU closes this way out. This kind of opposition to Europe takes an extreme form that cannot be comprehended in existing categorizations.[3] The British citizens decision to leave the EU opens a new chapter in the discussions about the future forms of differentiated integration in Europe and, interestingly, inside the UK as well. Britain may end up differentiately integrated with the EU—some parts of it may find themselves out of the EU, whereas some others may remain (or get re-integrated) inside the EU, whereas even some others may be positioned in some kind of a grey zone to be defined in the coming years after the referendum.

2 Differentiated Integration As a Scholarly Concept

Differentiated integration as a scholarly concept is a relatively new phenomenon in the European studies, or wider: international relations, legal studies, political science, or economy.[4] It grew together with the real-life increase in differentiation (opt-outs, exemptions, enhanced cooperation, constructive abstention, special clauses, additional protocols, etc.) and London was an unquestioned leader in it. In the last two decades, differentiation has been a dominant feature of European integration. It is argued that approximately half of the EU policies are implemented in different ways.[5] Undoubtedly studying differentiated integration contributes to the better and more refined theoretical and empirical understanding of the European integration process as such.[6] Differentiated integration can be best understood as the institutional response to the increasing heterogeneity of the Member States

[3] See also Leruth (2015).

[4] Compare with Andersen and Sitter (2006) and Mohler and Seitz (2012).

[5] For more details see Leruth and Lord (2015).

[6] See also Genschel and Jachtenfuchs (2014).

preferences and capacities resulting both from the widening and the deepening of the EU.[7]

In the case of the UK it is not the capacities but the preferences that kept London outside of the European core. It simply belongs to the category of the less willing countries, together with outsiders like the quasi-members: Switzerland or Norway (all of them having different legal status however). Some Member States opt out (internal differentiation), whereas some non-Member States opt in (external differentiation), which results in the need for reconciling heterogeneity inside and outside of the union.

The political idea of differentiated integration can be tracked back to the famous Tindemans report (1975), whereas as a legal concept it appeared in the Single European Act (1986). The academic debates on the topic find their roots in Dahrendorf's formulation of *Europe a la carte* (1970s). Already by the 1980s, scholars have identified several variations of differentiated integration and the scientific discourse has exploded ever since. From that moment on many various conceptualizations can be traced in the literature, including flexible integration, multi-speed Europe, Europe as an empire, Europe of variable geometries, concentric circles, hemispheres, etc.[8] Yet, differentiated integration is understudied in comparison with the huge literature on integration in general. The reason for it may be it has been limited by an assumption that differentiated integration would erode over time.[9] That Member States (and their neighborhood) would converge over time, the same variously applied policies would find their cohesive end. However, this assumption was challenged by the crisis.[10] The new one suggests that we are heading towards some more diversified forms of integration. It is John Eric Fossum who claims that the EU of tomorrow may combine all three of the following: accelerated integration for some, outright disintegration for others and greater differentiation for the rest.[11] The idea that differentiated integration amounts to little more than a process of convergence on similar outcomes at different speeds, seems increasingly questionable. Instead we observe a growing consensus among the observers and analysts that differentiated integration is a permanent organizational principle of the EU. The need to manage divisions or disagreements will no simply go away.[12]

There are many ways of analyzing this multifaceted phenomenon, from the analysis of the primary and secondary law,[13] through multilateral negotiations,[14] up to the party politics[15] in the domestic contexts. It can be studied as a phenomenon,

[7]See further Leuffen et al. (2013) and Schimmelfennig (2014).

[8]See also Jensen and Slapin (2012), De Neve (2007), Zielonka (2007) and Kölliker (2001).

[9]Leruth and Lord (2015).

[10]See further Lemke (2014).

[11]For details see Fossum (2015).

[12]Compare with Leruth and Lord (2015).

[13]For an illustration of this approach see Szwarc (2015) and Zhelyankova (2014).

[14]For example, see Winzen and Schimmelfennig (2015).

[15]For an exemplification go to Leruth (2015).

concept, process or as a system.[16] The complexity and plurality of approaches is justified by the very nature of differentiated integration. This chapter offers a scholastic approach that tries to integrate the national level, which appeared to be decisive in the British case, together with the sub-national level and supra-national level of analysis.

Britain is loosely integrated with the EU both horizontally and vertically. Vertical differentiation refers to the policy areas that integrated at various speeds and reached various levels of centralization over time. Whereas horizontal differentiation means that many integrated policies are neither uniformly nor exclusively valid in all the EU Member States.[17] The UK does not participate in all the EU policies (horizontal differentiation) and in some others, it participates at its own speed and extend (vertical differentiation).

Considering the above stated, logically speaking, it makes little sense for the UK to exit the EU in the hope of gaining some greater autonomy—re-entering the single market with similar obligations but fewer decision rights. However, renegotiating the UK membership answered some other need—the need for the reconfiguration of the relationship between the UK and the EU. In his January 2013 speech, the British Prime Minister David Cameron (2016) set out a plan to ask for a mandate from the British people to negotiate a new settlement with Europe (at that time this operation was seen as a method of strengthening his position in the Conservative Party, but apparently it ended with his resignation after the referendum). At the same time an audit was launched to calculate the costs and benefits of the UK's membership in the EU. The key issues that David Cameron focused on were the following: allowing the UK to opt out from the EU's declared ambition to forge an "ever closer union", restricting access to in-work and out-of-work social benefits to the EU migrants (until they have been resident for 4 years), giving greater powers to national parliaments (in their competences to block the EU legislation), securing explicit recognition that the euro is not the only currency of the European Union.

The Brexit question put in front of the UK citizens in June 2016 can be seen just as a battle in the long-lasting war between the competing visions of the UK's relations with the wider world, in this case Europe.[18] The Brexit issue tests differentiated integration in new ways. Practicalities of disentangling the UK from its existing membership may form the substance of a qualitatively different relations to any in which differentiated integration has been used before. Britain may be the first case of differentiated disintegration. Paradoxically both British exit and staying in would increase the importance of differentiated integration. Consequently, the EU may need an institutional re-settlement that makes its own character as a union of unions explicit.[19]

[16]See also Dyson and Sepos (2010).

[17]For details see Schimmelfennig et al. (2015).

[18]Compare with Kenny and Pearse (2016).

[19]For details see Leruth and Lord (2015).

What consequences does the Brexit bring for the differentiated Europe? First, potential strengthening of the center—the core of integration, which is Germany without any balancing power (considering France's status after the economic crisis). Secondly, the EU without Britain means also the EU without *free marketeers*—it was the UK (no matter if ruled by the Labor or Conservatives) who brought the liberal component to the European integration project. Less Britain in Europe means also less liberal ideas. Thirdly, we have learnt the limits of internal differentiation. Simply speaking David Cameron has overbid. The British political elites got lost in the attempts to gear in Brussels into domestic politics. Playing with egoistic interests, nationalisms and xenophobia went out of control—as a result Britain placed itself outside of the united Europe. The British exit potentially also widens the circles of differentiated integration. It goes beyond the known schemes of inner and outer core, as well as inner and outer peripheries. To the already existing categories of members and non-members, it adds the category of the former-member, unknown so far in the European studies.

3 Referendum As a British Way of Formulating Its European Policies

The first referendum on a (surprisingly not very) similar question was held in 1975 and concerned whether to stay in the European Economic Community. The integration project was still in its early and immature phase and the UK was a freshman in the community. Over the period of 40 years the EU has acquired a directly elected and influential parliament, substantially reduced the veto power of individual Member States, engaged in civilian and military operations abroad, launched a border-free traffic area and—finally—established its own currency inter-connecting the national economic policies even stronger. The Britons have not chosen to participate in all the above mentioned in 1975.[20] But they participated in the process of creation of every single element of the European integration project. None of the UE competences appeared in Brussels without the legitimation of the UK.

The 23rd June 2016 referendum was supposed to deal with the renegotiated position of the UK in the EU. The growing public frustrations about the UK-EU relations were the effect of the long-lasting failure to consult the British citizens about Britain's place in Europe and the changing EU that was undermining the relationship between London and Brussels. Despite of countless vetoes, opt-outs and constraints, many British governments (both labor and conservative) moved the Britain's involvement in the European integration project ahead of the British public understanding.

However, the Brexit referendum did not manage to bring stability to the European debate in the UK. On the opposite: the misunderstandings grew on both—the

[20]Glencross (2015), p. 306.

opponents and supporters—sides. The 23rd June referendum was another example of the misuses of direct democracy mechanisms with quite auto-destructive outcomes. The balance of pros and cons related to referendums have been investigated extensively in the literature, it will suffice here to provide a short overview. On one side the referendums make it possible to confront the problematic issue, spark the public discourse, debate the arguments, and build the democratic legitimacy of the decision. However, on the negative side, the referendums very often lead to oversimplification of the issue in question. They offer binary solutions only, very often too complicated, nuanced problems. The referendum questions can be manipulated and they get politicized very easily or even used for purely political (or party) strategic reasons. In the end the technical problem—the results of the referendum will need to be implemented by the representative democracy institutions (like the parliament). The decision makers will need to act against their own will or the will of their constituencies.

In the case of the UK, the 23rd June referendum was supposed to refresh the British people's understanding of European integration. As a result (and in opposite), it brought about even more polarization, more myths (both positive and negative about Brussels) and less objective knowledge in general. As it happened before in many other UE Member States, like the Netherlands, France, Ireland or Denmark, the referendum did not help to bring the EU citizens closer to the EU, but rather sparked Euroscepticism and the EU-confusions. Instead of offering a solution, the Brexit referendum generated even more problems. Initially, the commitments to hold this referendum have been used to manage tensions within the Conservative Party. Intra-party problem spilled over to the nationwide, or even Europe wide scale. Short-term tactics emerged into strategic continental concerns.

Britain's relations with the EU returned to the forefront and by doing this they addressed not only the uncertainties about the direction of the EU evolution but also put the question of the *EU's finalite* at the center of the debate. Just *market friendship* or fully fledged political union? The very perspective of a potential Britain exiting the EU sparked the public debate about the future of the European integration project, as well as about its future form, including various forms of differentiation.

The pro-European campaign focused on the positive agenda stressing practical, pragmatic, and utilitarian involvement in the EU that benefits Britain's economy security and power. It was stressed that leaving the EU would not stop British business facing regulations agreed in Brussels. Even immigration would remain a contentious issue because of the demands of the British labor market.[21] A vote to withdraw did not create a fixed "end-point" in the UK-EU relations. Not only that doubts will remain about public consent. But also, the process will take years—years in which the public opinion will be dynamic and the same with the negotiations of the future status of London-Brussels relationship. The British chose between some relatively known future that they were not totally keen on and, on the other side, totally unknown, however predicted by vast majority of analysts, as a rather

[21]For details see Oliver (2015).

negative, settlement. Not only the UK-EU relations remain unclear, the same with the Britain's international position. Most probably London will become even more peripheral and at the mercy of decisions taken by other powers.

A proper contextualization of the Brexit referendum is vital for clear understanding of how the public preferences are formed and expressed on the topic of options for differentiation available to the citizens. In diplomacy, the "splendid isolation" is known as a British tradition of being an outsider, which dates from imperial past to the much more modest present. The UK's sitting on the sidelines of integration is not only geographical but also emotional and political. It has had many manifestations from *Atlantism*, through *pro-Commonwealthism*, up to *Anglospherism* but has never been truly isolationism or desinteresment.[22] British imperialist discourses that date back to the nineteenth century were rather focused on the question how Great Britain could influence the world, instead of how to defend itself from external pressures. This reverse of logics suggests that it is also a mental problem nested in the change of the UK's position globally. Subordination to Europeanization impulses represents the end of splendid imperial past. The historical context need to be supplemented by the most recent history, that is Margaret Thatcher's attitude to Europe that was so much forming Britain's anti-Europeanism. One of the reasons why the UK is such an awkward partner in Europe is the distinctive personal influence of the "Iron Lady", whose individual action and legacy generated and magnified the core dynamics that soured the UK's ties to Europe so bitterly.[23]

To flee the chains of Brussels is the expression used by those who argue that the regulatory burden imposed on businesses by Brussels has sapped competitiveness and costs jobs. The economic crisis, followed by the long-lasting stagnation has given a gloss to claims that the UK would do better outside the EU—by expanding its trade with the Commonwealth. Additionally, the fast-growing Asian economies have the appearance of mirror images of neoliberal Anglo-Saxon ones. In this vision, the Great *Britannia*, reunited with the Anglosphere and trading with Asia, would be simultaneously unchained from Europe and prosperous in its Anglo-Saxon way.[24]

Most of the analytical reports on the effects of Britain leaving the EU were rather pessimistic (and, in some cases, apocalyptic), suggesting negative outcomes for the household incomes, economic growth, gross domestic product or trade.[25] But it is usually not the rational choice that is decisive for the referendum results, but rather political emotions. As it was framed by Antony Hilton: "Brexit is not about economics, it is about the kind of country people think they want to live in and the kind of people they think they are. It is not a factual matter, it is like faith: you believe or you don't—and that's why the outcome is uncertain."[26]

---

[22] Also see Daddow (2015).

[23] Fontana and Parsons (2015), p. 89.

[24] Also see Kenny and Pearse (2016).

[25] Compare with Hodgson (2016).

[26] Hilton (2016).

The political force that was and still is the strongest supporter of Brexit is the UK Independence Party (UKIP) led by Nigel Farage. Once a moderate actor on the British political scene, it evolved into a xenophobic, right wing party, attacking migrants, religious, sex, ethnic and racial minorities. Its leaders, aware of the huge potential of the emotions and fears that were likely to be the deciding factor influencing the British referendum decision. Still in April 2016, the Economist Intelligence Unit forecasted that the UK electorate would reject Brexit on the 23rd June referendum on the UK's membership in the EU. It was expected that the voters' fears about leaving the EU would rise as the referendum approaches and the economic arguments in favor of staying would prevail.[27] On the other side we have observed in Britain some growing public frustrations at the UK-EU relations that resulted from the longstanding failure to consult the UK citizens about their country's place in Europe. Two weeks before the referendum, the opinion polls gave the supporters of Brexit a 10% lead that suggested quite a safe victory of the isolationists camp to be predicted. After the murder of Jo Cox, a British politician campaigning for the UK remaining in the EU, there was an observable shift towards the supporters of membership camp. However, the final results of the referendum showed a moderate 51.9% for leaving and 48.1% for remaining.

The binary nature of referendums overshadowed the modest victory of the leave camp. It was an earth quake not only in British politics and economy but also in the European ones. The initiator of the referendum, prime minister David Cameron, in his speech on the post-electoral day morning declared his resignation in the perspective of 3 months. However, he tried to calm down the panicking markets that the trade of goods and services would continue, in the post-Brexit scenario, on contractual basis like the terms that exist as part of the EU. Britain would no longer have a say in the development of the EU laws and regulations but the whole British economy would still be bound by it. It would not solve the problem of the supremacy of the EU legal order or the free movement of workers together with accompanied rights to welfare. All these issues were to be settled in the upcoming negotiations between London and Brussels.

Among the intra-UK, domestic politics issues that need to be observed is the relations between the four parts constituting Great Britain—England, Scotland, Northern Ireland, and Wales. The referendum map showed that the Scots and the Northern Irish, as well as the metropolitan England, voted to stay in the EU, whereas peripheral England and Wales voted for leaving. Predominantly, it is the Scottish issue that is an important factor in the Brexit debate. The two processes are interrelated: London's potential leaving the EU and Edinbourgh's leaving the UK, consequently. The political casualty is evident—Brexit might give the Scottish nationalists an argument to hold another independence referendum (which was proclaimed in Nicola Sturgeon's speech directly after the referendum day). The Scots are predominantly pro-European and therefore very much interested to stay in united Europe, maybe even more than in the United Kingdom. Scotland's first

[27] Also see Haralambous (2016).

minister claimed that Brexit requires the Scottish Parliament agreement and, since it is against the Scots' will and interest, it will never happen. This potential legal blockage shows the complexity of the situation in which the UK found itself.

Another geographical location for which Brexit generates potential problems as a side effect is the Irish island—both the Republic of Ireland and Northern Ireland. British exit may create a certain investment dislocation and uncertainty. The agreement between the Northern Ireland and the Republic of Ireland is a fragile one and London's decision to go out of the union could move back the process that positively developed in the last two, three decades. What is worse, the new settlement would be negotiated not between London and Dublin but between London and Brussels, which may be a hard bargaining, since the EU negotiators may want give a clear signal and to discourage any other members states from considering such a move. Worth noticing, a couple of hours after the official announcement of the referendum results (which showed the Northern Irish support for remaining in the EU), the leaders of Sinn Fein declared that the British government lost its legitimacy and mandate to represent the people of Northern Ireland.

Concluding, one may observe an interesting pattern across Great Britain, where the Scots and the Irish are more often decided to stay in the EU, and where it is the English and the Welsh that are more likely to leave. Considering how the UK is governed after the Devolution Act, the Brexit would mean a substantial change leading to reassessment of the previous framework. If a narrow majority consisting of the English predominantly would decide about the future of Scots, Irish or even Welsh who voted differently, such a situation could even result in renegotiation of the constitutional setting inside the UK.[28] Openly speaking, it would mean the beginning of the end of the United Kingdom.

And finally, one must remember some general principles, patterns, and tendencies about referenda as such. The voters are inherently skeptical and tend to vote negatively whenever given the opportunity ('if in doubt vote no' principle). The voters are also seemingly willing to trust the recommendations of the political parties of their preference. The wording of the question becomes critical, especially in the context of growing Euroscepticism.[29] And it is not direct but indirect democracy that underlies at the heart of British politics. The British monarchy is a parliamentarian democracy, not one driven by referenda. It is not a mistake or coincidence that in many political systems (for example in Germany at the federal level) referendum is not an option as a method of decision making.

---

[28]The potential success of separatisms like Scotish or Irish may stimulate the separatist movements in other parts of Europe, including the Basqes or Cathalans in Spain, Waloons or Flanders in the Netherlands or Silesians in Poland.

[29]Also see Qvartrup (2016).

4 Conclusion

Rather than being solely an explanatory piece exploring why the British oppose Europe so strongly, the main objective of this chapter was to shed light on the UK's position in integrating Europe in relation to the main conceptualizations of differentiated integration.

It was not the demand for differentiation that drove the Brexit referendum dynamics. It was the desire to leave the European Union among the large parts of British publics and political elites. Historically speaking, London was one of the major diving forces behind the increased differentiation. It was treated as a kind of a compromise between the strong independence needs of the British and the consistency of the European project. However, it soon appeared that this is a short-term tactics that do not offer solid fundaments on which the UK presence in the EU could be grounded.

Although the United Kingdom has always been on the positive side about the balance of discriminatory and exemptive differentiations, it appeared not enough for quite a portion of the British citizens and political elites. The UK, before the referendum, enjoyed a status of a preferential membership—the opposition of discriminatory membership—a case in which a Member State is exempted from my rights and benefits of integration).[30] The UK was released from many undesired obligations that most of the other Member States took. The rest of the EU was not determined enough to demand the full adoption of the EU law. The UK was strong by its Euroscepticism, economic, as well as political power and, as a result, enjoyed a positive discrimination in the community.

The story of European integration can be told as a story of its deepening and widening—these two dynamics found the mechanics of differentiation. Consequently, the progress in integration meant the increase in differentiation over time.[31] Up to a certain point, the UK supported the widening of the European Communities (later the European Union) as a "panacea" for the deepening. The interplay between the two dimensions of integration seemed to effectively answer the British allergy to "ever closer Union". However, after integration advance in the 1990s, followed by the *big bang* enlargement (as well as subsequent waves in 2007 and 2013) and accompanied with the economic crisis,[32] which hit the British economy severely, the critical mass was achieved, and the dissatisfaction with the membership in the EU became dominant in the public discourse. The party system reacted to it on the supply side, giving the Brexit scenario its own dynamics.

At the preset, from the British perspective, the European integration project is not only a game of deepening and widening but also of differentiation of a new generation. The Brexit referendum—in its supranational dimension—was not only about Britain's position on the map of the EU (and its peripheries). It was also about

[30]Further see Schimmelfennig (2014).

[31]Also see Schimmelfennig and Winzen (2014).

[32]Compare with Allemand (2005) and Schweiger and Magone (2014).

the future of the integration project as such. The UK switched from an integration-tolerant country, to integration unfriendly country, which—by its behavior and attitude—endangers the very fundaments of the integration process. It produces externalities to be consumed by other Member States and non-members no matter if they are pro- or anti-integrationist.[33] Following the logic of the integration evolution from one crisis to another one, it is possible to interpret the Brexit decision as an opportunity for the EU's reform. The reformist impulse of Brexit may enhance the European integration in two various possible ways. First, it may help to reform the EU into a more differentiated system, which will allow accommodating countries willing to integrate at various speeds and extends. Secondly, once "getting rid" of the major troublemaker and marauder, that is Britain, the EU may accelerate now towards the "ever closer union".

The British have never felt the negative externalities of exclusion from the largest market in the world (by purchasing power standards). This makes the *British anomaly* even stranger. The other reluctant Europeans, like Switzerland or Norway had to find a solution to the risks associated with the economic isolation and reached a state of a "membership without accession" or "unfinished integration". After calculating the costs and benefits of membership and non-membership they decided to gravitate closer and close to the EU core. The British case is different. The difference can be portrayed in the metaphor of a "marriage and divorce"—the Swiss and Norwegians are hesitating and are still before the wedding ceremony, whereas the British are already after the divorce. The atmosphere in the family is different in these two situations, especially if the divorce ruins the whole family consistency. Not getting married is substantially different from getting divorced and so is the British situation in its relations with the rest of the EU (compared with Switzerland or Norway). There is a huge difference between quitting full membership and hitching up selectively to the EU policies from outside, especially having the negative history of cooperation (the losers of Brexit will never forget). The time before the referendum was seen as a game in which London could have won even more beneficial conditions inside the EU. However, the time after the lost referendum is the time in which the UK will try to build a status of a preferential non-membership. Whether Brussels allows this is a questionable hypothesis. Directly after the referendum the atmosphere for negotiations was rather cold. The successful UK outside of the EU could give a very negative signal for other potential Member States considering leaving the EU. Brussels has no interest into making the transition to non-membership soft and smooth for London.

The UK's European question was more than a question of whether to be or not to be in Europe. It was a question about party politics, identity, political economy, globalization and, finally, a changing Europe. The problem is that it can never be entirely answered.[34] It will come back in a reframed form with every new generation,

[33]Directly after the Brexit referendum, in several EU Member States (Slovakia for example) some political forces started to collect citizens' signatures for the initiative to organize an EU-exit referendum.

[34]Compare with Oliver (2015).

every new treaty, and every new enlargement. Although it is discussable whether it is the referendum that is the most optimal method of dealing with it. At the same time, the Brexit is not a one-day-event that will simply mean the walking out of Europe. Instead, it rather means a lengthy (most probably 2 years) and complex process of negotiations to begin.[35]

We know there is life outside of the EU (in Norwegian or Ukrainian variants). Now the British will need to seek answer to the question what life they will build outside of united Europe. The other important question is what united Europe (but for now it is beyond the British reach). Differentiation in Europe has reached such a phase, scale, and depth in which it is legitimate to agree to the argument that it is a systematic characteristic of the European integration project as seen in twenty-first century. Frank Schimmelfenning, Dirk Leuffen and Berthold Rittberger wrote even about the system of differentiated integration, in which differentiation is essential and enduring characteristic of the EU.[36] Directly after the Brexit referendum, the initial six founding states (Germany, France, Italy, Belgium, Luxemburg, and the Netherlands) met in Berlin to discuss the new circumstances generated by the Brexit earthquake, as well as to identify the options ahead. Symptomatically, the rest of the EU was called to a meeting in Warsaw a day later for the same purpose. The new divisions in Europe became even clearer in the sharp picture after the British decided to leave. Brexit gave the differentiated integration new impetus and dynamics. Hopefully it was not a turning point, reversing the trend towards disintegration.

References

Allemand F (2005) The impact of the EU enlargement on economic and Monetary Union: what lessons can be learnt from the differentiated integration mechanisms in an enlarged Europe? Eur Law J 11(5):586–617

Andersen SS, Sitter N (2006) Differentiated integration: what is it and how much can the EU accomodate? Eur Integr 28(4):313–330

Bernstein A (2016) To brexit or to brexit?, "News Extra" April 2016, p 7

Cameron D (2016) The future of the EU and the UK's relationship with it, London, 23 Jan 2013, https://www.gov.uk/government/speeches/eu-speech-at-bloomberg. Accessed 20 June 2016

Daddow O (2015) Interpreting the outsider tradition in British European policy speeches from Thatcher to Cameron. J Common Mark Stud 53(1):71–88

De Neve J-E (2007) The European onion? How differentiated integration is reshaping the EU. Eur Integr 29(4):503–521

Dyson K, Sepos A (2010) Differentiation as design principle and as tool in the political management of European integration. In: Dyson K, Sepos A (eds) Which Europe? The politics of differentiated integration. Palgrave, Basingstoke, pp 3–23

Fontana G, Parsons C (2015) 'One woman's prejudice': did Margaret Thatcher cause Britains' anti-Europeanis? J Common Mark Stud 53(1):89–105

Fossum JE (2015) Democracy and differentiation in Europe. J Eur Publ Policy 22(6):799–815

[35]Also see Bernstein (2016).

[36]Schimmelfennig et al. (2015).

Genschel P, Jachtenfuchs M (2014) Introduction: beyond market regulation. Analysing the European integration of core state powers. In: Genschel P, Jachtenfuchs M (eds) Beyond the regulatory polity? The European integration of core state powers. Oxford University Press, Oxford, pp 1–23

Glencross A (2015) Why a British referendum on EU membership will not solve the Europe question. Int Aff 91(2):303–317

Haralambous D (2016) The cost of Brexit, financialdirector.co.uk, http://web.a.ebscohost.com/ehost/pdfviewer/pdfviewer?sid=d2e58bc6-cfa2-47a9-ad49-69ac1e1347e2%40sessionmgr4005&vid=0&hid=4112 (05.05.2016)

Hilton A (2016) Statement in: "The London Evening Standard" 25 February 2016

Hodgson P (2016) Complying with Brexit, "Complience Week" May 2016, pp 53–55

Jensen D, Slapin J (2012) Institutional hokey-pokey: the politics of multispeed integration in the European Union. J Eur Publ Policy 19(6):779–795

Kenny M, Pearse N (2016) After Brexit. The Eurosceptic dream of an Anglosphere. Juncture 22(4): 304–307

Kölliker A (2001) Bringing together or driving apart the union? Towards a theory of differentiated integration. West Eur Polit 24(4):125–151

Lemke C (2014) Challenging the "ever closer union": political consequences of the Eurozone crisis. Am Foreign Policy Interests 36:18–24

Leruth B (2015) Operationalizing national preferences on Europe and differentiated integration. J Eur Publ Policy 22(6):816–835

Leruth B, Lord C (2015) Differentiated integration in the European Union: a concept, a process, a system or a theory? J Eur Publ Policy 22(6):754–764

Leuffen D, Rittberger B, Schimmelfennig F (2013) Differentiated integration. Explaining variation in the European Union. Palgrave, Basingstoke

Mohler L, Seitz M (2012) The gains from variety in the European Union. Rev World Econ 148: 475–500

Oliver T (2015) To be or not to be in Europe: is that the question? Britains' European question and an in/out referendum. Int Aff 91(1):77–91

Qvartrup M (2016) Referendums on membership and European integration. Polit Q 87(1):61–67

Schimmelfennig F (2014) EU enlargement and differentiated integration: discrimination or equal treatment? J Eur Publ Policy 21(5):681–698

Schimmelfennig F, Winzen T (2014) Instrumental and constitutional differentiation in the European Union. J Common Mark Stud 52(2):354–370

Schimmelfennig F, Leufen D, Rittberger B (2015) The European Union as a system of differentiated integration: interdependence, politicisation, differentiation. J Eur Publ Policy 22(6): 764–782

Schweiger C, Magone J (2014) Differentiated integration and cleavage under crisis conditions. Perspect Eur Polit Soc 15(3):259–265

Szwarc M (2015) Zróżnicowana integracja i wzmocniona współpraca w prawie Unii Europejskiej, Warszawa 2005

Winzen T, Schimmelfennig F (2015) The choice for differentiated Europe; Why European Union member states opt out of integration. Paper prepared for the 14th biennial conference of the European Union Studies Association, 5–7 March 2015, Boston MA, USA

Zhelyankova A (2014) From selective integration into selective implementation: the link between differentiated integration and conformity with EU laws. Eur J Polit Res 53:727–746

Zielonka J (2007) Europa jako imperium. Nowe spojrzenie na Unię Europejską. PISM, Warszawa

Part III
The UK Inside the European Communities/Union

Enlargement to the UK, the Referendum of 1975 and Position of Margaret Thatcher

Archil Chochia, David Ramiro Troitiño, Tanel Kerikmäe, and Olga Shumilo

Abstract The negotiations for the British accession were successful in the early 1970s only after de Gaulle left his position as President of France. The French blockade to the British accession was removed only after the British Premier had reassured his French colleagues about the British commitment to Europe and secured concessions on specific French concerns. The enlargement of the UK, Ireland, Denmark, and Norway had become a difficult challenge for all the parties involved. The financial contribution to the European Budget was also a major issue during the negotiations. The official reason for the referendum of 1975 was that the UK citizens needed to express their opinion and decide about such an important issue linked with their individual and collective freedoms. Margaret Thatcher's vision about European Communities covered such diverse areas as Europe and the EU; the Cold war, the USA, and the EU; the European Communities belonging to all its members; the Community not being an end in itself; national power against supranational constructions; weak bureaucracy; policies of the EU; European Market; European defence and relations between Europe and the USA.

1 Introduction

In this chapter, the authors shall attempt to study the issues related to the enlargement of the European Community to the UK, the referendum of 1975, and the position of Margaret Thatcher. Since de Gaulle was in power, the French tried to blockade the British out of the European Communities. After de Gaulle, the British government lobbied hard for the inclusion of the United Kingdom (UK) into the European Community. The enlargement of the UK, Ireland, Denmark, and Norway

A. Chochia (✉) · D. Ramiro Troitiño · T. Kerikmäe
Tallinn Law School, Tallinn University of Technology, Tallinn, Estonia
e-mail: archil.chochia@ttu.ee; david.troitino@ttu.ee; tanel.kerikmae@ttu.ee

O. Shumilo
Yaroslav Mudryi National Law University, Kharkiv, Ukraine
e-mail: shumiloolja@gmail.com

D. Ramiro Troitiño et al. (eds.), *Brexit*,
https://doi.org/10.1007/978-3-319-73414-9_7

had become a difficult challenge for all the parties involved. The British proposal related to the enlargements wanted to ease the access for further future applicants. It was also used to outline the importance of the enlargement for the Community and its positive effects. It also emphasised the negative aspects of unsuccessful negotiations for the Communities and the applicants. The financial contribution to the European Budget was a major issue during the negotiations.[1] The UK accepted most of the Communitarian claims or delayed the decision about the most problematic issues because it needed access to the European market to reinvigorate its economy, but this generated problems afterward, especially under the premiership of Margaret Thatcher.

The British elections of 1974 brought a change in the government. Surprisingly, the new government called for a referendum on the British membership in the European Communities. The official reason was that the citizens needed to express their opinion and decide about such an important issue linked with their individual and collective freedoms. During the 1975 campaign, the three major political parties were supporting the UK inside of the Communities and lacked a public leader agglutinating the sympathy of the voters. The British government strongly supported the Yes in the referendum of 1975. On the side of the No, the funds were scarce, there were no centrist public figures and the campaign was much more chaotic. The referendum itself was not binding upon the government in the strict legal sense, because of the principle of parliamentary sovereignty, but the electorate expressed significant support for the EEC membership, with 67% in favour on a 65% turnout. This was the first ever referendum that was held throughout the entire UK.[2] This stands in stark contrast to the referendum of 2016.

Margaret Thatcher has been one of the most influential politicians in the European building process. Many people in the current crisis of the European integration still today support her opinions, and her participation in issues such as the Single European Act or the solution of the British question influences still the daily life of European citizens.[3] Her basic idea was related to popular loyalty and the transfer of sovereignty from the national to the European level, a utopia according to Thatcher that could endanger European societies, liberties, and way of life. Her influence continues to this date and her words are worth re-reading to help us perhaps better understand the scepticism towards the EU in many circles—as she is still regarded as a symbol for euro sceptics, a defender of national sovereignty and the independence of the Member States of the EU from the dictatorship of European institutions.

[1] Saunders (2016), pp. 318–322.
[2] Sárlvik et al. (1976), pp. 83–113.
[3] Fuchs (2016), pp. 163–188.

2 Enlargement to the United Kingdom

The negotiations for the British accession were resumed again in October 1969 after de Gaulle left his position as President of France after losing an internal referendum link with the internal organisation of the French Republic. The new president, Pompidou, was more open to the British petition.

The UK organised a negotiation team divided into two main units, the Foreign Office, servicing the negotiations and providing information to the government, and the Cabinet Office, responsible for the negotiations. Geoffrey Rippon as Cabinet Minister was the British leader in the talks for the enlargement. He was a British Conservative politician, Chairman of the European-Atlantic Group and a prominent member of the Conservative Monday Club that made a resolution opposing Britain's accession to the European Communities in 1971.[4] His involvement in the European affairs led to his appointment as President of the European Documentation and Information Centre from 1979 to 1982. The negotiation team was assisted by Sir Con O'Neill, a British civil servant with long experience in the Foreign Office and the British representative to the Community from 1963 to 1965, and his deputy, John Robinson, a diplomat Head of European Economic Integration Department, Foreign and Commonwealth Office from 1968–70 and present in the previous negotiations in the two previous failed requests.[5]

The British Premier, Edward Heath, Prime Minister of the UK from 1970 to 1974 and Leader of the Conservative Party from 1965 to 1975, assisted in a summit with Pompidou in May 1971 removing the French blockade to the British accession.[6] The British Premier reassured his French colleague the British commitment to Europe and secured concessions on four specific French concerns:

- The use of majority voting within the Council of Ministers.
- The devaluation of the British pound.
- The relation between the Communities and the French ex-colonies.
- A compromise to keep the leading role of the French language in the working system of the European Communities.

The British negotiators, on the other hand, were concerned about three main issues:

- The financial contribution to the European Budget
- New Zealand
- Fisheries

The UK also included in the negotiations two general issues related to Communitarian aspects, the Role of the Enlarged Community in the World, and the reform of the enlargement system for future applications.[7]

---

[4]Sharp et al. (1998), pp. 33–56.

[5]Ramiro Trotiño (2013).

[6]Daddow (2003).

[7]Dinan (2014).

The French president had a general personal concern, like that expressed previously by de Gaulle, about the real intentions of the UK inside the Community, the real commitment of the British to the European integration process, as Pompidou expressed during the summit:

> Britain had really decided to become European. Whether Britain, which is an island, had decided to moor itself to the continent and if she was therefore ready to come in from the wide seas which had always drawn her.

Pompidou wanted guarantees for the European independence in terms of economy and politics in a world dominated by the USA and USSR.[8] As the UK was closely aligned with the Americans, the danger of English becoming the dominant language of the Communities and replacing the French, was very high. Both issues were related to the special relation between the UK and the USA and the construction of Europe as an alternative to a bilateral world.

Other minor issues discussed between the French president and the British Premier was the Community preference, the creation of European companies operating in the whole Community, the coordination of investments between Member States and the relation with the EFTA countries.

The use of majority voting within the Council of Ministers was motivated by previous French concerns to the introduction of majority voting system in the European Communities that led to the Empty Chair crisis and the Luxembourg Compromise. According to this solution given to France, if any Member State believed a vital national interest to be at stake, the Council must operate based on unanimity, thus ensuring a continuing right of veto. It was a big step back in terms of integration, providing the European Communities with an important intergovernmental aspect. Pompidou wanted a clear acceptance by the UK of this agreement. The respect of the national sovereignty in case of vital interest did not seem a big obstacle as the British had shown before their support to cooperation rather than integration. The inclusion of the issue in the negotiations was linked with the French fear of losing influence inside the Communities, because an alliance between the UK and Germany could outvote France in the European decision-making process working by qualified majority. Hence, the real problem was not the essence of the Community, integration or cooperation, or the real involvement of the UK in the European integration process, but to keep the French hegemony inside the Communities.[9] Heath agreed on the issue invoking the common sense, the reality that the Community could not take decisions against the national interest of its members without collapsing in the long term.

The devaluation of the British pound was linked with the role of the British currency as a world reserve and the British deficit in the balance of payments. If Britain was to experience balance of payments difficulties as a member of the Community, it could request financial assistance from the other member-states

[8]Parr (2009), p. 87.

[9]Haftendorn (2006).

under articles 108 and 109 of the Treaty of Rome. Also, the French were concerned about the advantage in this field of British economists included in the negotiation team that could have led to a beneficial agreement for the UK against the benefit for the whole Community.[10]

The French government wanted an equal treatment of all the currencies of the Member States and the abolition of the Basle facility that endured the predominance of the British pound. The UK assured its compromise but the reforms were to be implemented in a long-term perspective. The British government wanted a general agreement on the issue and continue discussions after the enlargement.[11]

The relation between the Communities and the French ex-colonies was threatened by the British accession because the UK counted with numerous ex-colonies that could join the Lomé agreements and benefit from the economic aid from the Communities. The financial support was not just a humanitarian help but a way to keep the influence of France over its ex-colonies.[12] As France did not have enough financial muscle to subsidise the former colonies, the solution was to use Communitarian funds for this purpose. The enlargement to the UK and the accession of the British ex-colonies to the agreement would have dissolved the financial support as similar money had to be shared among much more members. The main discussion was about Nigeria, a large country in terms of population. Pompidou wanted a clear British commitment on exceptions on the financial support to the country. On the other hand, Heath already knew the future economic possibilities for Nigeria because of the vast oil reserves, and agreed with the French position to limit the financial support to the country but continued providing technical support and training.[13]

A compromise to keep the leading role of the French language in the working system of the European Communities was needed because the UK, Ireland and Denmark were conducting their international relations using the English language.[14] Inside the Communities, Dutch and Germans also preferred English as the vehicular language for economic operations. The Foreign Office, however, had a British concession prepared: that in the future all British officials deployed to Community institutions can work in French. It was just a gesture, but in the right direction to overcome the French suspiciousness.

The British idea of the international role of the European Communities was linked with a basic Common position in international affairs to act more effectively and recover the position of Europe in the world affairs. It included common policies on such sensitive issues as economic and monetary affairs, international political issues, defence, and relations with the ex-colonies. It seems like an embryo of the current Common Foreign and Security Policy, but the British proposal was based on the

[10]Daddow (2003).

[11]Schenk (2002), pp. 345–369.

[12]Maitland (2001), pp. 1–8.

[13]Wauthier (1972), pp. 23–26.

[14]Ginsburgh et al. (2005), pp. 946–965.

coordination of the members of the Community when their interest was common and working with a system based on consensus rather than unanimity or majority.

The enlargement of the UK, Ireland, Denmark, and Norway had become a difficult challenge for all the parties involved. The British proposal related to the enlargements wanted to ease the access for further future applicants. It was also used to outline the importance of the enlargement for the Community, and its positive effects. It also emphasised the negative aspects of unsuccessful negotiations for the Communities and the applicants.

The financial contribution to the European Budget was a major issue during the negotiations. The British Premier wanted to ensure the lowest initial British contribution as possible, and gradually increase it till its normal leverage during the longest period as possible. Heath desired three corrective years, to follow the basic 5-year transitional period, to secure a good financial deal for the UK to adapt to the European market. The original British position during the first application was based on a permanent agreement on the financial contribution, changing to long transitional periods (over 13 years), afterwards to short term temporal exceptions and finally to an acceptance of the Communitarian claims but to be changed from inside once a member, in an internal reform.[15]

New Zealand was considered a main obstacle for the negotiations because securing a high rate of imports from that country faced the opposition of France. The UK wanted a transitional period granting at least 70% of the existing imports at that time and the allowance of the exceptions afterwards. France, on the other hand, wanted a much-reduced figure for the transitional period and no exceptions after the transitional period.[16]

The discussion about fisheries did not generate major problems in the initial meetings. The reform of the 1960s expanding the national sovereignty on the national waters and the exclusive economic rights had been adopted by the British government to secure the access to the new reserves of oil located in the North Atlantic. It provided exclusive access to traditional international fishing grounds to the British fleet that was under a restructuration after the Cod Wars with Iceland.[17] France adopted similar measures and faced an identical situation, being the most affected by the Spanish fishing fleet, traditionally stronger than the British and the French that lost access to the previously international waters. Hence, the agreement in the field was not complicated.

The negotiations were not finally concluded until January 1972 but the agreement between Pompidou and his British colleague was crucial to solving the main obstacles for the British accession. On July 1972 the British government initiated a year-long campaign to obtain enough parliamentary support for the agreement that was finally obtained with 112 positive votes.

[15]Rossbach (2009).

[16]Brownie and Dalziel (1993).

[17]Mitchell (1976), pp. 127–138.

Since the French veto of December 1967, British diplomacy towards the Community had centered upon the need to overcome de Gaulle's opposition to the British accession making a priority an understanding with Paris and a commitment to the French claims.

Finally, the third application was accepted after the retirement of de Gaulle and the final approval for the CAP. The British had asked for membership under a government of Conservatives, and under a government lead by Labour, so there was a common agreement between the main political parties of the UK about joining the European Communities. Hence, they were willing to accept most of the petitions of the European Communities, including the CAP and the end of the Imperial Preference system, as both British parties wanted to obtain the political gain of the membership in terms of domestic support. The UK accepted most of the Communitarian claims or delayed the decision about the most problematic issues because it needed access to the European market to reinvigorate its economy, but this generated problems afterwards, especially under the premiership of Margaret Thatcher.

Nevertheless, the enlargement meant the inclusion of Ireland and Denmark in the European Communities, and the application of Norway was also accepted, but a domestic referendum in that Scandinavian country had a negative result for the European aspirations of its government, keeping Norway outside the Community.[18]

3 The Referendum of 1975

Historically, the UK has been a parliamentary democracy for a very long time with little recourse to means like referenda. In 1975 Margaret Thatcher (in a similar vein as Clement Attlee before her) referred to them as "devices of dictators and demagogues".[19] Before the recent referendum of 2016, there have been only two referenda (in 1975 and in 2010), both of which were strictly advisory in nature, with the final authority being vested in Parliament.[20]

The British elections of 1974 brought a change in the government, the political domestic gains of the Communities membership were just an illusion for the conservative government. Harold Wilson won back the premiership and called for a referendum about the British membership in the European Communities. The official reason was that the citizens needed to express their opinion and decide about such an important issue linked with their individual and collective freedoms.[21]

[18]Archer (2004).

[19]How referendums can go wrong. Herding cats, 15 October 2015. Access mode: https://www.economist.com/news/special-report/21673504-referendum-results-are-notoriously-unpredictable-herding-cats.

[20]Ryan (2016), pp. 531–537.

[21]Pierce et al. (1983), pp. 43–63.

The Labour government wanted to renegotiate the terms of the agreement between the European Communities and the British government led by Heath, and then present it to the British citizens for their agreement. This strategy on renegotiating was later used by numerous Member States, such as Greece when Papandreou won the Greek national elections right after the enlargement, and has some similarities to the position of David Cameron. The conservative Prime Minister emphasised the necessity to find a new agreement between the European Union (EU) and the UK to present it to the British citizens and obtain their support.

The Labour party under the leadership of Wilson was divided on the European issue and a referendum could settle all the internal differences and assure the internal cohesion of the party before it could affect its real functionality by an internal political civil war. Again, there are similarities with the position of the Conservative government of Cameron that faced a strong division inside its party between supporters of the EU and the supporters of the Brexit as a better alternative for the British necessities.

Harold Wilson had himself applied for membership to the European Communities and was familiar with the internal development of the accession negotiations and the results. Obviously, he wanted the UK inside the Communities but thought the accession agreement could have been better for the British interest. On February 1974 the Labour party issued a manifesto to renegotiate the terms of British accession to the European Communities and a new agreement was reached during the Dublin summit of 1975 that included minor changes more cosmetic than effective, but at least enough to be presented to the British people as a success (Again another similarity to the Cameron claims to renegotiate the British involvement with the EU).[22] Nevertheless, the House of Commons voted 396 to 170 to continue within the Common Market on the new terms but the Labour party and the government were divided about the issue.

The question to be asked to the British electorate was:

Do you think that the UK should stay in the European Community (the Common Market)?
Permitting a simple YES/NO answer (to be marked with an (X)).

The majority of the British government and the opposition, including Margaret Thatcher newly elected leader of the conservative party, supported the permanence in the Communities. The government backing included personalities such as Denis Healey, the Chancellor of the Exchequer; James Callaghan, the Foreign Secretary; and Roy Jenkins, the Home Secretary. Denis Healey was Secretary of State for Defence from 1964 to 1970 and supported the first British accession petition, James Callaghan became British Prime Minister from 1976 to 1979, and Roy Jenkins became president of the European Commission from 1977 to 1981 overseeing the development of the European Monetary System, embryo of the Monetary integration in Europe.

[22]Broad and Geiger (1996), pp. 82–105.

On the side of the No, the funds were scarce, there were no centrist public figures and the campaign was much more chaotic. The referendum itself was not binding upon the government in the strict legal sense, because of the principle of parliamentary sovereignty, but the electorate expressed significant support for the EEC membership, with 67% in favour on a 65% turnout. This was the first ever referendum that was held throughout the entire UK.

Obviously, the referendum of 2016 did not reproduce the same circumstances, as the EU has grown to 28 members and the integration has deepened the relations between the states and the Union. The supranational power of the European institutions has grown after each Treaty, there is a common currency, although the UK is not part of it, and overall, the necessity for deeper integration to solve the current problems of the organisation makes possible a much more politically advanced model of integration in the close future.

The renegotiation was in both occasions a milestone in the government strategy, and in both cases, was vague without real influence in the relations between the UK and the EU. In reality, what the renegotiation looks forward is to accommodate the British interest inside of the Union, something unlikely to occur, as the necessities of the majority of the members are different from the British. It is not possible to give what Britain wants without endangering the whole process of integration.

The case of the media, perhaps was the main difference between both referendums, as on the first occasion there was a massive support to the Yes beside the exception of the left-wing Morning Star. During the 2016 media was more divided and the massive media channels offered much variety in opinions.[23]

During the 1975 campaign, the three major political parties were supporting the UK inside of the Communities and lacked a public leader agglutinating the sympathy of the voters. The situation in 2016 was different, with much more division among the members of the political parties and different popular politicians supporting the exit of the country, as Boris Johnson, major of London from 2008 to 2016 and who was a possible candidate to the leadership of the conservative party.

The British government strongly supported the Yes in the referendum of 1975 but in 2016 its position was more ambiguous as the ministers had freedom to support either side and Whitehall also was more cautious about getting actively involved in the referendum.

4 The Vision of Margaret Thatcher About European Communities

Margaret Thatcher has been one of the most influential politicians in the European building process. Her opinions are still today supported by many people in the current crisis of the European integration, and her participation in issues such as

[23]Hobolt (2016), pp. 1259–1277.

the Single European Act or the solution of the British question, influences still the daily life of European citizens.

From late 1970 until the mid 1980s, Thatcher and her combative attitude towards the EU were the mainstay of the UK-EEC relations. She fought with full vigour for a proportionate budgetary rebate for the UK. Because of this political battle, a settlement was finally reached at the June 1984 Fontainebleau European Council meeting.[24]

Thatcher is still a symbol for euro-sceptics, a defender of national sovereignty and the independence of the Member States of the EU from the dictatorship of European institutions.[25,26] Her basic idea was related to popular loyalty and the transfer of sovereignty from the national to the European level, a utopia according to Thatcher that could endanger European societies, liberties, and way of life. She thought that centuries of history had made the national states the natural recipient of popular loyalty, and hence the natural defender of people's liberties, and it would be unnatural to transfer that loyalty to an artificial upper level created in the European Communities by civil servants and irresponsible dreamers, a clear attack on federalism and neo-functionalism in their roles in European integration, and supporting Intergovernamentalism as the only responsible way to build a lasting Europe. She had a general approach like that of Charles de Gaulle towards the European construction, and Thatcher, as the French president also, was involved in Europe, and did not have the UK retreat from the European Communities. Both leaders were conscious of the benefits for their countries of membership in the European Communities. Thus, neither of them wanted to destroy the European building process; they just wanted to redirect its path from a supranational movement to national cooperation and hence to control it.

4.1 Facts About Thatcher

Margaret Thatcher was born in October 1925 in Grantham, a small town in eastern England. Her childhood, (she lived in a small and religious community), could explain her conservative approach. During those years the UK was still one of the major world powers, with colonies all over the world; by 1922 the British Empire held sway over a population of about 458 million people, one quarter of the world's population; also, more than 38 countries were included in the British Empire. Considering that during her childhood her country was the biggest in the world, it is easier to understand her pride and nationalistic approach.[27]

During the Second World War, Thatcher studied chemistry at Oxford, where she became president of the student Conservative Association, linking her life for always

[24]Westlake (2017).

[25]Buller (2000), pp. 319–327.

[26]Forster (2002).

[27]Moore (2013a).

with this political party. In the 1950s she ran unsuccessfully for Parliament twice and finally in 1959 was elected. She was given a junior office in the administration of Harold Macmillan between 1961 and 1964. The next conservative government lead by Edward Heath in 1970 gave her a more important position, Education Secretary, and she obtained cabinet rank.

Edward Heath and the conservatives were defeated in the elections of 1974, and Thatcher, a year later, became the leader of the party. She was the first woman ever to lead a Western European political party in a major State. Some people thought of her just as a temporal substitute, a bridge towards a new leader, but she reinforced her position during the following years and won the next parliamentary elections in the UK, becoming the first woman Prime Minister of the UK.[28]

Her first term, 1979–1983, was strongly influenced by the economic crisis and its solution in the UK. The Falklands War was another main point of her first term, winning her the respect of many Britons.[29]

The second term, 1983–1987, was influenced by a huge strike by the British Trade Unions that were defeated, enhancing Thatcher's economic reforms and determination. Many reforms were done during this time trying to achieve a more privatised economy and reducing the role of the state in the British economy. Thatcher sold state assets during this period; the privatisation was looking for a more liberal economic system and set a precedent that many other countries of the world were to follow. The Irish question and the IRA were also important in the domestic agenda. Even Thatcher herself suffered a terrorist attack in October 1984.

Her third term, 1987–1990, meant more reforms, especially in education, taxation, and the health system. The end of the Cold War was another milestone during these years of Thatcher as British Prime Minister. Her tough behaviour, too strong personal leadership, and her ideas about Europe led to an internal revolt in the conservative party, with the result of substituting John Major for Thatcher in November 1990. After her Premiership she was a member of Parliament and made important interventions about Bosnia and about Maastricht, retiring officially from public life in 2002.

The main ideas of Margaret Thatcher about the European building process have been taken mainly from a speech by the British Premier at the College of Europe in Bruges, Belgium, on 20 September 1988.

4.2 Europe and the EU

Margaret Thatcher thought that Europe was much more than the EU, and complained about the identification of both. She protested about the use of the adjective anti-European for people who did not support European Integration following the

---

[28]Young and Sloman (1986).

[29]Moore (2013b).

model of the EU, mainly because Europe was a wider concept, and because another kind of Europe was also possible. According to Thatcher, Europe is history, religion, culture, language, and politics:

- History: Because Europeans have had similar historical development, influencing each other, similar goals, similar threats, growing together, spreading the ideas of Europe all over the world.
- Religion: Because of the Christian roots of European society, because once Europe was united by a religious link that transfers to Europe the ancient wisdom of Greece and Rome, and especially because of the recognition by Christianity of the unique and spiritual nature of the individual. On the other hand, this affirmation is polemic in the frame of the rejected European Constitution and the intention of some countries, especially Poland, to include in the preamble of it a reference to the Christian roots of Europe, and the supporters of secularism in Europe, plus the possible enlargement of the EU to Muslim countries like Turkey. The debate is not about the Christian roots of Europe, because it is a historical fact, but about its influence nowadays in politics.
- Culture: Thatcher speaks about European cultural movements that spread similar ideas and similar tastes all over the continent. It is clear that this idea of a European culture is not homogeneous, but it is real.
- Language: Even though Europe has many different languages, most of them come from the same family, the Indo-European, with roots in Anatolia or Central Asia, divided into five main groups: Baltic, Celtic, Germanic, Romance, and Slavonic, plus other languages like Finno-Ugrian, Maltese, and Basque that belong to other families. Nevertheless, in this diversity, we find European influences that show our common roots, like Latin, once a common language for millions of people living in the Roman Empire, and still, nowadays many European languages, such as French, Spanish, Italian, and others show the important influence of this language.
- Politics: The French Revolution, the development of the national states, the concept of democracy, are mainly European ideas not developed just in one country, but all over the continent. Napoleon spread the ideas of the French Revolution all over Europe with his wars, and even when he lost against an alliance of European powers, he won the fight of the ideas, changing Europe for always. The rise of the national state is a European creation, and with the expansion of Europe all over the world this idea also was adopted by other states, and even the concept of state itself is European. Many countries in Europe contributed to the creation of all these political concepts and structures that nowadays seem universal for us.[30]

According to Thatcher, the idea of Europe rests in these five main pillars, and is much wider than the concept of the EU and its European building project. Being a participant in these pillars means that you are part of Europe, no matter whether you

[30]Ramiro Troitiño (2014), pp. 119–136.

support the EU or are against it. To prove it, she spoke about the links of the UK and the rest of Europe: Celts, Saxons, and Danes, the ancestors of the current British came from continental Europe, as did also the Normans, the religion, the rule of law, etc. Also, she thought that the commitment of the UK to Europe was also clear, with the numerous wars where Britain fought in Europe. Thatcher emphasised the role played by the UK to protect freedom in Europe against different powers that tried to conquer the continent and unite it under one sole power. Napoleon and his wars in Europe, the First World War, and the Second World War are examples of her idea. These wars devastated Europe and were won thanks to, among other factors, the help and the sacrifice of the British. Of course, Margaret Thatcher, as the British nationalist that she was, thought about the role of the UK as a determinate factor, but no one can deny the involvement of the UK in the European affairs as a major actor.

This idea of Thatcher about the usurpation of the concept of Europe by the EU is very clear, and was used to defend herself from the attacks by integration supporters to her policies towards the EU. But it also shows the manipulation by the EU supporters, calling the followers of other ways of integration, as cooperation or just national supporters, anti-Europeans, when they are just against a specific model of integration, the EU.

4.3 The Cold War, the USA, and the EU

The ideas of Margaret Thatcher about this topic made clear her position in the Cold War and her alignment with Ronal Reagan, president of the USA, and her intransigent position towards the USSR. The Prime Minister of the UK declared that the European Communities were one manifestation of the European identity, but were missing an important part of Europe that was behind the Iron Curtain. Thatcher made clear on numerous occasions that Europe was divided by force, as against the people who accepted the status quo of the Cold War and thought of Europe as Western Europe, as Charles de Gaulle, president of France, who, in his attempt to make France a third and independent power in the context of a battle between the USA and the Soviet Union, accepted the division of Europe as something natural in his obsession of distancing his country from the influence of the USA.

Nevertheless, the influence of the USA is clear in the creation of the European Communities and in their development. First, it was the American government and its intention to liberate West Germany from the occupation of the Allies that was the principal motor of the creation of the European Coal and Steel Community, the embryo of the current EU. The USA wanted to have a strong Germany in the context of the Cold War as it would be, in case of war, the first European battlefield against the Soviet Union; there was also the necessity to help the Germans to have economic development strong enough to block the expansion of the communists in Europe. To achieve that, the USA decided to give West Germany full control of the Ruhr area, rich in coal and steel, the basic elements for producing weapons. France was against that plan and wanted to repeat the system after WWI, international rule over the Ruhr area, but after WWII the power of France had decreased.[31] As the intentions of the USA were clear, the French government had just one option by which to control in some way the problematic area: the creation of a European Community. Also about the USA at this time of the twentieth century, it is important to remark that it was the country that held the Soviet Union in its position, keeping free France itself, as well as the rest of Western Europe.

So, these historical facts, plus the traditional link between the UK and the USA, made Thatcher a strong supporter of collaboration with the Americans. She even called the Americans the Europeans of the other side of the Atlantic, even proposing some kind of Community between Europe and the USA. It would have been difficult to have a Community between both powers in terms of equality, but the ideas of Thatcher were based more on a Free Trade Area, and political cooperation based on the same cultural values.

4.4 The European Communities Belong to All Its Members

Margaret Thatcher was against the domination of any one state over the EU, or a privileged position of any country inside the Community. The influence of France in the Communities since their foundation was clear with decisions as to the CAP and the Lomé agreements. The first, the agricultural policy, was designed for the benefit of France, where at that moment 25% of the labour was employed in the farming sector, and the state was near bankruptcy because of the payment of huge subsidies to farmers to keep the social peace of France and avoid the movement of workers from the countryside to the cities with the consequent lack of work, social unrest, and communist movements. The second was an agreement between the European Communities and the ex-colonies of its members, France being almost the only founding Member State with ex-colonies. The concept was clear: to keep the influence of France in the world using the means of the European Communities because France could not afford it alone.

According to Thatcher, this was inadmissible; all the members should have the same duties and the same rights, all of them should benefit from the European organization, and all of them should have the same obligations. This thought can be linked with the discussions that Thatcher had in the meetings of the European Council, especially with the representatives of France, with the intention to increase the benefits for the UK from the European Communities, to equalise them with the benefits France was getting. On this issue it is important to point out that the influence of France since the creation of the European Communities until the present day has been decreasing with each enlargement, depending nowadays completely on its bilateral cooperation with Germany. The more countries there are in the Union, the less important is the individual position of each single member.

[31] Hogan (1987).

4.5 The Community Is Not an End in Itself

Thatcher's ideas of the meaning of the organisation were quite clear: the European Communities could not become the objective of an intellectual concept, a tool for the creation of the European State. The EU should be, according to her, just a practical means for Europeans to enjoy prosperity and security in a world of powerful nations and groups of nations. It shows the practical approach of Thatcher; in improving the life of the people of Europe, the Communities have a sense of being, and the way to do it is by promoting individual initiative and enterprise, in other words, encouraging private action and reducing the role of the state to a supervisor of the system. The other two pillars of her conception of development were trade and industry. Thatcher thought that progress in Europe could be achieved just by promoting the economy to increase the wealth of Europeans.[32] The creation of any political entity should not be the main aim in the European building process, and Europe had to focus on providing Europeans enough and fair chances to develop their private initiative.

On the other hand, the issue of European security supported by Thatcher, a clear bet on a European Defence Community, but not of the kind of the 1950s when France proposed a Security Defence Community among the members of the European Communities with common institutions, but finally was rejected by its own French Parliament. Thatcher believed more in a close cooperation between European states and the USA, where no common independent institutions could be found, and where the decision making would be unanimity or consensus in a way to protect both Europe from external threats and the national sovereignty from international institutions. Also, security should be a way to keep Europe independent from rising powers like China, India, or Russia, a way to have a say in the international world, and enough muscle to back European decisions.

4.6 National Power Against Supranational Constructions

Margaret Thatcher assured that there were no substitutes for national states, and hence, Europe should be built on a union of European states, and not on the concentration of power in the European institutions. This means a clear attack on other theories of integration, mainly Federalism and Neo-Functionalism and a support of intergovernmental cooperation. The three models of integration have the same targets, avoiding wars in Europe and creating a peaceful and harmonious social system, but they differ in their way to do it. Federalism and Neo-Functionalism are based on the creation of European institutions that will outweigh national states, because the latter have proven ineffective in keeping peace and have not been able to create an international structure to keep away wars and miseries, because the essence of nationhood is building on the differences between people, emphasising the

[32] Wall (2008).

divergence instead the common needs of people.[33] To achieve a society where people can live together peacefully it is necessary to transfer the loyalty of the people of Europe from the national level to the European level.

Margaret Thatcher, as de Gaulle did before her, attacked both theories of integration and actively supported the third option, *Intergovernamentalism.*[34] This theory is based on agreements between states, good faith between them, common institutions as common forums, and always agreements and consensus, even unanimity. It means that there is not a voting system, there are just agreements, or, in case there is any voting system, unanimity would be required.

One of her main objections to Federalism and Neo-Functionalism was based on the national state because she thought it was the only institution that really had the loyalty of the people and hence the only one keeping values as important as freedom.

Thatcher also thought that a concentration of power in some kind of supranational institutions would be highly damaging and could jeopardise the objectives of the European process because the real power of European integration was the sum of the strong points of all the nationalities that took part in the process. As each nation in Europe had its own traditions, customs, and identity, it would be a mistake to build Europe on a European identity that did not exist instead of on something real, as are the nations, according to Thatcher.

She was, as well, against the ideas of the fathers of Europe, and mainly the idea of the USA as a model of integration, because for her the history of the United States was different, because the USA was built on emigrants from Europe that were escaping intolerance and looking for the creation of a new society. This purpose helped to create a new unity and pride in being American, a process never developed in Europe, where the unity and pride are still united with the national state. Thatcher thought that some kind of integration was needed in Europe to keep some predominance in world affairs, and she wanted Europeans working in the same direction, but through national pride in each country and parliamentary powers of the states, not through the European Parliament or other European institutions. This raises the questions of the good faith of the states and their natural egoism to reach a solution of their own problems, as we have seen nowadays when some important countries of the EU are trying to face the world crisis with a nationalist approach, not respecting their compromise with the EU, as the French government promoting a plan to help their car industry with the condition that the companies cannot reduce the workers on French soil, thus affecting other countries of the Union, such as the Czech Republic or Slovakia.

Nevertheless, the title of the speech Margaret Thatcher gave at the College of Europe in Bruges, Belgium, has the illuminating title of A Family of Nations, expressing all her ideas about European integration. However, according to Thatcher Britain was at risk of losing its independence and sovereignty because of the transfer of decision-making power to Brussels.[35]

[33]Börzel and Risse (2007), pp. 483–504.

[34]Puchala (1999), pp. 317–331.

[35]Polgár (2016), pp. 83–93.

This was even though since as early as 1964, there was increasing awareness among politicians and lawmakers in Europe that gaining membership of the European Community would result in curtailment of a permanent nature of the legislative powers enjoyed by the Member States. This was clear from the ECJ judgments of Van Gend en Loos v Nederlandse Administratie der Belastingen (1963) Case 26/62 and Flaminio Costa v E.N.E.L. Case 6-64. [36]

4.7 Weak Bureaucracy

Another point of her criticism against Federalism and especially against Neo-Functionalism was the role of civil servants. The idea of Margaret Thatcher about any kind of government, national or international, was based on supervisory powers. The state was merely a supervisor of the social and economic systems; it established the rules and looked after the social and economic agents. The state provided just the legal and social framework whereby the society could develop by itself; the state provided the structure whereby the people could develop and grow, the state was just for giving the citizens the same chances to succeed, and after that, it was a matter related to individual capacity to utilise these chances. So, the state provided security to private initiative. This idea of society is like the USA model, but not exactly the same, because Thatcher took power from minor institutions, as counties or city halls, to increase the weight of the British central government, something unthinkable in the USA, where the powers of the federal government and the states are more defined.

Nevertheless, the vision of Thatcher was very different from the model of the Member States of the European Communities in the 1980s, especially France and Germany, where the conception of the state was very different, not as a supervisory power, but as a proper agent of the system. The State tried to provide equality, not the same chances, which meant a bigger state, more technocracy and bureaucracy, more enrolment in the system, reducing the role of private initiative and regulation of the market by itself, increasing the role of the state.

The institutions of the European Communities were small in the first Community, the ECSC, but afterwards, the implementation of new treaties and the inclusion of increasing policies on the European level, made the European institutions grow bigger. Now the European Commission counts a staff of 33,000 people. In reality, this is not a huge number if we compare it with the number of civil servants in the Member States, as in France, where there are around two million, as there are in Germany. Civil servants nowadays in the UK, more than half a million, are considerably fewer than in Germany and France, but more than in the EU. If we consider that the EU is dealing on the European level, much wider than the national level, the number of civil servants working in the European institutions does not look excessive. Nevertheless, as Margaret Thatcher was decreasing the role of the regional institutions of the UK, and increasing the power of the central state, she did not like the idea of

[36] Kim (2016), p. 551.

growing numbers in the European institutions because her domestic policies were boycotted on the European level. Her dislike of the European institutions was also related to her idea of the central role of the national states in the European Building process. It made no sense to give power to a European technocracy that was not elected by the European people, that did not respect national positions, and that could become an alien power to the people of Europe, forcing and leading them towards the creation of an artificial political structure.[37] So, according to Margaret Thatcher, the institutions of the EU should be minimal, enough to assure that the common system is working, but never a substitute of the national institutions.

4.8 Policies of the EU

Margaret Thatcher had a clear idea about which policies should be European and which ones national. The main reason for having a European policy should be the benefit of the states, and hence, the benefit of the people of Europe represented by the states. Thatcher thought that any policy that was ineffective or benefiting only a non-representative portion of European states should be at the national level. She wanted a reform in the existing policies of the European Communities, mainly the Common Agricultural Policy, that was spending most of the money of the EU budget, transferring the money just to some countries, and of course, not to the UK. The situation was clear for her: if this policy cost the EU a great deal of money, and the UK was an important contributor to the finances of the European organisation, and the British did not get any benefit from it, this policy was wrong. According to this idea, a reform was needed inside the EU and its policies, reducing the policies included in the area of influence of the Communities, and giving back the sovereignty on these policies to the Member States. Her intentions were obvious and simple: the EU should not move towards the creation of a supranational state, taking increasing policies from the Member States as it was clear that these were not effectively managed on the European level. The European power should be just a structure to deal with the Commonwealth, in the policies where common agreement between governments would provide a benefit for all of them, in other words, a pragmatic union, never political.[38]

4.9 European Market

Margaret Thatcher wanted the European Communities to encourage enterprise to improve the economic situation of its members. For doing so, the best option for her

[37]Dahl (1999), pp. 19–36.
[38]Thatcher (1995).

was giving power to the market; it could develop itself in a more effective way than if it were to be highly regulated by political institutions. Her ideas about the market changed radically with the last economic crisis that Europe is still enduring. Nevertheless, from the time of Thatcher's governance until the present, her proposal for the economy has been the most popular and important, especially after the collapse of the Soviet Union and the lack of alternatives to the extreme capitalism of our days.

Her main proposal for the EU was the creation of a real interior market in Europe, to improve the effectiveness of the Common Market approved by the Treaty of Rome, that in reality was just a free trade area in industrial production and a highly regulated market in agricultural production. Thatcher wanted free enterprise within a framework of European law, a much better way, according to her, to speed up the growth of the European economy.

Thatcher's aim was clear: deregulate and remove the barriers to trade, most of them national. The barriers built up by the Member States of the European Communities to protect the national economical agents were numerous and were a brake to the economic development of Europe and its members. Thatcher was one of the promoters of a new treaty, the Single European Act, thinking that it would lead to a minimum legal agenda to improve economic integration and dismiss the political influence of the European institutions. It was a great miscalculation on the part of Thatcher, because what she thought would be mainly economic became eventually highly political. The Single Market approved in the Single European Act in 1986 meant, because almost all economic fields were then under the supervision of the European institutions, great powers to the European institutions, that, instead of deregulating and removing the barriers to trade, as Thatcher had thought, engendered deeper regulation of the Market to end the national distortions to it.

Moreover, the Single European Act meant bigger responsibilities for the European Commission, something translated in a huge increase of civil servants working for the organisation, something against the will and beliefs of Thatcher.

So, one can see that Thatcher's beloved Single European Act did not create the free market as she had hoped. Instead, it progressively replaced the Common Market within Europe with a Single Market. The difference between these two Markets is that the Common Market was based on mutual recognition of national diversity, albeit subject to some basic minimum standards. It was a result of negotiations made predominantly by the individual Member States. The Single Market, on the other hand, promotes harmonisation from the top to the bottom and gives all the power of regulation to the European Commission and the Court of Justice. This nature of regulatory regime imposes uniform standards across all the Member States. This is in sharp contrast to earlier approaches where EU directives required minimal harmonisation of laws in Europe and focussed more on banning restrictive regulation in Member States if it interfered with the four freedoms of people, goods, services, and capital. Thus, one could attribute the current problems of unmediated movement of capital and labour within the EU on the UK's insistence on the rapid enlargement of the EU and on the extension of the single market to many more sectors. This approach of the UK has led to the weakening of the mutual protection between regions and nations as was originally envisaged by the European project.[39]

The last consequence of the Single European Act and the creation of the Single Market has been the adoption of the Common Currency by most of the members of the European market. Thatcher in her great miscalculation did not pay attention to the consequences of her actions and the power of European integration. The Single Market was created to eliminate barriers to trade between the Member States of the European Communities, the same reasoning can be applied to the creation of the Common Currency, the Euro: to eliminate any distortion in the market produced by the exchange rate of the European currencies, or the uncertainty of the future rate of the currencies, something that reduces the trade between holders of different currencies, among other reasons. The British premier, after leaving office, became a bitter enemy of the Euro and the inclusion of the British currency, the Pound, in the European Common Currency.

Another consequence of the Common Currency, hated by Thatcher but a consequence of her polices, is the proclaimed end of the economic integration in Europe and the beginning of political integration, another nightmare for Thatcher. The creation of the Euro meant a Common Currency for most of the members of the EU, but the European market is not fully integrated, in some sense the market is still divided into national markets, with some economies more integrated, and others much less so. This means a great danger of an asymmetrical crisis, as Europe is facing currently, a crisis that could affect just a part of the market, but not spread to all the members of the market. In that case, the European Central Bank establishes a monetary policy for the majority of the system, not helping the affected economies, because doing so could damage the rest of the European economies. The problem is the loss of sovereignty in the monetary field of the Member States of the euro zone, reducing the number of tools to be used in case of a national crisis. The next logical step in the European building process will be the creation of some kind of European economic government, a step closer to a European state. It is clear that Thatcher did not want that when she supported the Single Market, or that the Euro and a possible European federal government is not only a consequence of the Single Market, but the SEA can be considered a basic and necessary step to achieve European political integration.

4.10 European Defence

Margaret Thatcher thought that the European Communities should focus on two main points, economy and security. The UK has one of the main armies of Europe, and its role in a future EU army would be predominant.

[39]Pabst (2016), pp. 189–201.

Margaret Thatcher, a great supporter of a close alliance with the USA, also thought of the idea of the European Army, but controlled, of course, by the national states; for her it would have been unthinkable that someone in Brussels could send British soldiers to fight, and maybe die, in an external war. She proposed to develop the army through the Brussels Treaty, signed in 1948 between the Benelux countries, France, and the UK as an expansion of the Treaty of Dunkirk signed the previous year between France and the UK.[40] Originally this was a defence Treaty against possible aggression by Germany, but as the Cold War intensified, it became an instrument against Communist expansion. The parties of the Treaty decided to create the Western Union Defence Organization. Its main institutions were a Committee at Prime Ministerial level, and a WU Combined Chiefs of Staff committee, including all the national chiefs of staff, which would direct the operative organisation; clearly an inter-governmental organisation where collaboration substituted for integration, as Thatcher liked. In 1954 other countries, West Germany and Italy, joined the organization that was renamed the Western EU. Its main institutions were a council and an Assembly. The most powerful institution and leader of the organisation was the Council of Ministers, assisted by a Permanent Representatives Council on the ambassadorial level. Again, we can see that no supranational institutions were created, and the main role was played by the states. Social and cultural aspects of the Brussels Treaty were handed to the Council of Europe to avoid duplication of responsibilities within Europe. The Assembly was just an advisory organ, without any real power.

This organisation was fully acceptable to Margaret Thatcher and her ideas, because developing a European army through the Western EU and not through the European Communities would prevent any control by any supranational body, such as the European Commission, and would keep all this process under the supervision of the national states, plus resolving the problem created by some members of the EU that were neutral and did not desire to develop any defence policy.

The difference between Thatcher and other supporters of the European Army is the relation with NATO and the USA; Thatcher imagined WEU as a complement to NATO, and never as a tool against the predominance of the USA in the world.

Nevertheless, the idea of Thatcher is still alive, and the WEU is getting more attention from some states of Europe as the best way to develop the European Army and the common defence.

4.11 Relations Between Europe and the USA

Thatcher was a supporter of a close alliance between both sides of the Atlantic, between the Europeans of Europe and the Europeans of the other side of the Atlantic. For her, one of the most important issues in the political agenda of the European

[40]Evans (2004).

Communities was keeping the traditional ties between the USA and Europe. She clearly disliked the idea of building Europe against the power of America in a futile attempt to become the next world power.[41] Margaret Thatcher was a loyal ally of Ronald Reagan, and supported fully his approach against the Soviet Union, his far from mild positions. She was thankful for the effort of the USA in defending Europe and thought the roots of American values were European. So, the similarities of both areas were much more numerous than were the differences.

Many Europeans, especially in Western Europe, wanted to build Europe as a power balance to the USA in the world, an alternative, complaining about the unilateralism of the American government, and a unipolar world where the USA decides and Europe has no influence; France has been a champion of this vision, starting with de Gaulle until almost nowadays, with the politics developed by Chirac.

Meanwhile in Central and Eastern Europe, the views about America are different and friendlier. These differences were clear in the last war in Iraq, when many countries of Western Europe, like France and Germany, were against the war, and new members of the EU and the UK supported the Americans. These differences can be explained by the fact that the new members of the EU achieved their independence thanks to the USA, because of its victory over the Soviet Union in the Cold War.

The UK, before Thatcher and after her, has had a special relationship with the USA, sharing the common language, cultural aspects, economic similarities, military cooperation, and a constant transfer of people and ideas between both sides of the Atlantic.[42] It was even one of the reasons given by Charles de Gaulle to reject twice the intention of the UK of joining the European Communities. Thatcher, following with this tradition, supported the creation of a European defence system, but working closely with the USA, never as an antagonist. This debate is still alive in the EU.

5 Conclusion

The authors' analysis of the issues related to the enlargement of the European Community to the UK, the referendum of 1975 and the position of Margaret Thatcher have hopefully helped to shed some light on the events of the day. In hindsight, it can now be clearly seen that in the 1970s the UK accepted most of the Communitarian claims or delayed the decision about the most problematic issues because it needed access to the European market to reinvigorate its economy, but this generated problems afterwards, especially under the premiership of Margaret Thatcher. Thatcher's basic idea was related to popular loyalty and the transfer of sovereignty from the national to the European level, a utopia according to her that could endanger European societies, liberties, and way of life. Thatcher's influence

[41] Jackson and Saunders (2012).

[42] Renwick (2013).

continues to this date and her thoughts and words have returned to haunt many in the modern EU.

The referendum of 2016 was very different from the referendum of 1975 and did not reproduce the same circumstances, as the EU has grown to 28 members and the integration has deepened the relations between the states and the Union. The supranational power of the European institutions has grown after each Treaty, there is a common currency, although the UK is not part of it, and overall, the necessity for deeper integration to solve the current problems of the organisation makes possible a much more politically advanced model of integration in the close future. The case of the media, perhaps was the main difference between both referendums, as on the first occasion there was a massive support to the Yes beside the exception of the left-wing Morning Star. During the 2016 referendum, media was more divided and the massive media channels offered much variety in opinions. The British government strongly supported the Yes in the referendum of 1975 but in 2016 its position was more ambiguous as the ministers had freedom to support either side and Whitehall also was more cautious about getting actively involved in the referendum.

The renegotiation was on both occasions a milestone in the government strategy, and in both cases, was vague without real influence in the relations between the UK and the EU. The necessities of the majority of the members are today different from those of the British. It appears that it is no longer possible to give what Britain wants without endangering the whole process of integration. The questions still remain as to how to satisfy the remaining euro sceptics in the EU, how to overcome tendencies to defend the rigid concept of national sovereignty and how to manage the independence of the Member States of the EU from the overarching influence of European institutions?

References

Archer C (2004) Norway outside the European Union: Norway and European integration from 1994 to 2004. Routledge

Börzel T, Risse T (2007) Europeanization: the domestic impact of European Union politics. In: Handbook of European Union politics, pp 483–504

Broad R, Geiger T (1996) The 1975 British Referendum on Europe. Contemp Br Hist 10(3):82–105

Brownie S, Dalziel P (1993) Shift-share analyses of New Zealand exports, 1970–1984. New Zealand Economic Papers

Buller J (2000) Understanding contemporary conservative Euro-scepticism: statecraft and the problem of governing autonomy. Polit Q 71(3):319–327

Daddow OJ (2003) Harold Wilson and European integration: Britain's second application to join the EEC. Frank Cass, London

Dahl RA (1999) Can international organizations be democratic? A skeptic's view. Democracy's edges, pp 19–36

Dinan D (ed) (2014) Origins and evolution of the European Union. Oxford University Press, Oxford

Evans EJ (2004) Thatcher and Thatcherism. Routledge, London

Forster A (2002) Euroscepticism in contemporary British politics: opposition to Europe in the British Conservative and labour parties since 1945. Taylor & Francis
Fuchs C (2016) Neoliberalism in Britain: from Thatcherism to Cameronism. Triplec (Cognition, Communication, Co-Operation) 14(1):163–188. Communication Source, EBSCOhost. Accessed 25 Aug 2017
Ginsburgh V, Ortuno-Ortin I, Weber S (2005) Disenfranchisement in linguistically diverse societies: the case of the European Union. J Eur Econ Assoc 3(4):946–965
Haftendorn H (ed) (2006) The strategic triangle: France, Germany and the United States in the shaping of the new Europe. Woodrow Wilson Center Press, Washington, DC
Hobolt SB (2016) The Brexit vote: a divided nation, a divided continent. J Eur Pub Policy 23(9):1259–1277
Hogan MJ (1987) The Marshall Plan: America, Britain and the reconstruction of Western Europe, 1947–1952. Cambridge University Press
How referendums can go wrong. Herding cats, 15 October 2015. Access mode: https://www.economist.com/news/special-report/21673504-referendum-results-are-notoriously-unpredictable-herding-cats
Jackson B, Saunders R (2012) Making Thatcher's Britain. Cambridge University Press, Cambridge
Kim K (2016) A long road to Brexit: how Britain came to leave the EU. J East Asia Int Law 9:551
Maitland D (2001) Britain, the Commonwealth and Europe: an overview. In: Britain, the Commonwealth and Europe. Palgrave Macmillan, Basingstoke, pp 1–8
Mitchell B (1976) Politics, fish and international resource management: The British-Icelandic Cod War. Geogr Rev (1976):127–138
Moore C (2013a) Margaret Thatcher: the authorized biography, volume one: not for turning. Penguin, London
Moore C (2013b) Margaret Thatcher: from Grantham to the Falklands. Vintage
Pabst A (2016) Brexit, post-liberalism, and the politics of paradox. Telos 176(2016):189–201
Parr H (2009) Transformation and tradition: Anglo-French Nuclear Cooperation and Britain's Policy towards the European Community, 1960–1974. In: The British way in cold warfare: intelligence, diplomacy and the bomb 1945–1975, p 87
Pierce R, Valen H, Listhaug O (1983) Referendum voting behavior: the Norwegian and British referenda on membership in the European Community. Am J Polit Sci, 43–63
Polgár I (2016) Euroscepticism, an increasing phenomenon among the member states. Road to Brexit. Revista Română de Geografie Politică Year XVIII, (2):83–93
Puchala DJ (1999) Institutionalism, intergovernmentalism and European integration: a review article. J Common Mark Stud 37(2):317–331
Ramiro Troitiño D (2014) The British position towards European integration: a different economic and political approach. Baltic J Eur Stud 4:119–136
Ramiro Trotiño D (2013) European integration: building Europe. Nova Publishers, Hauppauge
Renwick R (2013) A journey with Margaret Thatcher: foreign policy under the iron lady. Biteback, London, p 2013
Rossbach N (2009) Heath, Nixon and the rebirth of the special relationship: Britain, the US and the EC, 1969–74. Springer, Berlin
Ryan C (2016) Where does one start to make sense of Brexit? Int Econ Econ Policy 13(4):531–537
Sárlvik B, Crewe I, Alt J, Fox A (1976) Britain's Membership of the EEC: a profile of electoral opinions in the spring of 1974 -- with a postscript on the referendum. Eur J Polit Res 4(1):83–113. Political Science Complete, EBSCOhost
Saunders R (2016) A tale of two referendums: 1975 and 2016. Polit Q 87(3):318–322. Humanities International Complete, EBSCOhost
Schenk C (2002) Sterling, international monetary reform and Britain's applications to join the European Economic Community in the 1960s. Contemp Eur Hist 11(3):345–369
Sharp R, Lowe P, Ward S (1998) Responding to Europeanisation. In: British Environmental Policy and Europe: politics and policy in transition. Routledge, London, pp 33–56
Thatcher M (1995) The path to power. Harper&Collins, New York

Wall S (2008) A stranger in Europe: Britain and the EU from Thatcher to Blair. Oxford University Press, Oxford
Wauthier C (1972) France and Africa: "Long Live Neo-Colonialism". Issue: J Opin 2(1):23–26
Westlake M (2017) The inevitability of gradualness: the longer-term origins of the 23 June 2016 'Brexit' referendum. Bruges Political Research Papers 56/2017
Young H, Sloman A (1986) The Thatcher phenomenon. British Broadcasting Corporation, London

The British Rebate and the Single European Act: Political Ramifications of an Economic Reform

Liisi Keedus, Tanel Kerikmäe, Archil Chochia, and David Ramiro Troitiño

Abstract The UK rebate in the early days was largely devised and negotiated by Margaret Thatcher, yet its acceptance by the EC and the challenges that it posed to the union throughout the coming decades—or so this chapter will argue—have indirectly contributed to political reforms and new treaties that have in fact accelerated European political integration. Similarly, Thatcher's support for what she thought and advocated should remain a merely economic single market has had unforeseen political ramifications, mainly advancing elements of European federalism that she vehemently opposed. This article maps the role of economic integration in advancing political integration and traces both of their successes back to some at first seemingly unsuccessful visions to formulate a more integrated Europe.

1 Introduction

In October 1974, relationship troubles between the United Kingdom and the European Communities (EC) underwent an episode of intensification when the general election manifestoes of the Labour Party committed it to granting the British citizens the opportunity to cast their vote on whether Britain should stay in the Common Market on renegotiated terms or leave it altogether. After Labour's narrow victory, the new government called for a referendum to vote on Britain's membership in the EC.[1] The government campaigned for the country to remain in the EC, like did Margaret Thatcher as the new leader of the Conservative party. In the 1975 referendum, 67% of voters supported the UK's remaining a member in the EC. The

[1]For a standard study of the election, see Butler (1975).

L. Keedus (✉)
Department of Politics, University of York, York, UK
e-mail: lkeedus@tlu.ee

T. Kerikmäe · A. Chochia · D. Ramiro Troitiño
Tallinn Law School, Tallinn University of Technology, Tallinn, Estonia
e-mail: tanel.kerikmae@ttu.ee; archil.chochia@ttu.ee; david.troitino@ttu.ee

D. Ramiro Troitiño et al. (eds.), *Brexit*,
https://doi.org/10.1007/978-3-319-73414-9_8

membership terms' renegotiations mainly concerned the Common Agricultural Policy (CAP) and British contributions to the EC budget, at the time higher in relative terms than the contributions by other Member States. Harold Wilson, the Prime Minister, obtained some minor reductions in the British contribution, but the change was too insignificant to really offer a satisfactory solution.

When Thatcher became Prime Minister in the following elections in 1979, she was determined to change the situation, arguing that the UK's contribution to the EC budget was too high, while the EC payments channelled back to the member were too low. She placed the issue at the top of the Council agenda. Many of those meetings were reported to have led to confrontational situations between Thatcher, on the one side, and the German leader Helmut Kohl and French president Francoise Mitterrand, on the other. The president of the Council, the president or prime minister of the Member State that held the EC rotating presidency, compiled the agenda of the meetings, and usually excluded the British concerns. In disregard for the established protocol, Thatcher raised these issues nonetheless. She even threatened to withdraw her country from the EC if its concerns were not addressed.[2,3] While tensions were clearly a mutual responsibility, Kohl's retrospective reflections capture the antagonistic mood of the negotiations: "The British prime minister, who had completely isolated herself with her position, temporarily lost her nerves and completely lost her temper with me. She argued that Germany had to support Britain because British troops were stationed here".[4]

After years of ongoing effort and determination to address Britain's concerns, Thatcher succeeded in inching a budgeting reform. The new system was based on a reduction of British net contribution to the EC by approximately 66%.[5] It meant that the UK still paid into the EC budget more than it obtained, for example, in 2016 the British net contribution after the reduction was approximately 5.5 billion euros. The main problem with this compromise had been the contraction of the EC budget because of having to return a significant part of the UK contribution. Germany, one of the main net contributors to the EU finances, was initially to fill most of this budget cut. At the end, an agreement was reached that each year all the Member States contribute to the British rebate, and a complex system was devised that makes France the main beneficiary of the CAP, as well as the main contributor to the rebate.[6]

In the 1980s, CAP made up 80% of the EC budget and the aim of the UK rebate was to compensate for low agricultural redistributions to the UK. Today, it makes up for 40% of the budget and the previously undeveloped British farming sector has significantly increased and modernised, now obtaining a notable income from CAP.

---

[2]See Gowland et al. (2010), pp. 77–101, as well as Nugent (1999).

[3]Ramiro Troitiño (2014).

[4]Review of Kohl's memoirs, http://news.bbc.co.uk/1/hi/world/europe/4403002.stm, By Ray Furlong, November 3rd, 2005.

[5]Wall (2008).

[6]Ramiro Trotiño (2013).

This reduced the formerly negative effects of the policy on the British economy and increased the EC contributions to the UK.[7] Additionally, the differences between the British economy and other wealthy Member States have decreased. In fact, while the UK used to be the third poorest member of the Community of ten in terms of average income, after the recent enlargement waves, it has become one of its wealthiest members. Yet, the rebate has been preserved. There have been several attempts to adapt the rebate to the new circumstances but the UK has always rejected them, and since all changes requires unanimity, it has been successful in blocking any renegotiations.

The rebate was largely devised and negotiated by Thatcher, yet its introduction and the challenges that it has posed throughout decades—or so this chapter will argue—have indirectly contributed to reforms and new treaties that have accelerated what Thatcher most vehemently wished to prevent: European political integration. Similarly, Thatcher's support for what she thought and advocated should remain a merely economic single market has had enormous political ramifications, mainly advancing elements of European federalism that she fiercely opposed.

2 The Crises and European Integration in the 1980s

The 1980s were a critical period for the EC that challenged the integration efforts in several ways.[8] Indeed, the British demands were temporarily met by the British Rebate agreement reached in Fontainebleau. When Greece was opposed to the accession of Spain and Portugal, the Integrated Mediterranean Programme adopted by the Council in 1985 calmed the quarrels. Yet, both crises made it evident that decision-making processes in the EC were in urgent need of reform. Because of the unanimity principle it was too easy and likely for one member to pose demands on others by threatening to veto a decision. This meant that a single Member State could paralyse the entire enlargement process at the time when the Community was planning to expand. With more countries joining the organisation, such as Spain and Portugal, it was increasingly likely that enlargement might be hindered through the negative behaviour of any individual Member State, regardless of the size its population or economy.

Furthermore, the accession of Spain and Portugal constituted a significant change for the Community and highlighted the need for reform. Because of the complex political and economic situation of both countries—like Greece, both countries had recently emerged from dictatorships and suffered from outdated agricultural and industrial economies—the accession negotiations became protracted and ridden with difficulties.[9] It was clear that the Community was in dire need of reform, while the

[7]See especially Skogstad and Verdun (2010).

[8]A useful introduction is Winn (1997).

[9]McAllister (2009), pp. 107 ff. Baquero and Closa (2009); Tsoukalis (1981).

Greek example had shown that each new member would further complicate efforts undertake it. Hence, completing the new Treaty before the accession of Spain and Portugal became urgent—it was easier to reach an agreement between fewer Member States and more convenient to have Spain and Portugal simply accepting pre-existing treaties rather than becoming additional negotiating parties.

At the same time, relations between European institutions were not amicable, with tensions between the European Parliament and the Council running high. The two institutions often clashed in a struggle for control over the process of integration. Originally, decision-making power was in the hands of the Council, or the Member States, while the Parliament was acting mainly as a consulting assembly. Yet, the Parliament's powers were increasing. Most importantly, before the Single European Act (SEA) the Parliament controlled the ratification of the EC budget, even if this power was shared with the Council and there were frequent disputes over the size and distribution of the budget. There was fear that quarrels would result in the taking of unilateral decisions against provisions of the Treaties—and hence all parties perceived an urgent and obvious need for a new institutional framework that would meet the increasing ambitions of the Parliament and grant it a new role in the integration process.

Another significant challenge was that CAP was becoming overly burdensome for the budget and unduly prominent on the EC agenda. There was a widely shared sentiment that this policy ought to become more efficient and its predominance be ended. The Community needed a broader agenda and vision beyond being mainly an agricultural community—and the SEA was devised to delivered precisely this.[10]

Furthermore, in the 1980s, Europe was hit hard by a global economic crisis. Seemingly the simplest response seemed to be to counter the crisis with national policies—and this, instead of searching for a European solution, was the predominant approach during the crisis. Yet, the striking failures of the national policies to tackle the economic crisis once again highlighted the need for stronger European integration. It was obvious that some sort of reform was urgent and discussions began over a new treaty. At first, these concerned various proposals for reforming the EC institutional structures, and later came to include more extensive negotiations between the members of the Community, resulting in SEA, ratified in 1986.

3 The Spinelli Project and Genscher-Colombo Report: Setting the Path for European Integration

Altiero Spinelli (1907–1986), an Italian visionary for a united Europe, begun his political activism by joining the Italian Communist party in resistance against the Fascist regime of Benito Mussolini. In 1927 Spinelli was arrested and convicted to ten years in prison and six years in a confinement on the island of Ventotene. On

[10] McAllister (2009), pp. 135 ff.

Ventotene, he converted from a committed communist into a European federalist, writing a manifesto for a Free and United Europe. After the fall of Fascism and end of World War II, he became an active leader of the European federal movement and eventually, one of the most influential members of the European Parliament.[11]

Spinelli and other European federalists were at the forefront of a group of Parliament activists who pressed it into drafting a reform treaty for European integration.[12] In the 1980s, a special committee, with Spinelli as chairman, started to draft the treaty to establish European Union, and this venture became also known as the "Spinelli project". The committee proposed the creation of a European organisation based on the principles of integration rather than intergovernmentalism, aiming at transforming the decision-making process to being based on the principle of majority instead of unanimity. Spinelli's committee presented a detailed plan for the reform, highlighting the role of the European Parliament as the central institution of the Union. The plan was approved by a vast majority in the European Parliament and presented to the Member States. While some national parliaments voted on and indeed approved it, most Member States, however, were unwilling to take such a major step towards European integration and consequently rejected it. This initial setback notwithstanding, the draft triggered a debate over reforming the EC and became the basis of one of the most important treaties in the integration process, the SEA. This and later treaties entailed many ideas by Spinelli, who, despite having failed to create the federal European state, remains one of the founding fathers of the European Union.

In the late 1970s, Germany's and Italy's Foreign Affairs ministers, Hans Dietrich Genscher and Emilio Colombo[13] began drafting another reform treaty that emphasised three main points:

- Decision-making processes in the EC needed a reform. The draft proposed to replace the unanimity principle with a more flexible and less complex system based on a qualified majority, where Member States had a different number of votes corresponding to the size of their population, territory, economic power, etc.
- The second pillar of their report was a closer integration of political and economic cooperation. Cooperation within the EC had been mainly economic, with politics being only a residual part. The report proposed political integration on the premise that unless economic integration was not protected by legal and political regulations concurrent on the European level, it would risk collapse.
- The report also highlighted the importance of integration in security and defence. After the failure of the European Defence Community and the European Political Cooperation, this was a risky proposal that was almost bound to receive only lukewarm support from Member States. Even the United States, traditionally a

[11]For Spinelli's formative role, see esp. Burgess (2000) and Corbett (1998).

[12]For Spinelli's politics and its legacy, see also Glencross and Trechsel (2010).

[13]Hill and Smith (2003), pp. 120 ff.

supporter of integration in Europe, had distrusted this plan because in the Cold War context it could have meant dissension among the Allies.

The draft was not adopted by the Member States, but like Spinelli's project, it highlighted the need for reform and put forth ideas on possible future paths. The report prefigured the Stuttgart Declaration of 1983 and indirectly the SEA. Some of its ideas also feature in the Maastricht Treaty of 1992.

The European Commission similarly presented its own plan for reforming the EC. Under the leadership of its new and dynamic president, Jacques Delors, it presented a plan that included 279 legislative measures needed to complete the Common Market.[14] The plan outlined a timeline and proposed a deadline of 31 December 1992. Hence, the three major institutions of the European Communities—the Parliament through Spinelli's working group, ministers representing the governments of the Member States, and the European Commission—presented their own different but connected plans for advancing European integration.

4 National Leaders as European Visionaries

The 1980s saw major changes in the European national political arenas. New leaders came into office, introducing novel ideas and willing to further European cooperation.[15] Three most influential among them were Francois Mitterrand, Helmut Kohl, and Margaret Thatcher. The French socialist president seemed to breath fresh air into the relations between the EC and France. He was outspokenly pro-European and favourably disposed towards a new treaty. His approach towards the Community[16] can be summarised in the following main points:

- Rejection of any reform of the CAP. During the 1980s there was a widely shared willingness to reform this policy because of its high financial cost. But as France was its main beneficiary and any cuts would have harmed its agricultural sector, still a significant source of votes, Mitterand opposed changing it.
- An open attitude towards increasing multinational powers of the European institutions in some fields, even if it had minor negative effects on national sovereignty. It was expected that the French economy would significantly benefit from the expansion of the Common Market and the Communitarian rule, hence Mitterand accepted some loss of the French autonomy and sovereignty.
- Confidence that cooperation between France and Germany within the EC as was the most efficient means to consolidate and increase French influence in Europe and globally. Mitterand revitalised Franco-German relations to an unprecedented

[14]The plan is available at http://aei.pitt.edu/1007/1/monetary_delors.pdf, accessed 4 January 2017.

[15]Germond (2012).

[16]Haywood (2008).

level, encouraging them to be even more intense than in the period when de Gaulle and Adenauer governed.
- Setting out France's mentorship in Africa. Mitterand included the EC's closer relations with Africa in his political agenda, understanding the EC as a means of France's future influence in Africa. A similar policy was developed by de Gaulle before him and by Sarkozy afterwards.

Helmut Kohl similarly represented a new, outspokenly pro-European current in German politics. His vision for Europe was based on a profound trust in the positive effects of integration and he became a spokesman for a united Europe that would be closer to a federation. Kohl believed integration would be crucial for the further development of the European Communities. He also insisted that in this process, Germany and France should assume a central role.

A configuration of events and developments in the 1980s, such as the economic crisis, the challenges posed by Greece, the accession of Spain and Portugal, the British rebate, conflicts between the European Council and the European Parliament, debates over CAP, the federalist approach taken by the European Parliament after the draft of Spinelli, the contributions of Genscher and Colombo, the integration report of the Commission, and the emergence of new leaders as Mitterrand, Kohl, and Thatcher, made possible the elaboration of a new treaty that changed the way the EC was previously understood and imagined, and laid out the way for the SEA.[17]

5 The Single European Act (1986)

The Single European Act aimed at advancing European integration to both solve the institutional problems of the community as well as to meet key needs of the Member States. It had many contributions from different sources, but essentially was focused on the creation of a single market in Europe. The Common Market failed to exhaustively tackle the multiple obstacles still restricting trade inside the Communitarian area. SEA aimed to solve these problems and hence create a genuinely common economic area in Europe.

The meeting of the European Council in France in 1984 summoned a committee to discuss different proposals and recommendations for reform. The committee was chaired by James Clement Dooge and its report became the basis for the new Treaty and the creation of the European Single Market.[18] The final report of the committee identified the main obstacles to creating a functioning genuinely common European market, including[19]:

[17]Cf. the argument presented in Dyson and Featherstone (1999).

[18]Maynard (1988).

[19]Salmon (1997), pp. 190 ff.

- Technical problems: differences in legislation in Member States had a restrictive effect on trade. According to the national legislation of the Member States, a product could be legal in one Member State but illegal in another—and problems of this kind constituted a significant barrier for the growth of the common economic area. This could be tackled by elaborating common legislation across Europe.
- Free movement of people: There was no cooperation in important fields such as security, delinquency, or immigration between states that sought to abolish internal borders. The creation of a common economic area also meant the free movement of products and economic agents, companies and people. Similarly, criminality could move freely inside the area, and hence increased cooperation to counter its free movement was needed before creating the common area. Previously, the common area existed mainly for goods, which could pass borders without major controls, yet checked in the city of arrival—now, internal borders needed to be eliminated completely. The Schengen agreement abolished permanent controls in the inner borders of the Union, with some exceptions because of security reasons.
- A common economic area needed a common currency to increase and facilitate commercial exchanges. The problem was pointed out after the ratification of the SEA and the creation of the Single Market. This eventually led to the creation of the Euro, which came to be shared by many of the members, eliminating hence another barrier to Communitarian trade.
- The common economic area also needed common access to the sources of energy. There were no European electricity and gas networks—only national energy markets lacking almost any connections between the Member States. Access to energy as a crucial component in any industrial and commercial activity, it was argued, should be similar in the entire common area to ensure similar production conditions. If companies of one Member State enjoy lower energy costs or superior access to energy they gain an unfair advantage and the market is distorted. The creation of European gas and electricity networks has been a priority area for the European Union since the Single Market, but it has remained a major challenge.
- Fiscal barriers deriving from differences in taxation systems. One of the four freedoms of the Single Market is free movement of capital, but it has still not been achieved in the context of finances being channelled to Member States where taxation is lower, such as Luxembourg, with the consequent loss for the original country. Also, different taxation levels influence the competitiveness of companies and their choice of geographical location. This can lead to significant market distortion: when taxation is lower in a particular state within the common economic area, its companies can sell their products with a lower price and consequently sell more. At the same time, if the economic area is without borders, companies can move their production freely within it and thus their geographical position becomes irrelevant. Businesses are more likely to move to a Member State with a lower level of corporate taxation like for example happened when many moved their operations to Ireland. Indirect taxes like the rate of VAT

similarly influence the free movement of goods. Hence, additional harmonisation would still be needed, but Member States are reluctant to renounce any sovereignty in these matters—which admittedly remains essential, for example, for preserving their social security and other policies. Because of the Single Market, a debate on the standardisation of taxes in Europe has begun and is likely to remain an important component of the planning of European integration.

The creation of a functioning common market and the elimination of the still existing distortions can be achieved with two different kinds of measures:

- Affirmative actions: Legislation on the European level, harmonisation of the different regulations in Member States. The EC could launch their own legislative initiatives in the Single Market after the adoption of the SEA. When the Community adopts any new legislation, it becomes automatically binding on Member States and any national legislation in conflict with the European legislation is amended accordingly. After the SEA, the EC legal initiatives increased substantially, and its main aim has been to overcome national barriers to free trade.
- Negative actions: The European institutions can sanction actions against the principles underlying Single Market. These actions are mainly prohibitions of state actions with a restrictive effect on Communitarian trade. Normally these measures are consequence of the litigation between different parties and the judgements of the European High Court of Justice.[20]

6 The Single Market and Political Integration

The single market is the main achievement of the SEA. When previously the Member States had national markets with national rules and freedom for the economic agents to act in the entire state, the single market aimed to do the same on the European level.

To create an internal market, one of the starting tasks was to define what “a good” was, or in other words, what can be traded in the common area. In the European Communities, “a good” was defined as any product valuable in money and used for trading.[21] After defining “a good”, it was determined that goods could be traded freely on entire the internal European market: the goods produced or substantially transformed in a Member State, as well as foreign products after customs taxes. The next step was abolishing customs inside the Communities and having common borders for products from outside the common area. The main challenge here was to abolish measures—of a variety of different names and forms—that all were of the

[20]An example is the conclusion of the European Commission that Estonia granted inappropriate state aid to its national air carrier, Estonian Air, and the subsequent order to repay the state aid, summarised in the EC statement: http://europa.eu/rapid/press-release_IP-15-6023_en.htm.

[21]Barnard and Scott (2002).

equivalent effect to customs. Mainly these comprised of discriminatory internal taxes that protected national production against the competition of other European companies. Finally, to build a functioning internal market also fiscal cooperation was needed. However, this was still being planned and would become one of the major steps in European political integration in the coming years.

Margaret Thatcher was an outspoken advocate of the single market and of abolishing the still many barriers to free trade between states. Yet, she had little interest in political integration, in fact, she was openly hostile to the idea. In this sense, given that the integration of the European market led finally to the common currency, and indirectly also contributed to the expansion of the qualified majority system and granting of more power to the EU institutions, her support of the market seems self-contradictory and surprising. Even if Thatcher indeed obtained the British rebate, this seems like a minor compensation for the partial loss of sovereignty of the British Parliament. Thatcher's support could also be explained by a miscalculation of the political ramifications of what seemed like a merely economic treaty or by an over-calculation of her own influence. Also, further political implications and developments unfolded after Thatcher had passed on the premiership and the next prime ministers did not use their vetoes to block political integration. Thatcher herself, indeed, as we can see from her speeches as member of the British parliament, became a fierce critic of the Treaty of Maastricht and the Common Currency—reforms ironically unthinkable without the SEA.

References

Baquero J, Closa C (eds) (2009) European integration from Rome to Berlin, 1957–2007. History, law and politics. Peter Lang, Brussels

Barnard C, Scott J (eds) (2002) The law of the single European market: unpacking the premises. Hart Publishing

Burgess M (2000) Federalism and European Union: the building of Europe, 1950–2000. Routledge, London

Butler D (1975) The British general election of October 1974. Macmillan, Basingstoke

Corbett R (1998) The European Parliament's role in greater EU integration. Palgrave

Dyson K, Featherstone K (1999) The road to Maastricht: negotiating economic and monetary union. Oxford University Press, Oxford

Furlong R (2005) "Review of Kohl's memoirs", available at: http://news.bbc.co.uk/1/hi/world/europe/4403002.stm, 03.11.2016

Germond C (2012) Dynamic Franco-German Duos: Giscard-Schmidt and Mitterrand-Kohl. In: Jones E, Menon A, Weatherill S (eds) The Oxford handbook of the European Union. Oxford University Press, Oxford, pp 193–205

Glencross A, Trechsel A (2010) EU federalism and constitutionalism: the legacy of Altiero Spinelli. Lexington, Plymouth

Gowland D, Turner A, Wright A (2010) Britain and European integration since 1945: on the sidelines. Routledge, New York

Haywood E (2008) European agenda. The European policy of Francois Mitterrand. J Common Mark Stud 31(2):269–283

Hill C, Smith K (eds) (2003) European foreign policy: key documents. Routledge, London

Maynard G (1988) The economy under Mrs. Thatcher. Blackwell, Oxford
McAllister R (2009) European Union: an historical and political survey. Routledge, London
Nugent N (1999) The government and politics of the European Union. Macmillan, Basingstoke
Ramiro Troitiño D (2014) The British position towards European integration: a different economic and political approach. Balt J Eur Stud 4:119–136
Ramiro Trotiño D (2013) European integration: building Europe. Nova Publishers, New York
Salmon T (1997) Building European Union: a documentary history and analysis. Manchester University Press, Manchester
Skogstad G, Verdun A (eds) (2010) The common agricultural policy: policy dynamics in a changing context. Routledge, London
Tsoukalis L (1981) The European community and its Mediterranean enlargement. George Allen & Unwin, London
Wall S (2008) A stranger in Europe: Britain and the EU from Thatcher to Blair. Oxford University Press, Oxford
Winn N (1997) European crisis management in the 1980s: the inherent tension between bilateralism collectivism and national interest. In: Jørgensen K (ed) European approaches to crisis management. Kluwer Law International

British Approach to the European Union: From Tony Blair to David Cameron

Holger Mölder

Abstract Prime Ministers Tony Blair, Gordon Brown, and David Cameron all were supportive towards the European integration, but as they attempted to combine it with the powerful images of British otherness and island nation, British foreign and security policy doctrines have paid tribute to the British exceptionalism and the special relationship policy with the United States. The exceptionalist neo-conservative doctrine of the George W. Bush administration of the United States produced a gap between Atlanticist and community-oriented EU nations. In sum it forced the British government to develop more Atlanticist stand in its foreign and security policy and gave rise to the integration dilemma with the Franco-German alliance. Following the Global War on Terrorism, national security issues became more prevalent and pushed cooperative politics of the 1990s into the background. Later, the Euro-zone crisis and the migration crisis weakened the European unity and nationalist movements became stronger. In Britain, euroscepticist UKIP has met success in the European Parliament elections. As follows, the Conservative Party adopted more eurocritic positions on the European Union and David Cameron decided to lead the British nation to the secessionist referendum—Brexit.

1 Introduction

The process of Europeanisation, which aimed multifaceted and comprehensive integration for ensuring welfare, security, and stability among the European nations, started after the World War II and since the 1950s prevailed in the continental Europe. The United Kingdom (UK) has traditionally practiced more independent policy and distanced itself from the timely processes of continental Europe. The image of "island nation" frequently appears in political discourses emerging in the UK, which emphasises their unique role as balancer in the European political

H. Mölder (✉)
Department of Law, School of Business and Governance, Tallinn University of Technology, Tallinn, Estonia
e-mail: holger.molder@ttu.ee

D. Ramiro Troitiño et al. (eds.), *Brexit*,
https://doi.org/10.1007/978-3-319-73414-9_9

landscape. The British political identity stresses their otherness, which places them somewhere between the rest of Europe and the United States (US). Moreover, the British foreign policy strategy strongly relies on the doctrine of special relationship with the United States, which was born during the World War II, when two nations led the anti-Nazi coalition and attached themselves as architects of the new post World War II world order. In his famous speech in Fulton on 5 March 1946, Winston Churchill stated that a special relationship between the British Commonwealth and Empire and the United States . . ..

> . . .requires not only the growing friendship and mutual understanding between our two vast but kindred systems of society, but the continuance of the intimate relationship between our military advisers, leading to common study of potential dangers, the similarity of weapons and manuals of instructions, and to the interchange of officers and cadets at technical colleges.[1]

Security-related discourses have strongly influenced global politics in the twentieth century, which survived two world wars and Cold War's arms race caused by ideologically driven bipolarity. During the Cold War the US, despite not being geographically linked to Europe, became a major regional power in the Western Europe after taking responsibility to defend Europe against the potential Soviet attack. The US was considered to be the only power, which was able to balance Soviet military capabilities. Since World War II the British governments have been rather keener to develop transatlantic partnership with the United States than to build a strong strategic link with continental powers of Europe. Such policy in many ways favoured eurosceptic discourses, which appeared in the UK society. The British otherness, which particularly affected eurosceptic attitudes, was strongly related to historical memory of the British Empire as probably the first global power in the world history. Otherness has always been valued in the different formations of the British society and produced popular images that the British identity is something unique, much different from the continental Europe. It is favouring cautiousness towards pro-European narratives and is portraying such narratives as a threat to traditional values and identity based on the British national pride and sovereignty.[2]

The post-World War integrationist model of Europeanisation, based on a new Franco-German alliance, prevailed in continental Europe and left UK bystander on European issues. The UK joined the European Economic Community (EEC) after heated debates just in 1973, which was confirmed by the referendum of 1975. The decision to move closer to the rest of Europe and to promote closer economic ties with the continental Europe was mainly favoured among the political and business elites, while a big part of the British society felt shy towards the entire process of Europeanisation. In the 1960s–1970s, the Conservative Party led by Edward Heath became the strongest advocate of the British membership in the EEC, but the eurosceptic wing of the Conservatives, which characterised mostly Conservatives

[1]Harris and Tichenor (2010), p. 252.

[2]Shaw (2015).

outside of establishment, who did not occupy high-ranking positions in the party leadership, was always strongly manifested in these debates and year after year became more powerful. After being defeated in the next parliamentary elections of 1974, Edward Heath was replaced by Margaret Thatcher as a new leader of the Conservative Party. Thatcherite Conservatives were critical towards the further integration of Europe, but never opposed it. The Labour Party at the same time was split by supporters and oppositionists of the European integration. Especially its left wing opposed joining the continental integration and the Labour Party became more pro-European since Neal Kinnock leadership of the 1980s.

Tony Blair and David Cameron can be identified as politicians representing opposite poles of the British political tradition, but there are some common features in their political agenda—though being overall pro-European politicians supportive to further integration and community-building in Europe, they both were committed to the concept of British exceptionalism, an exclusive political doctrine, which is perfectly manifesting otherness described before. Exceptionalism is a political ideology, which believes that one nation can be regarded differently from other members of international society because of their own specific values, which could be served as a model for other nations. There is no a central political or legal concept, which may be used in definition of exceptionalism, therefore in the IR-literature exceptionalism is primarily related to the American exceptionalism, widely used as a model of exceptionalism.[3]

The British exceptionalism[4] pretends to the role of pivotal nation, which has always characterised British policy towards the European community in the post-World War II era and manifests its exclusiveness from continental Europe with its unifying integration policy wave. Wallace[5] refers to the myth of British exceptionalism—a free country confronting an unfree European continent, as a cornerstone of the British political culture. The presence of adversarial and confrontational myth-induced narratives can explain why the British euroscepticism was able to retain its core public support for 40 years after joining the EEC. By Andrew Glencross,[6] the British euroscepticism has traditionally set upon two fear-based narratives: first the EU membership would be somehow unfair or restrictive to free trade and global interests of the United Kingdom, and the second one refers to lacking consent in European integration among the public opinion of the British society. This chapter looks at how the British exceptionalism never disappeared from the British foreign policy doctrines during the last 20 years and finally led the nation to Brexit.

---

[3]Nolte and Aust (2013), p. 409.

[4]See Ash (2001), Eatwell (2016), Gifford (2008), Glencross (2014), Nugée (2013) and Tournier-Sol and Gifford (2015).

[5]Wallace (1991).

[6]Glencross (2014), p. 3.

2 Tony Blair and his Exceptionalist Doctrine

Even pro-European and integrationist politicians like Tony Blair were not able to completely distance themselves from the societal power of British otherness and paid tribute to the British exceptionalism. The fear of centre's (Brussels's) dictate and losing sovereignty in the integrated EU decision-making process has always been a handful political tool for promoting populism. The Labour Party was split on the European integration issue for years. In the 1970s the left side of Labour led by Michael Foot and Tony Benn opposed joining the EEC and at that time they were supported by a young Jeremy Corbyn, which may now explain why the current leader of Labour Party has been inconsistent in his support to the Remain campaign during the Brexit referendum.[7] The leftist circles of Labour complained that EEC rules constrain statist solutions to UK economic woes, fearing that Brussels can overrule nationalisation and other realms of leftist industrial policy.[8] In the 1970s and early 1980s, the Labour Party was much more committed to eurosceptical policies than their Conservative opponents. In 1981 the moderate and more European-friendly wing of Labour left the party and formed the Social Democratic Party, which later joined to the Liberal Democratic Party. Since 1983, after Neil Kinnock was elected a new leader, the Labour Party mostly gave up from its former steady euroscepticism and started to manifest pro-European stands, while Margaret Thatcher and the Conservative Party under her leadership became increasingly eurocritic.

Anthony Charles Lynton (Tony) Blair was elected a Labour Party leader in 1994. His political agenda stressed on moving towards change and national renewal. After 20 years of domination of the Conservative Party led by Margaret Thatcher and John Major, the British society was tired from Thatcherism based on support to free markets, financial discipline, tax cuts, small government, privatisation, restraints set to labour unions and tight control over the public expenditures that offered a momentum for alternative approaches. Thatcherism has proved success in improving national economy and gained popularity in the UK rebate issue by reducing British contribution to the EU budget, but the macroeconomical success was accompanied by social constraints, which drove the potential electorate off. British sociologist Anthony Giddens[9] said on Thatcherism:

> The theory underlying the policies of Margaret Thatcher's and successive Conservative administrations (1979-97) was that cutting tax rates for individuals and corporations would generate high levels of economic growth, the fruits of which would then 'trickle down' to the poor. Similar policies were implemented in the USA. But the evidence does not support the 'trickledown' thesis. Such an economic policy may generate an acceleration of economic development, but it also tends to expand the differentials between the poor and the wealthy and increase the numbers living in poverty.

[7]Wilson (2016).

[8]Glencross (2015), p. 556.

[9]Giddens (2009), p. 513.

Young and ambitious Blair seemed to be a suitable person for delivering hope to the British people. In May 1997, he became a new Prime Minister after the Labour Party had a landslide victory in British parliamentary elections. Under Blair's leadership the Labour Party promoted the concept of "New Labour", which was more tolerable towards market economy and intended to build a synthesis from socialism and capitalism influenced by Anthony Giddens and his Third Way concept.[10] Blair's New Labour doctrine was based on social justice, the equal worth of each citizen, equality of opportunity and community.[11] The new leadership of the Labour Party did not completely reject Thatcherism, which proved success in increasing the UK's economic capabilities, and maintained the core principles of political economy of previous cabinets of Thatcher and Major.[12] Blair, in his goals to combine old-style socialism and free-market oriented neoliberalism, attempted to make it more socially oriented and acceptable for those parts of public audience, who had not met economic success during the Thatcherite leadership of the country. Besides being economically more moderate than previous leaders of the Labour, he was deeply committed to the Atlanticist principles of foreign policy. Hereto, Blair was a confirmed proponent of interventionism, who believed that violations against human rights justify external interference and involvement of military forces for that purpose. Blair's commitment to humanitarian interventionism revealed during the Kosovo crisis when he urged reluctant US administration of Clinton to intervene.[13]

In the parliamentary elections of 1997 Blair's campaign carried out probably the most pro-European rally in the British political history, which made him distinct from Thatcherite moderate euroscepticism practiced by previous Conservative governments. His foreign minister Robin Cook declared that the British EU policy will stand on "a constructive spirit of partnership, not in the sterile spirit of oppositionalism."[14] However, in the 1990s, the European integration has been based on the idea of Kantian community widely shared in Western political elites, by which interdependence of liberal-democratic European states has no alternative, because it brings stable peace to Europe. The idea of European community was built on the shared belief on a Kantian peace, common democratic institutions and close economic interdependence.[15] Traditionally the focus on community building and grand projects would best describe the Franco-German view on the European integration, which does not correspond to British "visionless pragmatism."[16] In 2000, Tony Blair made a speech in the British Parliament in which he emphasised the need for modernisation and the European Union would be a key tool for realising it. He said:

---

[10]See i.e. Giddens (1998, 2000).

[11]Tansey and Jackson (2008), p. 97.

[12]See Hay (1999).

[13]Wright (2002).

[14]Dryburgh (2010).

[15]Lucarelli (2002).

[16]Nugée (2013).

> On Europe, standing up for Britain does not mean being anti-Europe. It is not pro-British to be anti-Europe. The EU is part of the modern world. Britain is part of the EU. Standing up for Britain means fighting for British values, getting the best for Britain, whether it is economic reform, moving Europe closer to the USA or protecting the British rebate.[17]

Nevertheless, Blair may sound pro-European in Britain, but in defending the movement towards better integrated European Union, Blair demonstrated his consistent commitment to British exceptionalism: his famous expression of "a bridge between East and West between the United States and the EU" and his support to the UK rebate of 1984.[18] He also emphasised the peculiarity of British otherness in the European context and justified hegemonic world led by the United States, where the fate of Europe will be determined through alliance with the United States because of security requirements.

In his beliefs Blair has always remained a strongly pro-European politician and constantly supported British further integration to the European Union, but his adherence to the special relationship with the United States caused tensions between him and influential politicians from continental Europe, which could be the reason, besides perhaps personal fears in endorsing a strong politician, why German Chancellor Angela Merkel later opposed him becoming the first president of the European Council, the new post created by the Lisbon Treaty. British exclusiveness in the European Union with its numerous opt-outs, including the single currency Eurozone, the passport-free Schengen zone, the Atlanticist foreign policy and active support to the United States on Iraq's war, downplayed Blair's chances in playing significant role in the EU political establishment.[19] Despite toning down in eurocritic rhetoric and presenting integrationist views, Blair retained the core rudiments of British traditional exclusiveness on European matters and the image of island nation, which defines itself neither a European nation nor outsider. This arguably corresponds to the core principles of British exceptionalism.[20]

3 Cooperative Security Dilemma in Europe

Another influential paradigm heading British society towards Brexit would be a cooperative security dilemma emerging between the United States and the Franco-German alliance. It would be argued that exceptionalist policies caused the emergence of integration dilemma in Europe in the 2000s. The Iraqi intervention of 2003 strengthened a split between security-driven Atlanticism favoured by the UK and the European community option favoured by France and Germany. Exceptionalist policies traditionally had a strong influence in the United Kingdom and Nordic

---

[17]Blair (2000).

[18]Ibid.

[19]Traynor (2009).

[20]Ash (2001), p. 5.

societies. Primarily Denmark, Norway and Iceland felt more proximity to the United Kingdom than to the European integration pushed by Franco-German alliance, therefore Norway and Iceland never joined the EU and Denmark similarly to the UK has several opt-outs to the Maastricht Treaty. Later, the American and British exceptionalism influenced the Eastern European nations, which joined EU in 2004, to build their security strategies more on bandwagoning with the US military power than on strengthening common European values and cooperative security capabilities through the EU community-building.

Mouritzen[21] explains the emergence of contrasting views on security with the doctrines that followed a realist tradition of IR theory. The United Kingdom has traditionally balanced any continental power hegemony emerging in Europe throughout Napoleonic France, Nazi Germany and the Soviet Union during the Cold War, therefore Franco-German attempts to build a security and defence union based on community-building model may awaken their "balancing instinct". The George W. Bush administration of the United States in conducting his Global War on Terrorism trusted "coalition of willing" type of interest-based coalitions more than cooperative security mechanisms, was strongly committed to the US national interests and thought little of community-building efforts favoured by the European Union. This strategy easily promoted misperceptions in the EU as in NATO as well and contrasted with the core principles of the Kantian community, to which direction both institutions moved a decade before.

In the 1990s, NATO and EU started to develop cooperative frameworks, in which focus was set on Eastern European nations by enhancing democratisation and supporting security reforms there. Both institutions focused on managing the Balkans crisis, which was the last major obstacle for ensuring stable peace in Europe except some frozen conflicts in the former Soviet republics (e.g. Transnistria, Nagorno-Karabakh, Abkhazija and South Ossetia). For the year of 2003 Europe has entered to the stage of mature anarchy. Barry Buzan[22] identifies mature anarchy as a highly ordered and stable system, where institutionalised norms are regulating relations among actors. Cooperative security dilemma—if some states cooperate to decrease their security fears, this may decrease security of others excluded from cooperative security arrangements—may appear in the security environment, which is highly institutionalised, best describes the European security environment after the Cold War.[23] The integration dilemma would manifest a specific form of cooperative security dilemma, where the state may fear being entrapped in the process of integration, but there also will exist a risk of abandonment from benefits of it.[24] The dissonance on the European further integration and different views on security and defence strategies between the UK and the continental Europe would describe at least some propensity for potential integration dilemma in the future.

[21]Mouritzen (2006), p. 151.

[22]Buzan (1991), p. 77.

[23]Mölder (2011), pp. 148–149.

[24]Wivel (2000), p. 335.

The integration dilemma has been gradually developing among the EU nations after the Maastricht Treaty was signed. Some nations favoured a community method in security and defence matters and had ambitions to include security and defence matters to the strategic agenda of the European Union. Other nations preferred to leave defence matters out of the Union and to rely on individual and US/NATO capabilities as usual. This would characterise the Atlanticist option. Italy, Greece, Spain and Belgium tended to support the community method while the UK, Denmark, Portugal, Ireland and Netherlands moved to the Atlanticist direction.[25] Throughout the 1990s, including the initial period of the Blair government, the United Kingdom opposed the Franco-German attempts to promote a co-ordinated EU approach to common defence.[26] However, during the British EU presidency in the first half of 1998, the UK took more integrationist view on security matters and started to cooperate with France to abolish the Western European Union (WEU) and to transfer its political functions over to a new fourth pillar of the EU.

Consequently, Tony Blair has become a co-founder of the Common Security and Defence policy. In December 1998, he met President of France Francois Mitterrand in Saint-Malo and United Kingdom and France signed a joint declaration, which made a commitment to build the credible military capability of the European Union able to conduct autonomous actions. Both countries recognised the need of the EU to exercise its full capabilities to response to international crises (Joint Declaration, 1998).[27] Next year, the European Union launched a military component to its political and economic power and decided to increase its crisis management capabilities.[28] The active involvement in the development of the security and defence pillar of the European Union indicates that Blair at least intended to overcome a gap between US and EU in security matters and believed to the availability of synchronised mechanisms that would join EU and NATO capabilities without producing mutual misperceptions between two institutions that would finally lead to cooperative security dilemma.

During the Cold War, the United States has taken much responsibility on defence of the European nations. Starting from the 1990s the Americans started to criticise Europeans as they might be not very dedicated on raising self-defence capabilities and too much burden have been placed on US taxpayers. In February 1991, France and Germany stated on Common Foreign and Security Policy that the construction of the European Union would remain incomplete without a common European defence system, which should rely on WEU capabilities. France and Germany agreed that EU should play a more important role and take more responsibilities on security and defence matters and their contribution should also strengthen NATO.[29] The US administration of George Bush and its neo-conservative doctrine

---

[25]Laursen (1996), p. 162.

[26]Williams (2002).

[27]Joint Declaration on European Defence Joint Declaration issued at the British-French Summit (1998).

[28]Giegerich et al. (2006).

[29]Laursen (1996), p. 159.

made significant changes to US security strategies that finally influenced the emergence of cooperative security dilemma in Europe. Following the terrorist attack of 11 September 2001, the US not just focused on its national security, but became more concerned on global security issues, particularly spreading of US national interests supported by their military power, which returned US exceptionalism to the global arena.

The Iraqi intervention of 2003 induced fundamental disagreements between the Western nations. Neo-conservative challenge to the post-Cold War community building process produced that transatlantic link between the United States and the continental Europe led by Germany and France was seriously damaged. United Kingdom and the Blair's cabinet sided in the emerging cooperative security dilemma with the United States.[30] Mouritzen[31] distinguishes transatlantic and continental approaches to European security, in which first approach recognises a specific role of the United States as a world hegemon by identifying itself primarily as an US ally in the unipolar world. This option in the European Union was led by the United Kingdom and supported first by Denmark, Poland, and the Baltic states. These nations emphasised a central role of national security in their particular strategic cultures, which led to practicing exceptionalist policies. NATO was to the Atlanticists nothing more than just a military alliance of nations with similar interests. Another way, which characterised France, Germany, Belgium, and later Spain, became critical on US hegemony and its military interventionism forced by the Global War on Terrorism, especially on the light of Iraqi war of 2003.

The Euro-Atlantic integration dilemma stems from post-Iraqi intervention consequences that the US and EU are no longer allies if it concerns their willingness to wield their power to coerce other states.[32] It is widely believed that Blair's involvement in enhancing areas for EU integration made him "the most pro-European British Prime Minister in a generation."[33] Just few years after the Saint-Malo declaration the United Kingdom suddenly found itself on the other side from its continental partners in the European Union. Blair's government, instead of building bridge between contrasting strategies and mitigating the emerging cooperative security dilemma, went along the new trends of its major ally and distanced itself from continental Europe and unwillingly facilitated the emergence of integration dilemma produced by the US-EU relationship. However, as Dryburgh[34] argues "the policies of New Labour represented more a form of tactical adaptation than a seismic shift in British policy."

Peterson[35] claims that Blair's government though believed to be pro-European was probably the most critical towards Brussels than any other government of large

---

[30] Mölder (2011), pp. 149–150.

[31] Mouritzen (2006), pp. 138–139.

[32] Peterson (2006), p. 7.

[33] Howorth (2003–2004).

[34] Dryburgh (2010), p. 258.

[35] Peterson (2006), p. 11.

EU members states at that time. The image of "weak and fading" Europe has gotten strength from the Atlanticist strategies if to refer Robert Kagan's[36] powerful image on differences between Europeans of Venus and Americans from Mars. In his own way Blair, though a strong supporter of the European integration, played the cards down to the political forces joined under the Brexit slogan. Consequently, the United Kingdom was rather committed to the role of faithful US ally in the Global War on Terrorism than it attempted to build bridge between two shores of the Atlantic Ocean as it was declared by Prime Minister Blair in his speech.[37] The integration dilemma driven by the US interventionist strategy divided Europe into two and strategic differences on security and defence matters between those two opposite perspectives were capable to lead the European community building process, which in the 1990s seemed unstoppable for many, to a dead end.

4 From British Otherness to Re-Birth of English Nationalism

The first decade of twenty-first century has been characterised by the wars in Afghanistan and Iraq and followed by the global economic crisis, which brought along the rise of nationalism. The US administration of George W. Bush became critical to liberal institutionalism, which dominated the global politics in the 1990s. The neo-conservative doctrine, which strongly influenced the US foreign policy during the Bush administration, called for heroic vision of national interests and national greatness.[38] While conservative views traditionally tend to be more supportive to isolationism in their foreign policy doctrines, the neo-conservatives adopted interventionist principles and tied them to the principles of American exceptionalism. The rising trend of US exceptionalism promoted by Bush and his administration was expressed by the negative positions taken towards the US participation in several multilateral international agreements (i.e. the Kyoto Protocol on Climate Change, the International Criminal Court). The contrasting views on the Iraqi intervention were not the only ones that produced gap between the United States and the Franco-German alliance. Their views diverged on missile defence, Kyoto Protocol, trade policy and the Middle East.[39]

The new emerging nationalist trend accompanied with anti-liberal views in domestic policy and opposition to liberal institutionalism in foreign policy gained popularity among some conservative politicians in Europe. The integration dilemma was not just a purely foreign or security policy issue, but was expanded to the integrationist-nationalist debates, which appeared in several European societies.

[36]Kagan (2003).

[37]Blair (2000).

[38]Williams (2007), p. 106.

[39]Wright (2002).

Already in 1999, after the parliamentary elections in Austria, Jörg Haider's far right the Freedom Party was included in the coalition government that caused tensions between Austria and the rest of European Union. In 2002, a French nationalist politician Jean-Marie Le Pen surprisingly finished second in French presidential elections, which gave a clear sign of new trend of nationalist and anti-integrationist sentiments is emerging in Europe. Most significantly the rebirth of nationalist ideology appeared in Poland under the government of Law and Justice Party since 2005 ruled by Kaczynski brothers. The rise of Vladimir Putin with his national rebirth oriented doctrines in Russia also corresponds to the trend described above.[40]

Though returning nationalism of European nations may be boosted by the US neo-conservative ideological challenge to integrationist trends of the 1990s, the core of European nationalism tends to have more isolationist character and excludes spread of democracy and humanitarian interventionism typical to neo-conservative patriotism from its agenda. Britishness built on traditional values of the British society has become an attractive response to the European integration, which covered different groups of society and was able to seize the crowds. Moreover, unlike in the continental Europe, in Britain euroscepticist views have been loudly supported by the British media and members of political establishment. In 2001, openly eurosceptic Ian Duncan Smith won in the Conservative Party leadership elections. Glencross[41] points out that "the pro-EU constituency in Britain cannot count on the unwavering support of established elites." Daddow[42] claims that "UK politicians have effectively handed over ideational leadership on European matters to a press-dominated UK media which has found since the Maastricht Treaty that there are increasing numbers of opportunities to express opposition to the European project."

Narratives favouring exceptionalism in the European discourses often emphasise the centre and periphery dichotomy in which imperialistic ambitions of anonymous Brussels have been balanced by the sovereign rights for self-government. In his speech "Britain and Europe", Prime Minister David Cameron[43] clearly emphasised the distinction between the national own and the European other. Such associations have been widely used by nationalist politicians representing eurosceptic circles in Britain and elsewhere in Europe—good national policies could oppose the dictate of anonymous Brussels. The agenda of harsh criticism towards integrationist ambitions of Brussels has become widely practiced in British political debates and gained much public popularity. However, the constant presence of euroscepticism in the British political environment was never formed into a strong political party able to victoriously run in national elections. The Conservatives, once leaders of joining the EEC, started gradually to move to the eurosceptic side of the political spectrum. During the Brexit campaign, the Conservative politicians representing the party

[40]Mölder (2010), p. 156.

[41]Glencross (2014), p. 8.

[42]Daddow (2015), p. 152.

[43]Cameron (2013).

establishment like Boris Johnson or Michael Gove successfully took a lead in the anti-EU movement and left pure euroscepticist movements like UKIP or British National Party to play just supportive secondary roles.

In the United Kingdom, the Conservative Party has represented distant views on European integration, but before the Brexit campaign started they never were willing to take a strong euroscepticist lead. Such a role largely remained to minor parties like the United Kingdom Independence Party (UKIP), which represents a large section of political interests in the UK that are hostile to the European Union.[44] UKIP was founded already in 1993 based on small eurosceptic party the Anti-Federalist League and promoted eurosceptic traditionalism, which was traditionally omitted to the right wing of the Conservative Party. In 1999, UKIP met its first success in the European Parliament elections after winning three seats. Support to UKIP significantly increased in next elections to the European Parliament as in 2004 they were able to get 12 places, which made them third UK party after the Conservatives and Labourites by the number of representatives in the European Parliament. The Liberal Democrats got also 12 seats, but had fewer votes.

The trend of growing influence of UKIP was gradually increasing. Five years later, because of the next elections of 2009, UKIP had already 13 seats in the European Parliament. In 2014, UKIP was already a winner with 24 seats in the European Parliament, followed respectively by the Labour Party with 20 seats and the ruling Conservative Party found itself just in the third place with 19 seats. The strong appearance of UKIP in the European Parliament elections strengthened positions of eurosceptic views in the Conservative Party, which was a traditional leader of moderate euroscepticism composed of the Thatcherite economic policy and the rejection of the single currency. However, UKIP was less competitive in national elections, unable to win any seats in the British Parliament in elections of 2005 (2.2% of votes) and 2010 (3.1% of votes). First representative of UKIP was elected to the House of Commons in 2015, when the party was placed third in total votes with 12.6%. This can be explained with the different voting system. The proportional system, practiced in the European Parliament elections, supported the brand UKIP, although it was not covered by respected politicians. Another factor ensuring their success in the European Parliament elections may indicate that a typical British voter has had fewer interests on European matters, which allowed interest groups with particularly strong views on these issues to make a better result.

Schnapper[45] notes that British euroscepticism has recently become less exceptional in the European Union as it was in the 1990s as similar movements have strength both in France (*Front National*) and Germany (*AfD*). However, while the continental anti-European parties tend to represent political fringes from left or right, concerning mainly protest parties almost never except for *Fidesz* in Hungary or *Lega Nord* in Italy are represented in ruling coalition, the British euroscepticism has spread among the mainstream political parties. There was a momentum of the

---

[44]Gifford (2008), p. 143.

[45]Schnapper (2015).

growing wave of euroscepticism for the United Kingdom to leaving the European Union and the Conservative government of David Cameron unwillingly, but skilfully used this momentum for that purpose.

Besides the traditional British euroscepticism, a new trend of English nationalism got up steam and gave a major boost to the rise of UKIP. Since 2006, after Nigel Farage was elected to lead the UKIP, it applied for support of economically distressed British working class, who was worried of the increasing presence of primarily Eastern European immigrants in the British soil. England, especially its rural areas, which have been more disappointed by the economic situation and more influenced by local nationalism, formed the strongest basis for the pro-Brexit voters in the referendum of 2016. The traditional conservatism, which characterises US supporters of Donald Trump and the UK supporters of Brexit, relies on defensive nationalism of preserving traditional values, while neo-conservativism encourages offensive patriotism of expanding the influence of values. The Brexit was overwhelmingly supported by rising trend of defensive English nationalism, which is different from moderately eurosceptic conservative Britishness. The English nationalism includes "more nativism and more "Little England" nationalism, which can veer into xenophobia."[46]

5 The Failure of Gordon Brown

The failure of New Labour policy was another significant factor that caused the movement towards Brexit. Although in the 1970s the Labour Party led the opposition to the entering European Economic Union, during the Blair's government Labour Party together with Liberal Democrats became strongest advocates of the European integration in the British soil. The Labour Party won the parliamentary elections of 2005 despite widely unpopular involvement into the Iraqi intervention of 2003. This happened mainly because the British economy maintained a good condition, which guaranteed advantage over the Conservative Party led by Michael Howard at this time. However, it was the last success of the Labour Party for a long time. The threat of international terrorism started to occupy headlines of media channels. Moreover, the United Kingdom witnessed first major evidences of terrorist threats in the London bombings of 2005. When the international system becomes more unstable as it happened after the September 11 attacks in the United States, people tend to value national security guarantees over economic and social benefits. National values will be preferred to universal values. If national security assets will become to play more decisive role in society, the extreme parties will get a chance to enhance their constituencies. It can be seen on the case of UKIP that made its first strong results in the European Parliament elections in 2004. Tony Blair was replaced in 2007 with Gordon Brown as the leader of the Labour Party and the Prime

[46]Erlanger (2016).

Minister. Under the leadership of Blair, the Labour Party managed to win three parliamentary elections in succession. At the same time, his government took Britain to the unpopular Iraqi intervention, which implications were inherited to Gordon Brown.

Brown was considered to be a main architect of the economic success of Blair's government and was therefore a logical choice to succeed Blair. There were rumours spread in the British media that in 1994, when Blair was first time elected to the leader's position, he and Gordon Brown concluded an agreement if Brown supports Blair as a new leader, he will be hold an influential position of Chancellor of the Exchequer and after Blair resigns, he would become his successor as a party leader. In the British political landscape, the New Labour policy promoted by Blair and Brown, despite their strong commitment to the Atlanticism in foreign and security issues, manifested integrationist views especially in comparison with their Conservative opponents. Therefore, the failure of Labour can be related to the weak competitiveness of pro-European politics with British exceptionalism and the growing strength of euroscepticism, which can demonstrate their strength during the crisis. The euro-zone crisis followed by the migration crisis reduced the naturally low attractiveness of the European integration among the British electorate.

The arrival of the Great Recession of 2008–2009, which started shortly after the Brown leadership, turned political winds once again against the Labour Party. While the global economic crisis was in its peak, the United Kingdom failed in economics under the Brown's leadership—public spending was out of control and polls indicated that the electorate felt the state has been allowed to grow too big.[47] With nationalist and security-oriented views getting more support in the British society and global economic crisis downplaying efforts made for improving welfare of the electorate, it finally caused the move of support towards more protectionist policies offered by the eurocritic movements. In the Europarliament election of 2009, the Labour Party became just a third by votes after the Conservative Party and UKIP, which was a clear sign from growing trend of euroscepticist and protectionist attitudes spreading in the British society.

Strengthening positions of British exceptionalism over the European integration were in fact admitted by the Labourite leadership and in several occasions appeared in their political discourses. In 2006, before he was elected a new leader, Gordon Brown delivered a speech at the Fabian Society meeting, in which he portrayed the Labour Party as a modern patriotic party, which should emphasise Britishness. Brown highlighted the US example to follow, as he said: "And what is our equivalent of the national symbolism of a flag in the United States in every garden?"[48] Nevertheless, despite all efforts to shape it accordingly to the newest trends in the British political environment, the project of New Labour promoted by Tony Blair and later by his successor Gordon Brown failed to meet success in redefining the way the British see themselves in their relation to Europe. Neither Blair nor Brown was

[47] Prince (2010).

[48] BBC News (2006).

willing to challenge the narratives promoted in continental Europe.[49] British exceptionalism was able to create numerous obstacles to prosper pro-integrationist policies in the UK. The patriotic spectrum based on eurocritic and protectionist views was already fulfilled by the Conservative Party and UKIP and there was no place for "mild otherness", which is generally supportive to the European integration although emphasising traditional values of British society. Gifford[50] concludes that Blair and Brown have been reluctant to take on right-wing euroscepticism and searched ways of legitimisation for British engagement in the evolving European order.

The failure of Gordon Brown, the Labour Party faced after a landslide defeat in the elections of 2010, marked the failure of New Labour. Next leader of the Labour Party Ed Miliband attempted to hold distance from Blair's and Brown's heritage. He claimed for a new policy, but was not able to establish a new and successful brand competitive to his predecessors. Finally, Miliband remained just a transitional leader and the failure of New Labour was finalised in 2015, when the party after some misleading journeys in its self-searching attempts turned left again, when a prominent politician representing the rebellious left side of the party Jeremy Corbyn with support of trade unions was elected a new leader of the Labour Party. During the Blair and Brown leadership, Corbyn was a backbench parliamentarian, who often disagreed with the leadership. The triumph of Corbyn marked the return of leftist spectrum of the Labour Party, which has traditionally supported more euroscepticist positions.

6 The Pyrrhic Politics of David Cameron

In 2010 the Labour Party led by Gordon Brown lost general elections to Conservatives led by David Cameron. Since the end of 2009 the rapidly evolving Euro-zone crisis influenced the stability of the European Union as several members of Euro-zone met difficulties to repay or refinance their governmental debts. The United Kingdom, although being outside the Euro-zone, still suffered under the negative impact of the crisis through its extensive business contacts, but the worst consequence of the crisis was in promoting distrust against the European integration, which emerged not just in always eurocritic Britain, but all over the European Union. The idea to renegotiate the UK's future membership in the European Union to avoid dealing with the EU's shortcomings gained popularity among the post-Thatcherite generation of Conservative leadership, who successfully integrated with the anti-European trends rising in Europe. The Euro-zone crisis, later followed by the migration crisis, helped to reinforce fear-based narratives that the European integration will jeopardize the British sovereignty.

[49]See Daddow (2011).

[50]Gifford (2008), p. 144.

After relatively young and inexperienced David William Donald Cameron was elected in 2005 to succeed Michael Howard as a new leader of the Conservative Party, he was often compared with Tony Blair. In 2005, Cameron shocked the audience, when at a dinner with newspapers executives he allegedly stated: "I am a hair of Blair."[51] Likewise Blair intended to change the ideological basement of the Labour Party, Cameron was suspected to throw Conservative away from their Thatcherite heritage, while he represented more liberal side of the Conservative Party and stressed on need to modernisation in his leadership campaign. Moreover, and similarly to Blair, he was a staunch supporter of humanitarian intervention and spread of democracy. Cameron[52] said in his speech delivered at the Conservative Party conference:

> I'm not a neo-conservative. I'm a liberal Conservative. Liberal - because I believe in spreading freedom and democracy, and supporting humanitarian intervention. That is why we cannot stand by and watch further genocide in Darfur. But Conservative - because I also recognise the complexities of human nature, and will always be sceptical of grand schemes to remake the world. We need more patience, more humility in the way we engage with the world.

Nevertheless, at the beginning there was nothing, which could predict that Cameron will lead the United Kingdom to Brexit. However, after first signs of crisis appeared, the euroscepticist stronghold in the Conservative Party started to demonstrate its strength and forced the leadership to change policy in the EU direction, where the possible withdrawal from the Union rose again on the agenda after 40 years of first EU referendum in 1975. At the threshold of 2015 election campaign, Cameron made a promise to renegotiate the EU membership and later hold a referendum, hoping to attract eurocritic electorate. He delivered a significant speech on 23 January 2013, in which he introduced the decision to announce the referendum on British withdrawal from the European Union if the renegotiation process on renewed membership conditions will fail. In his speech Cameron[53] referred to well-known narratives traditionally representing the doctrine of otherness: Britishness as the manifestation of an island nation, which identity can be characterised by the image of independent and forthright nation, passionate in defence of its sovereignty. Cameron practiced exclusive view of Europe by referring to Europeans as to collective neighbours representing entity outside of Britain, who live near but not in Britain.[54]

Cameron's appeal to growing nationalist moods in the British society was supposedly an easy opportunity to enforce British otherness on behalf of political support to the Conservative Party. Through contrasting narratives he emphasised self and other logic that would determine relationship between the UK and Europe.[55] The

[51]Pierce (2005).

[52]Cameron (2006).

[53]Cameron (2013).

[54]Spiering (2015), p. 20.

[55]Nugée (2013).

populist rhetoric, which stressed "legal judgments made in Europe" versus "impact on life in Britain" refers to outsider position to the European integration, but at the same time, Cameron never clearly identified Britain as a part of Europe nor as outsider.[56] The message, delivered by Cameron in his speech, was followed by the introduction of the draft of EU Referendum Bill, which was passed by the votes of Conservative majority in the House of Commons, but rejected by the House of Lords. These practical steps were also manifested in political discourses, where powerful narratives of British exceptionalism successfully opposed and neutralised integrationist sentiments.

Cameron's speech strongly emphasised the British exclusiveness towards the European Union and was foremost related to his political survival.[57] Cameron[58] recognised that EU has achieved it first goal to secure peace, but according to his words the overriding purpose of the Union is altogether to secure prosperity. Glencross[59] provides to the debate contrasting views that pushed David Cameron to play risky games between pragmatic Europeanisation and populist otherness.

> The desire for economic self-government, however, pushes free-market ideologues into a contradictory coalition with anti-immigration eurosceptics, whose goal is less market openness, at least when it comes to free movement of workers. Cameron's EU renegotiation gambit is designed to head off this improbable alliance. He needs to demonstrate that the opt-out from the single currency secures Britain against closer union within the euro zone and that EU labour migration is compatible with UK preferences over welfare spending.

The Euro-zone crisis and the European migration crisis have been two fundamental cornerstones of growing euroscepticism among the European nations. The British otherness may see the nation outside the European processes, but nonetheless the euroscepticism in the UK has strength from supporting trends emerging in usually more integrationist continental Europe. Without emerging crisis in the European Union that provided supportive environment, the Brexit referendum would be hardly realisable.

Nevertheless, Cameron has failed to strengthen British positions in the European Union and finally the United Kingdom may lose its credibility as a pragmatic partner to EU's leading nations Germany and France following the renegotiation gambit played by Cameron.[60] The trap of integration dilemma forced Cameron to lead the United Kingdom out from the European Union, to which his predecessor and fellow Conservative Edward Heath has led the nation 43 years earlier. The narrow but clear victory in the Scottish independence referendum of 2014 could also strengthen beliefs that the British electorate will avoid "unreasonable exit" from the European Union. At first glance the Conservative Party reinforced its positions as a leading party. The Conservatives seized the lead in victorious Leave-campaign and

[56]Spiering (2015), p. 19.

[57]Möller and Oliver (2014), pp. 27–30.

[58]Cameron (2013).

[59]Glencross (2015), p. 556.

[60]See Möller and Oliver (2014), Rasmussen (2015) and Oliver (2016).

maintained its positions after the referendum, but their win might also be defined as a Pyrrhic victory, which in many ways forced insecurity in public discourses. The leaders of the Leave campaign Boris Johnson and Michael Gove were excluded from the party leadership competition. David Cameron, who desperately campaigned for Remain, had to step back, and was forced to withdraw from the British politics. However, he put to the shoulders of the new Prime Minister Theresa May a burden, which eventually may significantly weaken political positions of the Conservative Party after the initial euphoria calms down.

7 Conclusions

The concept of British exceptionalism, which endorses otherness feelings towards the rest of Europe, has become increasingly visible in the UK's political discourses after the World War II. Instead of prioritising the European integration representational to the continental powers, it tends to more trust special relationship with the United States, which first bases on shared cultural and historical heritage, but is also often enforced by common security interests. During the last decade misperceptions against prospective benefits of the European integration have been reinforced through the Euro-zone crisis and the migration crisis. Paradoxically a pro-European politician Tony Blair has made a first step in direction that took the country finally out from the European Union. In 2003, the UK government decided to go along the George W. Bush administration and supported the Iraqi intervention, which caused the integration dilemma between Atlanticist and community-oriented nations of the European Union. The UK's Atlanticist foreign policy tradition valued national security assets more than cooperative security options based on further institutionalisation of political decision-making process.

The growing success of UKIP strengthened eurosceptic attitudes in the Conservative Party, which forced David Cameron to conduct Pyrrhic policies that led to the Brexit. Cameron aimed to put Brussels under the pressure, hoping that the Franco-German alliance will be more liable for indulgences and the British status in the Union will be renegotiated. Insecurity has been another supportive factor for the pro-Brexit campaign. The culture of fear based on increasing migration and sovereignty misperceptions definitely played a central role in decision making and forced the majority of British voters to vote for Brexit. British position on European integration has always been exceptionalist and all the governments from Tony Blair to David Cameron have been not able to overcome the natural otherness the British electorate feels towards the continental Europe.

British exceptionalism accompanied with moderate euroscepticism has traditionally characterised the British society, but the crisis within the European Union, primarily manifested by the Euro-zone crisis and the migration crisis, fuelled British euroscepticism and made it stronger. Nationalism took a lead in the British identity politics and enhanced basis for anti-integrationist moods emerged in the period from the Blair's government to the Cameron's government, when national security threats together with economic problems appeared to be among the main concerns in the British society. Nigel Farage succeeded in enhancing social basis of the euroscepticist movement and more exclusive English nationalism raised its head. In conclusion, Brexit seems to be a logical result of politics the UK carried out during the last two decades. Political elites with support of otherness-induced narratives often used to emphasise negative trends related to continental Europe and imperialistic ambitions omitted to Brussels, which strengthened opposition to the European Union.

References

Ash TG (2001) Is Britain European? Int Aff 77(1):1–13

BBC News (2006) Brown speech promotes Britishness. 14 January, http://news.bbc.co.uk/2/hi/uk_news/politics/4611682.stm. Accessed 17 Jan 2017

Blair T (2000) British identity and society. Tony Blair's Britain speech. The Guardian, 28 March, https://www.theguardian.com/uk/2000/mar/28/britishidentity.tonyblair. Accessed 19 Mar 2017

Buzan B (1991) People, states and fear: the National Security Problem in international relations. Harvester Wheatsheaf, New York

Cameron D (2006) The full text of David Cameron's speech to the conservative party conference. BBC News, 4 October, http://news.bbc.co.uk/2/hi/uk_news/politics/5407714.stm. Accessed 18 Mar 2017

Cameron D (2013) The danger is that Europe will fail. Spiegel Online, 23 January, http://www.spiegel.de/international/europe/the-full-text-of-the-david-cameron-speech-on-the-future-of-europe-a-879165.html. Accessed 19 Mar 2017

Daddow O (2011) New labour and the European Union: Blair and Brown's logic of history. Manchester University Press, Manchester

Daddow O (2015) Performing Euroscepticism: the UK press and Cameron's Bloomberg speech. In: Tournier-Sol K, Gifford C (eds) The UK challenge to Europeanization: the persistence of British Euroscepticism. Palgrave Macmillan, New York

Dryburgh L (2010) Blair's first government (1997–2001) and European security and defence policy: seismic shift or adaptation? Br J Polit Int Relat 12(2):257–273

Eatwell R (2016) The extreme right and British Exceptionalism: the primacy of politics. In: Hadsworth P (ed) Politics of the extreme right. From the margins to the mainstream. Bloomsbury Academic, London

Erlanger S (2016) European? British? These 'Brexit' voters identify as English. The New York Times, https://www.nytimes.com/2016/06/17/world/europe/european-union-britain-brexit-voters-english.html?_r=2. Accessed 17 Mar 2017

Giddens A (1998) The third way: the renewal of social democracy. Polity Press, Cambridge

Giddens A (2000) The third way and its critics. Polity Press, Cambridge

Giddens A (2009) Sociology, 6th edn. Polity Press, Cambridge

Giegerich B, Pushkina D, Mount A (2006) Towards a strategic partnership? The US and Russian response to the European security and defence policy. Secur Dialogue 37:385–407

Gifford C (2008) The making of Eurosceptic Britain. In: Identity and economy in a post-imperial state. Ashgate, Aldershot, Hampshire

Glencross A (2014) British Euroscepticism as British Exceptionalism: the forty-year "Neverendum" on the relationship with Europe. Studia Diplomatica LXVII(4):1–12. Various shades of federalism: Which responses to the rise of populism and euroscepticism?

Glencross A (2015) Going it alone? The choice of political Union in British politics. Polit Q 86(4):555–562

Harris RA, Tichenor DJ (eds) (2010) A history of the U.S. political system: ideas, interests, and institutions, vol 1. ABC-CLIO LLC, Santa Barbara
Hay C (1999) The political economy of new labour: labouring under false pretences? Manchester University Press, Manchester
Howorth J (2003–2004) France, Britain and the euro-Atlantic crisis. Survival 45(4):173–192
Joint Declaration on European Defence Joint Declaration issued at the British-French Summit (1998) Saint-Malo, 4 December, http://www.cvce.eu/obj/franco_british_st_malo_declaration_4_december_1998-en-f3cd16fb-fc37-4d52-936f-c8e9bc80f24f.html. Accessed 17 Mar 2017
Kagan R (2003) Of paradise and power: America and Europe in the new world order. Alfred A. Knopf, New York
Laursen F (1996) The common foreign and security policy of the European Union: words vs deeds. In: Peters I (ed) New security challenges: the adaptation of international institutions. St. Martin's Press, New York, pp 153–178
Lucarelli S (2002) Peace and democracy: rediscovered link the EU, NATO and the European system of liberal-democratic security communities. NATO EAPC fellowship final report. http://www.nato.int/acad/fellow/00-02/Lucarelli's.pdf. Accessed 24 Mar 2017
Mölder H (2010) Cooperative security dilemma – practicing the Hobbesian security culture in the Kantian security environment. Tartu Ülikooli Kirjastus, Tartu
Mölder H (2011) The cooperative security dilemma in the Baltic Sea region. J Balt Stud 32(2):143–168
Möller A, Oliver T (eds) (2014) The United Kingdom and the European Union: what would a "Brexit" mean for the EU and other states around the world? DGAPanalyse. Deutsche Gesellschaft für Auswärtige Politik e.V, Berlin
Mouritzen H (2006) Choosing sides in the European Iraq conflict: a test of new geopolitical theory. Eur Secur 15(2):137–163
Nolte G, Aust HP (2013) European exceptionalism? Glob Constitutionalism 2(3):407–436
Nugée J (2013) British exceptionalism and the European Union. Why does the United Kingdom rely so much on an adversarial and confrontational model of political discussion? The Globalist, 7 February, https://www.theglobalist.com/british-exceptionalism-and-the-european-union/. Accessed 19 Mar 2017
Oliver T (2016) European and international views of Brexit. J Eur Publ Policy 23(9):1321–1328
Peterson J (2006) In defence of inelegance: IR theory and transatlantic practice. Int Relat 20(1):5–25
Pierce A (2005) Horror as Cameron brandishes the B word, The Times, 5 October, http://www.thetimes.co.uk/article/horror-as-cameron-brandishes-the-b-word-rfjm9v3xhsh. Accessed 18 Mar 2017
Prince R (2010) Labour lost election because voters turned against big state. The Telegraph, 3 August, http://www.telegraph.co.uk/news/politics/labour/7922677/Labour-lost-election-because-voters-turned-against-big-state.html. Accessed 17 Mar 2017
Rasmussen MK (2015) Heavy fog in the channel. Continent cut off? British diplomatic relations in Brussels after 2010. J Common Mark Stud 54(3):709–724
Schnapper P (2015) The dilemma of pro-European parties in the UK: the case of labour and the liberal democrates since 2010. In: Tournier-Sol K, Gifford C (eds) The UK challenge to Europeanization: the persistence of British Euroscepticism. Palgrave Macmilllan, New York, pp 117–133
Shaw M (2015) Discourses on European integration in the UK Press: an assessment of the new labour era. PSA Annual Conference, Sheffield
Spiering M (2015) The essential Englishman: the cultural nature and origins of British Euroscepticism. In: Tournier-Sol K, Gifford C (eds) The UK challenge to Europeanization: the persistence of British Euroscepticism. Palgrave Macmillan, New York, pp 17–32
Tansey SD, Jackson NA (2008) Politics: the basics, 4th edn. Routledge, New York
Tournier-Sol K, Gifford C (eds) (2015) The UK challenge to Europeanization: the persistence of British Euroscepticism. Palgrave Macmillan, New York

Traynor I (2009) How Angela Merkel quietly sank Tony Blair's bid to become EU president. The Guardian, 29 October, https://www.theguardian.com/world/2009/oct/29/merkel-sank-blair-eu-bid. Accessed 17 Mar 2017
Wallace W (1991) Pride and prejudice, Marxism Today, October, 28–31. http://www.unz.org/Pub/MarxismToday-1991oct-00028. Accessed 19 Mar 2017
Williams P (2002) The Europeanization of British Foreign Policy and the Crisis in Zimbabwe. Paper given to the FORNET workshop at the London School of Economics, 5 June, http://www.lse.ac.uk/internationalRelations/centresandunits/EFPU/EFPUworkshop2002/paper%20-%20Williams.pdf. Accessed 17 Mar 2017
Williams M (2007) Culture and security. Symbolic power and the politics of international security. Routledge, Oxon
Wilson J (2016) Jeremy Corbyn wants Britain to remain in the EU — but here are all the times he said it was bad. Business Insider, 14 April, http://uk.businessinsider.com/jeremy-corbyn-is-making-a-big-speech-saying-we-should-remain-in-the-eu-heres-all-the-times-he-said-the-eu-was-bad-2016-4. Accessed 24 Mar 2017
Wivel A (2000) Theory and prospects for northern Europe's small states. Coop Confl 35(3):331–340
Wright B (2002) Analysis: Anglo-American special relationship, BBC News, 6 April, http://news.bbc.co.uk/2/hi/americas/1913522.stm. Accessed 17 Mar 2017

The Single Currency and the UK

Andres Tupits

Abstract While being part of the European Union, the United Kingdom is under a looser obligation in relation to economic and fiscal policy coordination, it has retained control over its monetary policy and it is not part of the euro area. It has also retained responsibility for the supervision of the United Kingdom banks.

1 Introduction

The United Kingdom occupies a special position outside the euro area. The legal basis for the different treatment of the United Kingdom is the The UK Protocol on certain provisions relating to the United Kingdom of Great Britain and Northern Ireland (hereinafter: '*the UK Protocol*'), which recognises that unless the United Kingdom notifies the Council that it intends to adopt the euro, it shall be under no obligation to do so.[1] The UK Protocol is an integral part of the Treaty on the Functioning of the European Union (TFEU).[2] Notably, Article 282(2) TFEU second sentence "The primary objective of the ESCB shall be to maintain price stability" does not apply to the United Kingdom; neither is the United Kingdom subject to Article 282(5) TFEU regulating the right of the ECB to be consulted on draft legislative instruments of the Union or national authorities and to give an opinion, to name a few. As a result of the exceptions under the UK Protocol, the United Kingdom retains competence for its monetary policy,[3] its fiscal rules are different from other EU Member States subject to European Semester. Further, the United

[1]It has also been suggested that in some regards the United Kingdom can be compared to a Member State with a derogation (Kapteyn and VerLoren van Themaat 2008, p. 941), however such comparison is not entirely accurate.

[2]Article 51 Treaty in European Union (TEU).

[3]It has also been suggested that the United Kingdom's opt-out (and that of the Denmark), constitute and important obstacle to the international projection of the euro (Lastra and Louis 2013, p. 62).

A. Tupits (✉)
Estonian Business School, Tallinn, Estonia
e-mail: Andres.Tupits@ebs.ee

D. Ramiro Troitiño et al. (eds.), *Brexit*,
https://doi.org/10.1007/978-3-319-73414-9_10

Kingdom has distanced itself from the Banking Union,[4] while some of the legal rules that underpin the Banking Union do need to be transposed by the United Kingdom.

2 Economic and Monetary Union

2.1 Single Currency

The European Central Bank (ECB) and the national central banks (NCBs) of the Member States make up the European System of Central Banks (ESCB). As long as not all Member States have adopted the single currency, the ECB and the NCBs in the monetary union together form the Eurosystem.[5] Full participation in the Eurosystem means that the participating Member States have limited their sovereign rights in the field of monetary policy, have submitted their national central banks to the governance of the ECB and transferred national competences in this field entirely to a supranational level (Zilioli and Selmayr 2000, p. 604). Under Article 282 (1) TFEU, the Eurosystem conducts the monetary policy of the Union.[6] Within this system the ECB's Governing Council is in charge of formulating the monetary policy. The ECB's Executive Board implements this policy through the Eurosystem NCBs.[7]

During the negotiations over the Maastricht Treaty, the United Kingdom opted from the commitment to adopt the single currency and join the Eurosystem. Therefore, the Bank of England is part of the ESCB, and its Governor belongs to the ECB's General Council, which comprises the Governors of all NCBs, as well as the President and Vice-President of the ECB.[8] While not being a decision-making body for the Eurosystem or ESCB, the tasks of the General Council under Article 141 TFEU, Articles 43 and 46 of the ESCB Statute are the following:

1. strengthening cooperation between the national central banks;
2. strengthening the coordination of the monetary policies of the Member States, with the aim of ensuring price stability;
3. monitoring the functioning of the exchange rate mechanism;

[4]The Banking Union can be defined as a transfer of responsibility for banking policy from the national to the EU level and entailing the following components: (1) uniform supervision by the European Central Bank; (2) prudential regulation; (3) reorganisation and resolution with common funding; (4) lender of last resort function; (5) deposit insurance.

[5]Article 282(1) TFEU.

[6]Case C-370/12, *Pringle* (27 November 2012), paragraph 49.

[7]Article 12.1 of the ESCB Statute, which from the legal point of view is also a protocol annexed to the EU Treaties, see Protocol (No 4) on the Statute of the European System of Central Banks and of the European Central Bank.

[8]The four other Executive Board members, as well as the President of the EU Council and a member of the European Commission may also participate in General Council meetings, but they do not have a right to vote.

4. holding consultations concerning issues falling within the competence of the national central banks and affecting the stability of financial institutions and markets;
5. carrying out the former tasks of the European Monetary Cooperation Fund, which had subsequently been taken over by the European Monetary Institute;
6. giving advice in the preparations for the entry to the euro area by Member States with a derogation;
7. contributing to the opinions on draft legislative acts of the Union and the Member States;
8. contributing to the collection of statistical information;
9. contributing to the reporting activities of the ECB;
10. contributing to the establishment of the accounting rules for the ESCB;
11. contributing to all other measures necessary for the application of the ECB capital key;
12. contributing to the laying down of the conditions of employment of the staff of the ECB.

While contributing to the above tasks, the Bank of England retains competence for its monetary policy in the United Kingdom,[9] and is not subject to the basic tasks of the ESCB in Article 127(2) TFEU.[10] The United Kingdom's 'out' position vis-à-vis the single currency also means that there is no right to participate in the appointment of the President, Vice-President and the other Members of the Executive Board and that there is no obligation for the Bank of England to fully pay up its part of the ECB's share capital, transfer to the ECB foreign reserve assets and to contribute to its reserves.[11]

2.2 *Primary Objective*

It is unclear whether under the EU law the primary objective of price stability would apply to the Bank of England.

The objectives and tasks of the ESCB as set forth in Article 127(1) to (3) and (5) TFEU,[12] do not apply to the Member States with a derogation under Article 139 (2)(c) TFEU. However, Article 282(2) TFEU and Article 2 of the ESCB Statute, which also refer to the primary objective, do not enjoy a similar derogation, which would therefore mean that the Members States with a derogation are bound by this duty.[13] Article 282(2) TFEU second sentence "The primary objective of the ESCB

[9]Article 3 of the UK Protocol.

[10]Article 4 of the UK Protocol.

[11]Articles 6 and 7 of the UK Protocol.

[12]Also repeated in Article 282(2) TFEU and Article 2 of the ESCB Statute.

[13]Article 42.1 of the ESCB Statute, which provides that a derogation referred to in Article 139 TFEU does not list Article 2 of the ESCB Statute; similarly, there is no exemption regarding Article 282(2) TFEU.

shall be to maintain price stability" does not apply to the United Kingdom. However, it is not clear whether Article 2 of the ESCB Statute applies as this provision is not exempted under the UK Protocol.[14]

Therefore, one might argue that the aim of the UK Protocol was not to bind the central bank for the United Kingdom with the duty to maintain price stability and the omission of reference to Article 2 of the ESCB Statute could have been a mistake.

However, it should be noted that price stability as an objective is mentioned in the Bank of England Act of 1998,[15] which would suggest that Article 2 of the ESCB Statute does in fact apply to the Bank of England, although it is also clear under the UK Protocol that it shall be the Bank of England that shall define its monetary policy.

2.3 *Central Bank Independence*

The principle of central bank independence is derived from Article 130 TFEU and Article 7 of the ESCB Statute. These two articles prohibit the ECB, NCBs and members of their decision-making bodies from seeking or taking instructions from Union institutions and bodies, offices or agencies, from any government of a Member State or from any other body; in addition, they prohibit Union institutions and bodies, offices or agencies and the governments of the Member States from seeking to influence those members of the ECB's or NCBs' decision-making bodies whose decisions may affect the fulfilment of the ESCB-related tasks.[16] These two articles apply to the Member States with a derogation but not to the United Kingdom.[17]

As a result, the United Kingdom NCB is the only member of the ESCB that is not subject to the central bank independence requirement.

2.4 *Independence in National Tasks*

Further to the exception described above, the ECB's Governing Council has no influence over the Bank of England's tasks under national law. Under Article 14.4 of the ESCB Statute NCBs may perform functions other than those specified in the

[14]It is noteworthy that while Article 4 of The UK Protocol provides that, among other, Articles 127 (1) to (5) TFEU and Article 282(2) TFEU, except for the first and last sentences thereof, shall not apply to the United Kingdom, there is no such corresponding duty in Article 7 of The UK Protocol.

[15]See Article 11 of the Bank of England Act of 1998. Notably, the Bank of England's objectives are not determined by the Bank itself but the Treasury under Article 12 of the Bank of England Act of 1998.

[16]Other authors have referred to this prohibition as "'No' to instructions and 'Yes' to dialogue" (Arda 2006).

[17]See Articles 4 and 7 of the UK Protocol.

ESCB Statute. While Article 14.4 of the ESCB Statute applies also to the Member States with a derogation under Article 42 of the ESCB Statute, it does not apply to the United Kingdom under Article 7 of The UK Protocol.

2.5 *Monetary Financing Prohibition*[18]

The monetary financing prohibition is laid down in Article 123(1) TFEU, replicated in Article 21.1 of the ESCB Statute, which prohibits overdraft facilities or any other type of credit facility with the ECB or the NCBs in favour of Union institutions, bodies, offices or agencies, central governments, regional, local or other public authorities, other bodies governed by public law, or public undertakings of Member States, and the purchase of debt instruments directly from these public sector entities by the ECB or NCBs. The precise scope of application of the monetary financing prohibition is further clarified by Council Regulation (EC) No 3603/93[19] (European Central Bank 2016, p. 29).

The prohibition does not apply to publicly owned credit institutions that, in the context of the supply of reserves by central banks, must be given the same treatment as private credit institutions.[20] Therefore, lending by a central bank, including the provision of emergency liquidity assistance for a credit institution owned by public institutions, would not normally fall within the prohibition of monetary financing. This is by analogy with the level playing field for public and private enterprises that has been laid down in Article 106 TFEU, confirming the applicability of the Treaties and, in particular, rules on competition for actions of the Member States in relation to undertakings in conjunction with Article 345 TFEU, establishing the principle of ownership neutrality.

Moreover, Article 21.2 of the ESCB Statute provides a further exception to the prohibition on monetary financing to the extent that it permits the ECB and the NCBs to act as fiscal agents for the entities referred in Article 21.1 of the ESCB Statute.

In accordance with Article 139 TFEU and Article 42 of the ESCB Statute and the UK Protocol the above provisions of TFEU and the ESCB Statute are applicable to all NCBs in the ESCB.

---

[18] Also known as the 'prohibition of monetization of government debt' (Lastra and Louis 2013, p. 97).

[19] Council Regulation (EC) No 3603/93 of 13 December 1993 specifying definitions for the application of the prohibitions referred to in Articles 104 and 104b (1) of the Treaty, OJ L 332, 31.12.1993, p. 1.

[20] Article 123(2) TFEU.

Therefore, the monetary financing prohibition as defined in Article 123 TFEU and Article 21.1 of the ESCB Statute shall apply to the United Kingdom and to the Bank of England with the exception that the Government of the United Kingdom may maintain its 'ways and means' facility[21] with the Bank of England.

2.6 *Consultation of National Laws with the ECB*

Pursuant to Article 127.4, Article 282.5 TFEU and Article 4(2)(a) of the ESCB Statute, the European Central Bank shall be consulted on any proposed Union act in its fields of competence, and by national authorities regarding any draft legislative provision in its fields of competence, but within the limits and under the Conditions set out by the Council in accordance with the procedure laid down in Article 129.4 TFEU and Article 41 of the ESCB Statute.[22] Pursuant to Articles 4 and 7 of the UK Protocol, such duty of consultation shall not apply to the United Kingdom.

2.7 *Subjecting the Bank of England Under the ECB's Supervision*

Article 271(d) TFEU and Article 35.6 of the ESCB Statute enable the ECB to open infringement proceedings directly against a national central bank which it considers to have acted in breach of the Treaties or the ESCB Statute.[23] It concerns the fulfilment by national central banks of obligations under the Treaties and the ESCB Statute and in this connection the powers of the Governing Council in respect of national central banks under Article 271(d) TFEU shall be the same as those conferred upon the Commission in respect of Member States by Article 258 TFEU. If the ECB Governing Council considers that an NCB has failed to fulfil an obligation under the Treaty and the ESCB Statute, it shall deliver a reasoned opinion on the matter after giving the NCB concerned the opportunity to submit its observations. If the NCB concerned does not comply with the opinion within the period laid down by the ECB Governing Council, the latter may bring the matter before the

---

[21]The 'ways and means' facility is the central governments overdraft facility at the Bank of England.

[22]Such as Council Decision 98/415/EC on the consultation of the European Central Bank by national authorities regarding draft legislative provisions, OJ L 189, 3.7.1998, p. 42.

[23]Zilioli and Selmayr note that this is the only instance in Community law where a 'national' authority can directly be sued before the Court of Justice, which is normally only competent to settle disputes between the Community institutions and the Member States (Zilioli and Selmayr 2001, p. 77). In accordance with Article 139 TFEU, Article 42 of the ESCB Statute and The UK Protocol there are no derogations and the above provisions of TFEU and the ESCB Statute are applicable to all NCBs in the ESCB.

Court of Justice of the European Union. Under Article 271(d) TFEU and Article 35.6 of the ESCB Statute, the Court of Justice shall have jurisdiction in disputes concerning the fulfilment by NCBs of obligations under the Treaty and the ESCB Statute. If the Court of Justice finds that an NCB has failed to fulfil an obligation under the Treaties, that bank shall be required to take the necessary measures to comply with the judgement of the Court of Justice.

However, bearing in mind the UK Protocol, the number of issues that could potentially raise concerns over the Bank of England's compliance with its Treaty obligations is close to zero, and there are no records of such procedure ever being launched against the Bank of England.

2.8 Banking Union

From the legal point of view, the Banking Union is relying on Article 114 TFEU,[24] an Intergovernmental Agreement,[25] an Interinstitutional Agreement,[26] an International Treaty,[27] a Memorandum of Understanding,[28] a Commission communication,[29] legislative measures adopted by co-legislators,[30] legislative measures adopted by the Council alone,[31] as well as non-legislative measures adopted either by the Commission or by the ECB.

---

[24]In contrast, most EU agencies have been established under Article 352 TFEU, under which most Member States have veto powers. A further issue under Article 114 TFEU may arise from the fact that while the Banking Union is not restricted to the euro-area, most of the Banking Union participants are euro-area Member States.

[25]For example, Intergovernmental Agreement on the single resolution fund (Council Document 8457/14), available at http://register.consilium.europa.eu/doc/srv?l=EN&f=ST%208457%202014%20INIT.

[26]Interinstitutional Agreement between the European Parliament and the European Central Bank on the practical modalities of the exercise of democratic accountability and oversight over the exercise of the tasks conferred on the ECB within the framework of the Single Supervisory Mechanism, OJ L 320, 30.11.2013, p. 1.

[27]The Treaty Establishing the European Stability Mechanism (the ESM Treaty), available at http://www.esm.europa.eu/about/legal-documents/ESM%20Treaty.htm.

[28]Memorandum of Understanding between the Council of the European Union and the ECB on the cooperation on procedures related to the Single Supervisory Mechanism (SSM) 11.12.2013, available at http://www.ecb.europa.eu/ecb/legal/pdf/mou_between_eucouncil_ecb.pdf.

[29]For example, Communication from the Commission on the application, from 1 August 2013, of State aid rules to support measures in favour of banks in the context of the financial crisis ('Banking Communication'), available at http://eur-lex.europa.eu/legal-content/EN/ALL/?uri=CELEX:52013XC0730(01).

[30]Directive 2014/49/EU of the European Parliament and of the Council of 16 April 2014 on deposit guarantee schemes, OJ L 173, 12.6.2014, p. 149.

[31]For example, Council Regulation (EU) No 1024/2013 of 15 October 2013 conferring specific tasks on the European Central Bank concerning policies relating to the prudential supervision of credit institutions, OJ L 287, 29.10.2013, p. 63.

Article 127(6) TFEU and Article 25.2 of the ESCB Statute set forth that the Council, acting by means of regulations in accordance with a special legislative procedure, may unanimously, and after consulting the European Parliament and the ECB, confer specific tasks upon the European Central Bank concerning policies relating to the prudential supervision of credit institutions and other financial institutions with the exception of insurance undertakings. Furthermore, this is also confirmed by Article 25.2 of the ESCB Statute,[32] which provides that in accordance with any regulation of the Council under Article 127(6) TFEU and Article 25.2 of the ESCB Statute, the ECB may perform specific tasks concerning policies relating to the prudential supervision of credit institutions and other financial institutions, with the exception of insurance undertakings.

It is noteworthy that under Article 139(2)(c) TFEU, Article 127(6) TFEU shall apply to all members of the ESCB, not just the Eurosystem. In addition, Article 42 of the ESCB Statute, which specifies the provisions not applicable to the Member States with a derogation, does not list Article 25.2 of the ESCB Statute. Even Articles 4 and 7 of the UK Protocol do not exclude the applicability of Article 127(6) TFEU or of Article 25.2 of the ESCB Statute to the United Kingdom.

However, this EU-wide supervisory competence has no EU-wide regulatory backing from the ESCB Statute. While the first indent of Article 132(1) TFEU and Article 34.1 of the ESCB Statute authorise the ECB to make regulations to the extent necessary to implement the tasks defined in, *inter alia*, Article 25.2 of the ESCB Statute, those regulations would only be applicable to the Member States that have adopted the euro. In particular, Article 139(1)(e) TFEU provides that acts of the European Central Bank issued under Article 132 TFEU shall not apply to Member States with a derogation.[33] The same is also true for the United Kingdom.[34] Therefore, while being lawfully competent to carry out prudential supervisory tasks throughout the EU once the Council has issued its regulation, the ECB's power to issue legal acts in this field would unfortunately be limited to the euro area Member States.

Further issue with the Banking Union arises from the fact that while Banking Union is open to all EU Member States, supported by the another fact that SSM/SRM is applicable to participating Member States (in other words, not restricted to the euro-area), ESM is only available to euro-area Member States. As a result, the BRRD applies for all EU banks, while the SRM Regulation applies only to the euro-area banks, the latter being related to the SRM's Intergovernmental Agreement, which has been adopted outside the EU's law-making procedures. The Intergovernmental Agreement governs part of the Single Resolution Fund, which is

[32]Remarkably, the task of prudential supervision has not been placed in Article 3 of the ESCB Statute together with other tasks of the ESCB. The rationale may be that this was a task foreseen for the ECB alone and not for the entire ESCB. However, Smits points out that Article 127(6) TFEU is not a separate article but a paragraph in an article describing the tasks of the ESCB (Smits 2000, p. 355). Smits' observation is supported by the language of Article 132(1) TFEU, which stipulates, among others that '[I]n order to carry out the tasks entrusted to the ESCB, [...]', while one of the legal bases for the ECB regulations is also Article 25.2 of the ESCB Statute.

[33]See Article 42.1 of the ESCB Statute and Article 34 of the ESCB Statute respectively.

[34]See Articles 4 and 7 of the UK Protocol.

an element of the SRM but lies outside the EU's harmonised regime. At the same time the Intergovernmental Agreement is to be applied and interpreted in accordance with EU law. When the ECB Governing Council will decide on SSM-related issues, it will do so in its original composition (i.e. composed of Governors of euro-area national central banks and the ECB Executive Board), thereby leaving out any Governor from a 'close cooperation' Member State.

Member States outside the euro area have the option to become a member of the Banking Union by entering into the close cooperation with the ECB in accordance with the SSM Regulation and subsequently join the SSM and SRM.

With regard to non-participating Member States, the supervision will remain exercised in accordance with the regulatory rules set in the CRD IV,[35] CRR[36] and BRRD.[37] With regard to cross-border institutions, the ECB could be involved in the supervision, either as a home supervisor or a host supervisor in colleges of supervisors.

If a resolution affects banks established only in participating Member States, the resolution process under the SRM will apply, whereas if a resolution affects banks established only in non-participating Member States, the resolution process under the BRRD will apply.

The United Kingdom is not part of the Banking Union. However, the United Kindom has to transpose the so-called Single Rulebook that includes capital requirements legislation, resolution and recovery legislation and the legislation on deposit guarantee schemes.

2.9 *Coordination of Economic Policies*

Under the EU Treaties, economic and budgetary matters remain within the competence of the Member States[38] and the latter 'shall regard their economic policies as a

[35]Directive 2013/36/EU of the European Parliament and of the Council of 26 June 2013 on access to the activity of credit institutions and the prudential supervision of credit institutions and investment firms, amending Directive 2002/87/EC and repealing Directives 2006/48/EC and 2006/49/EC, OJ L 176, 27.6.2013, p. 338.

[36]Regulation (EU) No 575/2013 of the European Parliament and of the Council of 26 June 2013 on prudential requirements for credit institutions and investment firms and amending Regulation (EU) No 648/2012, OJ L 176, 27.6.2013, p. 1.

[37]Directive 2014/59/EU of the European Parliament and of the Council of 15 May 2014 establishing a framework for the recovery and resolution of credit institutions and investment firms and amending Council Directive 82/891/EEC, and Directives 2001/24/EC, 2002/47/EC, 2004/25/EC, 2005/56/EC, 2007/36/EC, 2011/35/EU, 2012/30/EU and 2013/36/EU, and Regulations (EU) No 1093/2010 and (EU) No 648/2012, of the European Parliament and of the Council, OJ L 173, 12.6.2014, p. 190.

[38]Article 120 TFEU provides that the 'Member States shall conduct their economic policies', which is further confirmed by Article 127(1) TFEU referring to the task of the ESCB to 'support the general economic policies in the Union' indicating that it is possible to have a number of economic policies in the EU.

matter of common concern and coordinate them within the Council'.[39] The Member States committed themselves for the Stability and Growth Pact.[40]

Under Article 5 of the UK Protocol the United Kingdom is not subject to Article 126(1), (9) and (11) TFEU; as a result that the United Kingdom remains subject to the (second stage of the Economic and Monetary Union) obligation to *endeavour* to avoid excessive government deficits, whilst the euro area Member States are under an *absolute* obligation to avoid such deficits.

About the EU's economic governance, the main rules are introduced by the so-called "Euro Plus Pact",[41] "Six Pack",[42] the "Two Pack"[43] and by the Treaty on Stability, Coordination, and Governance.[44] These rules are implemented through the European Semester.

Under Article 8 of Directive 2011/85/EU the United Kingdom is not obliged to have in place numerical fiscal rules. Under Article 23(13) of Regulation (EU) 1303/2013,[45] the United Kingdom cannot be sanctioned by suspending of commitments or payments under the European Structural and Investment Funds.

---

[39]Article 121(1) TFEU.

[40]Resolution of the European Council on the Stability and Growth Pact Amsterdam, 17 June 1997, OJ C 236, 2.8.1997, p. 1.

[41]Available at http://www.consilium.europa.eu/uedocs/cms_data/docs/pressdata/en/ec/120296.pdf.

[42]Council Regulation (EU) No 1177/2011 of 8 November 2011 amending Regulation (EC) No 1467/97 on speeding up and clarifying the implementation of the excessive deficit procedure; OJ L 306, 23.11.2011, p. 33; Regulation (EU) No 1176/2011 of the European Parliament and of the Council of 16 November 2011 on the prevention and correction of macroeconomic imbalances, OJ L 306, 23.11.2011, p. 25; Regulation (EU) No 1175/2011 of the European Parliament and of the Council of 16 November 2011 amending Council Regulation (EC) No 1466/97 on the strengthening of the surveillance of budgetary positions and the surveillance and coordination of economic policies, OJ L 306, 23.11.2011, p. 12; Regulation (EU) No 1174/2011 of the European Parliament and of the Council of 16 November 2011 on enforcement measures to correct excessive macroeconomic imbalances in the euro area, OJ L 306, 23.11.2011, p. 8; Regulation (EU) No 1173/2011 of the European Parliament and of the Council of 16 November 2011 on the effective enforcement of budgetary surveillance in the euro area, OJ L 306, 23.11.2011, p. 1; Council Directive 2011/85/EU of 8 November 2011 on requirements for budgetary frameworks of the Member States, OJ L 306, 23.11.2011, p. 41.

[43]Regulation (EU) No 473/2013 of the European Parliament and of the Council of 21 May 2013 on common provisions for monitoring and assessing draft budgetary plans and ensuring the correction of excessive deficit of the Member States in the euro area, OJ L 140, 27.5.2013, p. 11; Regulation (EU) No 472/2013 of the European Parliament and of the Council of 21 May 2013 on the strengthening of economic and budgetary surveillance of Member States in the euro area experiencing or threatened with serious difficulties with respect to their financial stability, OJ L 140, 27.5.2013, p. 1.

[44]Available at http://www.consilium.europa.eu/european-council/pdf/Treaty-on-Stability-Coordination-and-Governance-TSCG/. This Treaty is not applicable to the United Kingdom.

[45]Regulation (EU) 1303/2013 of the European Parliament and of the Council of 17 December 2013 laying down common provisions on the European Regional Development Fund, the European Social Fund, the Cohesion Fund, the European Agricultural Fund for Rural Development and the European Maritime and Fisheries Fund and laying down general provisions on the European Regional Development Fund, the European Social Fund, the Cohesion Fund and the European

The United Kingdom is required to treat its exchange rate policy as "a matter of common interest",[46] which is understood as preventing the United Kingdom from taking deliberate steps designed to depreciate its currency with a view to securing a competitive advantage over the euro area Member States.[47] Also, the United Kingdom remains entitled to take unilateral protective measures in the event of a sudden crisis in its balance of payments, or to enlist the assistance of the Commission in the case of less serious difficulties.[48]

References

Arda A (2006) Objectives and tasks of the European System of Central Banks and the European Central Bank: a commentary on Article 105 TEC. SSRN website. September 5, 2006. http://papers.ssrn.com/sol3/papers.cfm?abstract_id=928148. Accessed 15 Aug 2016

European Central Bank (2016) Convergence Report. European Central Bank's website. June 2016. https://www.ecb.europa.eu/pub/pdf/conrep/cr201606.en.pdf?a91977931874a7c6c63d80305b651394. Accessed 15 Aug 2016

Kapteyn PJG, VerLoren van Themaat P (2008) The law of the European Union and the European Communities, 4th edn. Kluwer Law International

Lastra RM, Louis J-V (2013) European Economic and Monetary Union: history, trends and prospects. Yearb Eur Law 32(1):57–206

Smits R (2000) European Central Bank institutional aspects. Kluwer Law International, Hague

Zilioli C, Selmayr M (2000) The European Central Bank: an independent specialised organisation of community law. Common Mark Law Rev 37:591–644

Zilioli C, Selmayr M (2001) The law of the European Central Bank. Hart, Oxford

---

Maritime and Fisheries Fund and repealing Council Regulation (EC) 1083/2006, OJ L 347, 20.12.2013, p. 320, as amended.

[46] Article 142 TFEU read together with Article 5 of the UK Protocol.

[47] However, the applicability of such legal provision in the world where value of sterling is not set by the authorities but it is subject to external or market factors is arguable.

[48] Articles 143 and 144 TFEU in conjunction with Article 5 of the UK Protocol.

The British Role in the Emergence of Multi-Speed Europe and Enhanced Cooperation

Liisi Keedus, Archil Chochia, Tanel Kerikmäe, and David Ramiro Troitiño

Abstract The idea of the European Union as a lasting association of European democracies warranting a stable yet constantly evolving institutional framework was formulated in the Schuman Declaration and has remained the political corner-stone of the Union. Although the EU has enlarged through successive waves, this has also generated new tensions between its members, including among those willing to move towards closer integration and those determined to preserve the intactness of national sovereignty in core areas. Here, a multi-speed Europe, or at least a double-speed Europe, has the potential to advance further integration among only interested members. Also, institutionalizing a multispeed Europe would in fact simply recognize the existing working system in the EU.

1 Instruments of Differentiation in Integration

European integration is based on the rule of common law and Communitarian Treaties, which have been democratically ratified by all member countries. National approval may take the form of either by parliamentary vote, the most common procedure, or a national referendum, occasionally held by only a few Member States, such as Denmark (1986, 1992, 1993, 1998, 2014, 2015), Ireland (1986, 1992, 1998, 2001), Italy (1989), France (1992, 2005), Spain (2005) and the Netherlands (2005, 2016). The Treaties define areas over which the European Union has political influence and legal power. If a policy is not included in the Treaties, it belongs to the national jurisdiction and European institutions must not interfere. In areas under the treaties, EU institutions can adopt legislation, which the member countries then

L. Keedus (✉)
Department of Politics, University of York, York, UK
e-mail: lkeedus@tlu.ee

A. Chochia · T. Kerikmäe · D. Ramiro Troitiño
Tallinn Law School, Tallinn University of Technology, Tallinn, Estonia
e-mail: archil.chochia@ttu.ee; tanel.kerikmae@ttu.ee; david.troitino@ttu.ee

D. Ramiro Troitiño et al. (eds.), *Brexit*,
https://doi.org/10.1007/978-3-319-73414-9_11

implement. The most important treaties in the EU history have been the Treaty Establishing the European Coal and Steel Community (1951), the Treaties of Rome (1957), Merger Treaty (1965), The Single European Act (1986), Treaty on the European Union (1992), Treaty of Amsterdam (1997), Treaty of Nice (2001) and Treaty of Lisbon (2007). With each enlargement, the treaties are amended to accommodate new members.[1]

The treaties require the unanimous approval of all Member States to be approved and implemented, and for each enlargement there a treaty that needs to be approved and the new member accepted. In principle, approval of treaties requires the unanimity of the Member States, even if this was not always the case. For instance, the Treaty of Maastricht was rejected by the Danish voters in June 1992. The referendum had a turnout of 82.9% but approval was denied by a slim margin, with only 49.3% favorable votes. Following the idea of unanimity, the Treaty of Maastricht should have been rejected by the entire community, but the importance of its contents and the support of the key Member States led to further efforts and eventually an innovative solution—a new referendum on a modified form of the Treaty. The European Union offered the Danish government the following four opt-outs from the policies included in the Treaty: Economic and Monetary Union, European Union Citizenship, Justice and Home Affairs and Common Defense issues. These exceptions warranted the presentation of a modified Treaty for another referendum in May 1993. With a turnout of 85.5%, 56.8% voted in favor of the renegotiated treaty.[2] Similarly, in 2001 Irish voters rejected the Treaty of Nice by 53.9%, but with only 34.8% turnout, while in 2002, after an added guarantee for Ireland's military neutrality, they accepted it by 62.9% with 49.5% of the electorate voting.[3]

These precedents challenged the EU to explore new ways to strive for a closer union between the Member States more committed to integration, while in parallel allowing exceptions or opt-outs to a minority of members who would otherwise impede further integration. The successive enlargements of the Union, from the 6 founding members to the current 28 Member States, have made it increasingly difficult to reach a consensus on the extent and intensity of integration. On the one hand, there are countries keener on accelerating the process, while on the other, there are also members more reluctant to renounce any aspect of sovereignty. The opt-out clauses have eased the integration process for the majority of the Member States by allowing others to remain out of new policies included in the new treaties.

Currently there are four Member States with opt-outs: Denmark, Poland, Ireland, and the UK. The Schengen agreement does not apply to Ireland and the UK (Romania and Bulgaria have not yet been accepted to participate in the Schengen agreement), Denmark and UK are not part of the Economic and Monetary Union, the Defense Development does not apply to Denmark, the Charter of Fundamental

[1]Ramiro Troitiño (2013).

[2]Miles and Wivel (2013), p. 18.

[3]For an analysis, see Habermas (2013).

Rights of the European Union does not apply to Poland and the UK, and Denmark, Ireland and the United Kingdom have obtained opt-outs from the Area of freedom, security, and justice policies. The most reluctant countries in terms of further integration are the UK (4 opt-outs), Denmark (3 opt-outs) and Ireland (2 opt-outs)—interestingly, all these three countries are members since the first enlargement wave of the EC.[4]

The rejection of the European Constitution by the Netherlands (61.5% against) and especially France (54.9% against) in 2005 similarly posed a new challenge for the Union. While all previous rejections and exceptions affected only smaller Member States in terms of population and economic weight who then were sometimes accused of lack of commitment to integration, the Netherlands is a founding member of the Union with considerable economic power, and France is a leading member since its founding. In the case of the vote against the Constitution, the EU could not follow a familiar multi-track path because of the central role of these two members.[5] Indeed, some members are crucial for further attempts of political integration while others can be left aside, or, in other words, the central members of the Union and the more peripheral ones. The European Constitution failed after the French and Dutch rejections, even if most of its proposed amendments were included in the following Treaty of Lisbon, ratified by all the Member States of the European Union.

A further procedural instrument for advancing integration without the approval of all the members is international agreements. The Schengen agreement was originally an international agreement between France and Germany for the free movement of people, but its implementation was delayed because of the reunification of Eastern and Western parts of Germany. The French government was concerned about possible mass immigration from East to West Germany, speculating that Eastern German workforce might replace the Turkish workers in the West, which in turn could trigger an emigration of unemployed Turkish migrants to France. However, this never happened and soon the agreement was ratified. Furthermore, an increasing number of Member States soon joined it. The agreement abolished internal controls and reinforced external controls. The Treaty of Amsterdam included the agreement in the Communitarian sphere and hence it became a significant measure for furthering European integration.[6] Again, there were some exceptions for some members, most importantly for the UK and Ireland. Britain wanted to keep control over its borders and opted to stay outside the agreement, and Ireland—that has a bilateral free movement agreement with its neighboring island—did not have much choice than lining with the latter.[7]

The Schengen agreement is a patent example of European integration being developed outside the European institutions, on the international level, yet

[4]For further details, see Holzinger and Schimmelfennig (2012).

[5]See more in Beloff (1970).

[6]On the history of the Schengen agreement, see Nanz (1995).

[7]Ramiro Troitiño (2014).

subsequently accepted by additional or even most members and then integrated into the Union regulations. It may be a used as a shortcut to advancing integration as it allows the interested Member States to proceed without the unanimity or qualified majority required in the case of EU Treaties, and hence avoids the situation wherein integration would be blocked by its opponents. On the other hand, as international negotiations are exempt from the European Union regulations regarding equality and national discrimination, proceeding through international agreements gives extensive influence to the core Member States.[8] For instance, Germany and France, by adopting common policies that would first be implemented among members on whom they have the most influence and only later on others, could impose their position as key actors on less influential members without being restrained by the Union rules.

2 Enhanced Cooperation

The Treaty of Amsterdam (1997) was originally designed as an amendment to the Treaty of Maastricht and aimed to reform the EU institutions with a view to the imminent enlargement to Central and Eastern Europe that in two waves included twelve new Member States. Among the key changes were an increased use of common legislative procedure in the decision-making process to make it more flexible and thereby avoiding possible blockades because of the unanimity-based voting system. With twenty-seven Member States it was obvious that many cases and situations would defy unanimity or consensus, which made further integration vulnerable to the risk of paralysis—if only a single member opposed it. It was similarly obvious that in a union of twenty-seven members it was much more difficult to meet the preferences of everyone. Yet, the community needed to focus on its common interests and strengths rather than particular demands from individual Member States.[9]

It was precisely for meeting such challenges that the enhanced cooperation procedure was designed, first introduced by the Treaty of Amsterdam, and later simplified by the Treaty of Nice. Its main aim was to address community, judicial cooperation and criminal matters and it allows a minimum of nine Member States, which effectively means one third, to establish advanced cooperation in an area within the community structures, even if other members choose to remain uninvolved. The latter can simply opt out from new policies, while unable to block others from adopting them.[10] Hence currently the enhanced cooperation allows different groups of Member States to move at "different speeds" and towards different goals in the integration process. The enhanced cooperation can be used as

[8]See the discussion in Coudenhove-Kalergi (2011).

[9]Grabbe (2014).

[10]See also Leech and Aziz (2013).

the last resort after deliberating with all the Member States about a new policy. It must not have any discriminatory effect on any member of the Union. The procedure needs a minimum of one-third of Member States filling a request to the European Commission, which the latter must approved and then a qualified majority of all Member States must agree to proceed.

The Treaty of Nice (2001) further completed the Amsterdam Treaty by including new measures for strengthening cooperation in key areas. Moreover, it established that if a Member State wants to block planned integration measures, it must turn to the Council that will form its decision by a qualified majority. Exceptions to this requirement are in the areas of Common Foreign Policy and Security Policy where Treaty of Nice allows enhanced cooperation only by unanimity. The possibility of national veto is thus still allowed in foreign policy because of concerns that some Member States might lose their neutral status in international politics. However, the Treaty of Lisbon (2007) extended cooperation to defense and additionally envisions the possibility for establishment of a permanent structured cooperation in defense.[11]

Presently there are several policies of enhanced cooperation in place, including divorce law and patent law. The divorce law, while its aim is to standardize divorce procedures for multi-national EU couples, does not include Denmark, Sweden, Finland, Estonia, Poland, Czech Republic, Slovakia, Croatia, the Netherlands, Ireland and the UK. The Nordic states' divorce laws are more liberal than the EU directive and these countries did not wish to participate in a policy that could restrict their system of freedoms. The equal inclusion of recent and earlier members of the Union suggests that it was not created and must not necessarily result in core members imposing increased integration on others.

The unitary patent is another policy of enhanced cooperation adopted by the European Commission and Parliament. Despite the common European market there was no common patent system apart from the European Patent Office, which was simply the sum of the individual countries' patents. The system of individual patents was costly and slow as agents needed to register their patents in each Member State to be protected in the entire market. This was obviously inefficient, yet attempts to launch a common patent system failed on several occasions.[12] By 2011, twenty-five Member States backed new European legislation in the field, with only Spain and Italy opposing the initiative. The Spanish and Italians were against the use of three languages in the system, English, German, and French, and wanted to include just one, English. This was an unusual situation in the practice of enhanced cooperation: only two Member States were left out, and this happened not because of the disagreement with policy but because of what may appear as merely linguistic issues. Furthermore, the incident caused more general unease regarding possible linguistic discrimination in the EU[13] as Spain claimed that the unitary patent undermined free competition in the internal market by making all procedures more

[11]Church and Phinnemore (2013).

[12]For a detailed account of these efforts, see Hilty et al. (2012).

[13]See esp. Dahl (2000).

expensive for companies and investors in countries where English, French and German were not official languages.

Currently, there are ongoing discussions about other initiatives that will probably be included in the enhanced cooperation in the coming years, such as the planned financial transaction tax and the Defense Policy. The enhanced cooperation policy will be crucial in the tackling of future disagreements within the European Union as, on the one hand, integration is expected to progress, and on the other, not all the members are willing to commit to this development. The UK was for a long time cautious about the new directions in integration, which, it feared, would turn it into a secondary actor, while France and Germany are clearly assuming leading roles.[14] This has clearly ceased to be an issue after 2016, but there are other sceptics on further integration, such as Poland and other Visegrad countries.

Enhanced cooperation is doubtless a useful instrument for accelerating the integration process and side-stepping national vetoes, but it may also result in considerably asymmetry in levels of integration. Currently it is impossible to foresee whether this system will be used in the most contested areas in case it is bound to affect significantly the economic or political status of some Member States. Its main challenge is the possible asymmetrical consequences that may jeopardize the principle of equality between Member States. However, the EU has been always been asymmetrical to some extent[15] and there are guarantees provided to the states not willing to participate in enhanced integration. The combination of the principles of openness, transparency and control make enhanced cooperation an interesting and powerful tool for tackling some of the challenges in the way of progressive integration.

3 Multi-Speed Europe

The idea of the EU as a long-lasting association of European democracies warranting a stable yet constantly evolving institutional framework was formulated in the Schuman Declaration and has remained the political corner-stone of the Union. Although the EU has enlarged through successive waves, this has also generated new tensions between its members, including among those willing to move towards closer integration and those determined to preserve the intactness of national sovereignty in core areas. Here, a multi-speed Europe, or at least a double-speed Europe, has the potential to advance further integration among only interested members.[16] Also, institutionalizing a multispeed Europe would in fact simply recognize the existing working system in the EU. In addition to examples of exemptions from the Eurozone and Schengen, Denmark has opted out from Europe's Common Security

[14] Ramiro Troitiño (2014).

[15] As argued in Dinan (2004).

[16] This is an argument further developed in Gaynor (1997).

and Defense policy, Poland joined the UK in opting out of the Charter of Fundamental Rights, and the Czechs stand with the British outside the Fiscal Compact. Hence the concept of a multi-speed Europe is actually a reflection of the existing reality, as well as a useful tool for improving the effectiveness and democratic credentials of further development of the community.[17]

At the same time, a multi-speed EC could evolve into a complex system even more difficult to understand both for its citizens and international partners. This might in fact have a negative effect on Europe's democratic credentials and the alienation of its citizens would certainly undermine any quests for further integration. Also, in international politics, different integration levels are likely to reduce Europe's influence in the world affairs, especially if differentiation translates into fragmentation, harming both its unity of action and its image as a partner in foreign affairs.[18]

While introducing different levels of integration can solve some problems, it can also generate an asymmetric Union where the practical ramifications of the membership status—or of the lack of it, like it happened during the UK referendum campaign leading to Brexit—may get blurred and diffused. Also, the concept and practice of a multi-speed Europe could perpetuate divisions between the so-called "first" and "second class" members of the community. This may lead to the emergence of blocs within the Union struggling for predominance over communitarian issues. It can similarly undermine solidarity between Member States, with France and Germany leading the integration processes and other members having little choice but to follow them—since any decision would have an impact on them with or without their participation in the decision-making process.

Indeed, the concept and practice of a multi-speed Europe has clearly in large part been a French-German initiative aiming to tackle the UK blockade on further integration policies. The attempts of the UK to renegotiate the terms of its membership gave a significant impulse to the debate over multi-speed Europe. The agreement reached in February 2016 between David Cameron and his European colleagues, centered on issues ranging from migrant welfare payments to financial services, was an attempt to keep the UK inside the organization. But it also fueled populism all over Europe, as in several Member States some political parties similarly emphasize differences between Member States and insist that these differences must be accepted by the EU institutions.[19] After the shock of Brexit and during the celebration of the anniversary of the European Union in Rome in March 2017, the concept has been officially granted green light, despite vehement objections from some major new members states. It is seen not only as an instrument for consolidating the prominence of the so-called core Member States but as a tool for very likely marginalization of especially the newest Member States—as an instrument for

[17]See also Blauberger and Kelemen (2016).

[18]As argued in Schutze (2016).

[19]For an analysis, see Martinico (2015) and Fabbrini (2013).

recreating the first and second rate Europe(s) and even likened to "a new iron curtain."

While the UK has been one of the main triggers in the development of the concept and practices constructing a two-speed Europe, one of the most decisive questions in the aftermath of Brexit is, what will be the spill-overs of the long history the "singularity" and "special status" of the UK for the future of the EU. The two-speed Europe has always been slightly unbalanced—almost as if with only the UK on one side and the rest of the Union, or at least the most influential states, on the other. At the same time, there are signs of integration fatigue too difficult and dangerous to ignore in an increasing number of the Member States. This brings new challenges that will probably be tackled, among other methods, via the multi-speed Europe concept and practices—in which finding the fine balance between its perils and its promise will be as crucial as ever for the future of the Union.

References

Beloff M (1970) The Anglo-French Union Project of June 1940. In: Beloff M (ed) The intellectual in politics and other essays. Weidenfeld, London, pp 172–199

Blauberger M, Kelemen D (2016) Can courts rescue national democracy? Judicial safeguards against democratic backsliding in the EU. J Eur Publ Policy:1–16

Church C, Phinnemore D (2013) From the constitutional treaty to the Treaty of Lisbon and beyond. Eur Union Polit:41–56

Coudenhove-Kalergi R (2011) Pan-Europa, vol 4. Encuentro

Dahl Ö (2000) Tense and aspect in the languages of Europe. Walter de Gruyter

Dinan D (2004) Europe recast: a history of European Union, vol 373. Palgrave Macmillan, Basingstoke

Fabbrini F (2013) Enhanced cooperation under scrutiny: revisiting the law and practice of multi-speed integration in light of the first involvement of the EU judiciary. Leg Issues Econ Integrat 40:197–224

Gaynor K (1997) Economic convergence in a multispeed Europe. Palgrave

Grabbe H (2014) Six lessons of enlargement ten years on: the EU's transformative power in retrospect and prospect. J Common Mark 52:56

Habermas J (2013) Democracy, solidarity and the European crisis. In: Grozelier A (ed) Roadmap to a social Europe 4

Hilty R, Jaeger T, Lamping M, Ullrich H (2012) The unitary patent package: twelve reasons for concern. Max Planck Institute for Intellectual Property & Competition Law Research Paper

Holzinger K, Schimmelfennig F (2012) Differentiated integration in the European Union: many concepts, sparse theory, few data. J Eur Publ Policy 19(2):292–305

Leech D, Aziz H (2013) The double majority voting rule of the EU reform treaty as a democratic ideal for an enlarging union: an appraisal using voting power analysis. In: Cichocki M, Życzkowski K (eds) Institutional design and voting power in the European Union. London, pp 59–73

Martinico G (2015) A multi-speed EU? An institutional and legal assessment. IAI Working Paper

Miles L, Wivel A (2013) Denmark and the European Union. Routledge

Nanz K (1995) The Schengen agreement: preparing the free movement of persons in the European Union. In: Bieber R, Monar J (eds) Justice and home affairs in the European Union. European University Institute Press, pp 29–48
Ramiro Troitiño D (2013) European integration: building Europe. Nova Publishers, New York
Ramiro Troitiño D (2014) The British position towards European integration: a different economic and political approach. Balt J Eur Stud 4:119–136
Schutze R (2016) Foreign affairs and the EU constitution. Cambridge University Press, Cambridge

Part IV
The British and European Future

Article 50 of the Treaty on European Union: How to Understand the 'Right' of the Member State to Withdraw the European Union?

Andrea Circolo, Ondrej Hamuľák, and Ondrej Blažo

Abstract This chapter focuses on legal aspects, respectively the constitutional assumptions of the departure of the Member State from the European Union. It offers an analysis of past debates and theoretical models that preceded the official introduction of the exit clause in today's Article 50 TEU. It also addresses the question of the nature of the withdrawal and casts doubt on the nature of the "right to withdraw." Article 50 is working with two alternatives on how to leave the Union—a consensual exit and unilateral withdrawal. Although the authors accept the theoretical extreme possibility of unilateral exit without agreement, they also point to the factual necessity of the agreement (that is necessary from the point of view of legal certainty, economic stability, political accountability, and international status of the outgoing state), which in fact makes the consensual exit the only possible way of terminating membership and therefore casts doubts on the existence of right to withdraw.

1 Introduction: The Problem of the Withdrawal from the EU Nowadays

'*Le retrait est un acte par lequel l'État membre d'une organization Internationale met fin à son appartenance à celle-ci.*'[1] It's the simple and straightforward message. States as sovereigns are free to choose their destiny and decide whether participate or

[1]Mehdi (2007), p. 113.

A. Circolo (✉)
Department of Economic and Legal Studies, Parthenope University of Naples, Naples, Italy
e-mail: andrea.circolo@uniparthenope.it

O. Hamuľák
Faculty of Law, Palacký University Olomouc, Olomouc, Czech Republic
e-mail: ondrej.hamulak@upol.cz

O. Blažo
Institute of European Law, Faculty of Law, Comenius University in Bratislava, Bratislava, Slovakia
e-mail: ondrej.blazo@flaw.uniba.sk

D. Ramiro Troitiño et al. (eds.), *Brexit*,
https://doi.org/10.1007/978-3-319-73414-9_12

not on the functioning of particular international organisation. However, when meeting the political reality of European integration today and considering the complexity of European project, the issue becomes challenging and rather open. Several years ago, it would have seemed untimely and rather scholastic to make an analysis of real case of withdrawal[2] in relation to the European Union, given that it has never been applied (and for a long time even forecasted) and that, rather, the process of European integration, as developed in last 60 years, has been marked by successive and repeated enlargements (not exempt from criticism) that led the Member States from the original 6 to 28[3] of today. The European Union's external borders, with periodic behaviour and seemingly inevitable, have been, in fact, gradually moved in the direction of all four cardinal points.[4] The continuing exception of Switzerland and Norway does not diminish the impression of an unstoppable march that concerned, and that progressively involves the entire European continent.[5] Geographical widening and material deepening of European integration[6] over the last six decades has given rise to assumption of unstoppable and unlimited existence of the European bond. The lack of attention of the doctrine on the issue of termination of membership could be justified by this reason. The scholars predominantly focused on the theme of the accession of the applicant countries and the existing membership in the EC/EU (position of the states, relation between EU and national law etc.), rather than on the withdrawal of the Member States.

As is known, no cases of withdrawal have so far yet checked, both before and after the Lisbon Treaty and to the Community or the Union. However, the question has been the focus of some discussions for many years before the upcoming Brexit. In 1965 France, disagreeing with the Commission on how to finance the CAP, after the breakdown of negotiations, which took place during the Board of Ministers of the EEC (June 30/July 1), re-called his organisation's delegates and refrained from participating in the Meeting of the Council of Ministers of 26 July 1965. "The French behaviour" of that time is known as the policy of *the empty chair* or *chaise vide* to the Council, which blocked *de facto* the institution. The United Kingdom too is not new to such situations. The *Royame Uni* entered the European Economic Community in January 1973, under the government of the Conservative Party (Tory). In 1974 the (most of the) Labour Party, just from the beginning opposite to the entrance of Britain in the EEC, printed several posters for the upcoming

---

[2]For terminological clarity, withdrawal, retreat, and exit will be used as synonyms. We do not believe we can consider in this way the noun secession, which is used to describe a country that acquires independence separating itself from a unitary state.

[3]The writers refer to a "Europe at 28" because, as established by Art. 50 TEU, neither any withdrawal agreement has yet been signed, nor have 2 years after the notification of intent by the United Kingdom passed away.

[4]For an historical perspective of the enlargement see Nelli Feroci (2005), pp. 597; for a legal perspective see Puglia (2014), pp. 333–338.

[5]Vellano (2007), p. 503.

[6]Wessels (2001), pp. 5–11.

elections, in which he promised to ask for a renegotiation of the terms of accession of the UK and hold a consultative *referendum* (but strongly binding) with which the British people would have decided the country's future in the Community. *Historical courses and resorts*. The negotiation was signed in Dublin in March 1975 by representatives of the EEC and the British Cabinet, who voted 16-7 in favour of the United Kingdom stay in the EEC. The referendum also took place on June 5 1975, the result of which, perhaps influenced by the government's vote, was a landslide victory for the YES - 67.2%—(the question put to voters was "Do you think the UK should stay in the European Community (Common Market)?". The presence of representatives of the Community in the negotiations, and the absence of questions raised on the legality of the *referendum* demonstrated the will on the part of the EU not to create an unwelcome precedent, as suggests the idea that the Member States did not find illegal the British behaviour from the point of view of EU and international law (it should however be noted that the only request to renegotiate the treaties, under the threat of the withdrawal, could not possibly devote the existence of the right of withdrawal either in Community law or in the international one). It remained only a purpose, instead, the new electoral will of the Labour party to leave the EEC (1981): *the party of the rose* promised that, if victorious, would have withdrawn the country from the Community, this time even without going through a popular *referendum*, convinced that the confidence gained at the polls constituted sufficient mandate to complete the exit. Even then the reasons were, mostly, economic: the high contribution due to the coffers of the EEC, the revaluation of oil in the North Sea reserves, the decline of British industry. Another "accident" like the British occurred in Greece. During the election campaign for the 1981 national elections, PASOK (*Panhellenic Socialist Movement*) promised to hold, in case of victory, a national *referendum* to determine the permanence or the output of the Greek State by the EEC. Despite the victory of the Socialist Party, the *referendum* was never realised: this could have been requested only by the President of the Hellenic Republic, which was then Constantine Caramanlis, totally favourable to membership of his country to the European Community. At the end deserves special attention also the precedent of Greenland. However, even in this case, we are far from being able to talk about a case of withdrawal: in fact, although it is also spoken of withdrawal for this hypothesis, actually a change of the legal system was made to which the territory of the Greenland is subjected (with a strong autonomy from the Danish state as early as 1979 with the obtaining of the *Home Rule*), without which no evidence of its membership has come out with respect to the then European Economic Community. Belonging that was, and continues to, headed to Denmark. Since 1985, after a special *referendum* held on February 23, 1982, art. 182–187 of the Fourth Part of the EC Treaty "Association of Overseas Countries and Territories", are applied to Greenland, except the specific provisions as contained in Protocol annexed to the EC Treaty. It was, in fact, the Brussels Treaty (13 March 1984) to amend the Treaties establishing the European Community with regard to Greenland, declaring naught, from that date, the application of the Treaties themselves, and by conferring the status of "associated territory". The procedure for the change is that in art. 236 EEC: it was not, in fact, Greenland to require a direct way for the withdrawal, but Denmark for it, through a proposal for a redefinition of the application of the Treaties submitted to the Council, then transmitted to the Commission and Parliament for consultation. The case must therefore be classified in the same way for a revision of the Treaty, which established the quality of "Overseas Territory" for Greenland: there was no unilateral termination, as all Member States, also making several changes to the initial proposals, agreed with the result achieved (Greenland gained a new *status*, designed to regulate fishing rights and to recognise the same right to the "free trade").

The renewed (it would be more sufficient to treat it as 'firstborn') interest on the topic of withdrawal is unquestionably connected with the process of 'formal' constitutionalisation of the EU. Primary, it was opened in connection to the negotiation and creation of the Treaty Establishing Constitution for Europe, which in its art. I-60 introduced for the very first time the explicit right of (voluntarily) withdrawal of Member State from the EU.[7] Later, more deep evaluation of exit clause continued after adoption of Lisbon Treaty, which confirmed the right for withdrawal in art. 50 TEU, and discussion accelerated during the multi-crisis which EU have been facing during last periods. The ongoing economic and political crisis, the *Brexit* (with attached *Grexit* and *Frexit* hypothesis), and so long, have placed such a constitutional issue at the centre of political and scientific debate in Europe and beyond. Finally, the issue left the 'black letter' space of scholarly research and becomes the great topic of our time since June 2016 and March 2017 respectively, when UK people in *referendum* and the UK government by official notification started the most vivid and most important question of the history of European integration—the withdrawal of the United Kingdom from the European Union.

This text intends to give the overview of the 'withdrawal question' within the evolution of European integration and to analyse the nature of prescribed path of terminating the membership as it stands in EU law today. We must admit that analysis of such a proceeding and advancing topic brings the risk of being '*passé*'. On the other side, it´s the challenging and interesting adventure to be the part of this big story. From the legal point of view, art. 50 of the TEU, even rightly criticised for the multitude of shortcomings and declared as being the vehicle, that was not intended to be driven,[8] could be understood as archetypal constitutional provision. The general and short in its wording, giving the space for flexible interpretation and establishment of the constitutional practice. But politically this is not the case. Abstractness of the provision dealing with such a dramatic question complicates the process of withdrawal and gives rise to serious level of uncertainty. It is quite a risky business to enter the uncharted territory in the crucial question like this.[9] The questions arise and solutions appear on the day to day basis. Art. 50 shall for sure obtain new legal quality once being used in the process of *Brexit*. But the end of story is not here now. People of Europe, politicians and institutions are facing the

[7]Herbst (2006), pp. 383–389; Friel (2004), pp. 407–428; or de Waele (2005) pp. 169–189.

[8]Amato (2016).

[9]Craig (2016), pp. 447–468.

unprecedented (regrettable) situations. But the lawyers are looking for establishment of constitutional practice, so needed relative to the vague and abstract Treaty proviso.

2 Setting the Scene: The Situation Before Lisbon

Nobody wants to speak about divorce on the wedding day

The popular motto, often attributed to Abraham Lincoln, portrays perfectly the situation about the right to withdraw pre-Lisbon. Before the entry into force of this Treaty in 2009, in fact, neither the EC Treaty nor the EU Treaty did regulate explicitly the possibility of a Member State to leave the EU. The most probable reason for this silence about withdrawal seems to be the intent of the founders to dissuade Member States from withdrawal.[10] However, the withdrawal itself was never denied by the Treaties and therefore open to be discussed at least on the theoretical base. Another line of interpretation of 'no withdrawal provision' in the Treaties, was connected with the understanding of the integration entity as indissoluble community, that could not be abandoned by its Member States using the international law tools.[11] Unless the Treaty establishing the ECSC (whose duration was limited to 50 years), the Treaties establishing the EEC, Euratom and EU have been concluded for an unlimited period.[12] The undefined commitment of membership was interpreted ambivalently about the theme of the withdrawal.

On the first interpretation, the unlimited duration of the founding Treaties would involve the implied possibility for Member States not having to wait for a "budgeted" expiry and to be able to withdraw at any time.[13] Some subordinated the activation of the withdrawal to the fulfilment of the conditions of application of the principle of *rebus sic stantibus*[14] (art. 62 VCLT); others justified this possibility as available through the withdrawal expressed in the Vienna Convention on the Law of Treaties (1969), *white elephant* of the rules encoded on the theme: under art. 56 of that "a treaty which contains no provision regarding its termination and which does not provide for denunciation or withdrawal is not subject to denunciation or withdrawal", unless it is satisfied that it was "established that the parties intended to

[10]Wyrozumska (2013), pp. 1385–1418.

[11]Ćapeta (2016), p. 7.

[12]Respectively, Art. 312 EC (which replaces the EEC), Art. 208 EAEC, Art. 51 TUE.

[13]In this regard, the words of Von Mises (1983, p. 34): 'No people and no part of a people shall be held against its will in a political association that it does not want'.

[14]It is better to remind that this clause does not exempt the withdrawing State from showing the actual change in those conditions, although it is a case of denunciation that is independent of the length of the Treaty and that lives its own ontological and conceptual autonomy. The exceptionality hypothesis, therefore, does not justify in any way the assessment of this option in terms of withdrawal *ad libitum*, but rather as a case of withdrawal *ad nutum*, using a dear distinction with regards to the contractual legal tradition.

admit the possibility of denunciation or withdrawal"; or that "a right of denunciation or withdrawal may be implied by the nature of the treaty."[15] Both exceptions lend themselves, obviously, to be admitted, or excluding, according to opposite subjective interpretations, but not for this unfounded. However, the argument was used mainly by the doctrine that believes that, even before the entry into force of the Lisbon Treaty, Member States had the right to withdraw from the Union under the codification of 1969 and according, therefore, to the customary international law expressed in the Convention,[16] confirming fully the affiliation of the European Union Law with the International Treaties.

In this line of thinking also adhered, even in filigree, several national constitutional courts, which were firmly opposed to the idea that the Member States, joining the Community, agreed to give up their sovereignty: along these lines, in fact, the participation in the Union entails *a mere transfer of shares of sovereignty*[17] and not a definitive failure of the same. Although, mind you, as *ultima ratio*, the German and Spanish Constitutional Courts have left, then, foreseeing the possibility of withdrawal, in the presence of an irreconcilable conflict between the provisions of the respective Constitutions and the primary and secondary law of the Union.[18] More prudent has been, however, the Italian Constitutional Court, but still deployed in defence of the values essential content, in particular, in Part I of the Constitution. In this regard, it is worth quoting the considerations of a consolidated approach that would consider necessary the prior amendment of the national Constitution, as far as it provides for the participation in the European integration process, before activating any procedure of withdrawal. Even in the case of Italy it would need to proceed with the amendment of Title V[19] insofar as the Constitutional Law n. 3/2001 has introduced compliance with the constraints deriving from EU.[20] That reference, although not explicit as in the constitutions of other Member States, seems, in fact, to constitute a constraint of belonging to the European Union: a more explicit anchor was foreseen in the draft constitutional reform to art. 116, but it has not been successful.[21] Therefore, according to this approach, joining the European Union would not affect the right of withdrawal by a Member State, as a natural consequence of the principle of sovereignty.[22]

[15]To these assumptions are added the provisions of Art. 54 of the Convention, according to which "the termination of a treaty or the withdrawal of a party may take place: (a) in conformity with the provisions of the treaty; (b) at any time by consent of all the parties after consultation with the other contracting States". Albeit difficult configurability, given the unanimity of the 28 Member States, it is still a hypothesis possibly workable.

[16]In this sense see Tesauro (2012), p. 93.

[17]Puglia (2014), p. 339.

[18]Vellano (2007), p. 508.

[19]The procedure for constitutional amendment is required by the Italian Constitution in the Art. 138.

[20]Vellano (2007), p. 509.

[21]About this, just see Strozzi (2005), p. 388.

[22]Nicotra (2003), p. 453.

However, according to an interpretation in the opposite direction, just the unlimited duration of the commitment assumed leans in favour of the indissolubility of the bond contract by Member State: the absence of a specific procedure of withdrawal would therefore be the logical consequence of this choice, to be honest a little pragmatic and crystallised in legal abstraction (the question has always been shown to have a "material" side, difficult to contain by regulations). This seems to be the approach adopted by the Court of Justice, obtainable indirectly from some historical judgments (above all, Case C 6/64, Costa v. ENEL[23]): a clearly restrictive view on the possibility to withdraw from the Community which it recalls the sovereignty freely chosen by the Member States with their accession to the treaties, establishing the basis of 'an ever closer union among the European peoples' (Preamble of the EC Treaty - art. 1 TEU). In this historical decision, the European judges had to say that "the transfer, by the States in favour of the Community, of the rights and of the obligations corresponding to the provisions of the Treaty, implies [...] a definitive limitation of their sovereign rights". Furthermore, although It does not omit to consider, even in subsequent judgments, the fact that the treaty has been concluded in the form of international agreement, the Court arises from the very beginning from the perspective of understanding the treaty as a genuine 'federal' constitution,[24] where the covenant of "the marriage" is characterised by the permanence and the unlimited time.[25] The attempt to formalise this interpretation would have been only postponed.

Nevertheless, the existence of a jurisprudential and doctrinal trend favourable to the possibility of withdrawing let open a debate on the "output" mode: the withdrawing State and remaining States would have contest for real diplomatic negotiations prior to formalise withdrawal. Negotiation necessary to verify whether the conditions for withdrawal (e.g., the change of the initial conditions), to determine the full legitimacy of the relevant proceedings (the absence of which may lead to the assumption of sanctions against the withdrawing State), to define economic issues, in and out, with respect to the Member State in question.[26] According to another theory, it could bring about a scenario completely new and different: the question could be brought to the attention of the Court of Justice by the Commission or by another Member State,[27] with the possibility that the withdrawing State implicated does not recognise anymore, specifically because of the withdrawal, the jurisdiction of the Court of Justice.[28]

---

[23] Costa vs. ENEL, 6/64, ECLI:EU:C:1964:66.

[24] To express clearly this idea, the Advocate General Lagrange spoke about "a single market based on the creation of a separate judicial system of the Member States, but intimately and even organically tied to it."

[25] Nicotra (2003), p. 452.

[26] Vellano (2007), p. 509.

[27] Infringement procedure, respectively, in Art. 226 and 227 TEC.

[28] Vellano (2007), p. 510.

3 An Express "Exit Clause": A Birth That Lasted Twenty-Five Years

The path, which has found the end with the express provision in the Lisbon Treaty, has been, without any doubt, so long and tortuous. Before art. I-60 TCE (forerunner of the art. 50 TEU), that would have regulated the withdrawal if the Union's constitutional process (2004) had had a good end, there are various "unofficial" proposals that provide an insertion of a provision of that way that should be carefully evaluated. The *Spinelli's Draft* (1984) and the *Oreja-Herman's Draft* (1994), both pre-ordered to create a possible Constitution of the European Union, not yet reflected in an express provision on the possibility to withdraw. But this conclusion would be simply synonymous and symptom of superficiality. Both art. 82 of the *Spinell's draft* and art. 33 of the *Guidelines in the negotiations of Maastricht* (1990) ventilate the hypothesis of a "constitutional breakdown"[29], resulting in withdrawal from the Community, for the States that do not ratify the Constitution, only if most of the Member States, consisting of the 2/3 of the population of the Community,[30] agrees with it. Like them, it is the provision of art. 47 of the *Oreja-Herman Bozza*, published in February 1994 at the request of the Institutional Affairs Committee of the European Parliament: in this case, however, the *ratio* was 4/5. We are faced with a provision requiring the withdrawal still occasional, linked to occasions merely contingent and away from the hypothesis of unilateral withdrawal by the will of the Union Member State. The first proposal in this regard comes from the academic environment: a group of students (*European Constitutional Group*) published a draft of the European Constitution, whose art. I-60 contained an express provision on the withdrawal: this is guaranteed to each Member State, provided that the complaint is notified a year before.[31] At the beginning of the new millennium appears in the same wake the draft published by the magazine *The Economist*, whose Art. 20 reads simply: "a member State may leave the Union at any time"; a more complex and detailed proposal also comes from a group of researchers at the European University Institute in Florence.[32] The assessed drafts differ for solutions to the issue, but they all have in common a limited impact and the general indifference of the political "environment" of the time: nevertheless, it is undoubted the utility that the same have as a starting point in the scientific debate on the right of withdrawal.

The situation changed radically in the first years of this decade, when the greatest actors on the European stage decided to introduce in the Treaties a clause dedicated to the withdrawal from the Union by a Member State. The proposal was advanced for the first time during the works of the European Convention at the *Laeken*

---

[29]De Witte (2005), p. 21.

[30]Zbiral (2008), p. 306.

[31]Ibid p. 307.

[32]Ibid p. 308.

European Council (14–15 December 2001) to outline the *Treaty establishing a Constitution for Europe.*

During the works they were presented numerous doctrinal contributions, all of which suggested to give different trims to the exit clause.[33] The most important theoretical models for the elaboration of a withdrawal clause were three: *State Primacy*, *Union Primacy* and *Union Control*,[34] the concepts flowing between federal and international mode of understanding of membership of state in some greater bond. The federal systems usually do not permit the unilateral withdrawal without necessary change of constitution. Federations are based on the notion of indissoluble unity. On the contrary the international law perspective when dealing with the membership of the states in the international organisations or when dealing with the international treaty regimes is more open and more tolerant to the autonomy of state's will (and the state´s sovereignty[35]) hence rules of international law, as stated above, allow a state to end up its commitments arising from the international treaties and analogically to end up the membership in the international organisations founded by the international treaty.

The first model, which not coincidentally was supported by a doctrinal contribution presented by the British government, attributed to the Member States complete freedom to withdraw, without the possibility of intervention or *veto* by the Union institutions.

The second model, by contrast, embodied a fatal membership concept: once inside the Union, it would no longer be possible to get out.

The third and final model, that of the Union Control, offered this possibility through a mutual decision, shared by all the parties, following the model of the Canadian Federation, thus revealing itself a real example of negotiation.

The later converged solution in art. I-59 of the draft Constitution, and finally adopted in art. I-60 of the Treaty establishing a Constitution for Europe, however, "escaped" from each of these three models. Despite the failure of the Treaty establishing a Constitution for Europe, foundered after the failed ratification by France and the Netherlands, the former withdrawal clause of art. I-60 was one of multitude of provisions which, far from being shelved, merged in an almost unchanged form in the Lisbon Treaty.

The latter, which entered into force on 1 December 2009, defines the current Union's institutional framework, regulating the withdrawal of a Member State with the art. 50[36] of the new Treaty on European Union. Explicit regulation of the right for unilateral voluntary withdrawal from the Union apparently finished the debates

[33]Snavely (2004), pp. 213–230.

[34]Friel (2004), p. 422.

[35]Voluntary membership in international organisations was always seen as a basis of state sovereignty. It was the case even with the historically first global integration organisation—League of Nations. Voluntary membership was also in its case the (positive) answer to the question whether states which joined an international organisation and so accepted certain limitations on their sovereignty can still be seen as sovereign subjects (Le Fur 1935).

[36]This is the current text of the Art. 50 TEU:

whether withdrawal from the Union should be perceived from constitutional (federal) of international point of view. Explicit regulation of the right to withdraw from the Union shifted the discussions towards later option and underlined the concept of the EU as the bound of sovereign states. Inclusion of such proviso into the treaties was perceived as positive notwithstanding the fact that it deals with the negative question (the termination of the membership). It was observed as the constitutional rule having the positive and promoting impact on the integration process.[37] The hypothesis was that Members States having the explicit right to determine their destiny in/out of the integration processes would be better prepared to cooperate and accept the outcomes of the functioning of the EC/EU on the quotidian basis. The withdrawal option could therefore lessen the federalisation tendencies and make EU more operable.[38] There are of course also opposite views understanding the inclusion of the explicit exit clause as too risky. They speak about the 'rule of possible' pointing on the abusive potential of declaration of right to withdrawal.[39]

---

1. Any Member State may decide to withdraw from the Union in accordance with its own constitutional requirements;
2. A Member State which decides to withdraw shall notify the European Council of its intention. In the light of the guidelines provided by the European Council, the Union shall negotiate and conclude an agreement with that State, setting out the arrangements for its withdrawal, taking account of the framework for its future relationship with the Union. That agreement shall be negotiated in accordance with Article 218(3) of the Treaty on the Functioning of the European Union. It shall be concluded on behalf of the Union by the Council, acting by a qualified majority, after obtaining the consent of the European Parliament;
3. The Treaties shall cease to apply to the State in question from the date of entry into force of the withdrawal agreement or, failing that, 2 years after the notification referred to in paragraph 2, unless the European Council, in agreement with the Member State concerned, unanimously decides to extend this period;
4. For the purposes of paragraphs 2 and 3, the member of the European Council or of the Council representing the withdrawing Member State shall not participate in the discussions of the European Council or Council or in decisions concerning it.

A qualified majority shall be defined in accordance with Article 238(3)(b) of the Treaty on the Functioning of the European Union;

5. If a State which has withdrawn from the Union asks to rejoin, its request shall be subject to the procedure referred to in Article 49.

[37]Herbst (2006), pp. 388; Weiler (1985), pp. 282–298.

[38]For example, Czech Constitutional Court noticed this conceptual change and used the right to withdraw from the Union as an argument in favour of preserving the sovereignty of the Czech Republic when participating on the European integration. It reminded that: '[...] the Treaty of Lisbon newly introduces, in Art. 50 of the Treaty on EU, the possibility of withdrawing from the organization. This can take place by agreement between the withdrawing state and the Council as a representative of the member states (i.e., not with the Commission, as a representative of the interests of the Union itself), and if an agreement is not reached, the Treaty itself gives the withdrawing state a notice period. Thus, the manner of termination membership is also typical for an international organization, not a contemporary federative state, and this possibility, on the contrary, strengthens the sovereignty of member states. [...]' Decision in case Treaty of Lisbon I, Pl. ÚS 19/08, ECLI:CZ:US:2008:Pl.US.19.08.1, point 146.

[39]Klabbers (2016), p. 555; Wessel (2016), p. 2.

Thus from 2009, within the complex legal framework offered by the European Union's primary law, there is an express possibility of withdrawal available to the Member States of the organisation. Nevertheless, the discipline offered by art. 50 TEU, as articulated, also opens the way to interpretation difficulties, doubts, and criticism because of its several dark traits in some steps and its lack of clarity about the means of implementation of such withdrawal. The doctrine has criticised the wording of art. 50 TEU in relation to four particular aspects: the absence of conditions for the start of the withdrawal procedure, making in this way possible abuses of the instrument; his lack of analyticity in defining the individual phases of the procedure leading to the withdrawal; the darkness of the status that the country would enjoy withdrawing during the negotiations; the minimum content that the withdrawal agreement should assume for the purpose of managing, as much as possible, an unproblematic withdrawal. The current structure of art. 50 TEU, and in particular the choice not to include any express condition (apart from being subject to compliance with constitutional requirements) to operate the withdrawal could make it easier the blackmailing by States wishing to obtain special concessions, under the threat of disintegration of the Union.[40] However, in front of the new art. 50 TEU, the doctrine has set from the beginning a preliminary application: this standard gives the States a right of unilateral termination or rather the exit from the Union must necessarily follow an agreed procedure?

4 Two Alternatives of Withdrawal? Really?

4.1 The Unilateral Withdrawal

As often happens, different doctrinal currents are deployed in favour of only one of these reconstructions.

Some authors, for example, have focused on individual parts of the rule to affirm that States have the right to leave the European Union unilaterally, without any obligation to conclude a withdrawal agreement.[41] According to a less radical thesis, indeed (however, it is still part of the same current of thought), the letter of the second paragraph of the rule would place an obligation to negotiate and conclude an agreement not so much on the State, which would still have the possibility to withdraw unilaterally at the expiry of the two-year deadline for the negotiations, but rather on the Union's shoulders.[42] Paragraph 3 of art. 50 TEU, in fact, expressly leaves open the possibility of implementing the withdrawal by the State concerned even without withdrawal agreement if the parties are unable to agree within two years after its notification to the European Council. Although the deadline for

[40]Hofmeister (2010), p. 599.

[41]Tatham (2012), p. 152.

[42]Łazowski (2012), p. 526.

conducting the negotiations may be subject to extension, the complexity of the issues at stake and the need for a unanimous vote of the European Council to obtain it make the failure of negotiations, and therefore the absence of withdrawal agreement, a realistic assumption.

As we said, the unilateral withdrawal, in the absence of an agreement, would seem possible from the wording of paragraph 3 of art. 50 TEU. However, in the absence of a proper legal framework governing the withdrawal, the issues raised by this would risk transforming the farewell of the Union in a catastrophic event. In the absence of a minimum reference standard, inevitably we would witness the birth of frictions and disputes (political, economic, and legal) between the Union and the former Member State, whose solution would lead to unpredictable results, especially for the leaving State. Unable to conduct fruitful negotiations with their former European partners, the withdrawing State would be obliged to take note of the loss of the access to the single market, to introduce—if it were a Member of the Eurozone—an independent currency (with adjoining issue of renaming the debt), to recalibrate its geopolitical position in a rapidly changing world, to manage the numerous loss of job by its citizens once used in the administration of the Union, to legislate anew in the many subjects once governed by European law having direct effect, and so long. All this, managing alone and in strong bargaining asymmetry with the European Union and its members.

Despite these possible drawbacks, based on these considerations and other elements, the cited doctrinal current deduces, inside art. 50 TEU, the existence in the hands of the Member States of a unilateral withdrawal from the Union.

4.2 *The Withdrawal Agreement*

Another part of the doctrine invites to undertake a systematic reading of the Art. 50 TEU, globally understood, which ponders the legal, economic, and political context in which it should operate. Considerations of this type may only highlight that the withdrawal by agreement is not only the hypothesis far preferable, but also the only viable *de facto*. An abrupt unilateral withdrawal, as we saw, would end making so difficult resolving the issues concerned.[43]

Going through the process outlined by art. 50 TEU, a Member State which take—in accordance with its own constitutional provisions—the decision to leave the Union shall notify their intentions to the European Council. The Union, according to the provisions of art. 218, par. 3 TFEU[44] (with the appointment of a team of negotiators who would follow the guidelines dictated by the EU Council), will negotiate and conclude with the State concerned an agreement, governing the

[43]Di Paolo (2016).

[44]We have just said that the Art. 50 TEU does not consider, itself the concrete procedure of the withdrawal negotiation.

withdrawal and the frame of future relations between the Union and the State. The agreement will be concluded, from the Union, by the European Union Council, who will vote by qualified majority after the approval of the European Parliament. The European Treaties will cease to be applied to the withdrawing State upon the date of the entry into force of the Agreement Withdrawal, or, in case of failure of the attainment of the agreement, two years after the notification indicated in the first paragraph of the article. However, it remains a possibility that, given the paucity of the period granted to the negotiations, in relation to the complexity of the issues to be addressed, the withdrawing State and the Council agree an extension of the same.

Art. 50, par. 2, TEU provides rather general indications about the content that the withdrawal agreement will have: the norm is limited to attribute the task of regulating the withdrawal at issue and to dictate the overall framework for future relations between the withdrawing State and the Union. The main purpose of the withdrawal agreement is to adjust in the best way an operation in itself traumatic, also because of the absence of rules able to respond to major legal, economic, and political issues, inevitably present and to be solved. These, that the parties will have to discuss and resolve during negotiations, are so numerous and complex that make potentially insufficient the two-years term. This period, in fact, will be necessary to provide for the reorganisation of all EU bodies (e.g. The Council) in which sit representatives of the withdrawing State, as well as fixing a date from which the latter ceases to participate in meetings of the first, including also the multitude of agencies, organisations and institutions that give each day life at the Union.[45] The parties should allow citizens of the withdrawing State to continue its work within bodies of the Union until the date of entry into force of the withdrawal. This solution, albeit shared, however, ends up raising a paradox: the risk that the Union's policies and priorities are decided or influenced by significant periods of time by officers now less sensitive to the common European interest. Art. 50 par. 4, TEU merely provides the only abstention of the members of the Council and the European Council representing the Member State wishing to withdraw from the deliberations and decisions that concern them, leaving no express provision for the condition of the other leaders or officers. The withdrawal agreement could not fail to regulate also the termination of the work of the members of the European Court of Justice (e.g., judges of the Court of First Instance, or the Advocate General - one of them is always from UK) having nationality of the withdrawing State, providing a suitable framework to coordinate it with any cases, concerning the withdrawing State, which are still pending until the entry into force of the withdrawal.

Sensitive issues mentioned in the previous pages are only a small part of the numerous issues that the withdrawal of a Member State from the Union would let emerging: just think about how the integration between European countries has become deep in the last few year (for example, the EU's law-making has become so impressive as to make unthinkable abandoning it abruptly).

---

[45] Łazowski (2012), p. 530.

For these reasons, the doctrine recommends almost unanimously that the possible withdrawal of a Member State must be brought to fruition through the signing of a withdrawal agreement.

5 Conclusion

The procedure under art. 50 TEU, therefore, provides the opportunity to leave the European Union along two different roads: while leading to the same terminal, each of them still presents a path and its consequences. However, based on these and other considerations, the majority of the commentators has concluded that, although art. 50 TEU makes it possible in theory both, in a realistic scenario the complications, which would inevitably encounter the first (*pathological path*), make it workable, in practice, only the second one (*natural path*).[46] Anyway, the procedure should be carried out by the parties following the principle of loyal cooperation, assisting each other and solving the tasks which flow from the Treaties.[47] A joint reading of art. 50 and art. 4, par. 3 TEU, should, therefore, further reduce the viability of the "pathological" hypothesis of unilateral termination, resulting this theoretically possible but unrealistic,[48] as the spirit of the treaties is aimed at promoting cooperation between the parties, even in the management of a withdrawal between them.

In conclusion, for the first time in the European history, after the entry into force of the Lisbon Treaty, the EU Member States have a clause that explicitly allows and regulates the possibility of withdrawal from the Union by one of them. However, the European Union's exit does not prevent the state to back off because of a future afterthought: if the former Member States expresses a will to resume its EU membership, it will still have to run from the beginning the whole process described in art. 49 TEU, in a manner similar to any other candidate for accession (art. 50, par. 5, TEU).

A state's withdrawal from the EU must be first a consensual process. A Member State wishing to withdraw notifies its intention to the European Council, which provides guidelines for the conclusion of an agreement setting out the arrangements for its withdrawal. These negotiations are on behalf of the EU conducted by a negotiator (Commission) and when the negotiations are completed, the agreement is concluded on behalf of the European Union by the Council, after obtaining the consent of the European Parliament. The EU institutions can thus affect the process of a state's withdrawal, but not the withdrawal itself. The participation of institutions on the withdrawal was labelled as a display of Europeanisation of residual national

[46]Some authors (Nicolaides, Athanassiou, Lazowski, Hofmeister) have serious doubts about the practical viability of the withdrawal totally unilateral because of the weight of the legal, political, and economic challenges that such a move concerns.

[47]Art. 4, paragraph 3 TEU. This rule introduces the so called "principle of cooperation".

[48]Łazowski (2016), pp. 1297, 300.

sovereignty.[49] The withdrawal agreement is not an absolute condition of membership termination. If the agreement is not agreed on or is not accepted, membership comes to an end two years after the Member State declared its intention to the European Council.

The Member States are the original holders of competences and act as a *Master of the Treaties* but moreover they remain as independent units capable to make the own decision about their future. Their right to withdraw from the Union, which was introduced by the Lisbon underlines this fact.[50] Member States must be understood as the "holders of their own destiny", the masters in the Schmitt's extreme situation. Carl Schmitt commences his Political Theology by famous sentence that 'sovereign is who decides on the exception', where exception means the stepping outside the ordinary state of things, to stand outside the legal rules. Within the supranational legal system, the Schmitt's exception means to stand outside the EU, not to be the one of the Member States. This crucial (and extreme) position is absolutely in the hands of every Member State, which should act as a sovereign when using the exit clause of art. 50 TEU. Accession and withdrawal are autonomous rights of the states and the membership is their privilege, which cannot be taken away by a decision of an institution or a decision of other Member States.[51]

References

Amato G (2016) Father of EU divorce clause demands tough stance on British exit. World News (21.07.2016). http://www.reuters.com/article/us-britain-eu-amato-idUSKCN1012Q8

Craig P (2016) Brexit: a drama in six acts. Eur Law Rev 41:447–468

Ćapeta T (2016) Brexit and the EU constitutional order: a three act tragedy. Croat Yearb Eur Law Policy 12:1–23

De Waele H (2005) The European Union on the road to a new legal order - the changing legality of member state withdrawal. Tilburg Foreign Law Rev 12:169–189

De Witte B (2005) The process of ratification and the crisis options: a legal perspective. In: Curtin D (ed) The EU constitution: the best way forward? Springer, The Hague, p 21

Di Paolo E (2016) L'uscita dall'euro e dall'Unione Europea: teoria e pratica del Brexit e del Grexit. Department of European Union Law of University of Pisa, Italy

Friel M (2004) Providing a constitutional framework for withdrawal from the EU: Article 59 of the draft European constitution. Int Comp Law Q 53:407–428

Hamuľák O (2016) National sovereignty in the European Union. View from the Czech perspective. Springer, Cham

Herbst J (2006) Observations on the right to withdraw from the European Union: who are the "Masters of the Treaties"? In: Dann P, Rynkowski M (eds) The Unity of the European constitution, Beiträge zum ausländischen öffentlichen Recht und Völkerrecht, vol 186. Springer, Berlin, pp 383–389

---

[49] Kumm (2005).

[50] Hamuľák (2016), p. 85.

[51] The extreme decision on withdrawal is the part of Member State autonomy even in constitutional structure like EU and therefore state cannot be prevented to do so. See Nicolaides (2013), p. 212.

Hofmeister H (2010) Should I Stay or Should I Go? A critical analysis of the right to withdraw from the EU. Eur Law J 16:589–603

Klabbers J (2016) Editorial: continent in crisis. Eur J Int Law 27:553–556

Kumm M (2005). To be a European citizen: constitutional patriotism and the treaty establishing a constitution for Europe. In: Eriksen EO et al (eds) The European constitution: the Rubicon crossed? Arena, Oslo, pp 7–63

Łazowski A (2012) Withdrawal from the European Union and alternatives to membership. Eur Law Rev 37:526–530

Łazowski A (2016) Unilateral withdrawal from the EU: realistic scenario or a folly? J Eur Public Policy 23:1294–1301

Mehdi R (2007) Brèves observations sur la consecration constitutionelle d'un droit de retrait volontaire. In: Demaret P, Govaere I, Hanf D (eds) Dynamiques Juridiques Européennes. Peter Lang, Bruxelles, p. 113. Quote in Salmon J (ed) Dictionnaire de droit international public. Bruylant AUF, Brussels, 2001

Nelli Feroci F (2005) L'Unione europea: tra la crisi del Trattato Costituzionale e i dilemmi dell'allargamento. In: Ferrari Bravo L (ed) La Comunità internazionale (LX), trimestrale, organo della Società Italiana per l'Organizzazione Internazionale. Editoriale Scientifica, Naples, p 597

Nicolaides P (2013) Withdrawal from the European Union: a typology of effects. Maastrich J Eur Comp Law 20:209–2019

Nicotra I (2003) Il diritto di recesso e il Trattato che istituisce la Costituzione europea. In: Lucarelli A. (ed) Studi sulla Costituzione europea, percorsi e ipotesi. A. Patroni Griffi. Edizioni Scientifiche Italiane, Naples, pp 452–453

Puglia M (2014) Commento agli artt 49–50 TUE. In: Tizzano A (ed) Trattati dell'Unione europea. A. Giuffrè, Milan, pp 333–339

Snavely AC (2004) Should we leave the backdoor open? Does an agreement Uniting States need a withdrawal provision: the European Union Draft Constitution. UMKC Law Rev 73:213–230

Strozzi G (2005) Diritto dell'Unione Europea. Parte Istituzionale G. Giappichelli, Turin, p 388

Tatham AF (2012) Do not mention divorce at wedding, Darling! EU accession and withdrawal after lisbon. In: Biondi A, Eeckhout P, Ripley S (eds) EU law after lisbon. Oxford University Press, Oxford, p 152

Tesauro G (2012) Diritto dell'Unione europea, Settima Edizione. CEDAM, Padua, p 93

Vellano M (2007) Espulsione e recesso dall'Unione europea: profili attuali e prospettive future. In: Ferrari Bravo L (ed) La Comunità internazionale (LXII), trimestrale, organo della Società Italiana per l'Organizzazione Internazionale. Editoriale Scientifica, Naples, pp 503–510

Von Mises L (1983) Nation, State and Economy: contributions to the politics and history of our time. New York University Press, New York, p 3

Weiler J (1985) Alternatives to withdrawal from an international organization: the case of the European Economic Community. Israel Law Rev 20:282–298

Wessels W (2001) Widening and deepening. Transatlantic Internationale Politik 2:5–11

Wessel RA (2016) You can check out any time you like, but can you really leave? On 'Brexit' and leaving international organizations. Int Organ Law Rev 13:197–209

Wyrozumska A (2013) Commentary on Art. 50 TEU. In: Blanke H-J, Mamgiameli S (eds) The treaty on European Union. A commentary. Springer, Heidelberg, pp 1385–1418

Zbiral R (2008) Searching for an optimal withdrawal clause for the European Union. In: Niedobitek M, Zemanek J (eds) Continuing the European constitutional debate, German and Czech contributions from a legal perspective. Chemnitzer Europastudien. Duncker & Humblot, Berlin, pp 306–308

From EFTA to EC/EU and Back to EFTA? The European Economic Area (EEA) As a Possible Scenario for the UK-EU Relations After Brexit

Christoph Schewe and Davids Lipsens

Abstract Brexit is announced to take place and it appears, that the most probable scenario for the UK is the "Norway-Option", i.e., to (again) become a member of the European Free Trade Association (EFTA) and join the EEA. The chapter identifies the major claims of the leave-campaign to analyse, whether by doing so, the Brexit proponents will achieve what they campaigned for. Furthermore, the paper explains the functioning of the EEA, exploring the potential changes for the UK, the EU, and the EEA/EFTA.

1 Introduction: What Could Life After Brexit Look Like?

Despite the indications of preceeding opinion polls, the results to the Brexit referendum took the wider EU public by surprise: On the question "Should the United Kingdom remain a member of the European Union or leave the European Union?", almost 52% opted for "Leave the European Union" while only 48% chose "Remain a member of the European Union".[1] As this question only asked for "leave" or "remain", without further formulating the conditions or aims of the leave, there are no other indicators for the UK apart from leaving the EU. However, when considering the viable options, the UK will need to consider the main reasons of the vote for leave. The leave campaigns provide some insight, when formulating their aims to "release Britain from the European Superstate",[2] to regain sovereignty[3]; to be able to

[1]Bloomberg (2016). "EU Referendum: Final Results." Accessed September 3. http://www.bloomberg.com/graphics/2016-brexit-referendum/.

[2]The only substantial reason for leave at: http://grassrootsout.co.uk/. Accessed September 3.

[3]Leave (2016). "Our vision." Accessed September 3. http://leave.eu/en/our-campaign#our-vision.

C. Schewe (✉)
University of Latvia, FHVD, Kiel-Altenholz, Reinfeld, Germany
e-mail: schewe@fhvd-sh.de

D. Lipsens
Sorainen Riga, Rīga, Latvia
e-mail: davids.lipsens@sorainen.com

D. Ramiro Troitiño et al. (eds.), *Brexit*,
https://doi.org/10.1007/978-3-319-73414-9_13

put in place our own policies and laws on immigration; to "put in place our own policies and laws on our economy, including industry and energy"; to "be able to take back control of our country"; to "be able to improve upon our position as the fifth largest economy in the world by taking back control of our finances and trade deals. We are now in a position to dictate our own trade agreements with the rest of the world."; to "stop sending £350 million every week to Brussels and instead spend it on our priorities, like the NHS and science research"; to "regain our seats on international institutions like the World Trade Organisation so we are a more influential force for free trade and international cooperation." Furthermore, they advertised as a benefit that "Agriculture and fishing will also benefit from falling under national administration for the first time in over forty years." In sum, the goal is to "negotiate a new UK-EU deal based on free trade and friendly cooperation." A vote to 'leave' would thus signify that "a better, friendlier relationship with the EU is much safer than giving Brussels more power and money every year."[4]

Apart from these claims there are no precise plans prepared for the UK regarding its relation towards the EU after Brexit. While the proceedings of the definite "leave" have not even been officially launched (Art. 50 TFEU) and it is currently estimated, that this will not happen before 2017, scholars and politicians have started to draw potential scenarios. Particularly three[5] potential scenarios are discussed for sketching a potential future: firstly, to join the EFTA and the EEA, secondly, to negotiate a variety of agreements with the EU similar to the relations between the EU and Switzerland[6] and finally, to remain a member of the WTO without any agreement with the EU.

None of these scenarios perfectly fits all issues addressed by the leave-campaign, which means that all options are theoretically viable but imply drawbacks for the UK. For the upcoming negotiations, the only clear mandate is the decision to "leave the EU". When pursuing this objective, the UK-negotiators should consider that the referendum is based on a very thin majority of 2%. For this reason, there is no obligation to adopt all claims of the leave-campaign to 100% but makes it probable to negotiate an agreement that would achieve a compromise reflecting the referendum, as well as the realistic options with a view to the political and economic priorities for the country.[7]

[4]Vote Leave, Take Control (2016). "The campaign." Accessed September 3. http://www.voteleavetakecontrol.org/campaign.

[5]Jean-Claude Piris proposes seven alternatives: If the UK votes to leave. The seven alternatives to EU membership, download at: http://www.cer.org.uk/publications/archive/policy-brief/2016/if-uk-votes-leave-seven-alternatives-eu-membership.

[6]European Union External Action (2016). "EU relations with Switzerland." Accessed September 3. http://eeas.europa.eu/switzerland/index_en.htm.

[7]In principle, British negotiators would also have to consider the motivation of the voters. See for instance: Matthew J. Goodwin, What Really Caused Brexit? Analysis reveals why Britain confounded the expectations of pundits and mainstream politicians. Newsweek, 22 July 2016, available at: http://europe.newsweek.com/brexit-causes-result-who-voted-leave-eu-analysis-matthew-goodwin-483100?rm=eu.

In the current debate, both sides—UK and EU—utter as a preference, to keep the UK in the single market. Notwithstanding the theoretic option for a "Swiss model",[8] i.e. a choice for the UK, which agreement with the EU it would like to sign, this is improbable to be realistic, given that it would amount to a "cherry picking" that, for the EU, would be unacceptable. Furthermore, this option reflects a decade-long negotiation process with Switzerland with a very peculiar geographic position in the heart of the EU.[9] For that reason, the most realistic option would be the UK joining the EEA, which might amount to a form of compromise for those who opted for "leave"and the "remainers". The participation would keep the EU and the UK together as close trading partners, conceding the UK more autonomy in a range of aspects, albeit—as will be elaborated in this contribution—not in every single field as envisaged by the "leavers".

Although the EFTA and the EEA have already existed for decades, its structure, decision-making process and the relation towards the EU are relatively unknown. For that reason, this article will sketch the basic structure of the EEA institutional law (II.1) before introducing the substantive law, which also provides an overview of the policies covered by this agreements (II.2). Subsequently, the article proceeds discussing the potential changes under the (unmodified) EEA for the UK (III.1) for the EU (III.2) and finally for the EEA/EFTA. In these regards, the article aims, to highlight relevant changes, commenting on the viability of aspects, advertised in the "leave"-campaign.

2 A Scenario for Institutionalising Brexit: The Legal Framework of the EEA

The EEA is not an international organisation but an economic area that brings together the EU and its 28 Member States on the one and the three EFTA-states on the other side, covering the four fundamental freedoms.[10] In line with this economic focus, the EEA furthermore covers the directly trade related areas of competition,[11] state aid[12] and transportation policy.[13] Furthermore, it also covers horizontal policies related to the four freedoms, such as social policy,[14] consumer

[8]This "à la carte" model has been developed over decades, concedes Switzerland a unique position, which might also consider Switzerland's unique geographic position in the centre of the EU and its (formerly) strong negotiation position. To prevent other Member States from following the UK, it is not probable, that the EU would agree to an "á la carte" option for the UK.

[9]Burke et al. (2016), p. 76.

[10]Articles 8-45 EEA.

[11]Articles 53-60 EEA.

[12]Articles 62 and 63 EEA.

[13]Articles 47-52 EEA.

[14]Articles 66-71 EEA.

protection,[15] environment[16] and company law.[17] Most of those areas are not regulated with the Agreement itself, but in Annexes to the EEA Agreement, which however rank on the same level.[18] These EEA agreements were concluded in 1992 but also comprise EEA-relevant EU legislation. This means that EEA is not static, but in contrast that, the EEA continuously evolves in parallel to the EU internal market, adopting relevant legal acts of the EU.

While one may tend to assume that the EEA internal market, as it comprises free movement of goods, would imply the existence of a customs union, this is not the case and, given that this has important implications, it needs to be stressed that it is neither a customs union nor does it cover a common commercial policy.[19] Other significant areas not comprised by the EEA Agreement are the common agriculture and fisheries policies.[20]

2.1 Institutional Law of the EFTA/EEA

The EEA is not an international organisation but a trade agreement, which partially explains that it is based on a somewhat peculiar structure.[21] It is firstly based on the EU with its bodies and institutions on the one side, and secondly, on the EFTA (see 1.1). For administering the EEA, these two "pillars" form joint bodies in between (see 1.2 The EEA),[22] for which the structure is described as a "two pillar system". It illustrates, that within this structure, the EEA-EFTA states have not transferred any legislative competencies to the joint EEA bodies,[23] but—jointly with the EU—directly participate.

Historically, the EEA needs to be seen in the context with the creation of the EFTA. Initially, noting the success of the European Communities, in 1960, seven other Western European countries created an alternative organisation, the EFTA which had a similar aim albeit without the purported deep level of integration and legal commitment as the ECs. Although membership rose to ten in 1970, it dropped to four, when six Member States left and joined the EU.

---

[15] Article 72 EEA.

[16] Articles 73-75 EEA.

[17] Article 77 EEA.

[18] Article 2 (a) EEA. Albeit, the latest jurisprudence of the EFTA Court seems to suggest, that there is in fact a hierarchical order between the main part of the Agreement and the acts referred to in the Annexes, see Case E-7/11, Grund, 2012, para. 82.

[19] Case E-2/97, Mag Instrument Inc. And California Trading Company Norway, Ulsteen (1997), para. 25. Hereinafter: Cases beginning with "E" signify EFTA Court judgments.

[20] EFTA (2016d). "The Basic Features of the EEA Agreement." Accessed September 3. http://www.efta.int/eea/eea-agreement/eea-basic-features.

[21] Baudenbacher (2003), p. 881.

[22] Pelkmans and Böhler (2013), p. 47.

[23] Case E-9/97, Sveinbjörnsdóttir v. Iceland (1998), para. 63.

The term European Economic Area, in a sense as we understand it now, first appeared in 1984, when the Luxembourg Declaration on broader cooperation between the EEC and EFTA was signed, in which the ministers were convinced of the need to create a dynamic European economic space.[24] Rooting in an initiative of the European Commissions' president Jacques Delors, the EEA was finally created with the signing of the EEA agreements in 1992 to better link/unite the markets of the EU/EC and the EFTA. This eventually was achieved with the EEA agreements (see below at 1.2), which were signed in 1991 and, in general, reflect the corresponding law of the EC treaties before the Treaty of Maastricht, the founding Treaty of the EU. Hence, the reluctancy of some states to suprantional integration and the date of the agreement explain, why, significant amendments made in the EU Treaties, such as for instance the introduction of EU Citizenship, were not incorporated in the EEA.

2.1.1 The EFTA

Rather than the EEA, it is the two pillars—EFTA and EU—which establish the institutional structure of the EEA. Given that the EFTAs institutional structure is less known than the EU, we will concentrate the on explaining strucure, functioning and decision making of the EFTA, as this is relevant for assessing the potential consequences for the UK, should it become a member of the EFTA and a contracting party of the EEA. It is Most of the bodies on the EFTA pillar were introduced with the inception of the EEA Agreement and to certain extent mirror the functions and competences of corresponding bodies within the EU.[25]

The EFTA Council[26] is the highest governing body of EFTA, which discusses substantive matters, particularly relating to the development of EFTA relations with third countries and the management of free trade agreements. Additionally, it manages relations between the EFTA States under the EFTA Convention. It usually meets eight times a year at the ambassadorial level and twice a year at Ministerial level. In the meetings, the delegations consult, negotiate and decide on policy issues regarding EFTA. Decision are usually reached through consensus,[27] with each Member State represented holding one vote. Furthermore, it reviews relations with the EU third-country policy and administration. With regard to these tasks, it necessarily holds a broad mandate to consider possible policies to promote the overall objectives of the Association and to facilitate the development of links

[24]Luxembourg: Ministerial meeting between EFTA countries and the EC and its Member States. Joint Declaration (1984), p. 2. See: http://www.efta.int/sites/default/files/documents/about-efta/EFTA-EC-joint-declaration-1984.pdf.

[25]An overview is provided by: EFTA 2015. "This is EFTA." Accessed September 3. http://www.efta.int/publications/this-is-efta-2015.

[26]See the self-presentation at http://www.efta.int/about-efta/efta-council.

[27]Article 43 (5) Vaduz Convention, however speaking of "unanimous decisions" Decisions or recommendations shall be regarded as unanimous unless any Member State casts a negative vote.

with other states or international organisations. However, questions relating to the EEA are dealt with by a different, though closely connected body, the Standing Committee (see below). The policies discussed about, are designed to promote the overall objectives of the Association and to facilitate the development of links with other states and international organisations. Furthermore, the Council is responsible for administrative and budgetary matters within EFTA. The Council normally meets twice a year at ministerial level to provide political guidance to EFTA's work. At their summer meeting, the EFTA Ministers discuss free trade relations and developments under the EEA Agreement. An additional meeting devoted to free trade relations is usually held towards the end of the year. Between the ministerial meetings the Council convenes at ambassadorial level. A number of specialised committees assist and report directly to the Council.[28]

Closely related to the objectives and functions of the Council is the EFTA Standing Committee, which is a forum in which ambassadors of the EEA-EFTA states meet to consult each other and to achieve consensus before meeting with the EU in the EEA Joint Commission. Its function besides administration, management, and consultations among the EFTA States,[29] is particularly its central position in the decision-making process, which is defined in Art. 6 Agreement on Standing Committee (SCA). According to this provision (1), "[. . .*the Standing Committee may take decisions, which shall be binding on all EFTA States, and may make recommendations to EFTA States.*" Paragraph 2 of this provision stipulates, that "*Decisions and recommendations of the Standing Committee shall be made by unanimous vote, unless otherwise provided for [. . .]. Decisions or recommendations shall be regarded as unanimous unless any EFTA State casts a negative vote. Decisions and recommendations which are to be made by majority vote require the affirmative vote of the majority of the EFTA States.*" Subsequently, this voting mechanism thus provides a veto-right for each of the EFTA-states (see below at 1.2.b.).[30]

The EFTA Surveillance Authority (ESA), is responsible for monitoring the fulfilment of obligations arising out of the EEA Agreement.[31] Art. 108 of the EEA

[28]The Committee on Third-Country Relations, for instance, oversees the functioning and development of free trade and cooperation agreements with countries outside the European Union. The Committee of Customs and Origin Experts deals with cooperation in the field of customs. The Committee on Trade Facilitation seeks to improve procedures and reduce costs in cross-border trade. The Committee on Technical Barriers to Trade advises the Council on policy and financial issues regarding standardisation, conformity assessment and other issues related to technical legislation. The EFTA Board of Auditors is the auditing authority for the EFTA Secretariat. The Budget Committee assists the Council in budgetary matters. Finally, a number of committees manage the updating of the EFTA Convention.

[29]See Article 3 Agreement on a Standing Committee of the EFTA States, signed in Oporto on 2 May 1992, available at: http://www.efta.int/media/documents/legal-texts/committee-agreements/agreement-on-a-standing-committee/AgreementOnStandingCommittee.pdf and http://www.efta.int/eea/eea-institutions/standing-committee.

[30]Yoichi (2014), p. 523. The author though indicates the factual situation that Pascal Lamy paraphrased as a "fax democracy", see: ibid. at 523 and footnote 31.

[31]Article 109 (1) EEA Agreement.

Agreement stipulates that "The EFTA States shall establish a surveillance authority with procedures similar to those existing in the Community including procedures for ensuring the fulfilment of obligations under this Agreement...",[32] thus directly drawing a parallel to the infringement procedures in the EU under Articles 258–260 of TFEU and indicating the similarity of the respective functions of Commission and the ESA.[33] Similar to the respective function of the European Commission, the ESA is also the competent authority to start infringement procedures in the fields of procurement, State aid and competition.[34]

The EFTA Court is the highest judicial body of the EEA regarding the EFTA States with competence in actions regarding surveillance procedure, appeals in decisions in the field of competition, and settlement of disputes between EFTA States.[35] Additionally to these legal actions, the introduction of the Agreement between the EFTA States on the Establishment of Surveillance Authority and a Court of Justice (Surveillance and Court Agreement, SCA), widened the EFTA Courts competence to the advisory opinion procedure, which is similar to preliminary rulings in the EU. Furthermore, similarly to the EU, any natural or legal person may bring an action to the EFTA Court against the decision of the ESA if it is addressed to that person, or if it is of direct and individual concern.[36] Similar to the CJEU proceedings, the decisions by the EFTA Court regarding infringements and actions for nullification are binding to the parties. However, a remarkable differences exists insofar as the EFTA Courts advisory opinions are not binding to the States. However, in practice the state whose national court has asked the advisory opinion has always followed the EFTA Court's reasoning.[37]

Apart from these institutions, the EFTA disposes of Advisory Bodies, which unfold activities in the EFTA pillar of the EEA. These are the Committee of the Members of Parliaments of the EFTA States or the EFTA Parliamentary Committee,[38] and the EFTA Consultative Committee, a platform for establishing dialogue and consultation between EFTA social partners and authorities in the EFTA States.

[32]Article 108 (1) EEA Agreement.

[33]During the initial negotiations of the EEA Agreement, Switzerland proposed that oversight of fulfilment of obligations under the EEA Agreement should be done by the Commission regarding the Community, and by an independent body in the EFTA pillar—the ESA, see EFTA document LA 33/91. Further details on the ESA's competence are laid down in the SCA, particularly, in Article 5 and its Protocols.

[34]Protocols 2-4 of the SCA.

[35]Article 108 (2) EEA.

[36]Article 36 SCA.

[37]Baudenbacher (2003), assumes that not doing so would otherwise lead to violation of the EEA Agreement, since the contracting parties have assumed "... the obligation to arrive ... at a uniform interpretation and application of this EEA Agreement...", Recital 15 of the Preamble to the EEA Agreement.

[38]EFTA (2016c). "Parliamentary Committee." Accessed September 3. http://www.efta.int/advisory-bodies/parliamentary-committee.

The latter also provides input to the Standing Committee on social and economic aspects of the free trade agreements and EEA.[39]

2.1.2 The EEA

As has been previously indicated, the EU and the EFTA respectively, constitute the two pillars that form the basis of the EEA. The two-pillar comparison indicates, that the EEA does not have a highly institutionalised structure but instead, decisions are taken by joint bodies which are formed by representatives sent by the EU and EFTA, i.e. from the two pillars.

2.1.2.1 Bodies

The first body mentioned among these joint EEA institutions is the EEA Council, which is the political body operating 'between' the two pillars. Functions and composition are stipulated in Article 89 and 90 EEA. According to the former provision "It shall ... be responsible for giving the political impetus in the implementation of the EEA Agreement and laying down general guidelines for the EEA Joint Committee." and thus reminds of the EU's European Council and its functions (Art. 15 (1) TEU). It is composed of members of the Council of the EU and Commission, and of one member of the Government of each of the EFTA States.[40]

The second EEA body mentioned, (Article 92 EEA Agreement), the Joint Committee shall "... ensure the effective implementation and operation of this [the EEA] Agreement".[41] It serves as a forum in which the representatives of both, the EFTA States and EU, meet to discuss and take decisions regarding the EEA. Each of the EFTA States is represented by its own representative, usually at ambassadorial level, speaking with one vote each. Furthermore, it is composed by the representatives of the EU,[42] represented by the European External Action Services (EEAS) and an observer from the ESA.[43] The Joint Committee is responsible for the legislative process within the EEA. In this function, it take decisions on adopting the secondary EU legislation within Annexes of the EEA Agreement (see below at b. EEA-Law and Decision Making).

---

[39]EFTA (2016a). "Consultative Committee." Accessed September 3. http://www.efta.int/advisory-bodies/consultative-committee.

[40]Article 90 EEA.

[41]Article 92 EEA.

[42]The agreements still speak of EC.

[43]Article 1 (3) of the Rules of Procedure of the EEA Joint Committee. Article 93 of the EEA Agreement states, that the Joint Committee consists of representatives of the Contracting Parties, however that does not automatically mean that there is a representative of every EU Member State within the Joint Committee, but rather that they are represented as whole by the EEAS.

The EEA Joint Parliamentary Committee is an advisory body comprised of members of national parliaments of EFTA States and members of the European Parliament, which is however, not directly involved in decision making.[44] The EEA Consultative Committee is another advisory body of the EEA which is composed of members of the EFTA Consultative Committee and the European Social and Economic Committee. It function is, to strengthen contacts between social partners on both sides and provide input on social and economic aspects of the EEA.[45]

2.1.2.2 EEA-Law and Decision-Making

Given that the making of EU secondary law is one of the controversial issues in the Brexit referendum, it is of interest, in how far the procedures differ under the EEA, particularly, if the UK would "regain sovereignty". EEA law is formed by the EEA Agreement, its Annexes and Protocols and acts referred to therein.[46] While one might consider this as the EEA primary law, there is no equivalent to EU secondary law (Art. 288 TFEU) in the sense that independent EEA institutions would be vested with legislative powers.[47] However, de facto the vast majority of legislation regulating the EEA is, secondary EU law, made binding through Joint Committee decisions and referred to in Annexes.

The decision making process is governed by Articles 97–104 of the EEA Agreement, according to which the Joint Committee holds a central position. As has been mentioned before, the EEA only reflects the legal situation from 1992 and thus provisions on the internal market necessarily need to be updated in parallel to the evolution in the EU. On the other hand, it was one of the objectives of the EFTA Member States, not to be directly bound by the supranational decision making process of the EU. This explains the necessity for a specific decision making procedure that aims at considering both interests, to regularly "...guarantee the legal security and the homogeneity of the EEA..."[48] while safeguarding the interest of the EFTA states, not to be directly bound by EU legal acts.

Accordingly, it is the core interest of the two pillars, to identify the issues of concern for the homogeneity of the EEA. Subsequently, the Commission informs the EFTA States as soon as it drafts new legislation (Art. 99 (1) EEA Agreement) and shall informally seek advice. Apart from informing each other, this mutual consultation process aims at reaching a smooth decision-making process from the very first

---

[44]EFTA (2016b). "EEA Joint Parliamentary Committee." Accessed September 3. http://www.efta.int/eea/eea-institutions/eea-joint-parliamentary-committee.

[45]EFTA (2016a). "Consultative Committee." Accessed September 3. http://www.efta.int/advisory-bodies/consultative-committee.

[46]Article 2 (a) EEA.

[47]The general categorisation depends on how one would define "secondary law"; see for instance: Markus Benzing. 2007. "International Organizations or Institutions, Secondary Law", MPEPIL, OUP at: http://opil.ouplaw.com/home/EPIL.

[48]Article 102 (1) EEA Agreement.

moment.[49] On the basis of the proposals reached under this mechanism, decisions are finally made by the Joint Committee by agreement (Art. 93 (2) EEA Agreement)[50] between the two pillars each speaking with one voice.[51] The EFTA pillar is represented by the Standing Committee which means, that each EFTA Member State may theoretically block a decision (Art. 6 SCA). From the EFTA perspective, the structure of the Joint Committee thus formally establishes a rather intergovernmental decision making procedure, given that each may veto the adoption under the Joint Committee. However, until now, none the EFTA States has ever vetoed any decision.[52] Notwithstanding, Art. 102 and 103 EEA Agreement provide for the case, that an act should not be adopted.[53]

Following this procedure, novel EU legislation is continuously being added to the Annexes of the EEA Agreement.[54] Since the inception of the EEA, more than 7900 EU secondary legal acts that have been deemed EEA relevant, have been adopted,[55] which explains why the EEA Agreement is commonly considered to have a dynamic nature.

Notwithstanding the *à priori* non-binding character of EU secondary law, it has been indicated that EFTA states nevertheless adopted 'EEA relevant' acts. Erikson/Fossum thus concluded that Norway's rather was a rule taker than a rule-maker,[56] a conclusion that stands in contrast to the self-presentation of EFTA.[57] This could very well be a scenario for Britain, in case of its accession to the EEA via EFTA, since the EEA EFTA States do not enjoy any representation within Commission, Council of Ministers or Parliament.

Apart from the procedure indicated above, there are only few options to reject an unbearable EEA-relevant EU rule, one of which are the safeguard measures, if serious economic, societal or environmental difficulties arise, however, other Contracting parties may introduce rebalancing measures on the safeguarding state, if its actions have created disbalance in the market, to remedy the situation.[58]

[49]Read Article 100 EEA.

[50]The EFTA website speaks of "The decisions within the Joint Committee are made by consensus", http://www.efta.int/eea/eea-agreement/eea-basic-features.

[51]Article 93(3) EEA.

[52]Fredriksen (2012), p. 869.

[53]In this case, the EU may suspend the corresponding part of the agreement, thus rejecting access to the internal market for the EEA-EFTA State in question.

[54]The EFTA website provides a list of adopted Joint Committee Decisions, available at: http://www.efta.int/legal-texts/eea/list-of-adopted-joint-committee-decisions-jcds.

[55]See EFTA website, see box on EEA Statistics, download at: http://www.efta.int/legal-texts/eea; The Report by the EEA Review Committee, op cit n 6 supra, 108 counted 6.000.

[56]Eriksen and Fossum (2015a, b).

[57]EFTA (2009). Influencing the EU - EEA Decision Shaping , available at: http://www.efta.int/eea/decision-shaping; EFTA Bulletin on Decision Shaping, March 2009, download at: http://www.efta.int/media/files/publications/Bulletins/eeadecisionshaping-bulletin.pdf.

[58]Articles 112-114 EEA.

In sum, the EEA might correspond to some of the Brexiteers claims for 'regaining our sovereignity'. However, in practice, rule-making would leave the UK much less influence than the present situation.

2.2 *Substantive EEA Law*

2.2.1 Norms Regulating the EEA Internal Market

Art. 1 (1) EEA stipulates as the aim of this Agreement "... to promote a continuous and balanced strengthening of trade and economic relations between the Contracting Parties with equal conditions of competition, and the respect of the same rules, with a view to creating a homogeneous European Economic Area...". Its second paragraph directly refers to the four freedoms which are specified in Art. 8-45 and are largely identical to the corresponding provisions in the TFEU. The EEA furthermore covers the directly trade related areas of competition,[59] state aid[60] and transportation policy,[61] as well as horizontal policies related to the four freedoms, such as social policy,[62] consumer protection,[63] environment[64] and company law.[65] Most of those areas are not regulated with the Agreement itself, but in Annexes to the EEA Agreement, which however rank on the same level.[66] Furthermore, as has been illustrated above, EEA relevant secondary law is constantly adopted by the Joint Committee.

The free movement of goods entails in itself abolition of any customs duties on imports and exports and any quantitative restrictions between the Contracting parties, on the precondition that they have originated within the EEA itself, with the exception of products of agriculture and fishery.[67] Given that the EEA is neither a customs union nor does it cover a common commercial policy, which explains the necessity of establixhing rules of origin.[68] Furthermore, the EEA does not participate at the EU's common agriculture and fisheries policies.[69]

[59]Articles 53-60 EEA.

[60]Articles 62 and 63 EEA.

[61]Articles 47-52 EEA.

[62]Articles 66-71 EEA.

[63]Article 72 EEA.

[64]Articles 73-75 EEA.

[65]Article 77 EEA.

[66]Article 2 (a) EEA.

[67]The rules of origin are regulated in Article 9 and Protocol 4 of the EEA Agreement.

[68]Case E-2/97, Mag Instrument Inc. And California Trading Company Norway, Ulsteen (1997), para. 25.

[69]See Articles 17-20 EEA Agreement.

Regarding the other fundamental freedoms, the provisions are in principle identical to those of the EU. However, regarding the free movement of persons noteworthy particularities may be relevant for Brexiteers, given that the ECJ/CJEU has interpreted this economic freedom in conjunction with EU Citizenship. Unlike the economic agenda of the EEA, the EU strives for "… an ever closer union among the peoples of Europe…" (Art. 1 TEU), for which EU Citizenship forms one important instrument. In contrast, the EEA Agreement, negotiated through 1990–1992, mirrors the corresponding provisions of the EC Treaty as they stood at that time and thus does not comprise EU citizenship, which was only introduced by the Treaty of Maastricht. Given that the EEA did not amend the treaties accordingly, there is not equivalent in the EEA to Art. 20 TFEU, which stipulates, that every citizen of the EU, has inter alia the right to move and reside freely within the territory of Member States. While in the CJEU jurisprudence, EU Citizenship as a non-economic freedom, has become one of the most important issues, the EEA however may, for lacking this very provision, not follow the respective developments in the EU. Notwithstanding, the EEA has also adopted the so called "Citizens Rights Directive (Directive 2004/38/EC)", which deals with the rights to free movement of EU Citizens. With regard to a potential contradiction to the above said, it needs to be stressed, that the Joint Committee decision no. 158/2007 incorporating Directive 2004/38/EC into the EEA Agreement explicitly excluded that political rights could be drawn from this legal act.[70] In the context of Brexit, this aspect may insofar become relevant, as recent cases regarding one of the most controversial aspects—so called "benefit-tourism"—are particularly related to EU Citizenship.[71] While the UK would have to adhere the rules of free movement of persons, it might[72] not be oblidged to pay social benefits to those who have never worked in the UK.

2.2.2 Homogeneity and Effect of EEA Law

First mentioned in the Preamble of the EEA Agreement, it is the objective of the EEA to create a dynamic and homogenous European Economic Area based on common rules and conditions.[73] While it is evident that the legal framework for economic activities in a single market must limit distortions to trade as extensively possible, ie achieve homogeneity, it is less clear, to what extent private actors may contribute to this aim and at the same benefit. This last aspect particularly brings up the questions, whether the EEA enjoys direct effect and primacy over national law and if individuals may claim for damages from the state resulting from EEA law breaches.

[70]Paragraph 8 and 9 states that the Concept of 'Union Citizenship' is not included in this Agreement and Immigration policy is not part of this Agreement, respectively.

[71]See for instance the CJEU-cases C-333/13, Dano, paras 56-61, C-67/14; Alimanovic; C-299/14, García-Nieto.

[72]More extensively on this aspect at II.1 and references in footnote 97; also see Christian (2015).

[73]Recital 4 of the Preamble to the EEA Agreement; Article 1(1) of the EEA Agreement.

2.2.2.1 Homogeneity

Subsequently, Articles 105–107 EEA Agreement are dedicated to this principle the first norm stipulating that, "In order to achieve the objective of the Contracting Parties to arrive at as uniform an interpretation as possible of the provisions of the Agreement and those provisions of Community legislation which are substantially reproduced in the Agreement'.[74] Apart from the decision making mechanism explained above, this includes a system of exchange of information concerning judgments of the EFTA Court and the CJEU laid down in Art. 106 EEA Agreement. This provision thus aims at achieving homogeneity of the EEA courts judgements, ensuring that the EFTA Court considers relevant CJEU case law, and that the two treaties are interpreted in the same way.[75]

Furthermore, Article 6 of the EEA Agreement supports homogenous legal interpretation in the EEA, as it stipulates that, provisions of the EEA Agreement must be interpreted in conformity with relevant rulings of the ECJ given prior to the date of signature of the EEA Agreement (May 2, 1992), thus making the ECJ case-law before this date part of the EEA *acquis*. Moreover, Art. 3(2) SCA stipulates that the EFTA Court shall pay due account to the principles laid down by the relevant rulings of the ECJ given after the date of signature of the EEA Agreement.[76] The EFTA Court may deviate from a relevant ECJ ruling after the signature of the Agreement, if substantial considerations speak against the latter's solution. Therefore, the EFTA Court will have to adopt novel case law of the ECJ in most cases, divergences may be possible in cases of difference in goals and contexts between the EU law and EEA law. Eventually, this contributes to a dynamic character of the principle of homogeneity, which, as Carl Baudenbacher has pointed out, manifests in the fact that "Nonetheless, the requirement to pay due account as expressed in Article 3(2) SCA will ensure that new ECJ case law will be adopted in most cases."[77] The homogeneity principle thus intends to guarantee a level playing field for economic operators within the whole of the Area and to avoid forum shopping between systems.

---

[74]Article 105 (1) EEA.

[75]Barnard (2014), p. 153.

[76]Article 3(2) of the Surveillance and Court Agreement reads as follows: In the interpretation and application of the EEA Agreement and this Agreement, the EFTA Surveillance Authority and the EFTA Court shall pay due account to the principles laid down by the relevant rulings by the Court of Justice of the European Communities given after the date of signature of the EEA Agreement and which concern the interpretation of that Agreement or of such rules of the Treaty establishing the European Economic Community and the Treaty establishing the European Coal and Steel Community in so far as they are identical in substance to the provisions of the EEA Agreement or to the provisions of Protocols 1 to 4 and the provisions of the acts corresponding to those listed in Annexes I and II to the present Agreement.

[77]Baudenbacher (1997), p. 207.

2.2.2.2 Direct Effect and Primacy of EEA-Law?

For the EU, direct effect and primacy of EU law have proven to be elemtary factors for economic and for European integration. The doctrine of direct effect and EU law supremacy was developed with CJEU judgments in Van Gend en Loos[78] and Costa v E.N.EL.[79] in the early 1960s. Therefore, from the viewpoint of Article 6 of the EEA Agreement, one might conclude that both principles also form part of the EEA legal order. However, this interpretation disregards the constitutional order of the EEA, which excludes this understanding. Furthermore, it can be derived from Article 7 and Protocol 35 of the EEA Agreement, which stipulate the course of action in a situation of conflicting EEA provisions and statutory provisions of an EEA EFTA State, which points to the absence of transfer of legislative powers[80] in the EEA, as opposed to EU, as stated in Van Gend en Loos and Costa v E.N.E.L.

The EEAs structure does not allow for a EU-style direct effect,[81] therefore, hypothetically offering less protection of individuals' rights in the EEA than in EU. However, the protection of individual rights[82] is of paramount importance and the Contracting Parties are under a duty to loyally cooperate within the framework of the EEA Agreement.[83] Therefore, individuals can invoke any rights derived from provisions of the EEA Agreement, if they are being or having been made part of[84] the respective national legal order, if they are unconditional and sufficiently precise,[85] thus creating a doctrine of quasi-direct effect.

Regarding non-implemented EEA provisions, the EFTA Court further developed the concept of quasi-effect, emphasising the national courts obligation to interpret national law in conformity with non-implemented EEA rules, by stating that it is the duty of the national court to do whatever lies in their competence, to ensure the effect of EEA law.[86]

Regarding the primacy of EEA law, the approach by the EFTA Court has been similar. In its judgment *Einarsson*, the Court noted that implemented, sufficiently precise and unconditional provisions of the EEA Agreement take precedence over contradictory national provisions.[87] This might be considered a palpable option for the UK, since UK courts would not be required to apply a rule of EEA law in the

[78]Case 26-62 NV Algemene Transport- en Expeditie Onderneming van Gend & Loos v Netherlands Inland Revenue Administration (1962).

[79]Case 6-64, Flaminio Costa v. E.N.E.L., 1964. para. 8.

[80]Bull (2014), p. 206.

[81]Fredriksen and Franklin (2015b), p. 661.

[82]See: Recital 1 of the Preamble to the EEA Agreement.

[83]Article 3 EEA.

[84]Regarding Article 7 EEA, see more on Bull (2014).

[85]Case E-1/94 Restamark (1994), para. 77.

[86]See: Fredriksen and Franklin (2015a), 668; Case E-18/11 Irish Bank, 2012, para. 124.

[87]Case E-1/01 Einarsson (2002), para(s). 53–55.

national legal order when that rule is not transposed, or is inadequately transposed, into domestic law.[88]

Moreover, the EFTA Court recognised the principle of state liability.[89] The Court did not see the fact that the EEA Agreement does not entail transfer of legislative powers and differences in EU and EEA legal orders,[90] as an obstacle in recognising State liability (as opposed to direct effect and primacy). As President of the EFTA Court, Carl Baudenbacher noted, it is one of the most important decisions up to date, because 'had the EFTA Court not taken that step 10 years ago, the EEA Agreement would have been one-sided, with unequal protection of individual rights in the European Community and the EFTA pillar'.[91]

2.3 *Potential Consequences of the UK's Accession to the EEA*

Brexit will have an impact on the UK, the EU and, potentially, on the EEA. While the economic effects mostly remain speculative, some of the political and legal consequences for the case, should the UK leave the EU to the EEA/EFTA, are more predictable. One of the guiding questions probably is, if the Brexiteers would achieve what they have campaigned for (1). However, it is also of great interest, what consequences a 'Brexit to the EFTA/EEA' would imply for the EU (2) and the EEA/EFTA (3).

2.3.1 What Would Change for the UK in the EEA?

As has been pointed out, the EEA constitutes an economic area that covers the four fundamental freedoms. It is no international organisation, which means that the EEA does not have members, but contracting parties. However, the EFTA is an international organisation with members and, becoming a contracting party of the EEA without becoming an EFTA Member State does not appear realistic. Formally, the bodies do not have any supranational competences, and the EEA is rather based on a form of intergovernmentalism instead of supranationalism,[92] as it is the case for the EU.[93] In this regard, the leavers' wish, to regain sovereignty, would (formally) come true and thus "release Britain from the European Superstate".[94] However, this

[88]Case E-1/07 Criminal proceedings versus A (2007), para. 40–41.

[89]Case E-9/97 Sveinbjörnsdóttir (1998), para. 63.

[90]Ibid, para. 44.

[91]Baudenbacher (2009), p. 333.

[92]ECJ, Opinion 1/91, para(s.) 20–23, 27–28.

[93]On this question see: Suami (2014), pp. 529–540.

[94]The only substantial reason for leave highlighted, at: http://grassrootsout.co.uk/. Accessed September 3.

implies the factual shortcomings described above, that the possibilities to influence the adoption of legal acts in the joint committee are limited. Formally, each of the EFTA members would have a veto, but would have to consider that the EU could suspend certain rights.[95] Accordingly, Erikson/Fossum concluded that Norway's was a rule taker[96]—an option that would probably be even more advers to the interests of Brexiteers. For the UK, the EEA/EFTA option would thus bring advantages and disadvantages.

Similarly, there is no easy general answer to the leavers' second claim, which aims at reducing immigration. Given that the EEA implies free movement of workers, immigration of workers and service providers from other EEA states would continue. While the EEA-option is frequently described as unfit for the Brexiteers because of these rights to free movements, one would probably need to differentiate the forms of immigration. However, the leave-campaign criticised immigration in general at some point, the so called "benefit tourism" seemed to be particularly controversial.[97] As elsewhere, people in the UK seem to be more relaxed to accept that foreigners migrate to work, especially, if it is difficult to find nationals applicants. The leavers' argumentation, to have more money for education and the NHS after Brexit insinuates, that they particularly refer to non-contributing immigrants while foreign workers pay taxes and contribute to the social system.

While the EEA comprises the economic freedoms, the legal situation differs, when it comes to immigration of EU citizens who do not work but receive social benefits. Generally, EU citizenship and the principle of non-discrimination prevent EU Member States from discriminating against other EU citizens when it comes to the payments of social benefits. Given that the EEA Agreements do not comprise EU citizenship, relevant EU law would *á priori* not be applicable to the non-EU EEA states. Accordingly, states would theoretically be free to take measures against alleged social benefit tourism, which the leavers might claim a partial success as they could reduce the number of the arguably most controvercial immigrants. Notwithstanding, one needs to bear in mind, that the EEA also comprises some of the related secondary EU law acts (Directive 2004/38/EC). Although the EFTA states explicitly excluded political and social rights from application, it is nevertheless conceivable that, that, with a view to the CJEU-friendly jurisprudence of the EFTA court to achieving homogeneity, EEA-law will develop similar obligations.[98]

Regarding the aspect, to becoming externally independent for concluding trade agreements, while still enjoying access to the internal market, Brexit and the

[95]Articles 102 and 103 EEA Agreement.

[96]Erik Oddvar Eriksen, John Erik Fossum Second−rate Europeans? Lessons from the European Union's non-member, download at: http://www.eurozine.com/articles/2016-06-10-eriksen-en.html; Eriksen and Fossum (2015a) and Yoichi (2014), p. 523; with a rather optimistic assessment: Burke et al. (2016), pp. 82–85.

[97]See for instance: The Telegraph, Britain's hospitality is being abused (2015), http://www.telegraph.co.uk/news/uknews/immigration/11323394/Britains-hospitality-is-being-abused.html.

[98]Reding (2014), pp. 199–200. provides some orientation about respective case law; see also: (Burke and Hannesson (2015), pp. 1111–1134 and Case E-26/13, The Icelandic State v. Atli Gunnarsson (2014).

accession to the EEA might indeed lead to a viable compromise. Given that the EEA is no customs union, the contracting parties are free, to negotiate trade agreements with third countries on their own.[99] However, it is a very different question, if the conclusion drawn by the campaigners, "to be able to dictate ... trade agreements with the rest of the world" is a realistic one.

The fourth aspect, to stop financially contributing to the EU, is rather of a political nature than of a legal. For that reason, it will be determined by the negotiations of the exit-agreement between the EU and the UK, respectively, the EEA parties. Furthermore, the calculations of payments highly depend on the calculation methods, for which this aspect cannot be predicted. However, Norway provides some orientation.[100] Finally, given that the EEA only rudimentarily covers the controversial fields of agriculture and fishery, the UK, by joining the EEA, would be able to reach a further objective campaigned by the Brexiteers.

All in all it appears, as if the leavers could—at least formally—achieve a variety of their aims: EEA-relations would be governed by an intergovernmental instead of supranationalist mechanism, which could be interpreted as "getting back sovereignty".[101] The UK would cease to be bound by the EU's agriculture and fishing policy and be able to ... taking back control of our finances and trade deals" and could independently negotiate trade agreements.

2.3.2 What Would Change for the EU with the UK in the EEA?

The changes Brexit will bring for the EU are difficult to predict, although some aspects and challenges are already clear. With one of biggest Member States, having a permanent seat in the UN and one of its top economies leaving, arguably, the EU's economic and political weight as a global player would somewhat decrease. Furthermore, the EU will have supplementary issues on the agenda that do not contribute to solving other imminent matters such as the refugee crisis, coping with weak economic growth, strained relations with some third countries, controversial negotiations on TTIP, etc. Instead, Brexit will oblige the EU to dedicate resources to the negotiations with the UK, reshuffle the votes in the institutions, discuss sensitive budgetary questions and commitments of other payments (for instance those made in Paris regarding climate change), discussing the status of the English language and organise the order of the upcoming Council presidencies, where it would not make much sense to have the UK as a 'lame duck' in July–December 2017.[102]

---

[99]Notwithstanding, it needs to be noted that the EFTA states jointly negotiated several free trade agreements, see the EFTA website at: http://www.efta.int/free-trade/free-trade-agreements.

[100]Burke et al. (2016), pp. 91–92.

[101]Leave (2016). "Our vision." Accessed September 3. http://leave.eu/en/our-campaign#our-vision.

[102]Politico (2016) "UK might relinquish EU presidency due to Brexit." Accessed September 3. http://www.politico.eu/article/uk-might-relinquish-eu-presidency-due-to-brexit-council-of-ministers-justus-lipsius-brussels/ and Lock (2016).

However, in the case the EU and the UK keep the close ties under the EEA, most of the more political challenges will be less dramatic than one might have feared. Given that the economies will stay closely linked, the UK will try to influence the economic direction of the EU as it did before although with less institutionalised political means. Probably, constrains of *Realpolitik* and common interests will keep the partners united, when it comes to aspects of security and defence.

2.3.3 How About the Non-EU EEA Parties?

Finally, there remains the important question, which has frequently been ignored in the discussions on the EEA-option, what the EFTA-states think about this option. With only three small, but relatively wealthy states, the last 20 years of the EEA relations were surprisingly calm and smooth. Notwithstanding a somehow old-fashioned design of the EEA and EFTA-states requesting a reform,[103] overall, the contracting parties seem to be content with the system. With regard to this status quo, would they only be happy, to welcome the British "giant"? Being one of the UN's P5 and a G7 member, the UK is a political and somehow peculiar global player with its own and distinct national interests, who might easily disturb harmony among the three EFTA states, both internally, and, in the peaceful relations with the EU. Homogeneity, among far more heterogeneous parties, will certainly be more difficult to be achieved. While some commentators so far interpreted the situation differently, that the UK would upgrade the importance of the EFTA/EEA and EFTA-states would thus welcome the UK,[104] recent comments from Norway sound rather reluctant.[105]

However, the legal framework would generally allow the re-accession of the UK (Art.56 EFTA Convention) and political pressure and political concessions from the EU and the UK might persuade sceptics. Nevertheless, it is one of the additional obstacles that make a Brexit in the next 2–3 years a real challenge.

3 Is There a (Orderly) Life after Brexit?

From 1952 to 1973 the European Communities have existed without the UK. And this sketch of the option of the UK joining the EEA indicates, a perspective that promises more order than one might have expected: Business might to a

[103]Since its conclusion, there has been no amendment to the EEA agreement, despite of the EFTA-states' requests, Fredriksen and Franklin (2015a, b), p. 635.

[104]Burke et al. (2016), p. 77.

[105]See for instance The Guardian, *Norway may block UK return to European Free Trade Association*, download at: https://www.theguardian.com/world/2016/aug/09/norway-may-block-uk-return-to-european-free-trade-association or Jonas O Bergmann in *the Independent*, Norway Isn't Thrilled About Britain's Norway Option, download at: http://www.bloomberg.com/news/articles/2016-06-30/norwegian-option-for-u-k-brexiters-is-not-so-clear-for-norway.

considerable extent go on as usual, given that four economic freedoms would continue to apply. Mostly, the two million UK workers could continue working abroad, probably the same applies to the three million EU citizens working in the UK. To certain extent, EU-related questions that had been discusses controversially in the UK would continue to be discussed in the UK. Formally, the Brexiteers might argue that they achieve some of the goals which were claimed in their campaign: While remaining in the internal market, formally, the UK would gain more sovereignty in decision making by holding a veto in the EEA Joint Commitee; it could negotiate its own free trade agreements; the UK would not anymore be bound by the EU's fishery and agriculture policy and potentially, the payments to the EU might be reduced. However, it is questionable whether these presumable gains would be beneficial for the UK: The exercise of a veto would bear the risk of drawbacks along, which means that, in practice the UK's influence on shaping EU law would decrease while they would still need to adopt internal market related law. Even if the UK would be free to negotiate FTAs, and, despite the relative global importance of the UK, it is questionable, that it is capable to "dictate" other states trade agreements, given that its bargaining power with third countries is limited compared to that of a EU28. Notwithstanding, a preset structure and continuance in the internal market would bring a certain stability and continuity for the UK, and also for the EU.

References

Barnard C (2014) Reciprocity, homogeneity and loyal cooperation: dealing with recalcitrant National Courts? In: EFTA Court (ed) The EEA and the EFTA Court: decentrated integration. Hart, Oxford, pp 151–168

Baudenbacher C (1997) Between homogeneity and independence: the legal position of the EFTA court in the European economic area. Columbia J Int Law 3(2):169–227

Baudenbacher C (2003) The EFTA court – an example of Judicialisation of international economic law. Eur Law Rev 28(6):880–899

Baudenbacher C (2009) If not EEA state liability, then what? Reflections ten years after the EFTA Court's Sveinbjiornsdottir ruling. Chic J Int Law 10(1):333–358

Bloomberg (2016) EU referendum: final results. Accessed 3 Sept

Bull H (2014) Shall be made part of the legal order: the legislative approaches. In: EFTA Court (ed) The EEA and the EFTA court: decentrated integration. Hart, London, pp 203–214

Burke C, Hanneson ÓÍ (2015) Citizenship by the back door? Gunnarsson. Common Mark Law Rev 54(4):1111–1134

Burke C, Hannesson ÓÍ, Bangsund K (2016) Life on the edge: EFTA and the EEA as a future for the UK in Europe. Eur Public Law 22(1):69–96

Case 26-62 NV Algemene Transport- en Expeditie Onderneming van Gend & Loos v Netherlands Inland Revenue Administration, 1962

Case 6-64, Flaminio Costa v. E.N.E.L., 1964. para. 8

Case E-1/01 Einarsson, 2002, para(s). 53–55

Case E-1/07 Criminal proceedings versus A, 2007, para. 40–41

Case E-1/94 Restamark, 1994, para. 77

Case E-2/97, Mag Instrument Inc. And California Trading Company Norway, Ulsteen, 1997, para. 25. Hereinafter: Cases beginning with "E" signify EFTA Court judgments

Case E-9/97 Sveinbjörnsdóttir, 1998, para. 63

Christian F (2015) Rights of third-country nationals under EU Association agreements. In: Thym D, Zoeteweij-Turhan M (eds) Rights of third-country nationals under EU Association agreements. Koninklijke Brill, Leiden, pp 127–143
CJEU-cases C-333/13, Dano, paras 56-61, C-67/14; Alimanovic; C-299/14, García-Nieto
E-26/13, The Icelandic State v. Atli Gunnarsson, 2014
EFTA, Influencing the EU - EEA Decision Shaping, available at: http://www.efta.int/eea/decision-shaping; EFTA Bulletin on Decision Shaping, March 2009, download at: http://www.efta.int/media/files/publications/Bulletins/eeadecisionshaping-bulletin.pdf
EFTA (2016a) Consultative Committee. Accessed 3 Sept. http://www.efta.int/advisory-bodies/consultative-committee
EFTA (2016b) EEA Joint Parliamentary Committee. Accessed 3 Sept. http://www.efta.int/eea/eea-institutions/eea-joint-parliamentary-committee
EFTA (2016c) Parliamentary Committee. Accessed 3 Sept. http://www.efta.int/advisory-bodies/parliamentary-committee
EFTA (2016d) The basic features of the EEA Agreement. Accessed 3 Sept. http://www.efta.int/eea/eea-agreement/eea-basic-features
Eriksen EO, Fossum JE (2015a) Second−rate Europeans? Lessons from the European Union's non-member, download at: http://www.eurozine.com/articles/2016-06-10-eriksen-en.html
Eriksen EO, Fossum JE (2015b) The European Union's non-members independence under hegemony? Routledge, Abingdon
European Union External Action (2016) EU relations with Switzerland. Accessed 3 Sept. http://eeas.europa.eu/switzerland/index_en.htm
Fredriksen HH (2012) Bridging the widening gap between the EU treaties and the agreement on the European economic area. Eur Law J 18:6868–6886
Fredriksen HH, Franklin CNK (2015a) 668.; Case E-18/11 Irish Bank, 2012, para. 124
Fredriksen HH, Franklin CNK (2015b) Of pragmatism and principles: the EEA agreement 20 years on. Common Mark Law Rev 52:629–684
http://www.bloomberg.com/graphics/2016-brexit-referendum/
Jean-Claude Piris proposes seven alternatives: If the UK votes to leave. The seven alternatives to EU membership, download at: http://www.cer.org.uk/publications/archive/policy-brief/2016/if-uk-votes-leave-seven-alternatives-eu-membership
Leave (2016) Our vision. Accessed 3 Sept. http://leave.eu/en/our-campaign#our-vision
Lock T (2016) "A lame duck for a member state? Thoughts on the UK's position in the EU after the Brexit vote." Verfassungsblog. On matters constitutional, July 1. http://verfassungsblog.de/lame-duck-united-kingdom-brexit-lock/
Luxembourg: Ministerial meeting between EFTA countries and the EC and its Member States. Joint Declaration (1984) p 2. See: http://www.efta.int/sites/default/files/documents/about-efta/EFTA-EC-joint-declaration-1984.pdf
Pelkmans J, Böhler P (2013) The EEA review and Lichtenstein's integration strategy. Centre for European Policy Studies, Brussels
Politico (2016) UK might relinquish EU presidency due to Brexit. Accessed 3 Sept. http://www.politico.eu/article/uk-might-relinquish-eu-presidency-due-to-brexit-council-of-ministers-justus-lipsius-brussels/
Reding V (2014) Free movement of people and the European economic area. In: EFTA Court (ed) The EEA and the EFTA court. Hart, London, pp 193–202
Suami T (2014) EU Law, EEA Law and International Law—The Myth of Supranational Law and Its Implications for International Law. In: The EEA and the EFTA Court: Decentred Integration, edited by the EFTA Court, pp 529–540
The Guardian. Norway may block UK return to European Free Trade Association, download at: https://www.theguardian.com/world/2016/aug/09/norway-may-block-uk-return-to-european-free-trade-association or Jonas O Bergmann in the Independent, Norway Isn't Thrilled About Britain's Norway Option, download at: http://www.bloomberg.com/news/articles/2016-06-30/norwegian-option-for-u-k-brexiters-is-not-so-clear-for-norway

The rules of origin are regulated in Article 9 and Protocol 4 of the EEA Agreement
The Telegraph, Britain's hospitality is being abused, 4 Jan 2015., http://www.telegraph.co.uk/news/uknews/immigration/11323394/Britains-hospitality-is-being-abused.html
Vote Leave, Take Control (2016) The campaign. Accessed 3 Sept. http://www.voteleavetakecontrol.org/campaign
Yoichi I (2014) EEA law, unexpected success: a Japanese perspective. In: EFTA Court (ed) The EEA and the EFTA court: decentred integration. Hart, London, pp 518–528

The Brexit and Private International Law: An Outlook from the Consumer Insolvency Perspective

Thomas Hoffmann

Abstract While private law as such has not yet been comprehensively harmonized on the EU level, this is—to a large degree—already the case for private international law. As these harmonized rules will cease to apply once the UK is not member of the Union any more, the Brexit will cause essential challenges when jurisdiction and applicable substantical law have to be determined for disputes between British and EU parties.

Consumer insolvency and consumer debt discharge are at present one of those fields where this harmonization has an especially significant impact, as the UK serves—based on the provisions of the European Insolvency Regulation—as a popular consumer insolvency tourism destination. This chapter analyzes the impact of Brexit on the UK's and EU private international law on UK and European parties and exemplifies consequences and feasible options of handling these shortcomings by the phenomenon of UK-based consumer insolvency tourism.

1 Introduction

In most fields of law, the impact of the Brexit is alleviated by the fact that European law rarely does fade out completely even after the UK will have left the EU, as it „lives on" in the implementations of European Directives in British law. This is different in these fields of law that are not mainly shaped by implemented directives (as it is the case for e.g. consumer law), but directly regulated by the EU in form of regulations. Still, the outcome is more complex than that, as also before harmonization by EU regulations the UK was bound by a multitude of conventions in the field of private international law, which were partly ratified before, partly after the UK's accession to the European Economic Community. This chapter in a first step elucidates how essential individual parts of private international law will be regulated once UK law will not fall any more under the Brussels Regime. In a second step, practical consequences will be analyzed at the example of consumer insolvency tourism.

T. Hoffmann (✉)
Tallinn Law School, Tallinn University of Technology, Tallinn, Estonia
e-mail: Thomas.hoffmann@ttu.ee

D. Ramiro Troitiño et al. (eds.), *Brexit*,
https://doi.org/10.1007/978-3-319-73414-9_14

Private international law by purpose asks for a high level of harmonization, and the EU met this demand by regulating the determination of international jurisdiction, of applicable law, and of recognition and enforcement of judgments and public documents extensively. Once these regulations do not apply any more on non-EU-UK, in general those mechanisms that were in force before the harmonization of these fields would directly apply again—which is generally British national private international law. Still, the outcome is more complex than that, as also before harmonization by EU regulations the UK was bound by a multitude of conventions in the field of private international law, which were partly ratified before, partly after the UK's accession to the European Economic Community.

This chapter in a first step elucidates how essential individual parts of private international law will be regulated once UK law will not fall any more under the Brussels Regime. In a second step, practical consequences will be analyzed at the example of consumer insolvency tourism.

2 What Follows the Brussels Regime?

2.1 Determining International Jurisdiction

At present, the Brussels Ia Regulation[1] provides a well-established system determining international jurisdiction (including for lis pedens-constellations) for cross-border disputes in civil and commercial matters within the EU. Since the recast of 2012, the Regulation also provides mechanisms for the recognition and enforcement of judgements.

The UK courts will not be bound any more by the Brussels Ia Regulation after a Brexit. Anyway, this does not necessarily mean that the UK courts will have to apply exclusively British law, as the Regulation was preceded by a "Convention on jurisdiction and the enforcement of judgments in civil and commercial matters",[2] which was drafted in 1968 and subsequently ratified by the then-members of the European Economic Community. As the number of Member States increased, it was respectively amended, the las consolidated version before the enactment of the Brussels Ia Regulation being of 1996.[3]

The Convention remained in force also after the Brussels Ia Regulation was enacted, as explicitly foreseen in recital 9 of the Regulation, stating that the 1968 Convention "continues to apply" in these territories that are not covered by the Regulation. However, the Convention covers only a fraction of the scope of the Regulation—in both substantial and territorial terms: There are no special regulations for sale of goods and services (the bulk of "civil and commercial matters"), and

[1]Regulation (EU) no. 1215/2012 of 12 December 2012 on jurisdiction and the recognition and enforcement of judgments in civil and commercial matters (recast) OJ L 351.

[2]Brussels Convention on jurisdiction and the enforcement of judgments in civil and commercial matters, signed 27 September 1968, OJ L 299–232.

[3]A consolidated version of the Convention is accessible at [1998] OJ C 27/1.

no privision on the recognition and enforcement of foreign judgments at all, meaning that the need for exequatur-procedures (which were finally made superflous by the Brussels Ia Regulation recast) would revive. Besides, the Convention was ratified only by those States that were EU-member-States in 1996, thus missing 13 Member States.

Perturbations would thus be considerable after the Brexit. The UK can—if it wishes—anyway use as a model some existing mechanisms regulating international jurisdiction and recognition/enforcement of foreign judgments the EU has already established for disputes between parties in EU and non-EU-Member States: For instance, the (new) Lugano Convention of 2007 implements the content of the Brussel I Regulation into this treaty concluded between the EU itself and the European Free Trade Association apart from Liechtenstein, i.e. Iceland, Norway, and Switzerland. If the UK is interested in keeping the benefits of the mechanisms developed in the Brussels Ia recast, but not interested in joining EFTA—as reasonable as it may seem,[4]—they could consider ratifying the Lugano Convention (provided that the EU and the other parties to the Convention agree, which ought to be expected).

2.2 *Determining Applicable Substantial Law*

2.2.1 Contracts

At present, the law applicable to contracts is determined by the Rome I Regulation.[5] The Rome I Regulation is the first directly binding regulation on contractual obligations, but it has been preceded by a treaty—the 1980 Rome Convention[6]—which covered contractual obligations just as well and which was signed by the UK and various today EU Member States. In terms of content, the Convention and the Regulation match to large degrees.[7]

Because of its congruent function along with the Rome I regulation, the Rome Convention is not only hardly dealt with in practice, but is sometimes even interpreted (Hess 2016, p. 417) as being expired when the Rome I Regulation came into force, which would make it thus unsuitable as a Rome I Regulation replacement for the UK after the Brexit as well.

This interpretation is based on Art. 24(1) of the Rome I Regulation, which states that the Regulation "replaces" the Rome Convention. The term "replacing" is

[4]See more in the chapter by Schewe and Lipsens (2017).

[5]Regulation (EC) No 593/2008 of 17 June 2008 on the law applicable to contractual obligations (Rome I), OJ L 177/6.

[6]Convention 80/934/EEC on the law applicable to contractual obligations, concluded at Rome on 19 June 1980, [1980] OJ L266/1.

[7]The Regulation is slightly more comprehensive as also insurance issues are covered, just as well as foreign overriding mandatory rules have been treated differently.

anyway far to vague to be interpreted as the termination of another treaty; it should rather be interpreted as a replacement in terms of functional scope and applicability. Besides, even if a respective termination clause had been included in the Regulation, a Regulation cannot make its predecessor expire by merely evoking such an effect; a respective expiration clause would have had to be included rather in the Convention itself—or within a separate agreement concluded between all States having ratified the Convention.

The 1980 Rome Convention thus did not cease to exist when the Rome I Regulation came into force.[8]

Anyway, the applicability of the Rome Convention on UK-related transborder transactions has been challenged also by another aspect, as the Convention addressed exclusively Member States of the then European Economic Community and had—according to the preambule—the explicit purpose to facilitate transactions within the internal market of just that community. The Convention may thus generally be in force, but not towards a non-EU UK.[9] Still, it has to be considered that the convention is technically a treaty among sovereign States, not an act of European legislation. The fact that the UK later will not match any more the circle of addresses intended by the treaty may eventually give substantial reason to revise the convention, but it does not affect the binding nature of the treaty as such under public international law.

In conclusion, the Rome Convention provides for a solid interim regulation of contractual transborder disputes that ought be able to prevent major confusion after the Brexit at least in this respect. Still, UK legislation should consider to fill existing gaps between the Regulation and the Convention by soon-to-be-taken measures to maintain legal certainty among practicioners.

2.2.2 Non-Contractual Obligations

The applicable law on transborder non-contractual obligations are at present determined by the Rome II Regulation.[10] These obligations—according to Art. 2 of the Regulation based on tort/delict, unjust enrichment, negotiorum gestio or culpa in contrahendo—provide each of them separately their proper determination criteria.

In contrast to Rome I, the Rome II regulation was not preceeded by any Convention; respective plans have been long time discussed, but never set into practice before the Regulation was enacted.[11] The consequence is that the UK would for non-contractual obligations simply re-apply its national private international law. These British rules are partly similar as those imposed by the Rome II Regulation—for torts, the principle of *lex loci delicti* (which also governs most of the remaining

[8]See also Dickinson (2016), p. 204.

[9]For details on the controversy see Lehmann and Zetzsche (2016).

[10]Regulation (EC) 864/2007 on the law applicable to non-contractual obligations, OJ L199/40.

[11]For background see O Lando, The EC Draft Convention on the Law Applicable to Contractual and Non-Contractual Obligations', ibid p. 6.

British private international law on non-contractual obligations[12]) is applied with respective exceptions for conduct and damage occurring in different countries just as in the Rome II Regulation—but do generally not go as far as the Regulation; for instance, IP law, product liability, competition law, unjust enrichment or pre-contractual liability are covered fa rless comprehensively than in the Regulation.

Applicable law determined by the UK judges on base of the UK private international law would thus start to considerable differ from today's practice after the Brexit—unless the UK would actively prevent this outcome herself.

3 Practical Consequences at the Example of Consumer Insolvency Tourism

3.1 The Brexit's Impact on Trans-Border Insolvency Proceedings

Just as the Bussels Ia Regulation does for civil and commercial matters, the European Insolvency Regulation of 2000, reformed in 2015 in form of a "recast" taking effect from 26 June 2017,[13] regulates international jurisdiction and recognition of foreign judgements, but it contains also—as the Rome Regulations—regulations on the determination of the applicable substantial law, providing thus a comprehensive framework for all PIL issues arising in trans-border insolvencies. Being rather efficient and well-received by practitioners already before thre reform, the "recast" will certainly remove further hurdles to smooth and comprehensive EU-wide insolvency proceedings, providing regulations on pre-insolvency, secondary and hybrid proceedings, shortcomings observed in connection with forum shopping schemes, and EU-wide disclosure mechanisms.

At present, the UK law provides in international comparison a rather liberal regime for both corporate and consumer insolvency, making the UK law often the favorable choice for foreign companies and consumers facing bankruptcy. Whether the UK law can be chosen indeed depends on the state of the procedure.

In the case where the opening of insolvency proceedings are seen as the ultimate measure, choice of law and recognition of respective judgements are regulated by the European Insolvency Regulation. These criteria have been interpreted quite liberally by the UK courts, setting up "core requirements" for the application of substantial UK law, which are relatively easy to meet[14] and thus make the UK even more attractive as an insolvency destination.

[12]See e.g. Private International Law (Miscellaneous Provisions) Act 1995, sec 11(1).

[13]Regulation (EU) 2015/848 on insolvency proceedings (recast), OJ L 141/19.

[14]Also, foreign companies can be object of schemes of arrangement (1) if they have a 'sufficiently close connection' to the UK, (2) if there is beneficial effect of the scheme to be expected for the creditors, and (3) if at least one of the creditors falls directly under the UK jurisdiction. These

In those cases where a voluntary agreement between the debtor and the creditor can prevent the opening of insolvency proceedings by re-structuring the company, the UK legal practice has developped the instrument of 'schemes of arrangement', which "arranges" debts also with non-approving creditors if at least 75% of the remaining creditors have agreed. While these schemes are not covered by the EIR present (Swierczok 2014), it is controversial whether they are recognized as binding beyond the UK in other Member States under the Insolvencz and Judgment Regulations (Eidenmüller and Frobenius 2011).

This constellation has spured a flourishing "insolvency industry" in the UK, providing various services to EU-companies in financial arrears.

After Brexit, nor the European Insolvency Regulation (EIR) neither the Brussels Ia Regulation will provide direct recognition of any of these decisions taken by the UK courts any more via Arts. 19 and 20 EIR. Judgements would have to be recognized according to procedures provided by national insolvency law, which in many cases will impose much higher thresholds for recognition: Under German law,[15] for instance, Art. 343 Insolvency Act (InsO) does not even automatically recognize the opening of proceedings, meaning that separate proceedings can be opened in Germany. Ongoing proceedings must be positively recognized as "insolvency proceedings" within the meaning of the German Insolvency Act.

The German court would further examine whether the courts of the third state are internationally competent from the perspective of German courts, which may diverge essentially from the current practice.

From the perspective of the UK courts, the Cross-Border Insolvency Regulations 2006[16] would regulate again EU-transborder insolvencies, as it does today with third country-related insolvencies. Besides, for many British Commonwealth Countries special forms of inter-court cooperation can alleviate the proceedings according to section 426 of the Insolvency Act 1986.[17]

As insolvency matters were excluded from the 1968 Convention on Jurisdiction and the Enforcement of Judgments in Civil and Commercial Matters,[18] between 1963 and 1980 a "Convention on bankruptcy, winding-up, arrangements, compositions and similar proceedings"[19] was drafted under the auspices of the Commission of the European Communities. Although the outcome was subsequently studied by an EC Council Working Party from 1982 until 1985, work was "suspended for lack of sufficient consensus" (EU Council Report on the Convention of Insolvency

criteria serve to interpret the central requirement for applying the UK law, being "liable to be wound up" as stated in 895(2)(b) Companies Act 2006. These three core requirements have been developed by British court practice already since Real Estate Development Co [1991] BCLC 210.

[15]For details on the German approach see Weller et al. (2016), p. 2382.

[16]Cross-Border Insolvency Regulations 2006, 2006 No. 1030.

[17]Insolvency Act 1986, 1986 c. 45.

[18]Convention on Jurisdiction and the Enforcement of Judgments in Civil and Commercial Matters, OJ L 299/32.

[19]On the entire Convention 81/1068/EEC and its reception in detail see Kegel and Thieme (1988).

Proceedings 1996, p. 15). There is thus no Convention that could replace the Regulation for insolvency issues from a EU perspective. The UK in fact has a Convention that provides reciprocal enforcements of judgements in civil and commercial matters, but as it does not entail recent insolvency practices (dating from 1934) and as it is only conlcuded with Belgium, its practical significance is low.

3.2 *Special Focus: Consumer Insolvency Tourism*

As consumer debts have increased EU-wide in the last decases, not only corporate but also consumer insolvency has become an international and partly industralized field of business.

3.2.1 Background

In contrast to corporate insolvency, the only feasible option in case of personal bankruptcy is to "restructure" the assets of the individual, i.e. granting a more or less complete discharge under certain conditions.

These proceedings are covered by the EIR as well, although with some essential discrepancies—mainly because of the fact that the EIR was "drafted with business bankruptcies in mind, and its scope of application being designed accordingly."[20] Another reason why consumer insolvency proceedings face certain challenges and provide for often unexpected results is the explicit heterogeneity of consumer insolvency proceedings not only EU-, but also worldwide, an outcome due to the specific nature of the discharge as a legal tool: The discharge—being a "pure concession to pragmatism and dogmatically alien to the basic principles of both common law and civil law legal systems (pacta sunt servanda)"—is short of "patterns for a dogmatically clean implementation of this tool in any European legal paradigms" (Hoffmann 2012).

Thus, discharge conditions differ in different EU Member States more considerably than rulings on corporate insolvency do: Some countries as Bulgaria or Croatia do not offer discharge possibilities for consumer at all or do so—as e.g. Ireland—only under very harsh conditions (no discharge before an elapse period of twelve years and after 50% of the debt have been paid), some others only when fixed percentages of debts have been paid in respective time frames (e.g. in Austria, within the "Abschöpfungsverfahren" according to § 199 f. Austrian Insolvency Act), or discharge is granted only if a respective agreement with the majority of debtors (e.g. in Portugal of those debtors who claim at least two thirds of all debts has been concluded). Free discharge is generally granted in the Nordic countries[21] and those

[20] European Council (2005), p. 39.

[21] For Norway and Estonia see Volens and Lilleholt (2016).

influenced by German law, although the duration of the "Wohlverhaltensphase" (i.e. the fixed period during which the debtor must assign his income exceeding a minimum wage to a court-appointed trustee) may differ considerably.

Together with the French regions of Alsace-Lorraine,[22] it is though the UK that offers the most debtor-friendly discharge regime in Europe: A discharge can be granted either on base of private settlement (either under a deed of arrangement or an individual voluntary arrangement according to sec. 252 Insolvency Act) or—if this agreement cannot be reached, which is most often the case—within a bankruptcy proceeding according to sec. 264 f. Insolvency Act. In this case, sec. 279 (1) Insolvency Act provides that discharge is granted automatically after 1 year, but in most cases in practice the official receiver declares a close investigation of the bankruptcy as unnecessary or concluded (sec. 279 (2) Insolvency Act), which results in immediate discharge after filing of the respective note at court.[23]

3.2.2 Recognition of a Discharge Granted in the UK

According to Art. 3 I EIR, the national insolvency law of that State is applied where the debtor has his or her "Centre of Main Interest" (COMI). "Application" includes here the recognition of any measures taken within the proceeding, see Arts. 19 and 20 EIR under the applicable law—including an eventual discharge. This concerns the law on opening and closure of the proceedings and on creditors' rights after the closure—rights that may be restricted by discharge provisions.

While the term "insolvency proceeding" in Art. 3 par. 1 is defined in annex A for every country respectively, this is not the case for the COMI (Weber 2010, p. 8). Anyway, recital 13 EIR states that the "centre of a debtor's main interest should correspond to the place where the debtor conducts the administration of his interests on a regular basis and is therefore ascertainable by third parties".[24] Since the Eurofood-decision,[25] it has been clarified that this determination has to be exercised in uniform manner and by criteria that are "both objective and ascertainable by third parties", and since the "Interedil"-decision[26] following definition has been established in the practice of the ECJ: "Where the bodies responsible for the management and supervision of a company are in the same place as its registered office and the management decisions of the company are taken, in a manner that is ascertainable by third parties, in that place, the presumption in that provision cannot be rebutted."[27]

For natural persons, the recast of the EIR in 2015 now finally clarifies from June 2017 in Art. 3 III EIR that the COMI "shall be presumed to be the place of the

[22]On the French consumer insolvency system see the both contributions by Köhler (2003a, b).

[23]A more detailed overview see at Hoffmann (2012).

[24]Art. 13 EIR, 1346/2000/EC.

[25]C-341/04, Eurofood [2006] ECR I-3813, para 33.

[26]ECJ, case Interedil Srl (in liquidation) v Fallimento Interedil Srl, C-396/09; [2011].

[27]ECJ, Interedil C-396/09; [2011], operative part of the judgment, III.

individual's habitual residence in the absence of proof to the contrary. This presumption shall only apply if the habitual residence has not been moved to another Member State within the 6-month period prior to the request for the opening of insolvency proceedings." In other words, if the debtor has really lived in the UK where insolvency proceedings should be opened for at least 6 months, his or her effective COMI is irrebuttably presumed there.

Whether a person "really lives" in the UK is examined by British courts respectively thoroughly, i.e. by indices as an employment contract at the alleged residence, proof for a rented/owned apartment including respective maintenance costs or even social contacts (memberships in local associations et al.). The decisive point of time for this examination has, after long controversy, finally EU-wide been determined in the Staubitz-Schreiber judgement,[28] now being the date of reception of the application to open the insolvency proceedings by the relevant insolvency court.

In the UK court practice, it must be remarked that the motives for a COMI change are not considered at all[29]; i.e. debts accumulated abroad or any other practical convenience is irrelevant for determining an effective COMI change.[30]

This very debtor-friendly policy has the UK made Europe's favorite consumer insolvency destination, a phenomenon often referred to as "consumer insolvency tourism" or—more drastic—as circumstances making the UK a "bankruptcy brothel" (although this term originally referred to corporate bankruptcy[31]). Bankruptcy tourism is supported by a more or less professionally acting "industry"[32]; provided services include usually registration of the client at the respective UK residence registry office, the preparation of lease contracts with British tenants, support within the formal discharge procedure and further legal assistance.

3.2.3 The Brexit's Impact on the Consumer Insolvency Tourism

Already before Brexit started dawning, the question whether forum shopping is an entirely legal option as a personal discharge strategy was controversial—especially as this practice could be interpreted as an abuse of the EIR. It has also been questioned whether creditors from legal systems not providing any form of discharge do indeed not deserve more protection than provided by the EIR when they suddenly face the complete discharge of their debtor, especially since most of the debtors seeking discharge abroad are middle class professionals and do thus not deserve considerably more protection than their creditors (Walters and Smith 2009).

[28]C-I/04 [2006], ECR I-701.

[29]Official Receiver vs. Eichler [2007], BPIR 1636.

[30]BPIR 1636, p. 12.

[31]See e.g. "London risks becoming "brothel" for bankruptcy tourists", The Guardian, 31 Jan 2010.

[32]For further information concerning firms acting in Germany see Hergenröder (2009), p. 310.

For that abuse, the ECJ had set up criteria in the judgement Emsland-Stärke,[33] requiring an "intention by the alleged abuser to benefit from an advantage as a result of the application of community rules by carrying out an artificial operation". Anyway, a genuine COMI change is already per definition not artificial[34]; if the EIR's objectives are otherwise ignored, courts should rather adapt criteria for habitual residence recognition than marking a genuine COMI change artificial. Applying for discharge after a genuine COMI change therefore cannot be seen as abuse. At present, the practice of consumer insolvency tourism is thus lawful.

After the Brexit, this practice will in this form end for various reasons.

First, the possibility of a relocation of the COMI to the UK is a direct consequence of EU freedoms, here the freedom of establishment, enshrined in Art. 43 and 48 EC Treaty. Since the ECJ's Centros-decision it has been established that "the fact, that a national of a Member State, who wishes to set up a company chooses to form it in the Member State whose rules of company law seem to him the least restrictive and to set up branches in other Member States, cannot, in itself, constitute an abuse of the right of establishment",[35] meaning that although practicing these freedoms to the direct detriment of creditors is covered 43 and 48 EC Treaty.

However, the Treaty provides these freedoms only within the EU. After Brexit, the ECJ will cease to support relocations to the UK by deeming these as a mere expression of 43 and 48 EC Treaty, just as the UK will not be obliged to welcome discharge seekers.

Second, even if a genuine COMI change to the UK has been successful, a subsequent discharge granted by the UK courts will after a Brexit not be recognized any more in EU Member States under Arts. 3 and 16 (respectively from June this year by Art. 19, 20 of the recast version) EIR.

It is more than questionable whether EU national courts will be fond of recognizing UK discharge decisions on base of their national PIL systems, especially since the current practice has been seen as a considerable disregard of the creditor's interests, as a comprehensive "discharge risk assessment" taking into account a comparison of all EU consumer insolvency systems is almost impossible to achieve (Anderson 2004, p. 672).

---

[33]ECJ, case Emsland-Stärke, C-110/99 [2000], ECR 1-11569, par. 39.

[34]Disagreeing D'Avoine (2011), p. 312, who assumes an abuse of the EIR in cases of obvious "return option" of the debtor.

[35]C-212/1997 [1999] ECR1-1459, p. 27.

4 Conclusion

Among the various detrimental impacts on current cross-border legal cooperation, the phenomenon of consumer insolvency tourism will quite probably be one of the legal practices hardest hit by Brexit. This outcome itself has as such not necessarily to be deplored, as this form of forum shopping has been subject to severe critic.

Deplorable is rather the outcome from a UK perspective, as insolvency tourism is a very good example demonstrating how European legislation provided essential advantages to the UK as legal venue—or, in other words, as an example of the ability of the UK legal practice to "enrich" EU law with the UK law exceptions and thus attracting clients from the entire EU.

On the other hand, it was these exceptions that also kept EU law alert and urged respective reforms—in this case, the recast of the EIR. The fact that the UK judgements were recognized EU-wide also ensured that the EU had to consider common law and thus the leading legal system in the rest of the world when regulations were drafted—the loss of the UK will in that respect certainly diminish the global compatibility of EU law as well.

References

Anderson K (2004) Review essay: "The Explosive Global Growth of Personal Insolvency and the Concomitant Birth of the Study of Comparative Consumer Bankruptcy". Osgoode Hall Law J 42(4):661–680

D'Avoine M (2011) Internationale Zuständigkeit des deutschen Insolvenzgerichts bei offenkundiger "Rückkehroption" des ehemals selbstständig wirtschaftlich tätigen Schuldners (Unternehmer, Freiberufler, Arzt, Anwalt, Notar etc.) mit dem Ziel der Restschuldbefreiung – Wann wird forum-shopping unerlaubt und verstößt unter Umständen gegen den Ordre public? Neue Zeitschrift für Insolvenzrecht:310–324

Dickinson A (2016) Back to the future: the UK's EU exit and the conflict of laws. J Priv Int Law:195–210

Eidenmüller H, Frobenius T (2011) Die internationale Reichweite eines 'Scheme of Arrangement, Wertpapier-Mitteilungen: 1210–1218

European Council, Niemi-Kiesiläinen J, Henrikson A-S (2005) Report in legal solutions to debt problems in credit societies, 11th rev. Niemi-Kiesiläinen, J. & Henrikson, A.-S., Strasbourg

European Council (1996) Report on the convention of insolvency procedures. Virgos, M. & Schmit, E. Brussels. Accessible online at http://aei.pitt.edu/952/. Accessed 20 Jan 2017

Hergenröder CW (2009) Entschuldung durch Restschuldbefreiungstourismus? Voraussetzungen, Grenzen und Verfahrensfragen der Anerkennung einer ausländischen Restschuldbefreiung im Inland nach der EuInsVO. Deutsche Zeitschrift für Wirtschaftsrecht: 309–322

Hess B (2016) Back to the Past: BREXIT und das europäische Internationale Privat- und Verfahrensrecht. Praxis des Internationalen Privat- und Verfahrensrechts: 409–417

Hoffmann T (2012) The phenomenon of "Consumer Insolvency Tourism" and its challenges to European legislation. J Consum Policy 35(4):461–475

Kegel G, Thieme J (1988) Vorschläge und Gutachten zum Entwurf eines EG-Konkursübereinkommens. Mohr Siebeck, Tübingen

Köhler MA (2003a) Entschuldung und Rehabilitierung vermögensloser Personen im Verbraucherinsolvenzverfahren: Ein Vergleich der Verfahrensreformen in Frankreich und Deutschland. Nomos, Baden-Baden

Köhler MA (2003b) Reform des Verbrauchersanierungsverfahrens in Frankreich – der lange Weg zur Restschuldbefreiung. Zeitschrift für Verbraucherinsolvenz:626–645

Lando O (1974) The EC draft convention on the law applicable to contractual and non-contractual obligations. Rabels Zeitschrift für ausländisches und internationales Privatrecht/The Rabel Journal of Comparative and International Private Law, 38. Jahrg., H. 1: 6–55

Lehmann M, Zetzsche DA (2016) Brexit and the consequences for commercial and financial relations between the EU and the UK. Eur Bus Law Rev, Special Edition, Forthcoming. Available at SSRN: https://ssrn.com/abstract=2841333 or https://doi.org/10.2139/ssrn.2841333. Accessed 20 Jan 2017

Schewe C, Lipsens D (2017) From EFTA to EC/EU and back to EFTA? The European Economic Area (EEA) as a possible scenario for UK-EU relations after Brexit. In this Volume

Swierczok A (2014) Recognition of english solvent schemes of arrangement in Germany. King's Stud Law Rev 5(1):78–91

The Guardian (2010) Newspaper article "London risks becoming "brothel" for bankruptcy tourists", published 20 October 2010, online accessible at https://www.theguardian.com/business/2010/jan/31/insolvency-uk-law-bankruptcy-foreign. Accessed 20 Jan 2017

Volens U, Lilleholt K (2016) Consumer insolvency law in Estonia and Norway: comparative aspects. Eur Rev Priv Law 24(5):759–789

Walters A, Smith A (2009) Bankruptcy tourism under the EC regulation on insolvency proceedings: a view from England and wales. Int Insolvency Rev 19:181–208

Weber J (2010) The rise of insolvency tourism. LL.M.-Thesis, Leiden. Accessible online at http://bobwessels.nl/wordpress/wp-content/uploads/2010/03/Weber-Thesis-January-2010.pdf. Accessed 20 Jan 2017

Weller M-P, Thomale C, Benz N (2016) Englische Gesellschaften und Unternehmensinsolvenzen in der Post-Brexit-EU. Neue Juristische Wochenschrift:2378–2383

Impact of the Article 50 of TEU on Migration of the EU Workers in Case of Brexit

Lehte Roots

Abstract BREXIT has created a new situation in the field on free movement of workers within the EU. It was the change introduced by Lisbon Treaty that gives the EU Member States the right to exit from the European Union. On 29 March 2017, Theresa May send a letter to President of the European Council Donald Dusk a letter with a wish to use the Art. 50 of TEU to exit from the EU, and from European Atomic Energy Community. Europe and Britain are now facing a new situation that has never happened before and therefore any decision of the further collaboration and co-existence gives precedents to potential new "dissociates" from the EU. The current situation affects also the EU citizens living in Great Britain and British citizens living in other EU countries, as the principles of free movement of persons will no longer automatically apply to either of those groups of people and new agreements need to be imposed.

This chapter analyses the application of Art. 50 of TEU and its impact on free movement rights of the EU citizens who are workers, from both perspectives the British citizens abroad and the other EU citizens living in the United Kingdom. What would be the options for further cooperation after Brexit to maintain the rights of workers? It elaborates on five different post Brexit solutions that can be introduced to resolve the questions of workers' rights that were created by EU legislation.

1 Introduction

This chapter elaborates on a new situation that Brexit has created in the field on free movement of workers within the EU. Brexit means that Britain wants to use the opportunity created by the Lisbon Treaty to exit from the European Union. Before changes made by Lisbon Treaty, it was not possible for a state to leave from European Union. On 29 March 2017, Theresa May send a letter to President of the

L. Roots (✉)
Tallinn Law School, Tallinn University of Technology, Tallinn, Estonia
e-mail: lehte.roots@ttu.ee

D. Ramiro Troitiño et al. (eds.), *Brexit*,
https://doi.org/10.1007/978-3-319-73414-9_15

European Council Donald Dusk a letter with a wish to use the Art. 50 of TEU to exit from EU, and from European Atomic Energy Community.

The decision of British citizens living in Great Britain has created a panic and unstable situation for the EU citizens in the United Kingdom and the UK citizens settled or living outside of the UK, as they do not know what will happen to their rights that they have obtained as EU citizens, living in another EU Member State. British citizens who were living outside of Britain could not participate in the voting process.

The number of people who plan to immigrate and emigrate in general is very difficult to predict. The analysis in this field is often done using data that has been collected posterior the action. Perhaps the most important question about a post-Brexit immigration rules and policy is to what extent policies towards EU citizens seeking to live and work in the UK and those British expatriates living in EU, would continue to be shaped by the relationship with the EU or individual EU Member States?

After the decision to leave EU, the UK and EU would need to work out together with the European Union to negotiate the terms of the UK-EU relationship. Free movement of workers would undoubtedly be on the table for this discussion. It is possible that the UK might agree to continue to allow free movement in return for access to the single market by joining the European Economic Area (EEA). In case the future EU-UK relationship do not include free movement, bilateral immigration agreements with specific EU countries might be another alternative.

This chapter analyses the application of Art. 50 of TEU and its impact on free movement rights of EU citizens who are workers, from both perspectives the British citizens abroad and the other EU citizens living in the United Kingdom.

2 Application of Art. 50 of TEU

To analyse the implications of Art. 50 of TEU on the rights of EU citizens, it is relevant to compare the application of Art. 50 of TEU with the relevant international law provisions. The procedure and consequences of a withdrawal from the EU are now governed by EU law and no recourse to international law is possible. International law cannot be applied in parallel to Article 50 TEU. CJEU in its Costa v. Enel decision has stated that EU has created a special legal order.[1] So, leaving EU must be done according to the EU rules but the new agreement between EU and Britain can be covered by international law.

This is even more important to understand the difference because Article 50 TEU lowers the conditions for a withdrawal as stipulated under international law. Under Article 62 of the Vienna Convention, a state party can withdraw from a treaty only, if

[1]Case C-6/64 Flaminio Costa v E.N.E.L, Judgment of the Court of 15 July 1964, ECLI:EU: C:1964:66.

there is a fundamental change of circumstances, which have occurred in relation to those existing at the time of the conclusion of that treaty. Article 50 TFEU does not establish any substantive conditions for a Member State to be able to exercise its right to withdrawal, but only states procedural requirements. The procedural character of the withdrawal clause does not even oblige the withdrawing Member State to state formally a reason for its decision.[2]

Article 50 of the Treaty on European Union allows a Member State to notify the EU of its withdrawal and obliges the EU to try to negotiate a 'withdrawal agreement' with that state. The Article 50 contains five points stated below:

> 1. Any Member State may decide to withdraw from the Union in accordance with its own constitutional requirements.
>
> 2. A Member State which decides to withdraw shall notify the European Council of its intention. In the light of the guidelines provided by the European Council, the Union shall negotiate and conclude an agreement with that State, setting out the arrangements for its withdrawal, taking account of the framework for its future relationship with the Union. That agreement shall be negotiated in accordance with Article 218(3) of the Treaty on the Functioning of the European Union. It shall be concluded on behalf of the Union by the Council, acting by a qualified majority, after obtaining the consent of the European Parliament.
>
> 3. The Treaties shall cease to apply to the State in question from the date of entry into force of the withdrawal agreement or, failing that, two years after the notification referred to in paragraph 2, unless the European Council, in agreement with the Member State concerned, unanimously decides to extend this period.
>
> 4. For the purposes of paragraphs 2 and 3, the member of the European Council or of the Council representing the withdrawing Member State shall not participate in the discussions of the European Council or Council or in decisions concerning it. A qualified majority shall be defined in accordance with Article 238(3)(b) of the Treaty on the Functioning of the European Union.
>
> 5. If a State which has withdrawn from the Union asks to re-join, its request shall be subject to the procedure referred to in Article 49.

The formal withdrawal process starts with a notification, from the Member State wishing to withdraw, to the European Council by declaring its intention to do so. The timing of this notification is entirely in the hand of the Member State concerned, and informal discussions could take place between it and other Member States and/or EU institutions prior to the notification. The European Council (without the participation of the Member State concerned) then provides guidelines for the negotiations between the EU and the state concerned, with the aim of concluding an agreement setting out concrete withdrawal arrangements. It should also cover the departing Member State's future relationship with the Union. The Union and the Member State wishing to withdraw have a period of 2 years to agree on these conditions of an agreement unless agreed upon otherwise. The form of any withdrawal agreement would depend on the negotiations and there is therefore no guarantee the UK or EU

[2]Terhechte (2008), pp. 143, 152. See also the debate Roots (2009), pp. 261–281.

would find the terms acceptable. The possible scenario is that the EU Treaties would cease to apply to the UK on the entry into force of a withdrawal agreement or, if no new agreement is concluded, after 2 years, unless there is unanimous agreement to extend the negotiating period.[3] In its letter to Dusk, May has declared that there will be new law that "will convert the EU law into UK law" but with the additional conditions "wherever practical and appropriate".[4]

In principle during the 2-year negotiation period, EU laws will still apply to the UK as they are still Members of EU and need to follow the rules of the Union. The UK continues to participate in EU as before, but it would not participate in internal EU discussions or decisions on its own withdrawal. From the EU side, the agreement is negotiated by the European Commission according to a mandate from EU ministers and concluded by EU governments "acting by a qualified majority, after obtaining the consent of the European Parliament."[5]

For the moment it is also not clear what will be the position of the European Parliament whose role is also to take care of EU citizens and the workers.[6] In case the agreement includes different policy areas such as elements of services, transport, investments, the agreement will classify as "mixed agreement" and this requires additional ratification by every national parliament of European Union.[7] One should bear in mind that not only the UK law and rules will change but also the EU Treaties need to be changed and amended to reflect the leave of UK from the Union. This means that the final deal at the end of negotiations needs to be ratified also by EU leaders via qualified majority vote, the majority of European Parliament and by the other 27 national parliaments of EU Member States.[8]

It demonstrates that the negotiations of this type of agreement will not be easy and fast. There is a need for consent of EU institutions, whose obligation is also to protect the rights of EU citizens.[9] Nevertheless, the notification from the UK to use Art.

[3]Art. 50 (3) TEU.

[4]Letter avaialble from http://news.bbc.co.uk/2/shared/bsp/hi/pdfs/29_03_17_article50.pdf; Accessed 31.03.2017.

[5]Art. 50 (2) TEU.

[6]See more about the role of the Parliament of EU.
http://www.europarl.europa.eu/atyourservice/en/displayFtu.html?ftuId=FTU_2.1.1.html; 22.03.2017.

[7]See more on mixed agreements in Cremona (2006).

[8]http://openeurope.org.uk/today/blog/the-mechanics-of-leaving-the-eu-explaining-article-50/; 08.03.2017.

[9]Articles 24 and 227, 228 TFEU, decisions 94/114, 94/262 and 2002/262 Citizens must be aware of their rights, to be able to defend them when they think that a Member State is not respecting them. EU citizens are entitled to defend their rights acquired through European law. They can take their case to the national courts, which can either issue a ruling or turn to the Court of Justice for a preliminary ruling or by simply and inexpensively lodging a complaint with the Commission or a petition with the European Parliament. The Parliament has a Committee on Petitions that examines the complaints of citizens. In case the complaint concerns instance of mismanagement in the activities of the European institutions or bodies, the citizen may address himself or herself to the Ombudsman appointed by the European Parliament.

50 has been agreed to be at the end of March 2017, which leads to the conclusion that Britain should officially leave EU by the April of 2019 as the negotiations must end within 2 years after the application to leave is launched in case other agreement is not reached for extension of these negotiations.

3 The EU Citizenship, Workers, and the Derived Rights

The vulnerable groups affected by BREXIT are the EU citizens living in the UK and UK citizens in other EU Member States is a consequence. The EU Member State citizens have enjoyed free movement for ages and planned their everyday lives according to these rights derived from the EU citizenship.

The citizenship of the EU was introduced by the Maastricht Treaty.[10] Article 20 of the Treaty on the Functioning of the European Union (hereinafter referred to as TFEU) states that "every person holding the nationality of a Member State shall be a citizen of the Union". The citizenship was created to lay down better grounds for the rights of movement, residence, and equal treatment of EU citizens. The ECJ has presented that the citizenship has strengthened the prohibition of discrimination on grounds of nationality both in EU Member States and the host EU Member States.[11]

There are several secondary legislation instruments applicable to EU workers like directive 2004/38/EC on the right of citizens of the Union and their family members to move and reside freely within the territory of the Member States[12]; Regulation (EU) No 492/2011 on freedom of movement for workers within the Union[13]; Regulation (EC) No 883/2004 on the coordination of social security systems[14] and its implementing Regulation (EC) No 987/2009.[15] Application of these rules now after the introduction of Brexit the treatment of EU citizens by Britain is under consideration. It is not any more secure which EU citizens' rights will be maintained and which not? As far as the conditions of new agreement between EU and Britain are not clear one cannot say whether those better ground for the rights of movement, residence and equal treatment are maintained. EU institutions have worked years to achieve the results that there is less discrimination on grounds of nationality but after Brexit there is no automatic consideration of those rights.

[10]See also Roots (2012).

[11]Craig and De Búrca (2011), p. 819.

[12]OJL 158/77.

[13]Regulation (EU) No 492/2011 of the European Parliament and of the Council of 5 April 2011 on freedom of movement for workers within the Union, OJL 141/1.

[14]Regulation (EC) No 883/2004 of the European Parliament and of the Council of 29 April 2004 on the coordination of social security systems, OJL 166/1.

[15]Regulation (EC) No 987/2009 of the European Parliament and of the Council of 16 September 2009 laying down the procedure for implementing Regulation (EC) No 883/2004 on the coordination of social security systems OJL L 284/1.

Article 20 of TFEU states the rights and duties of EU citizens. Those include right to move and reside freely within the territory of the Member State, right to vote and to stand as a candidate in elections to the European Parliament and in municipal elections in their Member State of residence, under the same conditions as the nationals of that State. It also gives a right to protection of the diplomatic and consular authorities of any Member State on the same conditions as the nationals of that State, in situations when in a third country there is not representation by their country of nationality. The last one is right to petition the European Parliament, to apply to the European Ombudsman, and to address the institutions and advisory bodies of the Union in any language of the Treaty and to get a response in the language of EU Member State. Job seekers have the right to reside for a period exceeding 6 months[16] without having to meet any conditions if they continue to seek employment in the host Member State and have a 'genuine chance' of finding work; during this time, they cannot be expelled.

After BREXIT British citizens cannot automatically benefit any more from those rights derived from the EU citizenship unless other type of agreement is reached during the negotiations with EU. But the problem does not arise only for the British citizens living abroad but also the EU citizens settled in Great Britain. The EU institutions have an obligation to protect the rights of EU citizens. These rights should not be degenerated because Britain has decided to leave European Union. So, any deal that is made with Britain in the process of leaving EU should protect EU citizens and their rights derived from their EU citizenship.

Free movement of workers is one of the fundamental rights guaranteed by the EU. It applies also in European Economic Area. The free movement of workers gives citizens of the 31 EEA countries a right to choose the place of residence and work, gives right to establish business and go to study in any of these countries. Before Maastricht Treaty free movement right was limited only to workers who contributed for the formation of common single market and not to all EU citizens. During the last 15 years Europe has contributed money, initiated projects and has placed political pressure to increase the free movement possibilities and increase interest of persons to move to work to another EU Member State. This has been a symbol and great success of market integration and more interaction between states of EU, which also contributes to the goals of EU to become a world leader in many areas of business, education, and innovation.

Barnard is highlighting that only few people took advantages of this opportunity to move to live in another EU Member State, because of social, economic, cultural, and linguistic constrains.[17] It is definitely not so easy to move to live and work in another country than the one you were born or you have lived before. It takes effort to learn a new language to get your qualification recognised and to integrate into new society were the rules are different than in your home country. So, it needs courage or real need, which might be financial or exploratory, to leave your country of origin

[16]C-292/89 - The Queen v Immigration Appeal Tribunal, ex parte Antonissen.

[17]Barnard (2013), p. 230.

to start up your new life in another EU Member State. Sometimes emigration is a choice and sometimes not. Now with the unclear situation of after Brexit rules the situation of EU citizens in Britain is put under very unclear situation as they had more preferential treatment in comparison with third country nationals living in Great Britain.

The European Union, by creating the EU citizens' rights has removed obstacles that were there before in 1960 and 1970s.[18] Freedom of movement and residence for persons in the EU is the cornerstone of Union citizenship, which was established by the Treaty of Maastricht in 1992 with the abolishment of further legal and technical barriers in the community and it became effective from 1993. Nevertheless, some free movement rights were still restricted. Only in 2004, the Directive 2004/38/EC on the right of citizens of the Union and their family members to move and reside freely within the territory of the Member States amending Regulation (EEC) No 1612/68 and repealing Directives 64/221/EEC, 68/360/EEC, 72/194/EEC, 73/148/EEC, 75/34/EEC, 75/35/EEC, 90/364/EEC, 90/365/EEC and 93/96/EEC, replaced the previous directives and codified the principles that were established by Court of Justice of European Union in the area of free movement.[19] The aim of free movement of workers is to remove all obstacles of the freedom of movement, and to give the same rights to nationals of EU Member State, not only in EU Member States but also in EEA states and their family members within the EEA by removing discrimination on the basis of nationality. After Brexit rest of the citizens of 27 EU Member States can enjoy rights of free movement of workers', as well as in three of those non-EU countries in the EEA and Switzerland. Although the principle of free movement is controversial and it was a key issue in Britain's referendum and became now a critical part of Brexit negotiations.

The EU leaders have made clear that the freedom of EU citizens to migrate to Britain is non-negotiable.[20] In the informal meeting on 29 June 2016 in Bratislava, the leaders of 27 EU country made a promise to discuss the rights of EU citizens in the situation of Brexit but unfortunately in the Roadmap and Declaration of 16 September 2016 we cannot see any discussion or opinion on Brexit or further steps. It is clear the time has not yet arrived to discuss issues that might happen when there is no clear letter from British Government to use Art. 50 of TEU.

As mentioned before access to the single market without free movement of workers is contrary to the principles of EU. The rights of free movement of workers are granted under Article 45 and the secondary legislation implementing it. These rights are granted to workers and their family members. In accordance with Article 45 free movement of workers are secured in the EU. It removes disadvantage like discrimination based on nationality between workers of the Member States as regard

[18]Ibid.

[19]See also in Roots and Dumbrava (2016).

[20]BBC News, Brexit: EU says no compromise on freedom of movement http://www.bbc.com/news/world-europe-36659900; 22.03.2017; See also Bratislava Summit 2016, Statement of Informal meeting of 27 EU Informal meeting at 27 Brussels, 29 June 2016.

employment, remuneration etc. but it is not applicable to employment in the public service.[21] According to EU secondary legislation, all EU citizens, including workers, have right to move freely any Member State in the EU and remain in a Member State 3 months without any special conditions.[22] Doherty is emphasising that EU established equal rights to social and tax benefits. It applies to workers and their family members who are moving from another Member State and to host State workers. The ability of family members to move with the worker, and be entitled to equal treatment in the host State, meant that it was not only economically active citizens that can move, but also, for example, children and elderly relatives. The existence of the latter groups on the territory of the host State has obvious consequences for social services like healthcare and schooling, language classes etc.[23]

In case a person wants to reside longer than 3 months, he needs to register himself in that Member State and identify their status in the host country. There are many statuses that a person can have. EU citizen can be a worker or self-employed, family member or a student, pensioner, or jobseeker and all of them have a right to stay in another Member State also after 3-month period if they fulfil the conditions set up by directive 2004/38/EC. As mentioned before, EU citizen must hold a citizenship of one EU Member State and citizenship is determined according to the domestic law of the Member State of EU. When Britain is leaving out of EU British workers will lose their EU citizen rights, but the same happens to EU citizens in Britain. The British citizens become non-EU nationals in another EU country, and should be treated as any other third country national is treated in the EU country where they stay.

Worker is generally an economically active person, who provides something for remuneration. There is no internationally agreed definition of the term of a worker and it is also missing from the EU Treaties, but the CJEU made it clear that, where union nationals are under control of the employer, they are workers. Court stated in Lawrie-Blum case[24] employment relationship means "if a person perform service for certain period under the direction of other and receives remuneration for that and it is called worker". In another case CJEU has said that there is no requirement for the work to be full time, hours, and minimum level of remuneration as well.[25] There should be no special rules for job-seekers who are coming from the other Member States of the EU. The general rules of host state applicable for job-seekers. The EU workers in Britain will lose this possibility to refer to the CJEU.

EU law and the principles that CJEU have created will lose their significance if no other deal will be made with Britain. Migrant workers and members of their families shall enjoy equal treatment with nationals of the host state. They also enjoy equal treatment in respect of trade union membership and exercise rights associated to trade, the right to vote or to be eligible for the administration or management posts of

[21] Foster (2014), p. 31.

[22] Art. 13 of Directive 2004/38/EC.

[23] Doherty (2016), p. 376.

[24] Case C-6/85, Lawrie-Blum v. Land Baden-Wurttemberg.

[25] Case C-53/81, Levin v. Staatssecretaris van justitie.

trade union.[26] Furthermore, workers enjoy all the rights and benefits accorded to national workers in respect of housing, ownership of property, child benefits[27] etc.

4 Impact of Brexit on Migration of Workers

Since the UK voted in a referendum to leave the EU, there has been legal uncertainty in several areas. Free movement of workers' rights is one the top agendas such as what does Brexit mean for employers, employees, and trustees? Currently, most employment rights of EU citizens in the UK are guaranteed by EU law. The rights include protection against discrimination in the workplace; health and safety regulations; dismissals and beyond; rules related to working time; protections of workers on transfers of undertakings and in insolvency; rules on the treatment of fixed-term contracts, agency and part-time workers; and other, more peripheral, rights such as data protection.[28] It can be concluded that Brexit will have huge impact on free movement of workers. This also affects EU employment, taxes, social security, and pension. Workers will feel influence that the changes will do to employment and pension law. After Brexit, EU citizens who would like to work or reside in the UK might need a work or residence permit.

Nevertheless, a distinction should be made between EU worker who is a resident in the UK for a period longer than 5 years and those who have been resident for less than 5 years. This is because, a person who has already been resident in the UK for a period longer than 5 years, he or she can apply for permanent resident permit in the UK, on the other hand, whose current stay is less than 5 years will be faced with the condition that British employers need to submit a separate work permit or he/she must go back to his/her own state. This principle is also coming from the EU secondary law that regulates the stay of EU nationals in another EU Member State. How this will be regulated in the future, must also be part of the Brexit negotiations.

Brexit will also have an impact for British living in other EU countries. Close to 1.2 million UK nationals live elsewhere in the EU. According to BBC the population of the UK is 63.7 million, of which 5.3 million (8%) are non-British, and just over half of those - 2.9 million (5%)—are from Europe. Of those 2.9 million EU nationals living in the UK, about 2.15 million are working.[29] So we are talking about the rights of workers mainly.

Large scale immigration has consequence on wages. For lower-paid occupations, a 10% rise in the ratio of immigrant workers to the UK born workers was associated

[26]ibid.

[27]ibid.

[28]Ford (2016), p. 399.

[29]http://www.bbc.com/news/uk-politics-uk-leaves-the-eu-36745584, Accessed 29.03.2017.

with a near 2% reduction in pay.[30] When immigration is too high and pace of change is too fast, it is quite impossible to build cohesive society because it is hard for social services like schools, hospitals, housing, and transport to cope with the situation. The UK has voted to leave and behind this, one of the most obvious reason, was immigration from European countries to the UK. It was a vote against free movement of workers within the EU—a vote to take back control over immigration policy.[31]

The issue of permanent residence and citizenship might also come to the Brexit dispute table as those who do not have a right to permanent residence might, be forced to leave from the EU or the UK, according to applicable national rules on immigration.

Brexit has impact on wage tax and social security as after Brexit the EU Social Security Regulations will not apply automatically to the British and to people living in Britain. As a result, the applicable social security legislation may have to be determined by using bilateral treaties or by using national social security laws or the new introduced act will take over the previous EU aquis. Initial legal impacts of Brexit will be relatively minimal for wage/personal income tax because of the fact that the right to levy tax is governed by bilateral tax treaties. Employment legislation has been transposed into the UK law and is deemed to be based on fundamental principles. Following Brexit, the UK would have to change employment legislation. Workers may get new working time rules, working hours, holiday pay and sick pay. However, Brexit might have a future impact on remuneration. After Brexit, the UK might not apply the Capital Requirements Regulations and Directive (CRDIV), the Alternative Investment Fund Managers Directive (AIFMD) and the Undertakings for Collective Investment in Transferable Securities (UCITSV), as a resulting in a ban on having a European passport.

It is also uncertain what will happen to pensions of workers. The British pensionaries who live in other EU countries have currently a right to transfer their pensions to the country where they live. Their health insurance covers their costs of healthcare and they enjoy other social benefits that are given to the citizens of that country where they live.

Cross-border pensions might become a big issue. Currently the EU law in respect of pension allows to link and sum up all years of work and pension rights. For example, if pension applicant is a national of an EU Member State, the applicant must apply for the state pension in the EU country where applicant last worked and the pension offices of all EU Member States will then exchange their information on basis of applicant employment history within the EU and calculate the full pension of an applicant based on this data. It is uncertain whether those options will remain post-Brexit. Brexit will affect applicant actual pension entitlement built up to date.

Brexit does not only have impact on workers and pensioners but also it changes the system in higher education and students who use their free movement rights.

[30]https://fullfact.org/immigration/does-immigration-reduce-wages/, Accessed 29.03.2017.

[31]Somervill (2016).

Nowadays, EU citizens including the British citizens can receive their education from any Member State, as a result they can gain knowledge in special fields. Students can go easily for exchange programs because of free movement of persons. British higher education is a business that is going to lose number of EU students if the new after Brexit policy does not give any benefits to them. It is already now quite expensive to study in UK and after Brexit Britain is not obliged to treat EU citizen students as their own, which means that the study fees can go up again to the amount that the third country nationals are paying. The same applies to other student allowances, loans, or benefits. After Brexit, they would be in a new legal situation that for now is very uncertain.

For example in 2015, UK universities contributed around 39.9 billion to the GDP in 2011–2012, which amounts to 2.8% of the GDP, 4 times that of agriculture.[32] Presently, there is free movement of EU students within the UK. EU students who are studying in the UK paying the level of fees and access to the same services as the UK students, including loans and grants. EU citizens currently make up 15% of the academic workforce and 5% of the student body. It is obviously noted that, EU students make a huge contribution to the UK economy. In 2011 to 2012, they generated £3.7 billion for the economy.[33] After Brexit fewer EU students will go to the UK for training. So, there will be substantial reduction in the availability of teaching staff and obviously the UK students may not have the opportunity to travel to other European countries to get education. It would affect the whole UK economy. The other concern of Brexit is that the UK has a plan to end rights given under freedom of movement rules already before, the UK triggers Article 50. This idea is based on fear and assumptions, that there will be increase of Romanian and Bulgarian migrants who would like to come to the UK before Brexit.[34] Although, the EU has argued that the cut-off date should be the same date as the day the UK actually leaves the EU.[35]

Furthermore, the UK is also going to lose the reference rights to CJEU. This is because Article 267 TEU allows only a request from Member State, to give preliminary rulings on EU law. It must be the court or tribunal of EU Member State that makes the passage.[36] This change might create big impact, because the UK appellate courts have ever given a social Directive a wide interpretation in favour of workers without the guidance from the ECJ.[37] In the absence of the assistance of guidance from the ECJ, the domestic appellate courts would return to their default position. So, it is also a loss for EU citizens living in the UK as they have less instruments to defend their rights. EU rules are strict on sanctioning employers for recruiting third country nationals who do not have lawful residence. After Brexit

[32]Furley (2016).

[33]Ibid.

[34]Johnston (2017).

[35]Ibid.

[36]Ford (2016), p. 404.

[37]Ibid. p. 405.

British citizens will become third country nationals who need residence and work permit in EU. They need to fulfil the criteria meant for third country nationals regulated by the law of the country of their stay and have no access to CJEU.

Many of the EU migrants living in the UK have been in Britain for some time. By early 2015, an estimated 39% of citizens of EEA countries had been in the UK for 10 years or more, and a further 32% had lived in the UK for 5–9 years. Most of EU citizens have been in the UK long enough and do qualify for permanent residence. EU citizens according to Directive 2004/38/ EC can gain permanent residence after 5 years of continuous residence. EEA nationals can apply for a permanent residence card certifying their right to permanent residence, although they are not required to do so. They can also apply for the UK citizenship after 6 years of residence. In practice, the numbers of grants of permanent residence or citizenship are low as a share of the EEA national population. Permanent residence grants to EEA nationals and their non-EEA family members have fluctuated between 15,000 and 23,000 per year since 2011, while citizenship grants to EU nationals have been between 7000 and 18,000. Both emaciated in 2013.[38] Despite widespread reports of greater interest in permanent residence and citizenship, the most recent data for 2015 do not show an increase in grants to EU nationals. However, these figures do not cover decisions made in 2016. Quarterly data show an increase in the total number of citizenship grants (to people of all nationalities) in the first quarter of 2016, although a breakdown of the 2016 data by nationality—separating EU from non-EU migrants—is not due to be published until May 2017.[39] Graduated students are usually welcomed by the employers who are looking for fresh new ideas and active employees. Limiting the access of students is limiting also the movement of workers to the UK.

There remains some uncertainty about how the status of EU citizens who have been in the UK for less than 5 years would be determined, although legal analyses suggest that EU citizens already living in the UK before Brexit, would not lose their rights. It is possible they might do so if they became unemployed, however, and it is unclear what rules would apply to very recent arrivals (such as people arriving after the date of the referendum but before new immigration rules were developed). These questions might be clarified as part of an agreement with the EU on the future UK-EU relationship.[40] Current UK immigration policy requires that, most non-EU labour migrants must be in graduate level employment, and provides very limited options for non-EU citizens to come to the UK for low-skilled work. At the same time many of the EU citizens working in the UK, under free movement rights, are holding positions in low-skilled level jobs (even if the individuals themselves often have relatively high levels of education). One can argue that the Brexit would have

[38]Migration Observatory, What would UK immigration policy look like after Brexit?, Published 09th June 2016, http://www.migrationobservatory.ox.ac.uk/resources/commentaries/uk-immigration-policy-look-like-brexit/ Accessed 29.03.2017.

[39]Ibid.

[40]Ibid.

more impact on low skilled workers than to highly skilled workers, who might nevertheless fulfil the criteria of right to stay or become a resident in the UK.

5 Alternative Solutions for Rights of the EU Workers' After Brexit

In case the Brexit deal stops the free movement of workers, another question about the future UK immigration system arises—whether and how the government would mitigate the potential impacts on UK employers, who have come to rely on EU workers by introducing a low-skilled worker programme.

In the past, there have been programmes that allowed employers to recruit non-EU nationals for work in certain low-skilled occupations, such as agriculture and food processing. From 2007 to 2008, participation in these programmes, known as the Seasonal Agricultural Workers Scheme and the Sectors Based Scheme, was limited to Romanian and Bulgarian nationals. They were closed entirely at the end of 2013, when nationals of these two countries gained unrestricted access to the UK labour market. The closure of the two schemes was explicitly linked to the fact that EU workers were available to meet labour demand in low-skilled jobs. Announcing their closure, the Immigration Minister stated that the unskilled and low-skilled labour needs "should be satisfied from within the expanded EEA labour market". This raises the question whether such programmes would be reintroduced as part of a new post-Brexit immigration policy that did not involve free movement.[41]

What would be the options for further cooperation after Brexit to maintain the rights of workers? One can look at the alternative models that are already in place to find a best solution for the case of BREXIT or create a completely new relationship. One can consider five working models of cooperation that are related to workers:

First model of Norway. Norway is full member of EU single market, accept free movement and makes free contributions to EU budget. Norway is not taking part of tariffs and customs union.

Second model of Switzerland. Switzerland is only partly member of the single market. Accepts free movement and makes smaller contributions to EU budget than Norway.

Third model of Canada. Canada does not take part of single market, does not accept free movement, is not in the customs union but has an agreement on reduced tariffs and does not make any contributions to EU budget.

Forth model of Turkey. Turkey is not a member of the single market, does not accept free movement to Turkey, has a special deal of Turkish workers in EU. Is in the customs union. Does not make contributions to EU budget.

[41] The Migration Observatory, What would UK immigration look like after BREXIT? University of Oxford 09.06.2016 http://www.migrationobservatory.ox.ac.uk/resources/commentaries/uk-immigration-policy-look-like-brexit/, 08.03.2017.

Fifth model of WTO. Where EU has a special deal on tariffs with WTO members. It is clear that whatever model is agreed upon it will change the current situation of workers who were moving around freely and had special treatment in comparison with third country nationals.

This article is not going to discuss further these models, as it seems that after the submission of the letter of notification to exit EU, the UK still needs to discuss different options within itself. Quite clear message that the letter gives us, is that UK seems not to opt for the single market access and there will be probably a different deal, that might not follow any of the above-mentioned models and the discussion should be switched to EU external relations with third country, as this is what UK seems to mature after Brexit.

6 Conclusion

Many issues, that need to be dealt after the initiative taken by the UK, are related to the political decisions. Nevertheless, whatever political decisions will be made the fundamental rights of persons including workers should be respected. Also, the principle of legal certainty, legitimate expectations and rule of law should be respected. It is clearly not the right time to say what will happen to rights of EU citizens to stay in the UK as their status has to be inserted in the exit agreement of Britain from EU.

On 29 March 2017, Theresa May sent a letter of notification to EU with a wish to use Art. 50 (2) of TEU.[42] In this letter May is looking for "deep and special partnership" with the EU after Brexit. The UK understands that they will not be able to have same access to Single European Market as before and that there will be "consequences" from Brexit. Britain also accepts that the four freedoms are "indivisible". In her letter to the EU she also had highlighted the need to have the transitional period "in order to avoid any cliff-edge as we move from our current relationship to our future partnership, people and businesses in both the UK and the EU would benefit from implementation periods to adjust in a smooth and orderly way to new arrangements." This shows that there is a possibility that the 2-year period indicated in Art. 50 TEU might not be used but the negotiations will be prolonged.

In her communication she also confirms that "the European Communities act of 1972 that gives effect of EU law in UK, will be repealed". It will be annulled by the legislation that converts the body of existing EU aquis to the UK law and "gives certainty for UK citizens and for anybody from the EU who does business in the UK". Nevertheless, the acquisition of EU aquis is not unconditional, as the words "wherever practical and appropriate" were used in the communication letter. The

[42]May's letter will be delivered at 12:20 BST on Wednesday by the British ambassador to the EU, Sir Tim Barrow. http://www.bbc.com/news/uk-politics-39422353; Accessed 29.03.2017.

new legislation comes into effect when the UK leaves the European Union. Taking in mind the limits of this article on rights of the workers, Art. 50 letter does not give us much guidance. It only states that "in the heart of our talks are the interest of all our citizens". It does not identify explicitly which citizens are in the first priority, the EU citizens or the UK citizens as it has not been specified. One can read from the next sentence of the letter that, "many citizens of the remaining Member States living in the UK and UK citizens living elsewhere in the EU", might be taken as a confirmation, that both the rights of the UK citizens and those EU citizens living in the UK should be determined soon.[43]

Currently there is only time to wait and see further developments, to understand and analyse, what will be the further steps, positions and the outcome of this new European Union without the UK and what consequences and changes it will bring to workers—UK and EU citizens. Because of BREXIT, the UK needs a large-scale review of its legislation, applicable principles, and legal policy. It is not a fast process to review all relevant legislation that has been applied since 1973 when the UK joined EU and make decisions which of those will be applied also in the future and what will be not any more relevant. It leads to the judicial reform and requests great political will, to make those decisions fast and without delay to find solutions to all. Year 2017 will be a memorisable landmark in the history of European Union as the UK has initiated a new precedent of exiting a Union from where in the past, it was only possible to enter.

References

Barnard C (2013) The substantive law of the EU: the four freedoms, 4th edn. OUP, Oxford

Craig P, De Búrca G (2011) EU law: text, cases, and materials, 5th edn. Oxford University Press, Oxford

Cremona M (2006) External Relations of the EU and the Member States: Competence, Mixed Agreements, International Responsibility, and Effects of International Law, EUI Working Paper, LAW No. 2006/22

Doherty M (2016) Through the looking glass: Brexit, free movement and the future. King's Law J 27:3

Ford M (2016) The effect of Brexit on workers' rights. King's Law J 27:3

Foster N (2014) Blackstone's EU treaty & legislation 2014–2015, 25th edn. OUP, Oxford

Furley J (2016) Brexit: What will be the effect on Dentistry? Linked in, 11th July, https://www.linkedin.com/pulse/brexit-what-effect-dentistry-julia-furley. Accessed 29 Mar 2017

Johnston L (2017) Theresa May to end EU citizens' rights to live in UK after fear 'half of Romania and Bulgaria' will come, Independent News, 27 February

Roots L (2009) The impact of the Lisbon Treaty on the development of EU immigration legislation. Croat Yearb Eur Law Policy 5(5):261–281

Roots L (2012) European Union citizenship or status of long-term resident: a Dilemma for third-country nationals in Estonia. Balt J Eur Stud 2(1/11):65–80

[43]See more http://www.telegraph.co.uk/news/2017/03/29/article-50-brexit-letter-read-full/, Accessed 29.03.2017.

Roots L, Dumbrava C (2016) E-Citizenship opportunities in the changing technological environment in Kerikmäe T. et al. The Future of Law and e-Technologies. Springer
Somervill W (2016) Brexit: the role of migration in the upcoming EU Referendum. Migration Policy Institute, 4th May, http://www.migrationpolicy.org/article/brexit-role-migration-upcoming-eu-referendum. Accessed 29 Mar 2017
Terhechte JP (2008) Der Vertrag von Lissabon: Grundlegende Verfassungsurkunde der europäischen Rechtsgemeinschaft oder technischer Änderungsvertrag?, Europarecht, Heft 2

Legislation

Regulation (EC) No 883/2004 of the European Parliament and of the Council of 29 April 2004 on the coordination of social security systems, OJL 166/1
Regulation (EC) No 987/2009 of the European Parliament and of the Council of 16 September 2009 laying down the procedure for implementing Regulation (EC) No 883/2004 on the coordination of social security systems OJL L 284/1
Regulation (EU) No 492/2011 of the European Parliament and of the Council of 5 April 2011 on freedom of movement for workers within the Union, OJL 141/1

Cases

Case C-6/64, Flaminio Costa v E.N.E.L, Judgment of the Court of 15 July 1964, ECLI:EU:C:1964:66
Case C-292/89, The Queen v Immigration Appeal Tribunal, ex parte Antonissen
Case C-6/85, Lawrie-Blum v. Land Baden-Wurttemberg
Case C-53/81, Levin v. Staatssecretaris van justitie

Websites

http://openeurope.org.uk/today/blog/the-mechanics-of-leaving-the-eu-explaining-article-50/; 08.03.2017
http://news.bbc.co.uk/2/shared/bsp/hi/pdfs/29_03_17_article50.pdf; Accessed 31.03.2017
http://www.bbc.com/news/world-europe-36659900; 22.03.2017;
http://www.bbc.com/news/uk-politics-uk-leaves-the-eu-36745584, Accessed 29.03.2017
http://www.bbc.com/news/uk-politics-39422353; Accessed 29.03.2017
http://www.europarl.europa.eu/atyourservice/en/displayFtu.html?ftuId=FTU_2.1.1.html; 22.03.2017
http://www.telegraph.co.uk/news/2017/03/29/article-50-brexit-letter-read-full/, Accessed 29.03.2017
https://fullfact.org/immigration/does-immigration-reduce-wages/, Accessed 29.03.2017
http://www.migrationobservatory.ox.ac.uk/resources/commentaries/uk-immigration-policy-look-like-brexit/. Accessed 08.03.2017

The Scope and Specificity of Economic Relations Between the EU and the United Kingdom in Brexit Case

Rasa Daugėlienė and Paulius Puskunigis

Abstract The *scientific research problem* was formulated: how to explain controversial UK position regarding the membership in the EU? The *aim* of the study is to prognosticate the future of economic international relations between the EU and the UK in Brexit case. *The tasks* of the study are to systemise the dynamics of the EU and the United Kingdom economic relations in the perspective of history; to predict possible EU-UK relations scenarios after the Brexit; as well as to investigate the opinion of experts regarding the research object. The *research methods used*: literature analysis, focusing on primary sources but also including secondary sources; survey of experts using structured questionnaires with closed questions. The design of the study is formed in chronological order. It includes a historical analysis of the UK's road to the European Communities, as well as the dynamics of the UK's membership in the EU. The study also includes analysis of secondary sources to identify the most conceivable Brexit strategy, and then analysing the possible impacts of the most probable scenarios, which are based on that strategy. The key results address a few propositions. To begin with, although British were among the conceptualists of European integration, it took almost 20 years when the UK finally became a member of the developing EU. Those two decades had negative economic implications for British economy as it missed out opportunities provided by the common market. The eventual UK membership boosted most of the numbers concerning the British economy, however, disagreements with the EU still existed, particularly through issues of EU Budget contributions and immigration. Moreover, the "hard" Brexit is understood as the most probable Brexit strategy. In this case, the future EU-UK relation scenarios range is very limited. It includes a presumable Free Trade Agreement or bilateral trade based on World Trade Organization rules. We conclude that neither of those two solutions would ensure the UK trade with EU without tariffs or quantitative restrictions.

R. Daugėlienė (✉) · P. Puskunigis
Faculty of Social Sciences, Arts and Humanities, Kaunas University of Technology, Kaunas, Lithuania
e-mail: rasa.daugeliene@ktu.lt; puskunigispaulius@gmail.com

D. Ramiro Troitiño et al. (eds.), *Brexit*,
https://doi.org/10.1007/978-3-319-73414-9_16

1 Introduction

On 23 June 2016, citizens of the United Kingdom (UK) with a small 2% margin voted to leave the European Union (EU). The decision was a surprise both for politicians and for financial markets as Pound Sterling currency rate immediately dropped to the lowest level in 31 years. It is not clear what will the economic relations between the UK and the EU be in the future. Therefore, "Brexit is risky and its impact would depend heavily on the terms negotiated".[1] Regarding this *scientific research problem* was formulated: how to explain controversial UK position regarding the membership in the EU? The *aim* of the study is to prognosticate the future of economic international relations between the EU and the UK in Brexit case. *The tasks* of the study are to systemise the dynamics of the EU and the United Kingdom economic relations in the perspective of history; to predict possible EU-UK relations scenarios after the Brexit; as well as to investigate the opinion of experts regarding the research object. The *research methods used*: literature analysis, focusing on primary sources but also including secondary sources; survey of experts using structured questionnaires with closed questions.

In this paper, scientific works of Ehring (2002), Dedman (2006), Johnson (2015), Daugėlienė (2011), Vitkus (2013), Gifford (2016), Holmes et al. (2016), Young (2015) and Begg (2016) are used to analyse a history of the UK in the European integration that reveal that roots of Brexit were long before the UK even became the member of European Communities. Moreover, papers of Crafts (2016), Webb et al. (2016), Kierzenkowski et al. (2016), as well as European Commission statistics database were important in analysing economic aspects of the UK Membership in the EU. Papers of Piris (2016), Kierzenkowski et al. (2016) and the HM Government were the major sources to analyse possible EU-UK relations scenarios after Brexit. However, neither of the authors had a clear answer which model of future UK-EU relations would be applied, therefore, more in-depth expertise is needed. *The scientific novelty of the paper* is based on the fact that Brexit is still a new issue and, as a result, it is still lack of studies focusing on Brexit. Consequently, it raises a problem how to explain and to prognosticate the scope and specificity of economic relations between the UK and the EU in Brexit case.

[1] See Crafts (2016), p. 1.

2 Role of the UK in the Origins of European Communities: Period 'til 1952

During the eighteenth to nineteenth centuries, the UK had been one of the most powerful maritime states in the world, therefore, British Government had very few interests in the continental Europe.[2] Basically, their main goal was to avoid a creation of anti-British coalition. Nevertheless, this attitude slowly started to change. In the beginning of the twentieth century, during the start of Pan-European movement, there were a lot of hopes that the UK would take a leading role in uniting Europe. The famous Winston Churchill, UK Prime Minister during the Second World War and during the post-war period, who had already been an influential British politician from the start of the twentieth century, "published articles supporting the idea of a 'United States of Europe' in 1930 and in 1938.".[3] Churchill was "a federalist" and in favour of the United States of Europe.[4] His first article was written after his trip to the United States of America (USA) in 1930—Churchill was impressed how an absence of borders and tariffs supports a growth of economy. "Churchill believed, however, that Britain was not part of Europe but should support it from outside and that the French and Germans should create it."[5]

On the other hand, during the Second World War, "British federalist literature had an enormous influence on continental federalists". The top of pro-European enthusiasm in the UK was probably in June 1940 when Churchill's Cabinet made "the offer of complete political union between Britain and France" <...> "With joint organizations for defense, finance, foreign affairs and economic policy" and even "a common dual citizenship." This idea had not been implemented because the same month France was occupied by Nazi Germany. "Enthusiasm for European federalism never again achieved 1939-1940 levels of interest in Britain."[6]

In 1940–1941 Churchill was focusing on attracting Americans to the European affairs to get their military support as the UK was feeling a danger of Germany.[7] The Prime Minister overcame US isolationism and signed a lend-lease although it was a painful agreement for the UK. In an exchange of military support from the USA, the UK gave Americans a right to interfere in its overseas trade. The UK was also forbidden to import salted beef from Argentina, had to restrict its commercial aviation development and even had to make payments for the US Government the last of which was made only in 2006. On the other hand, this British turn to the American side was essential defeating the Nazi Germany and was the origin of trans-Atlantic cooperation and NATO.

---

[2] Read Vitkus (2013), pp. 84–85 and Ehring (2002), p. 921.

[3] Dedman (2006).

[4] For details read Johnson (2015).

[5] See Dedman (2006), p. 16.

[6] See Dedman (2006), pp. 20–21.

[7] For a more detailed analysis read Johnson (2015), Chapter 17 "The Wooing of America".

Nevertheless, situation changed again just after the Second World War. Churchill made a speech about the 'United States of Europe' in Zurich in 1946 but this time he had more support. After a death of Roosevelt, the next US President Harry S. Truman announced the Truman Doctrine. "Truman committed the US to the worldwide containment of communism by means of American aid to counter both communist internal insurgency and external aggression. <...> This was followed by the connected initiative of the Marshall Plan"[8] The plan was introduced in 1947, at this time most of the Europe was still destroyed after the war, its countries also were hit by a very harsh winter and as a result, although their currencies were very strong, they had no goods to sell.[9] Eventually, the USA was the world power that gave a proper origin for European integration.

The Plan was "a four-year programme (1948-1952) of over 22$ billion in American aid to 16 European states started."[10] The UK got the biggest amount of financial support (3189 billion dollars). At the same time, it was a turn towards a regional cooperation as Marshall Aid was implemented by two agencies: Economic Co-operation Administration (ECA) and European Economic Co-operation (OEEC).[11] ECA was basically giving humanitarian aid (money for food, fuel, cars) to Europeans and supporting special projects, particularly infrastructural ones. Meanwhile, OEEC had to ensure that programme countries would commit to an implementation of policies, promoting a growth of trade and industry. Organisation also had to find out possibilities of creating either a customs union or a free trade area, as well as to improve payment systems, to set friendlier environment for labour and had some specific requirements for free movement of capital.[12] "The Americans hoped that the OEEC could be developed into a customs union for Western Europe." However, it did not happen. In 1949 "the British and Scandinavians <...> vetoed all such federalist recommendations from the Parliamentary Assembly" in November 1949 in Strasbourg.[13] Nevertheless, the Marshall Plan was still very successful. In 4 years in Western Europe Gross National Product (GDP) had grown by 30%, industrial production surpassed pre-war levels by 40%, there had been huge improvements in agriculture, trade balance and economic liberalisation.[14] Moreover, a few of the biggest US companies (Dupont", "General Motors", "IBM") started investing to Europe. Later, huge European companies ("Royal Dutch Shell", BP, EMI, "Unilever", etc) started doing the same in the USA. Therefore, there was an increase in concurrence on both sides of the Atlantic Ocean.

[8]See Dedman (2006), p. 25.

[9]For details read Vitkus et al. (2008).

[10]See Dedman (2006), p. 22.

[11]To find more numbers about the Marshall Plan read Daugėlienė (2011), pp. 18–19.

[12]To find more details about ECA and OEEC, read Vitkus et al. (2008), Daugėlienė (2011), Gifford (2016), Young (2015).

[13]See Dedman (2006), p. 28.

[14]Vitkus et al. (2008), p. 202.

The real origin of the European Communities was May 1950, when the Schuman Plan was presented. Winston Churchill was in favour of this plan but he had lack of support in the Parliament that was afraid of UK's sovereignty.[15] Therefore, "Britain declined to participate in the talks from the outset."[16] The Treaty of Paris was signed in 1951 and became into force in 1952 when the European Coal and Steal Community (ECSC) was established.[17] The ECSC laid a path for further economic integration (led by France and Germany) but the UK came back to pre-war level of nationalism and fear of giving some sovereignty to supranational institutions that led to staying outside the European Community for two more decades.

3 The UK Foreign European Economic Policy from 1952 'til 1973

In 1950s, the UK's foreign policy was focused on international security matters, particularly through NATO and the Western European Union (WEU). This "claim to superpower status was based on the global network of Empire which generated an interest in most regions of the world", although, "The Empire could not be sustained."[18] Meanwhile, the UK's foreign economic policy was very cautious. On the way towards Rome treaties of 1957, the UK sent their representative—a Board of Trade official, who "was initially briefed to try and steer the talks towards an OEEC free-trade area framework for West European commerce and trade."[19] Although the six members of European Steel and Coal Community "sought a close cooperation with Britain in moving towards the next step of economic integration",[20] the UK was afraid of supranationalism once again and eventually only was an observer in the talks. "Britain's refusal to join the EEC at the start is now seen as one of the biggest mistakes of post-war international statesmanship."[21] This was a mistake considering the internal economic situation in the UK. The country had "lost 25% of its wealth in World War II <. . .> Defence spending equalled 28.5% of total government expenditure in 1953, which meant very high tax rates". In this situation, the UK Government had to seek for options. With some pressure from states such as Sweden, Switzerland and Portugal, the UK mounted "a counter-initiative to the Common Market", which proposed "to convert the 16-state OEEC into a free trade zone."[22] However, this idea had been turned down by 'the Six'.

---

[15]Read Johnson (2015), Chapter 20 "Churchill the European".

[16]See Dedman (2006), p. 57.

[17]For more details read Pukelienė (2008).

[18]See Dockrill and Young (1989), p. 2.

[19]Dedman (2006) and Gifford (2016).

[20]Dockrill and Young (1989), p. 6.

[21]See Dedman (2006), p. 106.

[22]See Dedman (2006). pp. 107–110.

The following action was "setting up a European Free Trade Area (EFTA), as a rival organization to the EEC."[23] The EFTA Treaty, with an initiative from the UK, came into force in 1960 and was signed by seven countries: the UK, Denmark, Norway, Portugal, Sweden and Switzerland The main difference between EEC and EFTA was that the following had not sought for further political integration and had been aiming only for liberalisation of trade coordinated by national governments.[24] Seven participating countries abolished tariffs on industrial goods in 1967.

However, British government still had hope that EFTA and EEC eventually could merge into a big free trade area. However, it took very little time to realise that the Association was unprofitable for the UK and benefited smaller states (like Sweden and Switzerland). The UK was an only big market in the Association: 51 of 89 million of EFTA population had been provided by the UK and only 10% of British exports had been to EFTA.[25]

During 1950s and 1960s the EEC countries had a rapid economic growth. Meanwhile, the British Empire was going to an end. Without an economic boost from colonies British economy was in stagnation. The main reason for this was not being a part of EEC Common Market. In 1968, the EEC completely got rid of the last internal customs, non-tariff barriers and set common external tariffs. It indicates that the EEC began to coordinate security of its Common Market from the third countries, including the UK. In 1950s, British producers had been second-rated in Europe. Although they had partly less concurrence in domestic market, they had less innovations, productivity and growth comparing to European firms. Moreover, British automobiles producers lost Australian market when its Government introduced 35% import custom tax while in European market UK producers had been losing a competitive battle to Italian car producers whose production was cheaper because of its membership at EEC. According to statistics, the period outside the EC had a negative impact on British economy: in 1958–1971 EEC economy grew in total by 98% while the UK had a grow of only 48%: Gross domestic product (GDP) in 1950s and 1960s was growing on average, accordingly, 5.4% in EEC and 2.8% in the UK per year.[26] British standard of living in 1970, comparing to EEC countries, was higher only than Italy.[27]

When the UK decided to seek for EEC membership, the admission process was long because of Common Agricultural Policy (CAP) and commitment to take supranational decisions. (Dumčiuvienė 2010) However, the biggest obstacle for the UK's integration into the European Communities (EC) was its complicated relations with France. The UK submitted two applications in 1961 and 1967 but both times they were vetoed by France.[28] There were unilateral decisions by a

---

[23]Dedman (2006), p. 110.

[24]Vitkus et al. (2008).

[25]See Dedman (2006), p. 111.

[26]To read more see Dedman (2006).

[27]For more analysis read Young (2015), pp. 1253–1275.

[28]Vitkus (2013), p. 84.

president of France Charles de Gaulle. "He regarded Britain as America's 'Trojan Horse' in Europe allowing greater US penetration of the Common Market".[29] De Gaulle was worried about Britain's nuclear force, its close relations with the US through the NATO as a danger to France's role in Europe. After all, De Gaulle resigned in 1969 and the UK were able to resume negotiations with the EC. Finally, the UK became the Member of EC on January 1, 1973.

4 Economic Aspects of the UK Membership in the EU

Accession to the Single Market "has raised UK income levels appreciably and by much more than 1970s' proponents of EU entry predicted. These positive effects stem from the EU's success in increasing trade and the impact of stronger competition on UK productivity."[30] Trade tariffs for Britain were eliminated after a 4.5 year transition period: each year there were reduced by 20% until got totally lifted in July 1977.[31] In 1970s, the EC was erecting the majority of remaining non-tariff barriers, "including national import quotas, complex rules of origin and 'voluntary' export restraints".[32] Eventually, the Single European Market (SEM) was established in 1992, which "was simply a programme to enable the EU to complete the creation of a CM."[33] By that time, diverse national rules had been finally enough harmonised to complete this move.

Therefore, joining the EU (at that time still the EC) helped UK producers and traders to become more competitive inside and outside the SEM: "In the context of the 1970s at which point the UK had endured a long period of protectionism, the 'shock' of joining the EU had favourable effects on productivity and was part of an effective antidote to relative economic decline which worked through strengthening competition".[34] GDP growth and standard of living for British people had used to be behind the EC countries in 1970s and early in 1980s but integrating into the European market helped to boost a growth in GDP. By 1995, growth rate exceeded growth percentages in France and Germany. On the other hand, those statistics cannot be explained only by an effect of the SEM. EC economies had been growing very rapidly and it was expected to slow down naturally while the UK GDP was still growing by more than 2% despite its problems with colonies.

In fact, an empirical research about an effect of economic integration for countries of the EU stated: "GDP per capita of the EU-15 would be approximately one-fifth

[29]See Dedman (2006), p. 106.

[30]Crafts (2016), p. 1.

[31]For a more detailed information read Dedman (2006).

[32]See McDonald and Deardem (2005), p. 329.

[33]McDonald and Deardem (2005), p. 334.

[34]Crafts (2016), p. 15.

lower today if no integration had taken place since 1950."[35] Particularly for the UK, this impact would be 25.5%.[36] This growth effect is based on bilateral trade as the EU "is the UK's major trading partner, accounting for 44% of exports and 53% of imports of goods and services in 2015."[37]

Despite all of this, after the accession into the EEC the UK was already demanding an abatement for its contribution to the EC Budget.[38] The UK Government calculated that their contributions would exceed receipts the UK got from the EC (EU). This was based on two reasons. Firstly, there were relatively British farmers as majority of the financial support from the EU Budget is distributed for European farmers.[39] In 1970s, around 70% of food products in the UK were being imported while only 3% of country's workforce were in agriculture sector.[40] Secondly, the UK had great numbers in collecting Value Added Tax (VAT). The problem of contribution was a question of disagreement until 1984 while UK Prime Minister Margaret Thatcher negotiated a long-term agreement with the EC. The UK was given an exception, which "is calculated according to a formula which in essence used to mean that the UK's net contribution was reduced by 66%, relative to what it would be without the abatement. However, certain elements from the Budget are excluded from the deduction, including EU overseas aid, and from 2009 non-agricultural expenditure in new Member States. This latter development, the effect of which was phased in up to 2011, largely accounts for the sharp increase in the UK's net contribution."[41] By 2015, it exceeded 18 billion euro per year (Fig. 1).

Despite the rise in the UK's input, the EU expenditures for the UK during the period (2010–2015) were very constant. Consequently, UK input-revenue ratio concerning the EU Budget went extremely negative starting a year of 2010. In 2015 the UK was contributing 10.7 billion euro more than it was receiving from the EU Budget (Fig. 2).[42]

[35]Research made by Badinger (2005), p. 53.

[36]For a more detailed information read Crafts (2016).

[37]Webb et al. (2016), p. 3.

[38]Vitkus (2013), p. 85.

[39]For a detailed analysis read Vitkus et al. (2008).

[40]Dedman (2006).

[41]Webb et al. (2016), p. 9.

[42]Read Begg (2016), pp. 39–47.

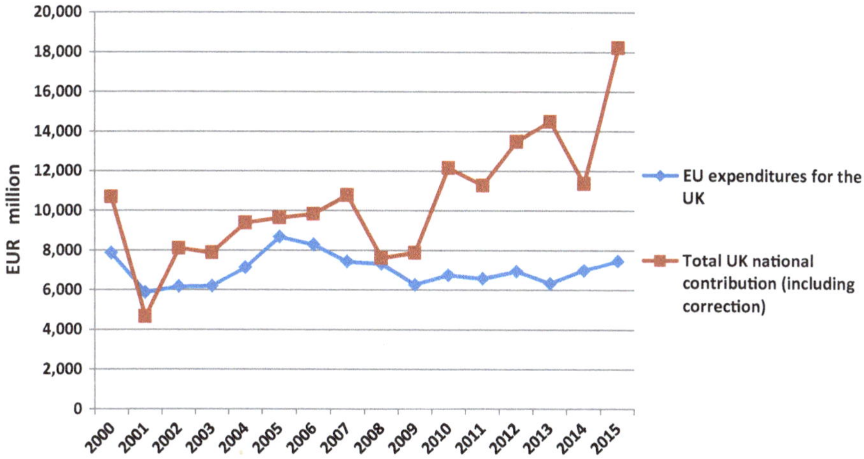

Fig. 1 Dynamics of the UK national contribution and EU budget expenditures for the UK (Numbers are retrieved from the interactive European Commission database)

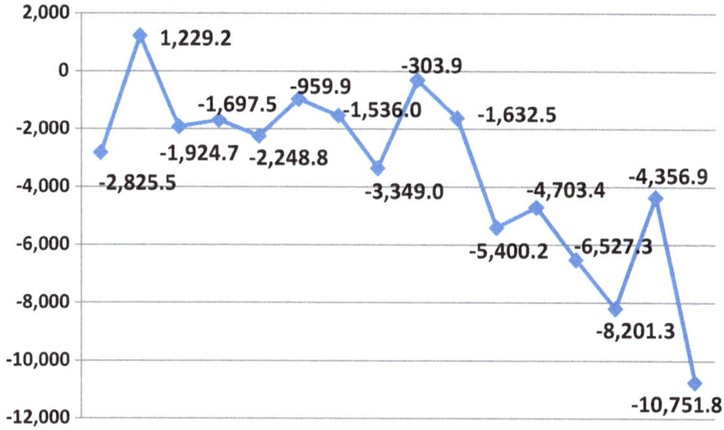

Fig. 2 UK balance dynamics (2000–2015) comparing its contribution to the EU Budget and EU Budget contributions for the UK (Numbers are retrieved from the interactive European Commission database)

Therefore, EU Budget contribution was a constant argument during the referenda campaign as "the UK makes a contribution equivalent to around £275 million a week".[43] The Vote Leave claimed that that money could be used for other purposes such as education or healthcare.

Talking about trade and investment between the EU and the UK, the latter is generally on negative side of trade balance in goods, however, the London City

[43]See Webb et al. (2016), p. 10.

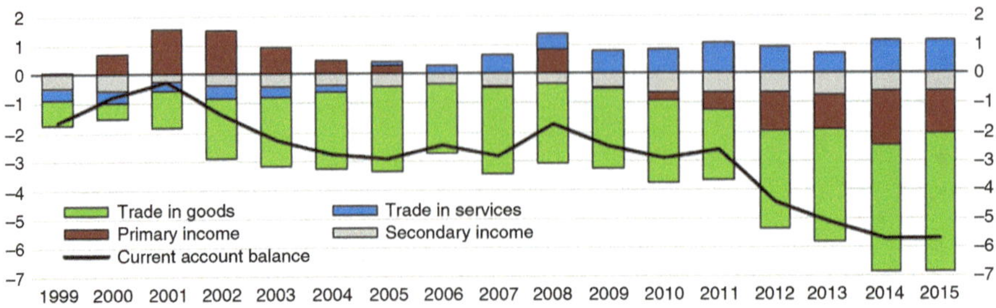

Fig. 3 UK account balance with the EU (This figure is retrieved from the OECD economic policy paper made by Kierzenkowski et al. (2016))

financial centre is putting the UK in positive territory concerning the services (from 2005 onwards):

Exports to EU countries account for about 12% of the UK GDP and about 45% of total UK exports, and for imports the EU is even a more important partner <…> "The UK has a deficit in goods trade *vis-à-vis* the EU, but a surplus in services <…>, in particular in financial services. <…> Exports of financial services amount to slightly more than 2.5% of GDP for the UK, against about 0.5% of GDP in EU peers."[44] (Kierzenkowski et al. 2016) (Fig. 3).

In terms of Foreign Direct Investment, the EU is not as important as the USA. For example, "The EU accounted for only 19% of net FDI flows into the UK in 2014 (compared to 55% from the US)." (Webb et al. 2016) However, according OECD, the UK is the most attractive country among the EU Member States for FDI. Therefore, a loss of it in the Single Market "would weaken fixed investment, reduce export capacity and hit innovation and productivity (technical progress) over time."[45] Speaking of that, Brexit negotiations will be crucial.

One more aspect to point out is the effect of immigration as it was the main argument for Leave Vote campaign. Although movement of labour force is the least implemented freedom, migration is considered as a huge problem in the UK.[46] "Migration has only been significant since the mid-1990s and has only become controversial since the accession of (relatively poor) eastern European countries in 2004 and 2007."[47] The EU takes only a small part in European social policy.[48] Because of relatively small EU budget, which amounts only 1% of total accumulated budgets in the Member States, the EU cannot perform redistribution policy like can individual countries. That is why its social policy is oriented towards a creation and adoption of common social regulation in the EU. However, the most arguing between the UK and the EU had been to a free movement of persons that ensures

[44]Kierzenkowski et al. (2016), p. 14.

[45]Kierzenkowski et al. (2016), p. 25.

[46]To get more information read Vitkus et al. (2008).

[47]See Crafts (2016), p. 8.

[48]For more analysis of European social policy read Vitkus et al. (2008).

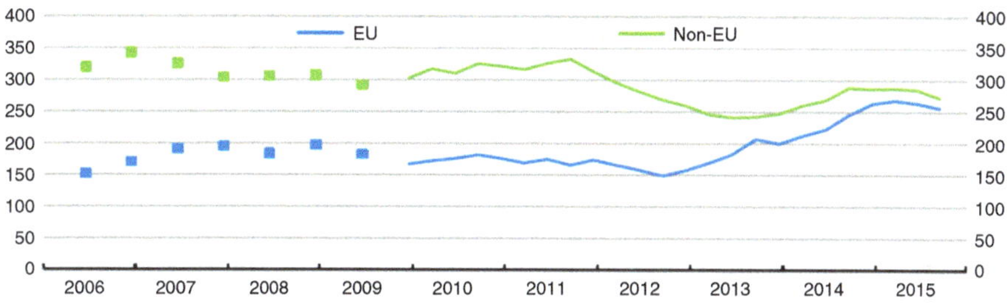

Fig. 4 Inflows of migrants to the United Kingdom in thousands (This figure is retrieved from the OECD economic policy paper made by Kierzenkowski et al. (2016))

that Member States pay for EU immigrants allowances that were their cumulated social security contributions in different states.[49] British society is feeling an anger that a part of the budget is spent on allowances for immigrants from Europe. However, "for immigrants that arrived since 2000, contributions have been positive throughout, and particularly so for immigrants from EEA countries. Notable is the strong positive contribution made by immigrants from countries that joined the EU in 2004."[50] Therefore, immigrants from the Eastern Europe (Poland, Lithuania, etc.) actually were useful for British economy. For example, "around 3.3 million jobs are linked, directly or indirectly, to UK exports to other EU countries."[51] According to the OECD paper[52]:

Immigrants, particularly from EU countries, have boosted GDP growth significantly in the UK. EU immigrants have higher employment rates than natives and almost all other migrant groups <...> Migrants from countries that acceded to the EU in 2004 (EU8 countries) have a higher employment rate than EU migrants in general. EU migrants also have a better education than in most other EU countries <...>, although wages of immigrants from EU8 countries are rather low. Immigration has been a key factor behind the strong labour market. Out of around 2.5 million jobs that were added to the UK in 2005–2015, 2.2 million were supplied by immigrants, with nearly 60% originating from the EU <...> Immigrants have contributed on average 0.7% points to GDP per year since 2005, accounting for roughly half of GDP growth, with a slightly higher contribution of immigrants from the EU than non-EU countries <...> Immigration should also provide longer-term economic benefits by mitigating population ageing (Fig. 4).

The figure above shows that many new immigrants in the UK from 2015 have been around 500,000 each year. Most of them were from the EU Member States. Therefore, if free movement is suddenly strictly restricted after the Brexit, it could be as a shock to the economic system.

[49]See Vitkus et al. (2013), p. 274.

[50]Dustmann and Frattini (2014).

[51]Webb et al. (2016), p. 7.

[52]Made my Kierzenkowski et al. (2016), p. 26.

5 Identification of the Most Likely Brexit Strategy

At first, British Prime Minister Theresa May said that she would seek for two, in EU law contradicting, goals: to restrict free movement of persons from the EU to the UK and to remain in the SEM. However, responses from Chancellor of Germany, Angela Merkel, Prime Minister of Luxembourg, Xavier Bettel and President of the European Council Donald Tusk were stern: the UK could only in the SEM only if free movement of persons is maintained. Consequently, in January 2017 May made a speech in which declared that the UK was leaving the EU, as well as that it would not stay in the SEM, the Customs Union, and the EEA. May's statement may sound risky but she, after statements of the EU officials, probably has only this approach to satisfy voters whose main concern during the referenda was immigration.

Piris (2016) analysed 7 possible Brexit scenarios. However, according to the speech by May, 5 of them (customised relationship with the EU; EEA; Customs Union; EFTA; Swiss model) are unrealistic.[53] The only two remaining options are either that "the UK negotiates a free trade agreement with the EU" or that "the UK does not conclude any trade agreement with the EU and relies on WTO rules to manage trade with it".[54] There is one more option, which is explained in the UK Policy Paper[55] called "the Norway model", however, it includes free movement of persons that is also unacceptable.[56]

The fact that the UK may definitely exit the SEM and the Customs Union should have a result that: "Trade between the UK and the EU would become more costly. Administrative costs related to customs controls would rise for any of the arrangements with the EU <...> leading to trade diversion outside the EU over time."[57] (Kierzenkowski et al. 2016) However, with both post-Brexit options (FTO and WTO rules) there is one extra factor, concerning the issue of UK trade with non-EU countries. As a legal entity, the EU could sign international treaties with the third countries, which must be ratified by all Member States and, eventually, binds all of them. This is one of EU legal sources (*Europos Sąjungos teisė.* 2007). Therefore, once the UK formally leaves the EU, it is no longer a part of FTAs or Preferential Agreements between the EU and the third countries. It must be a big issue for the Government to deal with as "at the moment UK companies get preferential access to many external markets thanks to EU trade agreements covering 53 markets."[58] About 12% of UK exports are linked with these Trade Agreements. Consequently,

[53]Read the article by Piris (2016) to get a more detailed information about each relation model.

[54]See Piris (2016), p. 10.

[55]*Alternatives to membership: possible models for the United Kingdom outside the European Union* (2016).

[56]Holmes et al. (2016).

[57]See Kierzenkowski et al. (2016), p. 17.

[58]See UK Policy Paper: *Alternatives to membership: possible models for the United Kingdom outside the European Union* (2016), p. 24.

Table 1 Length of FTA negotiations, examples (Retrieved from Kierzenkowski et al. (2016), p. 17)

Negotiation	Time (years)
Switzerland—China	4
EU—South Korea	4
EU—Mexico	4
US—Australia	3
EU—Canada	5
EU—Switzerland	10

a withdrawal would be both time and resource costly for the UK as "the time needed to negotiate recent FTAs was at least 3 years."[59]

6 Theoretical Implications of the Presumable EU-UK Free Trade Agreement

The EU-UK trade agreement negotiations would have a lot of complexity involved. On the legal side, it would require the agreement of 27 remaining Member States, as well as the ratification of the European Parliament, UK Parliament and in Parliaments in all EU Member States (in some cases, like in Belgium, even an approval of regional Parliaments). Each FTA could have different rules, on the other hand, it creates a landmark for future agreements and majority of them have most of things in common. But one landmark that is common for all FTAs is a long duration of negotiations. It may be quicker to achieve a bilateral Agreement between two individual states, though, the EU is a huge international organisation of 27 countries that makes negotiation process long-lasting (Table 1).

Regarding the trade itself, once the EU-UK FTA is achieved, "it goes back to the current zero-tariff regime for trade with the EU"[60] but not in all sectors. For example, although CETA is "the most comprehensive trade agreement the EU has ever negotiated"[61] and it eliminates 99% of import duties, it is the remaining 1% that remains. Those customs are in some parts of two industrial areas: agriculture and manufacturing of cars. There are also some quotas of custom-free agricultural products that limits the amount of free trade. The UK Policy Paper[62] summarises the remaining EU-Canada trade barriers in this sector and imagines how the same rules would affect the UK:

Canada will only be allowed to export limited quotas of processed shrimp and frozen cod, beyond which tariffs of 20% and 7.5% will be applied, respectively.

[59]Kierzenkowski et al. (2016), p. 17.

[60]See Kierzenkowski et al. (2016), p. 19.

[61]Piris (2016).

[62]UK Policy Paper: *Alternatives to membership: possible models for the United Kingdom outside the European Union* (2016), p. 33.

Quotas are introduced for export of other products, such as beef and pork. For example, Canada will only be able to export 50,000 tonnes of beef to the EU, beyond which it will have to pay tariffs. More than 90% of both the UK beef and sheep exports go to the EU (92,000 tonnes and 75,000 tonnes, respectively). Based on the Canada deal, whatever amount of beef the UK exported to the EU beyond the agreed quota (of the UK's £80 million annual beef exports to the EU) would face tariffs of more than 12%. In addition, they could face additional duties on top of several hundred Pounds for every 100 kg.

As far as cars are concerned, the EU common external tariff for them is 10%. Currently in the SEM, UK producers (Aston Martin, McLaren, Jaguar and all the others) sells their production without tariffs or any regulatory barriers. However, if Canadian model would be applied, "UK car manufacturers would still be subject to the bureaucracy and associated costs of complying with EU Rules of Origin. Furthermore, UK exporters could still face a 10% tariff when exporting to the EU."[63] (*Alternatives to membership: possible models for the United Kingdom outside the European Union* 2016).

It is a different story for services that are responsible for almost 80% of the UK economy. According to Piris (2016), "FTAs usually say very little about trade in services." (p. 9) CETA excludes financial services and government procurement "so Canadian retail and investment banks, insurance and pension companies, as well as investment funds, may not provide many services in the EU without establishing a subsidiary in Europe." Piris (2016) UK financial companies may lose the EU's passporting[64] rights that could have destructive impact for the London City as 40% of financial exports are intended for the EU countries. Currently, it is the financial centre in Europe and brings a notable contribution to British economy, "accounting 7% of UK output and 4% of employment in 2015." (Kierzenkowski et al. 2016) UK financial services have the biggest impact for GDP among the EU Member States. Taking CETA as an example, there could also be restrictions for other service sectors, for example audio-visual and air transport. "UK low-cost airlines currently benefit from full access to a liberalised EU air services market", however, they could lose part of their competitiveness.

Before summing it up, we should mention that the UK products may be bounded by Rules of Origin. In Canadian case, "companies have to prove that a sufficient proportion of the product was originally made in Canada to qualify for preferential tariff rates. Complying with these rules creates an extra burden for businesses."[65] Moreover, while products or services enter the SEM, they still have to comply with most of the EU Regulations, however, withdrawal from the EU means that the UK

[63]UK Policy Paper: *Alternatives to membership: possible models for the United Kingdom outside the European Union* (2016), p. 33.

[64]"The EU's financial services 'passport' means that financial services firms authorised in the UK can provide their services across the EU, without the need for further authorisations." (*Alternatives to membership: possible models for the United Kingdom outside the European Union.* 2016).

[65]See Kierzenkowski et al. (2016).

will not have a right to vote on EU Law. It might bring more obstacles for British firms, especially, if the UK Government decides to repeal most of the Laws based on EU Regulations and Directives. Consequently, the business would have to deal with a problem of how to comply both with local and Europeans rules if it wants to export.

7 Theoretical Implications of Economic Relations Based on World Trade Organization Rules

If no EU-UK agreement is concluded, they will simply have to rely on World Trade Organization (WTO) rules to manage trade. WTO rules "set limits on the maximum tariffs that countries can apply to trade in goods."[66] WTO became an official international organisation in 1995 and had evolved from the General Agreement on Tariffs and Trade (GATT), which was signed in 1947. GATT is based on three principles: reciprocity, prohibition on trade restrictions other than tariffs, non-discrimination. However, the latter has two main exceptions: developing countries; free trade areas and customs unions.[67] One of the non-discrimination principles is called the *Most Favoured Nation* (MFN). According to it, "if a GATT country grants a trade concession to another GATT country, this concession automatically applies to all other GATT countries as well."[68] Therefore, in most cases (except a few exceptions) countries cannot unilaterally set different import tariffs for each country. However, the EU falls into the category of exceptions: "If two or more countries decide to form a free trade area or a customs union, such as the countries of the European Union (EU), discrimination treatment is allowed, essentially because it is viewed as a move in the right direction of free trade." This exception allows the EU to manage free trade in the SEM and to set a common external tariff for all the countries.

As a result of this, if EU-UK economic relations are governed by WTO rules, the UK "face the EU Common External Tariff as EU exporters would face the tariffs adopted by the UK."[69] This would be a definitive break from the EU as "under WTO rules neither the UK nor the EU could offer each other better market access than that offered to all other WTO members."[70] The EU Common External Tariffs will affect the UK exporters if the Government does not reach any trade agreement with the EU—WTO based economic cooperation is the only Brexit option that do not require any agreement. Accordingly, WTO rules would bind from the very first day of formal Brexit (unless there would be a transitional period) and the UK would be treated as one of the EU third countries, like China, Russia, etc. Piris states: "The UK

[66]Piris (2016), p. 10.

[67]For a more detailed analysis read Van Marrewijk et al. (2012).

[68]See Van Marrewijk et al. (2012), p. 243.

[69]Lea (2017), p. 3.

[70]Piris (2016), p. 11.

would have to re-establish customs controls at borders with EU member-states. This would include establishing a border with the Republic of Ireland, unless the EU and the UK managed to conclude a special agreement on that issue before the date of the UK's withdrawal."[71] This would have a serious political issue as citizens of Northern Ireland and the Republic of Ireland would face border control procedures for the first time since 1920s. Starting in that decade, "the countries have operated a Common Travel Area, which allows for nationals of both countries to travel and live in each country without immigration controls."[72] There are no guarantees that it would not lead to the referenda in Northern Ireland, protests, riots or any other political tension that would certainly have further unpredictable economic impact.

As far as tariffs are concerned, it is clear that "if reciprocal tariffs were introduced on imports from the EU, these goods would become more expensive" for the customers in the UK. Therefore, an inflation in the UK would soar if the WTO-only model is applied. The other thing for the UK would be the issue of how to determine a single, universal set of tariff rates with the countries outside the EU as the UK would no longer trade with under the EU common external tariff. New tariffs would be required to be submitted to the WTO. Consequently, "this would be a complex exercise involving a review of every tariff line – over 5,000 – to determine what rate the UK would wish to apply."[73]

Moreover, many industries "rely on tariff-free imports of components from the Single Market to support complex supply chains. The individual price calculations behind these would change if tariffs were reintroduced. This would have considerable implications for the competitiveness of UK businesses."[74] For instance, according to the HM Government (2016) WTO model could be very stressful for UK's car industry as "components sourced from the EU would become more expensive for UK vehicle manufacturers. As over 40% of components purchased by these manufacturers come from the EU, this could place such exporters at further disadvantage."[75] As components become more expensive, the expenses required to make a product are also higher. Consequently, the production becomes less competitive as manufacturers must raise prices. On the other hand, "given that the EU is locked in to zero tariff treatment for so many non-agricultural products, many manufacturers in a country that exited the EU could face no change in tariff treatment in their exports to the European Union."[76] Of course, this is just a hypothesis. It may

[71]See Piris (2016), p. 10.

[72]UK Policy Paper: *Alternatives to membership: possible models for the United Kingdom outside the European Union* (2016), p. 16.

[73]See UK Policy Paper: *Alternatives to membership: possible models for the United Kingdom outside the European Union* (2016), pp. 35–38.

[74]UK Policy Paper: *Alternatives to membership: possible models for the United Kingdom outside the European Union* (2016), p. 38.

[75]UK Policy Paper: *Alternatives to membership: possible models for the United Kingdom outside the European Union* (2016), p. 35.

[76]See *Trade and Investment Balance of Competence Review* (2013), p. 55.

Table 2 EU maximum MFN applied duties on non-agricultural products (Numbers are retrieved from World Trade Organization database)

Product group	EU's maximum tariff (%)
Fish & fish products	26
Minerals & metals	12
Petroleum	5
Chemicals	13
Wood, paper, etc.	10
Textiles	12
Clothing	12
Leather, footwear, etc.	17
Non-electrical machinery	10
Electrical machinery	14
Transport equipment	22
Manufactures, n.e.s.	14

end up that the UK exporters would pay a maximum tariff as every solution is still possible (Table 2).

8 Empirical Approach to the Further Economic Relations Between the EU and the UK

A survey of experts using structured questionnaires with closed questions was made to examine the opinion of experts regarding the EU and the UK future relations. Questionnaires were distributed among two groups: for politicians—members of Committee on European Affairs in Seimas (Lithuanian Parliament) and for academics in social sciences. Those academics in social sciences were from different countries as their universities are in Piraeus (Greece), Gdansk (Poland), Prishtina (Kosovo), Warsaw (Poland), Riga (Latvia, there was also one Chinese PhD candidate studying in Riga), Kiev (Ukraine) and Mannheim (Germany). In total 17 responses were received: 8 from Lithuanian parliamentarians and 9 from international group of academics.

10 out of 17 respondents agreed that the "hard" Brexit is likely. However, while politicians believed either in "soft" Brexit or in softer options of the "hard" Brexit, foreign social scientists tended to think that the "hard" Brexit and WTO model would be chosen. However, almost everyone (16 out of 17) agreed that "some sort of transitional period is possible before moving on to a permanent relations model". Thus, there is a believe that Brexit will not be very sudden and both business and government will have some time to make changes before moving on to a stable EU-UK relations model. Moreover, Lithuanian politicians believe that the UK will have trouble maintaining the same trade provisions with non-EU countries that have any type of preferential arrangements with the EU while among the academic target group there was an almost equal scatter of opinions. What is more, two thirds of

respondents agreed that Brexit will "weaken UK's negotiation power in world politics".

Moreover, the majority answered that both restrictions of the EU free movement of persons and a return to bilateral customs policy in case of WTO model would have a negative impact on British economy. Four fifths thought that if UK financial companies lose EU passporting rights, it would slow down GDP growth. Two thirds also had an opinion that UK's withdrawal from the EU should have a negative impact on at least for some EU Member States that receive the most of support from the EU Budget. To sum it up, although there was not a unanimous opinion about future EU-UK relations, the majority of respondents felt pessimistic about Brexit's impact on British and European economies.

9 Conclusions

British were among the conceptualists of European integration but it took almost 20 years when the UK finally became a member of the developing EU. Those two decades had negative economic implications for British economy as it missed out opportunities provided by the common market. The eventual UK membership boosted most of the numbers concerning the British economy, however, disagreements with the EU still existed, particularly through issues of EU Budget contributions (despite the abatement) and immigration.

Furthermore, the main goal of the UK Government after Brexit is to retrieve immigration control, therefore, the "hard" Brexit scenario currently is the most likely outcome. In case of "hard" Brexit, either the EU-UK FTA or WTO rules based EU-UK trade future cooperation models are both possible. The FTA would give UK business more access to the Single European Market than WTO model, however, in both cases at least some tariff and non-tariff barriers would return. This would lead to inflation, especially for the imported goods because of import tariffs and administrative costs. It would also reduce competitiveness of UK producers that export into the EU market.

As the empirical research showed, there is not a unanimous opinion about the future EU-UK relations, the majority of respondents felt pessimistic about Brexit's impact on British and European economies. The "hard" Brexit is the most likely. Brexit will not be very sudden and both business and government will have some time to make changes before moving on to a stable EU-UK relations model.

References

Alternatives to membership: possible models for the United Kingdom outside the European Union (2016) 9781474129442. HM Government, London

Badinger H (2005) Growth effects of economic integration: evidence from the EU member states. Rev World Econ 141(1):50–78

Begg I (2016) The EU budget and UK contribution. Natl Inst Econ Rev 236(1):39–47

Crafts N (2016) The growth effects of EU membership for the UK: a review of the evidence

Daugėlienė R (2011) ES ekonominė integracija: priežastys, raida, perspektyvos. Technologija, Kaunas

Dedman M (2006) The origins and development of the European Union 1945–1995: a history of European integration. Routledge, Abingdon

Dockrill ML, Young JW (1989) British Foreign Policy, 1945–1956. Springer, Berlin

Dumčiuvienė D (2010) Europos ekonominė integracija. Technologija, Kaunas

Dustmann C, Frattini T (2014) The fiscal effects of immigration to the UK. Econ J 124(580):F593–F643

Ehring L (2002) De Facto discrimination in world trade law. J World Trade 36:921

Gifford C (2016) The United Kingdom's Eurosceptic political economy. Br J Polit Int Relat 18 (4):779–794

Holmes P, Rollo J, Winters LA (2016) Negotiating the UK's post-Brexit trade arrangements. Natl Inst Econ Rev 238(1):R22–R30

Johnson B (2015) Churchilio veiksnys. Kaip vienas žmogus lėmė istoriją. Tyto alba, Vilnius

Kierzenkowski R, Pain N, Rusticelli E, Zwart S (2016) The economic consequences of Brexit: a taxing decision. OECD Economic Policy Papers, (16)

Lea R (2017) Brexit update: and trade can thrive under WTO rules

Mcdonald F, Dearden S (2005) European economic integration, 4th edn. Pearson Education, Harlow

Piris J (2016) If the UK votes to leave. The seven alternatives to EU membership. Centre for European Reform, London

Pukelienė V (2008) Ekonominė integracija: teorija, ES politika ir procesai. Kaunas, VDU

Trade and Investment Balance of Competence Review (2013) London: Centre for Economic Policy Research Europos Sąjungos teisė (2007), 5th edn. Eugrimas, Vilnius

Van Marrewijk C, Ottens D, Schueller S (2012) International economics, 2nd edn. Oxford University Press, Oxford

Vitkus G (2013) Jungtinė Karalystė ir Europos integracija. Europos mozaika. 28 Europos Sąjungos valstybės. Eugrimas, Vilnius, pp 84–85

Vitkus G, Grikienis R, Maniokas K, Martikonis R, Sinkevičius E, Vilpišauskas R (2008) Europos Sąjunga. Enciklopedinis žinynas, 3rd edn. Eugrimas, Vilnius

Webb D, Keep M, Wilton M (2016) In brief: UK-EU economic relations. House of Commons Library Briefing Paper, 6091

Young AR (2015) Liberalizing trade, not exporting rules: the limits to regulatory co-ordination in the EU's 'new generation'preferential trade agreements. J Eur Public Policy 22(9):1253–1275

Kolibri 360 GmbH
Ferdinand-Jühlke-Straße 7
99095 Erfurt, Deutschland
produktsicherheit@kolibri360.de